Petfinder.com

The Adopted Dog Bible

Your One-Stop
Resource for Choosing,
Training, and Caring
for Your Sheltered or
Rescued Dog

COLLINS LIVING
An Imprint of HarperCollinsPublishers

A Stonesong Press Book

Petfinder.com

The Adopted Dog Bible

KIM SAUNDERS

Vice President of Shelter Outreach and Public Relations

This book contains advice and information relating to pet health. It is not intended to replace medical advice and should be used to supplement rather than replace regular care by your pet's veterinarian, who should always be consulted on questions specific to your pet.

While certain sections of the book contain advice for dealing with emergencies when a veterinarian is not available, it is recommended that you seek your veterinarian's advice whenever possible. The publisher, the proprietor, and the author expressly disclaim any and all losses, damages, and liabilities resulting from the application of the materials in this book. The author believes the information is accurate as of April 2008.

PETFINDER.COM. THE ADOPTED DOG BIBLE. Copyright © 2009 by THE STONESONG PRESS, LLC AND DISCOVERY PET ONLINE SERVICES, LLC. All rights reserved. Printed in the United States of America. No part of this book may be used or reproduced in any manner whatsoever without written permission except in the case of brief quotations embodied in critical articles and review. For information, address HarperCollins Publishers, 10 East 53rd Street, New York, NY 10022.

Petfinder and logo are trademarks of Discovery Communications, LLC, used under license

HarperCollins books may be purchased for educational, business, or sales promotional use. For information, please write: Special Markets Department, HarperCollins Publishers, 10 East 53rd Street, New York, NY 10022.

FIRST EDITION

Designed by Susan Walsh

Line art by Scott Nurkin

A Stonesong Press Book

All photographs courtesy of and copyright 2008 Discovery Pet Online Services, LLC except for the following:

Photograph on page xix courtesy of Betsy Saul
Photographs on pages 4, 49, 63, 77, 102, 271, 411 courtesy of Kim Saunders
Photograph on page 7 courtesy of Charles Saunders
Photograph on page 13 courtesy of Sharon Prushinski
Photograph on page 43 courtesy of Cindy Moran
Photograph on page 53 courtesy of Kristin Stevens
Photographs on pages 54, 121, 262, 265, 432, 451 courtesy of Carolyn Moran
Photographs on pages 65, 293 courtesy of Jodi Porretta
Photograph on page 105 courtesy of Paulette Feiereisel
Photographs on pages 116, 207 courtesy of Steve Surfman Photography
Photograph on page 132 courtesy of Greg Feiereisel and Ines Tu
Photographs on pages 161, 170 courtesy of Oriana Leckert
Photographs on pages 179, 217, 288 courtesy of Sara Lippincott
Photograph on page 211 courtesy of Cheryl S. Smith
Photograph on page 326 courtesy of Holly Kraska
Photograph on page 392 courtesy of Jared Saul
Photograph on page 419 courtesy of Sue Sternberg
Photograph on page 463 courtesy of Bonnie Baker
Photograph on page 471 courtesy of Sue Bertram
Photograph on back cover courtesy of Laura Moss Photography

Bach Flower Remedies Chart on pages 396-99 courtesy of bachflower.com

Recipe on page 182 courtesy of Kellyann Conway
Recipe on page 183 courtesy of Petfinder.com
Recipe on page 183 courtesy of Kellyann Conway
Recipe on page 184 courtesy of Carolyn Moran
Recipe on page 184 courtesy of Petfinder.com
Recipe on page 185 courtesy of Petfinder.com
Recipe on page 186 courtesy of Petfinder.com
Recipe on page 186 courtesy of Kellyann Conway

Library of Congress Cataloging-in-Publication Data has been applied for.

ISBN 978-0-06-143559-1

09 10 11 12 13 OV/RRD 10 9 8 7 6 5 4 3 2 1

This book is dedicated to the HEROES who dedicate themselves to making life better for homeless pets:

the staff and volunteers who run the shelters and animal rescue groups

the foster moms and dads who make room for "just one more"

the donors who make it financially possible

the good Samaritans who take the time to help a lost pet get back home, or to a safe place

the individuals who make the choice to ADOPT and save a life instead of purchasing a pet

and the dedicated Petfinder team I've had the honor of being a part of for these many years

And of course to Kona, who introduced me to the world of rescue and has been the truest partner I could ever hope for; Mocha, the princess I let go once, but found her way back; and Mojo, who reminds me every day to laugh and enjoy life and that there is good in the world.

Acknowledgments

Our Writers

We would like to gratefully acknowledge and thank all of the writers who contributed to various chapters in this book.

Sheila Boneham
Susan McCullough
Liz Palika
Cheryl Smith
Karen Stevens

Our Editorial Advisory Board

We at Petfinder.com gratefully acknowledge our esteemed advisory board who generously gave their time, wisdom, and expertise in reviewing many of the chapters in this book:

Veterinarians

Lila Miller, DVM
ASPCA
Vice President, Veterinary Outreach
Veterinary Advisor

Adjunct Assistant Professor at University of Pennsylvania School of Veterinary Medicine
Cornell University College of Veterinary Medicine

Kathleen V. Makolinski, DVM
ASPCA
Director of Veterinary Outreach

Kevin Fitzgerald, DVM, PhD
Diplomat, American College of Veterinary Practitioners
Alameda East Veterinary Hospital, Denver, Colorado
Host of the *Animal Planet* series "Emergency Vets" and "E-Vet Interns"
Adjunct Assistant Professor at the University of Denver
Writes monthly columns for American Kennel Club *Gazette*, American Kennel Club *Family Dog* magazine and *Police Dog* magazine Also has written chapters in medical texts on subjects such as emergency veterinarian medicine, toxicology, and reptile medicine and surgery.

Shelter Expert/Behaviorist/Trainers

Sue Sternberg
Founder, Executive Director Rondout Valley Animals for Adoption
Subject of the HBO documentary "Shelter Dogs"
Developed Assess-a-Pet™ method to evaluate animal temperament
Author of several books including, *Successful Dog Adoption*
animalsforadoption.org

Kellyann Conway
CABC Training Consultant

Nutritionist

Linda P. Case, MS
Owner, AutumnGold Consulting and Dog Training Center
Adjunct Assistant Professor, College of Veterinary Medicine, University of Illinois

Trainer, teacher and writer specializing in companion animal behavior, nutrition and health

Author of four books; including *Dogs and Cats: Understanding and Training Our Two Best Friends*, and *Canine and Feline Nutrition*

www.autumngoldconsulting.com

Holistic Care

Amy D. Shojai, CABC

Author of 22 pet care books including *New Choices in Natural Healing for Dogs & Cats* and *Petiquette: Solving Behavior Problems in Your Multipet Household*

Has been featured on ABC, NBC, CBS, CNN, and in *USA Weekend, The New York Times, Washington Post, Reader's Digest, Woman's Day, Family Circle,* and *Woman's World,* among others

www.shojai.com

Editorial Consultant

Paul Jolly

Executive Director and Vice President

The PETCO Foundation

The PETCO foundation was established in 1999 to manage the charitable efforts of PETCO in a wide variety of animal welfare efforts nationwide.

Our Photography Coordinator

Special thanks to Carolyn Moran, Petfinder.com Outreach Coordinator, for her time and skill in researching and selecting the perfect photographs of adopted dogs, coordinating the necessary permissions and finalizing fitting captions. The photos throughout the chapters and in the color insert make the text meaningful and bring the reality of adopting a dog to life.

Meet Our Models!

All of the dogs who appear in this book are adopted.

Acknowledgments

Contents

Foreword by Betsy Saul   xvii

Introduction   xxi

1. Shelters, Rescue Groups, Ads—Oh My! Where to
   Find the Right Dog   1

   Gimme Shelter   1

   Rescue Me!   6

   Puppy Personals   8

   The Story for Strays   11

   Dog Biscuits for the Soul: Kirby   15

   Resources   15

2. Pre-Adoption Preliminaries   16

   Will a Dog Fit into Your Life?   17

   Describing Your Dream Dog   24

   Dog Biscuits for the Soul: Boomer   40

   Resources   40

3. Breed All About It   41

   Doggie Group-Think   41

   Good Sports: The Sporting Group   42

   Elvis's Favorites: The Hound Group   44

   Busy, Busy, Busy: The Terrier Group   47

Great Big Dogs in Very Little Packages: The Toy Group 52

Take This Job and Fetch It: The Working Group 53

Movers (But Not Shakers): The Herding Group 55

Odds and Ends: The Non-Sporting Group 57

A Little of This and a Little of That: Mixing It Up 58

Dog Biscuits for the Soul: Feebee and Rosie 61

Resources 61

4. Getting Prepped for Parenthood 62

Checklist of Supplies 62

Dog-proofing Your Home, Inside and Out 74

Dog Biscuits for the Soul: Pinny 80

Resources 80

5. Choosing the Right Dog for You 81

Before You Go 81

What to Ask the Shelter Staff 84

At the Shelter: Guidelines for Making the Right Match 86

At a Foster Home or Adoption Event 91

Dog Biscuits for the Soul: Spike 95

Resources 96

6. Bringing Your New Hound Home 97

Picking Up Your Pup 98

The Drive Home 99

What to Expect During the First Twenty-four Hours 99

Sweet Dreams: Sleeping Arrangements 101

What to Expect During the First Week 102

Your Behavior: Managing Stress 104

Full House: Introducing the New Arrival to Your Other Pets 104

The Truth About Cats and Dogs 106

Doctor, Doctor! The First Vet Visit 107

What to Expect During the First, Second, and Third Months 109

Dog Biscuits for the Soul: Mia 111

Resources 111

7. Basic Re-Training 112

How Dogs Operate 113

Becoming a Benevolent Dictator 113

Basic Equipment and Management Tools 115

Training Techniques 119

Training Some Basic Behaviors 121

Make Your Dog a Good Canine Citizen 130

Dog Biscuits for the Soul: Gizmo 133

8. Modifying Undesirable Behaviors 134

Scary Sounds 134

A Touching Problem 137

House-training 138

Modifying Problem Behaviors 143

Enlisting Professional Help 150

Dog Biscuits for the Soul: Nike 153

Resources 154

9. Dinner's On 155

Where Should You Feed Your Dog? 156

How Often Should You Feed Your Dog? 156

How Much Should You Feed Your Dog? 158

The Diet Dilemma: What Should You Feed Your Dog? 161

Obesity—Is My Dog Fat or Just at the Top of His Weight Class? 176

What if Your Dog Is Underweight? 178

That's a Good Boy! Finding the Right Treats 179

Dog Biscuits for the Soul: Kiki 182

Resources 187

10. Walks, Workouts, and Play 188

Walking Basics 188

Meet and Greet 193

Workouts 203

Play 207

Dog Biscuits for the Soul: Nestlé 211

Resources 212

11. Washing and Grooming for Good Looks and Good Health 213

Grooming Essentials 214

Caring for Canine Coats and Skin 217

Bath Time 225

Ear Care 228

Eye Care 229

Oral Health Care 230

Foot and Nail Care 231

Anal Gland Care 235

	Dog Biscuits for the Soul: Louis	239
	Resources	239
12.	**Neutering Your Dog**	240
	What Does Neuter Mean?	240
	The Benefits of Neutering for Your Dog	241
	The Benefits of Neutering for Your Community	242
	Is My Dog Too Young to Be Neutered?	242
	Some Common Myths About Neutering	243
	The Future of Sterilization	245
	Dog Biscuits for the Soul: Buddy	246
	Resources	247
13.	**Anatomy 101: Your Dog, Her Body, and How It Functions**	248
	The Head	249
	The Nose and Mouth	250
	The Ears	251
	The Eyes	252
	The Neck and Body	253
	The Tail	254
	The Legs and Feet	255
	The Skin	256
	Coat Types and Textures	256
	Coat Colors and Patterns	258
	Dog Biscuits for the Soul: Bruno	260
	Resources	260
14.	**Health Basics for Your Adopted Dog**	261
	Infectious Diseases	261
	Vaccinations	265
	Signs and Symptoms of an Injury or Illness	270
	First Aid 411	278
	Emergency Procedures	280
	Dog Biscuits for the Soul: Sarah	286
	Resources	287
15.	**Helping the Healing Process: Caring for Your Sick or Injured Dog**	288
	Work with Your Veterinarian	289
	Work with Your Vet's Staff	292
	If Your Dog Is Hospitalized	294
	Nursing Your Dog	296

Contents

	Dog Biscuits for the Soul: Ralph	307
	Resources	307
16.	Managing Problems of the Outer Dog	308
	Eyes	308
	Ears	322
	Skin and Coat	326
	Allergies	334
	External Parasites	337
	Dog Biscuits for the Soul: Sam	343
	Resources	343
17.	Managing Problems of the Inner Dog	345
	The Circulatory System	345
	The Digestive System	351
	The Urinary System	362
	The Respiratory System	367
	The Musculoskeletal System	368
	The Endocrine System	376
	The Immune System	379
	Cancer	381
	The Nervous System	384
	Dog Biscuits for the Soul: Oscar	389
	Resources	390
18.	Holistic Medicine	391
	What Is Holistic Veterinary Medicine?	391
	How Is Conventional Medicine Different from Holistic Medicine?	392
	Types of Holistic Medicine	392
	Dog Biscuits for the Soul: Arnold	405
	Resources	405
19.	On the Road (or Plane, Train, or Boat) with Your Dog	407
	Canine Cruising	407
	Flying the "Furry" Skies	411
	Trains, Boats, and Buses	414
	Foreign Travel	414
	Time for a Break: Traveling Without Your Dog	415
	Dog Biscuits for the Soul: Belle	420
	Resources	420

20. Changes at Home   421
    Back to Work, Back to School   421
    Time to Move   426
    Your New Relationship: Dog Versus Date   429
    And Baby Makes . . . ?   430
    Dealing with Divorce or Death   432
    Dog Biscuits for the Soul: Koda   435
    Resources   436
21. When You Must Give Up Your Dog   437
    Can You Keep Her?   438
    Neuter Now!   440
    Finding Prospects   441
    Dealing with Applicants   443
    Finalizing the Adoption   445
    Using a Shelter   446
    Dog Biscuits for the Soul: Coby   447
    Resources   449
22. The Toughest Word: Euthanasia   450
    "How Do I Know When It's Time?"   452
    Euthanasia Versus a Natural Death   453
    Preparing for the Inevitable   454
    Saying Good-bye   455
    Coping with Your Loss   456
    If Your Dog Dies Unexpectedly   462
    Dog Biscuits for the Soul: Dexter   463
    Dog Biscuits for the Soul: Moose   465
    Resources   466
Appendix: Saving Dogs on a Larger Scale   469
    More Time than Money? Volunteer!   469
    More Money than Time? Donate!   472
    Resources   474
Index   475

Foreword

"When I adopted [my dog], I thought I was rescuing her. But it turns out I was the one who was rescued."

—a Petfinder visitor

It may come as a surprise to you that it was your very own dog that inspired us to create *The Adopted Dog Bible*.

It would be superficial to suggest that all shelter dogs are alike, but we couldn't believe more strongly that, when you find that special one—the one who becomes your perfect companion, with all her capacity for silliness, fear, love, depth, selflessness, creativity, and devotion—then to know her is to know them all. It is certainly the most motivating force we've ever experienced.

The idea for this book was born of equal parts: our desire to celebrate your dog and our heartfelt wish to thank you for choosing her. The book didn't feel complete, however, without introducing some of the characters that brought us here. These dogs stretched our hearts so much that they caused us to fall in love with all dogs. To us, they represented an awakening to the vast amount of love in furry bundles waiting in shelters everywhere, yearning to be discovered.

Meet Kobie. It was totally coincidental that I saw Kobie on Petfinder while doing some routine site maintenance. I can't imagine why the photo caught my eye. It showed a dark kennel run with a nondescript dog leaning against the door, his black eyes barely noticeable in his black face. But as his image flashed by, I had that déjà vu feeling that I already knew him. A finger that seemed no longer controlled by my brain punched in the shelter phone number. Within moments, Jared, my husband and co-founder of Petfinder, and I were on our way to pick him up. We planned to simply foster Kobie, but instead, he moved in. Now he never leaves our side. He is a clown, but also the consummate worry-wart. He alerts us (loudly) if any four-legged creature appears on the television, so try as we might, we can never watch *Animal Planet* in peace. One afternoon he yelled, "Intruder! Intruder!" and then courageously blocked the stairs to protect us from a giant, scary creature that was lurking on the landing. We hurried over to investigate and found that the "intruder" was a photo of a kitten printed on the front of a t-shirt hanging over the banister. (In Kobie's defense, it *was* a very large kitten.) He monitors the fax machines and fusses about the ceiling fans and anything else that might spring to life without permission. But most touching, if someone is sad or hurt, Kobie goes on duty. The weaker and smaller the person, the more aggressively he appoints himself chief caretaker. His method of making things better? Kisses. Lots of juicy kisses. He pins you down with his big feet and his bony elbows, using eighty-five pounds of dog to back them up, and slathers you with unstoppable, slobbery kisses. On your face, in your ears, on your neck, in your eyes, on the top of your head and—whoops!—he accidentally gets a tooth caught in your nose (these things happen), which is clearly justification for more kisses! It's impossible not to feel better when you are fighting for air under a furry beast. This is therapy, Kobie-style. No one can feel down when Kobie is around.

In contrast to worrywart Kobie, Mojo is a happy-go-lucky guy. He visits our farm on occasion, and across the paddock where he likes to run, I see his huge Pit Bull head pop up above the tall grass. Our eyes lock. I am now the center of the universe. He launches into the air and races toward me. In spite of his speed, his bowlegged, sideways lope gives the impression of a cartoon dog running in slow motion. The three remaining legs of a giant purple stuffed octopus wedged in his jaws stream behind him. His tongue lolls out the other side of his smiling face. I think, "No one has ever been so happy to see me!" immediately followed by, "Holy cow! Is he gonna stop?!" The answer used to always be "no," but keeping Mojo from body-slamming his friends at twenty miles an hour has been one of Kim Saunders's great achievements. When she adopted Mojo, he had apparently received no training from his previous owners. Although he still races through the house as if it were an

Foreword

agility course built just for him (his best dance move is the area-rug slide), he now greets visitors like a perfect gentleman, with an abrupt, plopping sit right at (sometimes on) their feet, and an open-mouthed grin.

Betsy and Kobie

Kim, Petfinder's first staff member and the author of this book, met Mojo in the emergency animal shelter in the aftermath of Hurricane Katrina. She went to Louisiana to help with the recovery efforts, and Mojo was one of the 10,000 animals whose lives were saved by the passionately dedicated volunteers who came from across the country. Mojo's previous family never claimed him, and he went to Arkansas to a foster home. There is no obvious reason why Mojo stood out among the thousands of Pit Bulls that passed through the shelter, but Kim couldn't get him off her mind. She tracked him down, and he made the journey from Arkansas to New Jersey to become the happiest member of Kim's pack. The disaster response took an emotional toll on all the recovery volunteers. They had to embark on their own journeys of recovery, and Kim was no exception. Mojo, the goofball Pit Bull who lives only in the present, turned out to be the perfect medicine.

And then there is Schweetu. Have you ever looked into a dog's eyes and had them look right back at you and into your soul? That is what Schweetu does. We call him the little man in a dog suit. Some pets are *fur babies* and some people are *pet parents*, but no such terms are appropriate for Schweetu and his place in the family. This Husky/Shepherd mix is more partner than pet. Though he loves to romp in the park with the other dogs, he will always gravitate back to his person, Teri White, Petfinder's longtime business manager and a dear friend. He positions himself with his back to her, facing the world, his watchful eye carefully scanning the landscape for danger or opportunity. When we walk together, I often sense that Schweetu thinks the leash serves *him* to keep *Teri* out of trouble. When Teri speaks to him, he returns her gaze, leans in, and widens his eyes in concentration. His desire to understand is palpable. Eventually, he starts playing the "hot/cold" game by going through his repertoire of tricks, watching her eyes to see if he's on the right track. He pokes Teri playfully with his nose, showing his sense of humor, if he can't get through to her. With Schweetu, you know it's only for lack of opposable thumbs and a common language that you can't sit down and enjoy a beer and a round of poker with him. He has clear self-awareness and is what psychologists would call self-actualized—enough to let himself out of the yard when he chooses to go for a stroll and enough to help himself to the sausage on the counter.

But Schweetu isn't your run-of-the-mill naughty boy. He ponders the consequences of his actions. You can see him weighing the options (his ears give him away when he's thinking about being naughty). It is hard to begrudge a guy of his intelligence a little freedom to make choices, and even harder to imagine him waiting in a shelter-run with an uncertain future—and no choices. For pre-Schweetu Teri, who was minding her own business one day and not feeling particularly in need of a dog, Schweetu was a surprise. First there was his face on the monitor, and then there was Teri in the car, heading to the shelter. Teri saved Schweetu's life, but Teri was the most changed. Getting to know Schweetu opened her to the possibility that other shelter dogs were as sentient as he was. The thought of them waiting in shelters, scared and alone, became the catalyst for major change in both Teri and her community. Ever since Teri came to know the little man in a dog suit, she has been rescuing and fostering dogs in his honor.

Kobie, Mojo, and Schweetu have been motivating forces in our lives, and they reveal an amazing treasure—the promise and potential that lie within the heart of every dog. When I first looked into Kobie's eyes, I felt as if I already knew him. Now, after knowing Kobie, I see a sparkle of him in all the dogs waiting to be adopted at shelters.

It is these dogs in shelters and foster homes, these treasures just waiting to be discovered, that grip our hearts. They are the next Kobies, Mojos, and Schweetus, and we can't help but love them. Each has a unique story, but all are familiar enough to us to know how very valuable they are. Several hundred thousand adoptable pets on Petfinder are waiting for homes. With you and your adopted pooch as ambassadors, we will fulfill our mission to make certain they all find families. I'm so excited and honored to embark on this new relationship with you!

—Betsy Saul, co-Founder, Petfinder.com

Introduction

Welcome to *Petfinder.com: The Adopted Dog Bible*. I hope you enjoy this book as much as I've enjoyed the journey—and the dogs—that led to it. I'm excited at the prospect of you finding the dog of your dreams and providing her with the adoptive home she deserves. I believe this book will help you every step of the way.

How I Got Here

In 1995, shortly after buying my first home, I stopped at a pet adoption event "just to look." I was ready. My yard was fenced. My schedule was flexible. I'd read everything there was to read on dogs. I'd practiced on the dogs of friends and family ever since I could walk, and I often stopped strangers to talk about or talk to their dogs. I had spent my entire childhood and early adult years pining for a dog. But adopting a dog seemed like such a monumental decision. I was sure it would take months to choose just the right one.

And then I saw him. Before I could catch my breath, I had completed the adoption questionnaire and stood, puppy in arms, facing the Noah's Ark volunteer who would interview me to decide if this was a good match. All was going well. After all, I really had all the makings of a caring, responsible pet parent. And then, without realizing what she was in for, the volunteer asked, "So how long have you been looking for a dog?" At that moment, all the anticipation, the excitement, and the nervousness welled up, and I (normally levelheaded and relatively sane) burst into tears and blubbered, *"All my life!"* Fortunately, the volunteer was not put off by my outburst, and after we packed the car with newly purchased food, treats, toys, a crate, and other supplies, my new puppy and I headed for home.

Kona. I really had waited all my life for him. And he was worth the wait. He has turned out to be the best friend I've ever had. He was also a heap of trouble—in ways only someone who has lived with a puppy can understand. The first year was tough as we maneuvered the rocky road from puppy teething to adolescent antics. And yet, when the holidays rolled around, there was no doubt what I was most thankful for. So I called Nancy, the founder of Noah's Ark, to express how grateful I was that she had rescued Kona and his littermates and to let her know how much Kona meant to me. An all volunteer, foster-based rescue group, Noah's Ark did amazing, lifesaving work, and Nancy told me about all the animals in their care that needed homes. Before I stopped to think about it, the fateful words were out there: "Is there anything I can do to help?"

I volunteered with Noah's Ark in a variety of ways, but the most meaningful opportunity arose after I read an article in my local paper about a new website started by a New Jersey couple to help adoptable pets find homes. I was skeptical. I wasn't much of a computer person. And really, I thought, would people look for a pet on the Internet? But our foster homes were over-full, as were local shelters, and there always seemed to be more pets in need than adopters. So I called the phone number in the paper and had my first conversation with Betsy Saul, the co-founder of Petfinder.com (and destined to become both my friend and my boss). As a result, Noah's Ark and our adoptable pets became the nineteenth group to join Petfinder.com and a part of the revolution in how adoptions would take place.

The Petfinder Story

Betsy and Jared Saul came up with the idea that became Petfinder.com on the way to dinner on New Year's Eve 1995. The World Wide Web was brand new, and the couple was discussing how people weren't maximizing this new technology's search capabilities. Most web pages were just replications of a company's print media. Betsy and Jared brainstormed about what kind of company or group could most benefit from searching. Suddenly a lightbulb went off. They both loved animals and had always wanted to do something to help them. What about creating a website to market adoptable pets and connect them with would-be adopters?

Animal shelters and rescue organizations, working furiously to save homeless pets, sometimes under terrible conditions and often with little or no money, were the perfect non-profit organizations to benefit from a searchable website.

To get the idea off the ground, each evening, after returning from her day job, Betsy called shelters and rescue groups in New Jersey and the surrounding states and invited them to try this new idea. Meanwhile, Jared, who was in medical school at the time, built a multi layered site that was easy for visitors to use. By entering the type of animal, breed, size, gender, age, and zip code, visitors could obtain a list of all the pets in the Petfinder database who matched their criteria. They could then read descriptions, see photos, and eventually view videos of these pets—all from the comfort of their homes. And when they felt a connection to a particular pet (the inevitable magic click!), they could contact the group caring for her directly to learn more and set up a meeting. As organizations signed up, Betsy and Jared posted information about the adoptable pets the shelters faxed to them. The site launched in early 1996—and, as they envisioned, the adopters followed.

In 1998, in response to requests from shelters and rescue groups across the country, Petfinder went national, and in 2000, it moved into Canada.

As the site expanded, Betsy sought corporate sponsorship so it could remain free of charge for both the animal welfare organizations posting pets and the visitors searching for the perfect addition to their families.

The Petfinder mission—then and now—is to increase the adoption of homeless pets so that no adoptable animal will be euthanized simply for lack of a home. Betsy, always a fan of benchmarks, wanted to set a standard against which they could gauge their success. She decided that if they could save the life of one homeless pet per month, all of the hard work they put in to Petfinder would be worthwhile.

Meanwhile in 1999, in what I believe to be a crash collision of fate and good fortune, I had the privilege of becoming Petfinder's first staff member. I never worked harder than I did in that position; but after all, the outcome had never been so important. All I had to do was look into Kona's eyes to know what was at stake.

Look How Far We've Come

Petfinder has become the largest searchable database of homeless pets on the Internet. Shelters and rescue groups from all fifty United States, each Canadian province, Puerto Rico, Mexico, the Bahamas, Costa Rica, the Virgin Islands, and Guam all post their adoptable pets. As of this writing, the shelter and rescue members number more than eleven thousand and continue to grow as new organizations form. Many of our Petfinder members tell us that more than 50 percent of their adoptions are a result of their Petfinder postings.

Petfinder staff grew from one employee (me!) to a dedicated team of thirty-five . . . and counting. And our recent acquisition by Discovery Communications, a company carefully selected as a good adoptive home for Petfinder, has brought additional resources for us to use to further our work on behalf of the pets.

Back to Betsy's benchmark: she thought the value of saving one life per month would be enough to keep it all going. Well, since that very first month, she has far exceeded her own goals. Today, Petfinder assists the animal welfare community in saving more than 1.5 million lives each year. In our twelve-year history, the lives saved total more than 12 million. It is an overwhelming honor to be a part of such an accomplishment.

To complement my work with Petfinder, I have continued to volunteer locally, acting as a foster parent for dogs and puppies, in addition to updating Petfinder pet photos and descriptions. Years ago, one of my foster dogs was turned in to a local shelter a year after her adoption. Luckily, they traced her back to me, and with Kona's blessing, we decided that Mocha would permanently join our family. (We've coined the term "foster failure" as an honorary title for a foster parent who winds up permanently adopting his or her charge.) Finally, I unexpectedly rounded out my canine pack following Hurricane Katrina when Mojo made mine his forever home as well. The joy that Kona, Mocha, and Mojo bring me each and every day fulfills me and adds meaning to my life.

Over the years, I have been repeatedly awed and amazed by the incredible staff and volunteers who work tirelessly on behalf of the pets in their care. They are true heroes—I count myself lucky to have the honor of knowing and working with them. As you begin your search to adopt the perfect dog for you, I hope you'll take a moment to recognize the sacrifices these folks make so that we can find and forge the relationship of a lifetime. They are experts, and, in addition to the information in this book, you should look to them for advice and resources as you and your newly adopted dog begin your life together.

Petfinder.com: The Adopted Dog Bible is the latest step in our journey. We wrote it with you and your new dog—or new dog-to-be—in mind. As you begin your quest to find just the right dog to add to your family, we want you to feel confident that you have all the information you need in these pages to choose, care for, and train your new best friend. We want to make sure that the dog you fall in love with (and you will fall in love), will make a great family member.

Share Your Happy Tails with Us

It is only fitting that since Kona started me on this journey thirteen years ago, he is sitting by my feet as I write to ask you about *your* dog. Is she smart and serious like Kona, anxious and pushy like Mocha, or joyful and carefree like Mojo? Without a doubt, she will have her own unique personality and her own unique story. Remember, as Betsy mentions in her foreword, it was *your dog* who led us to this book. So please, after a long day of care and training and playing, and after you've fed her dinner, settled her down for the night, and counted your blessings that she found you, take a moment to submit your Happy Tail at www.petfinder.com/happytails/ or simply drop me a note at adopteddogbible@petfinder.com. I really do want to hear her story.

Adoption is a great option.

1

Shelters, Rescue Groups, Ads—Oh My! Where to Find the Right Dog

You may have thought that deciding to adopt a dog rather than buy one from a breeder would be the toughest part of the whole dog acquisition process. But choosing to adopt a dog isn't the end of a process, it's the beginning.

You might feel a bit overwhelmed when you try to figure out where to look for your adopted dog. Lots of options confront you: animal shelters, rescue groups, advertisements, and even dogs that might choose you by following you home. But take heart! This chapter gives you all your adoption options to find the dog of your dreams.

Gimme Shelter

Your local animal shelter can be a great place to find your dream dog. Generally, shelters are run by local governments or local humane organizations. Almost every county and medium-to-large city in the United States has a shelter; some may have several.

However, all shelters are not created equal. Some are state-of-the-art facilities with climate-controlled apartments, piped-in music, and full-time trainers who socialize the canine guests, teach them some new tricks

Every shelter is full of dogs who long for your love.

(literally), and otherwise keep them as happy as possible until they're adopted. Such shelters are in the minority, though, because building, creating, and maintaining these ideal shelters requires funding and personnel that most communities don't have. These communities do the best they can with the relatively meager resources available to them, and they make every effort to provide a safe, clean refuge for the animals they shelter. And almost all shelters, regardless of the luxuriousness of their accommodations, have employees who do their very best to care for the unfortunate animals who need a shelter's services, and to find permanent homes for as many as they can.

Many local organizations go by the name of SPCA (Society for the Prevention of Cruelty to Animals). These groups are neither related to nor regulated by the American Society for the Prevention of Cruelty to Animals (ASPCA), the country's oldest humane organization, which is based in New York but has a national focus. The same is true for local humane societies that have no relation to the national organization, the Humane Society of the United States (HSUS).

In addition to paid staff, many shelters have volunteers who help with duties such as socializing dogs, screening adoption applications, and introducing applicants to available dogs. Some fortunate shelters have full-time trainers who show selected volunteers how to teach the dogs basic manners. A dog who responds to simple cues such as "come," "sit," and "heel" is much more likely to make a good impression on a prospective adopter than a dog who hurls himself at an approaching human in a joyous frenzy or hugs the rear wall of his enclosure when someone passes by. But keep in mind that just because a dog has not yet learned basic manners does not mean that he won't make an excellent companion once you put in some time socializing and educating him.

There are as many reasons for a dog to wind up in a shelter as there are dogs that need homes. According to Petfinder, purebred dogs make up at least 25 percent of the adoptable dogs available. While young puppies occasionally come to a shelter (often with their mother), many shelter dogs are adolescents—between six months and two years of age. Among these canine teenagers are dogs whose former families adored them when they were cute little puppies, but couldn't or wouldn't cope with their adolescent unruliness just a few months later. Other shelter dogs are senior citizens whose folks might not have wanted to be bothered with taking care of an elderly animal, or perhaps, whose people were seniors themselves and no longer able to provide their beloved friend with a home.

Shelter dogs also come in all sizes and shapes. One enclosure might house a high-strung silky-haired toy-sized pooch; in the next might be a big couch potato of a Pit Bull mix. When it comes to shelter dogs, diversity is the name of the game.

Regardless of their age, appearance, or temperament, many shelter dogs find themselves homeless due to circumstances beyond their control, or because they have minor issues that would respond to a little time and effort by a caring human being or a family.

Kill Versus No-Kill

Unfortunately, not all shelter dogs are lucky enough to find permanent homes. With some, initial evaluations indicate that they're not good candidates for adoption. Others fail to elicit potential adopters' interest. What happens to these dogs depends upon the shelter they're in.

There are two types of shelters: open-admission shelters, which must accept any animal in need, and limited-admission shelters, which will only accept as many animals as they have the capacity to care for (also known as "no-kill shelters"). Open-admission shelters may be forced to euthanize animals to make room for new arrivals, which is why they are sometimes labeled "kill shelters." However, while limited-admission shelters may choose not to euthanize animals, they also may refuse to accept animals they consider unadoptable or any animals if they are at capacity (and in doing so, they pass the burden of euthanasia to the open-admission shelters).

Knowing whether a shelter is a no-kill or open-admission facility shouldn't affect your decision to adopt a dog from them. Before judging any shelter for its policies, visit first, and evaluate what you see. See Chapter 5 for some help with deciding whether a particular shelter is the right place to find your new canine companion.

Most shelters have a three-part adoption procedure: preparing a dog for adoption, selecting an adopter, and following up after the adoption.

Typically, when a dog first arrives, shelter personnel evaluate his temperament, immunize him against rabies and other serious canine diseases, perform a heartworm test, and check for internal parasites. The dog then

Don't fall victim to the Big Black Dog Syndrome (large dark dogs are often bypassed in shelters even though they are just as loving as their lighter-colored counterparts).

goes to live in his own enclosure among the other canine guests. The enclosure may include a blanket, toys, or other goodies to help the dog feel more at home. During his stay, shelter employees and volunteers not only feed the dog but also try to spend some quality time with him: taking him for walks, playing with him outdoors, and even teaching him basic good manners such as coming when called and sitting when told. Such efforts not only help acclimate the dog to the shelter but also help prepare him to be adopted.

While the dog is being prepped for a forever home, other shelter staffers and volunteers work to find that home. They might photograph the dog and advertise his availability on Petfinder.com and/or on their own website. They also might place a classified advertisement in their local paper, or put up flyers on community bulletin boards or at pet supply stores. When prospective adopters show an interest in the dog—through phone calls, e-mail, or a visit to the shelter—employees usually ask them to fill out a questionnaire or application. Such applications can be quite extensive (see "So You Think You Can Just Adopt a Dog?" on page 9), but if used properly, they can open a constructive dialogue between shelter personnel and would-be adopters to make the best possible match between the dog and a prospective family.

Shelter employees evaluate each application, check references, and interview the applicant either by phone or in person. Based on those evaluations, shelter staff can help match the right dog with the right family. Some shelters will then perform a home evaluation in which a shelter staffer or volunteer visits the adopter's residence to make sure that it's a good place for the dog to live and to help the new pet-parent-to-be with dog-proofing tips.

If you think your dream dog may be waiting for you in a shelter, take these steps to advance your quest:

Find some shelters. Don't know where your local shelters are? Simply log on to the Internet and point your browser to www.petfinder.com/shelters.html. If you don't have access to the Internet at home, work, or through a friend, log on to a computer at your local library. There you'll find Petfinder's searchable database of animal welfare organizations. Decide whether you want to search by location or by state, and follow the prompts.

Visit online. Almost all shelters maintain a web page on Petfinder.com—along with a list of available dogs for adoption. Some also link to their own website. Whether on Petfinder or through an organization's website, you should be able to gain vital information about the shelter's visiting hours, adoption procedures, and how dogs are made available for adoption. You may also find the organization's adoption questionnaire or application.

Visit in person. Once you have all the information you need, pay the shelter a visit—even if their current listings don't include a dog who interests you. If you're a parent, try to make this visit on your own, so that you're not subjected to the nagging pleas of your kids. Visit the dogs there and fill out an application. Talk with the shelter employees or the volunteers who handle adoptions, and let them know about the kind of dog you're hoping to adopt. They may remember you when a dog who may be suited to your needs comes along. As you chat with the shelter staff and watch them at work, evaluate your experience: Do you feel welcome? Does the staff seem genuinely interested in helping you find the right dog for your family? Do they show real compassion and concern as they interact with the dogs in their care? (For more suggestions on what to look for in a shelter, see Chapter 5.)

Bring your checkbook. Although adopting from a shelter is a relatively economical way to acquire a dog, it's not free. If you find a dog and the shelter approves your application, there will be an adoption fee or donation. Adoption costs vary, depending on location and whether the dog needs to be spayed or neutered. Shelters need to charge an additional fee for any spaying or neutering they perform to recover some of their costs. For example, the Washington Humane Society, which operates the District of Columbia's animal shelter, charges $35 to adopt a dog who's already spayed or neutered, and $135 for one who needs the procedure. The Madison County Humane Society in Anderson, Indiana, charges $100 for all dog adoptions, and states on its website that the fee includes the cost of spaying and neutering. On the west coast, Sacramento (California) County Animal Care and Regulation charges a variety of fees, depending on the gender and spay/neuter status of a dog. An unspayed female costs between $106 and $126, plus $15 extra for a heartworm test. An intact male costs between $96 and $111, not including the $15 heartworm fee. Spayed females and neutered males each cost $50 less. Keep in mind that these fees help keep the shelters running and allow them to care for the dogs they have. See Chapter 2 for more information on the costs associated with caring for a dog.

Once the adoption is approved and your new dog joins your household, shelter personnel may phone or e-mail you to see how you're both doing. Many shelters also offer telephone and e-mail help lines as well as dog training classes that are discounted for shelter dog alumni and their adoptive families.

Rescue Me!

Shelters aren't the only places to find adoptable dogs. Rescue or adoption placement groups also give second chances to dogs who have lost their homes, but their working methods differ somewhat from those of shelters. While a shelter generally employs both staff and volunteers to house dogs in a single structure, rescue groups typically rely on networks of volunteers who provide temporary care for dogs from their own homes. In essence, rescue group volunteers provide temporary foster care to dogs who are awaiting adoption into a permanent home.

Some rescue groups focus on purebred dogs exclusively; there are groups for Labrador Retrievers, groups for Rottweilers, and so on. Others work with both mixed-breed dogs and purebreds. You can find rescue groups in your area by logging on to Petfinder's website at www.petfinder.com/shelters.html. There you'll find a database of animal welfare groups that you can search by distance from your zip code, or by state. If you're interested in a specific breed, search Petfinder.com for that breed and you will likely find some at general rescue groups and shelters and others in their own purebred rescue groups.

Generally, a rescue group's adoption procedure is similar to that of a shelter. While a dog's foster care-giver readies the dog for adoption, she or other volunteers will also search for a suitable permanent home. Like shelters, rescue groups require applications, references, and often, home visits. However, sometimes it takes rescue groups longer to respond to you. This is because most groups are made up of volunteers for whom this is a labor of love. These volunteers usually have full-time "real" jobs, families, and other commitments. They often create a second full-time job for themselves by fostering and finding homes for adoptable pets. Knowing that these big-hearted volunteers are doing the best they can may make the wait less frustrating.

Rescue groups often foster entire purebred litters—like these Pit Bulls.

While shelters' and rescue groups' adoption procedures may be similar, their caregiving approaches often differ. Because some shelters house a fairly large number of dogs in one place, shelter employees may have relatively little opportunity to get to know an individual dog. That can make it difficult for you to learn much about a dog's behavioral tendencies until you meet the dog yourself. By contrast, a rescue group foster caregiver lives with a dog in her own home 24/7. Moreover, a dog often remains in a rescue group's foster care network longer than would be the case in a shelter, mainly because a rescue group doesn't need to set a deadline for adoption to make room for additional dogs. Either way, the foster caregiver has more time than a shelter employee to develop considerable knowledge about the dog (or dogs) in her care—knowledge that she can share with you.

Some rescue groups aren't able to offer as many dogs to choose from as a shelter can. In addition, some rescue groups' adoption fees may be higher than those of a shelter. For example, Golden Retriever Rescue, Education and Training in southeast Virginia charges $350 to adopt a dog under four years of age, $300 for a dog between the ages of four and seven, and $225 for a dog eight years of age or older. Central Illinois German Shepherd Dog

Rescue charges $325 for a dog under one year old, $275 for a dog between one and six years of age, and $250 for dogs six years of age and over. Dogs Without Borders, an all-breed rescue group in Los Angeles, charges $250 for most adoptions, but raises the fee to $300 for puppies less than six months of age. Paws Animal Rescue, an all-breed rescue group in Alvin, Texas, charges a minimum of $125, while Save Our Setters, Inc., a setter rescue group in Denver, Colorado, charges adopters between $150 and $350, depending on a dog's age.

Before you balk at those higher prices, remember that a rescue group depends entirely on these fees and other donations to continue its work, whereas a shelter may be able to augment income from its adoption fees with money allocated in a city or county budget.

Look to both sources in your search for the dog of your dreams. In fact, many shelters work in partnership with rescue groups. If, for example, an adoptable shelter dog is slated for euthanasia due to overcrowding at the shelter, a shelter adoption director may ask a local rescue group to take that dog in. The same might be true if a newly arrived shelter dog has special dietary, training, or medical needs.

Puppy Personals

Once upon a time, the only people who advertised dogs in classified ads were not-so-reputable breeders and individuals who couldn't keep their dogs but didn't want to take them to a shelter. Nowadays, the ad game is different. In addition to the not-so-good breeders and the individuals who can't keep their pooches, you can find ads from shelters and rescue groups in the classifieds section of many larger newspapers, as well as online ads. (Petfinder populates online classified sites such as Oodle and Vast with adoptable pets from shelters and rescues, increasing their chances of finding a good home).

Sometimes such ads will feature individual dogs; in other cases, the ads might showcase an upcoming adoption event in which prospective adopters can meet and greet as many as a dozen (or more) dogs. Either way, you'll know that you're dealing with a shelter or rescue group because the name of the group and its telephone number or website will appear in the ad. You can

So You Think You Can Just Adopt a Dog?

Think again.

Sure, shelters and rescue groups want to find homes for the dogs in their care—but not just any home. They want to make good matches for these dogs, with folks who are willing to commit themselves to their well-being for as long as the animals live. Not every prospective adopter offers such a home and not every adopter is the right match for every dog. The only way to be sure that an adopter is the right match for a particular dog is to have an open discussion about your lifestyle and what you would like or need in a new canine family member.

It may feel as if you need to jump through plenty of hoops in your quest to adopt a dog from a shelter or rescue group. Adoption applications vary; some are very brief "conversation starters" and some are lengthy documents. You may be asked what your living situation is, whether everyone in your family wants a dog, and what's happened to any dogs that you've had in the past. You can count on questions about where the dog will sleep, where the dog will spend his time, and how long he might be left alone. You should not be surprised if you're asked for the name of a veterinarian who can discuss what kind of dog parent you have been in the past. There are not necessarily right or wrong answers to these questions, but they do open a conversation between you and the shelter staff that will help them find a perfect canine match for you and your lifestyle. That said, though it may not occur in every case, you should be willing to have a shelter staffer or volunteer schedule a visit to your home before the adoption is finalized, to help you ensure it is adequately set up for a dog.

All of the dogs in a rescue group, foster home, or animal shelter have lost their homes at least once. The people taking care of these dogs now want to make sure that the next home these dogs find themselves in will be their forever home. If that isn't enough to convince you of the need to go through the entire process, consider this: the shelter or rescue group doesn't simply want the dog to be happy with you. They also want you to be happy with the dog. By answering all their questions as fully and honestly as you can, you'll improve your chances of finding a dog with whom you can live happily ever after.

respond to such ads with the same confidence as when you go to a shelter or contact a rescue group directly. You can also find out about local adoption events by logging on to Petfinder's event calendar. PETCO, a longtime Petfinder.com sponsor, routinely hosts in-store adoption events. Locate one in a store near you by logging on to http://www.petco.com and following the prompts for Store Adoptions.

Advertisements placed by individuals require a more cautious response. You'll find such ads not only in newspapers, but also in grocery stores, libraries, veterinarians' offices, pet supply stores, or other public bulletin boards. These ads may appear to offer an inexpensive route to dog adoption; they may even say the dog is "free to a good home." But what you don't pay in adoption fees now might result in your having to pay more for that dog's care later. That's because shelters and rescue groups generally spay or neuter the dogs in their care, immunize them against rabies and other serious diseases, and dispense medications designed to combat parasites. Many shelters and rescue groups also socialize and train their dogs to live politely with human beings and other animals. Some individuals provide such care to their dogs, but many don't.

The easiest way to avoid a possible adoption disaster is to bypass ads placed by individuals, but if you are going to take your chances, be sure to do the following:

Listen for questions. An individual who cares about her dog's future will ask you almost as many questions as a shelter or rescue group would. She'll want to know about your living situation, the other members of your family, and your history with dogs. She'll want references—and when you provide them, she'll contact them. She'll ask where the dog will live, eat, and sleep. If the person you're working with doesn't ask you any questions, she probably wants to simply unload the dog as quickly as possible, and she might be withholding information about the dog's behavior and history. Don't let her unload that dog on you.

Ask lots of questions. Just as a caring person wants to know that her dog will be okay in your home, you'll want to know whether the dog's been okay in his current situation. Ask for the name of the dog's veterinarian, and find out whether the dog has had any training.

Ask, too, why the advertiser no longer wants the dog. Moving overseas, allergies, and changes in economic circumstances can force even the most devoted pet parent to relinquish her canine companion. Other reasons might reflect a careless attitude that's had a negative impact on the dog. A first-time pet parent may not want to deal with the effects that attitude might have had on this particular dog's health and behavior. On the other hand, if you have some dog experience and can commit some time, energy, patience and finances to working through his issues, you may make the friend of a lifetime.

Be firm with yourself. If you meet the dog, be very sure you want him before you agree to take him. Don't let sympathy overwhelm your judgment. See Chapter 5 for ideas on how to evaluate a prospective canine adoptee. If you have misgivings about adopting the dog, listen to your instincts—and walk away.

The Story for Strays

You weren't looking to add a dog to your household. But somehow, while you were taking a walk, running errands, or just venturing into your own backyard, a dog you have never seen before shows up out of nowhere. (Welcome to my world!) You don't see a collar or tags, his coat is a mess, and he looks so forlorn and sweet, begging you to take him in, that you just can't resist.

It's a hard situation, but for your sake and the dog's, you need to proceed carefully. Here's how:

Let the dog come to you. If his tail is wagging in a relaxed manner (low and relaxed, not high and stiff) and he's neither staring at you nor growling, try turning sideways while still standing, averting your eyes, smiling and speaking gently and lovingly to the dog. Then let him approach you. When he comes over, turn your face away slightly (no direct staring; dogs consider that impolite or even aggressive), and check to see if he has a collar with an identification tag. If he does, contact his family, who will probably be grateful that you've found their lost companion. Otherwise you'll have to figure out what to do with him. While your efforts to get a stray dog back home or to a safe place are to be commended, be sure not to jeopardize your own safety. Unknown dogs can react unexpectedly if frightened or feeling threatened. In the unfortunate event that you are bitten by an unfamiliar animal, it will be important to maintain control of the animal so that he can be quarantined to rule out rabies, a fairly uncommon but transmittable and fatal disease that dogs can pass on to people. To avoid such a situation, be sure to act carefully, use common sense, and trust your instincts.

Take him somewhere safe. If you think he'll fit in with your family (both human and non-human members), at least temporarily, bring him home. If you don't, consider having him stay at your vet's (if you have one) or at a boarding kennel for a few days. Either way, coax him into the backseat of your car and drive him to your intended destination. (If you are the sort of person for whom, like me, finding a loose dog is a regular occurrence, keep a slip lead and some treats in your car for just such occasions.) If you're not comfortable transporting him yourself, you will need to contact your local shelter or, if they are closed or can't help you, call the police department for assistance. Bear in mind, however, that the police will take the dog to the closest municipal shelter, which is likely to be an open-admission facility that may have to euthanize animals after a few days. If you are considering adopting the dog after he's been evaluated at the shelter or know someone who may be interested, find out which shelter he's being taken to and follow up with that facility immediately.

Publicize his plight. If the dog doesn't have any identification and you bring him home, you still need to make a reasonable attempt to find his family. Even if the dog clearly looks mistreated or neglected, you don't know anything about his history; perhaps he's been away from home for a long time, and his condition may be a result of his stay outdoors. Someone may be desperately searching for him.

Pet parents looking for their lost dog will likely contact their local shelters, so you need to do the same. Petfinder offers a free classifieds section where you can list information on the dog you've found—and check for lost dog ads that might be a match. You can also make posters, place some newspaper ads (sometimes offered free for found pets), and notify your local police department and other less local humane organizations, since there is no telling how far your newfound friend may have traveled. Also be sure to bring him to your vet (or any local vet) to be scanned for a microchip and checked for a tattoo.

Make a decision. If the dog's family can't be located in a week or two, you have the options of keeping the dog or finding him a new home. To start the ball rolling on finding a home that's not your own, contact a local all-breed or purebred rescue group. You can find a list for your area by logging on to Petfinder.com

"Look who followed me home, Mom!"

and using the searchable database of animal welfare agencies. When contacting groups for assistance in finding a home for your found dog, provide them with as much information as possible in your initial contact, including attaching a photo to your e-mail, if possible. Also let them know if you are willing to provide a temporary foster home for the dog while they assist you in finding him a "fur-ever" home. For groups who have a shortage of foster homes, this could be the deciding factor in whether they can help you. If you decide to keep the dog yourself, take him to a veterinarian right away for a health check, and see Chapter 4 for detailed information on how to get yourself, your family, and your home ready for your new family member.

From Backyard to Back Lot: A Real Life Story

Princess, a Spaniel-Pit Bull mix, spent most of her young life chained in a yard, with little or no attention from her owner. But when animal trainer Miriam Fields-Babineau first laid eyes on her, she saw much more than a lonely, neglected puppy. She saw the ghost of a canine thespian. "Her eyes were just like those of another dog I'd had years before, who was a fantastic production dog," recalls Fields-Babineau, who not only trains people's pets but also trains animals who appear in advertisements, commercials, live stage performances, television, and movies.

There was just one problem: Princess belonged to someone whom Fields-Babineau didn't know. "She was living in a house that was next door to one of my clients," explains Fields-Babineau, who lives in Amherst, Virginia. "I asked my client to talk to the owner and ask if she wanted to keep the dog or give her to me. A month later, the owner contacted me and said she would take Princess to the pound if I didn't come and get her right away."

When Fields-Babineau retrieved Princess and brought her home, she had intended to prepare her to be adopted by someone else. "But my whole family loved her and she became a permanent resident," she says.

Once the family decided Princess should be theirs, Fields-Babineau taught her the tricks of the canine thespian trade, including on- and off-leash behaviors such as sit/stays, down/stays, and coming when called. Princess also learned to shake hands, wave her paw, roll over, sit up, fetch and hold objects, twirl, and chase her tail. She loved performing, and didn't get fazed by the commotion that inevitably occurs during the filming of a commercial or feature film. Soon she developed an impressive list of credits, including commercials for the Washington DC Lottery, the Virginia Department of Transportation, and the Maryland Department of Transportation. She also nearly made her big-screen debut when she portrayed a dog who sees aliens abducting people on her street in Steven Spielberg's 2005 movie *War of the Worlds*—although, through no fault of hers, the scene ended up on the cutting-room floor.

Princess's burgeoning career places her in distinguished company. Other dogs who leaped from rescue groups or shelters to stage and screen include Pal, the rescued Collie who portrayed Lassie in all six of the 1940s and 1950s feature films about the beloved canine heroine; Moose, a rescued Jack Russell Terrier who portrayed Eddie on the TV comedy *Frasier;* and the shelter dogs that portrayed Benji in Joe Camp's original films of the 1970s and 1980s, as well as in *Benji Off the Leash,* which was released in 2004.

Dog Biscuits for the Soul: Kirby

Kirby

For three months my family had been searching for a new small, furry addition. I had been visiting local animal shelters and browsing the newspapers. So many pets needed good homes, but none seemed to fit into our family, due to size, temperament and other things we wanted in a companion. While perusing the Internet one evening, I stumbled across Petfinder.com. The website is excellent for thoroughly describing the pets that are up for adoption. It was so easy to "run down" the pros and cons. In less than two minutes I had found the cutest little Boston Terrier. It seemed as if he would fit well with the activities of our household. The next morning I went to visit him and wound up bringing him home! The ladies at the shelter were so friendly and informative. They were just as excited to find him a forever home as I was to adopt him. Kirby is the most precious little thing in the world.

Jessica Stallman, Murfreesboro, Tennessee
Kirby was adopted from Country K-9 in Lebanon, Tennessee

Resources

Collins, Ace: *Lassie: A Dog's Life: The First 50 Years*. Penguin Books, 1993
Internet Movie Data Base: www.imdb.com
McCullough, Susan: *Your New Dog: An Expert Answers Your Every Question*. Capital Books, 2003

2

Pre-Adoption Preliminaries

Dogs embody many characteristics that we humans value and enjoy. They love us and forgive us and accept us as we are. They're handsome, beautiful, or "so ugly they're cute." They're always ready for fun and they defend us with their lives. They are always happy to see us. And at the end of the day they lay their warm chins on our knees (or in the case of my adopted dog Mojo, all 75 pounds across my chest) and show us that they love us.

It's so easy to think of all the reasons to have a dog that people often forget that making a dog part of the family is more than cuddles and fun. In fact, one main reason so many dogs are available for adoption is that their previous people didn't consider that, while dogs fill many of our needs, they also have needs of their own—and those needs must be met every single day. Dogs need training, exercise, play, grooming, feeding, and companionship. They also bring an element of chaos into our lives. They break things, make noise, shed, and track in dirt. They can get injured or sick. They are, in short, living beings.

In later chapters, we'll talk about how to choose a dog that is a good match for you and your family. But before you decide to adopt a dog who has already lost at least one home, be certain you are able and willing to meet her needs. We hope that despite whatever baggage she may carry from her previous life, she'll do her best to be your best friend. Make sure you can return the favor, and then choose sensibly. Let's explore some of the things to consider.

Petfinder.com: The Adopted Dog Bible

For more great tips, watch our video on adopting the right dog for you at www.petfinder.com/dog-bible.

Will a Dog Fit into Your Life?

Can You Afford a Dog?

Like all good things, having a dog carries a price tag. As you learned in Chapter 1, if your new friend comes from a shelter or rescue program, you will almost certainly pay an adoption fee to help defray the cost of taking in unwanted or lost animals, including the one you take home. But even if you find your dog or she's given to you for free, rest assured you'll spend money on her. In fact, the fee you pay to adopt will be a tiny fraction of the money you will spend over the life of your dog.

Some expenses are mandatory for all dogs, including food, routine veterinary care, licensing according to local regulations, at least one collar, a leash, an identification tag, a way to keep your dog from roaming, and basic grooming equipment and supplies. Any reputable shelter, rescue program, or individual will require that your dog be altered (spayed or neutered) as a condition of adoption. Other expenditures may not be required, but are highly recommended for almost all dogs. These include permanent identification such as a microchip or tattoo, at least one training class, additional grooming supplies or regular professional grooming, a spare collar and leash, a comfy bed, toys, and at least one crate or carrier (preferably one for the house and a second one for the car).

When you budget for a dog, expect the unexpected expense from time to time. Accidents and illness can result in costly emergency veterinary care. Even the most careful and responsible pet parent can have a dog go missing, and you may have to spend money for posters, advertisements, rewards, and even "bail out" fees if you are lucky enough to have her land safely in a shelter. If you are considering adopting a dog with special physical or behavioral challenges, be sure you have a clear idea of how much specialized professional support may be needed to overcome her past, and for how long. Although we hesitate to put a price tag on love, it's important to know that you can afford the cost of regular care for your adopted dog, and that you have the resources to cover unexpected expenses from time to time. After all, if

No Such Thing As a Free Dog

Adopting a dog requires a financial commitment to her health and well-being. This chart will give you a rough idea of how big a commitment you should plan on. (These costs are estimates based on a survey of pet parents around the country—some may be higher or lower depending on where you live and the dog you adopt.)

	First Year	Each Year Thereafter
Adoption	$0–500	N/A
Food	$120–500	$120–500
Nutritional Supplements*	$0–100	$0–100
Food/water bowls	$10–40	$0–25
Treats	$20–200	$20–200
Dental/chew toys	$20–200	$20–200
Routine veterinary exam	$45–200	$20–100
Vaccinations	$60–150	$60–150
Emergency veterinary care	$0–2,000+	$0–2,000+
Heartworm test**	$0–35	$0–35
Heartworm prevention	($0)$24–120	($0)$36–132
Fecal exams	$10–30	$10–20
Worming	$10–25	$10–25
Spaying/neutering	$35–200	N/A
Professional teeth cleaning	$60–500	$0–500
Collar(s)	$7–50	$0–40
Leash(es)	$10–50	$0–50
Training	$30–250	$0–200
Grooming tools	$20–250	$0–25
Professional grooming	$0–1,200	$0–1,200
Shampoo	$5–50	$5–50
Fence	$0–2500	$0–2500
Stain/odor removers	$10–100	$10–100
Doggy bed(s)	$25–100	$0–100
Crate(s)	$20–250	$0–250
Toys	$10–200	$0–200
Boarding, per day	$15–50	$15–50

*Do not supplement your dog's diet without consulting your veterinarian.

**Heartworm tests and prevention are necessary wherever there is risk of exposure.

you can't, there's a good chance your dog could wind up back in a shelter, and that's not what anyone wants.

How Much Time Do You Have for Your Dog?

Taking care of a dog also requires time. At the very least, you will need to feed her two to three times a day (more often in the case of very young puppies or dogs with certain health issues), take her out to potty several times a day, and provide a constant supply of clean water. But that's just the start. To be a responsible pet parent, you must be happy to spend at least an hour a day training, exercising, grooming, and playing with your dog. Regardless of your other commitments, you will have to budget time for her without fail. Plan to spend a minimum of half an hour a day just to meet her basic needs—feeding, potty times, and minimal leg-stretching. If you adopt a dog with a long or heavy coat, you will need to spend at least twenty minutes a day on grooming. If your dog has an abundance of energy, you will need to devote anywhere from twenty minutes to an hour or more to exercising her. If your adopted dog comes to you with little basic training, you will need to spend at least fifteen to thirty minutes a day on that. You can combine some of these tasks—for instance, training and exercise. But even if your adopted buddy is the most laid-back, low-maintenance canine in the world, she still needs to spend at least several hours a day with you, just being your friend. In fact, many dogs find themselves up for adoption because their people didn't think about the time commitment. Dogs are social animals, and they thrive on companionship. Left alone, they often develop serious behavior problems or become depressed. Besides, why have a dog if you don't have time to spend with her?

That said, some dogs do need their people to dedicate more time to doggy pursuits than other dogs (see "Wall-Bouncer or Couch Potato" on page 27). If she's young, or has certain medical conditions, she will need attention every few hours, so you have to come home regularly, or arrange for someone else to be there. If you adopt a puppy or adolescent, you should plan to spend well over an hour a day socializing, exercising, and playing with her during the first year. As we've seen, mature adults vary in their requirements depending on their grooming and exercise needs, and all dogs need at least an hour or two of quality waking time with their people. Many "problem behaviors" are simply the expression of canine intelligence, instinct, and energy that people never channeled positively through training, exercise, and other types of care. If the dog you adopt comes from such a background, it will be especially important for you to devote whatever time she needs as an individual, whether ten minutes or two hours a day, to teaching her new habits and meeting her needs.

If you're a parent, be realistic about how much time your children will spend with the dog you adopt, and how much responsibility a child can reasonably assume. Kids have other commitments, and your dog needs to be cared for regardless of sports, school, and other childhood pursuits. Besides, as children grow, their interests change, and the dog-crazy ten-year-old may have other priorities at fifteen. There's nothing wrong with encouraging children to help, but ultimately, the responsibility for your dog's daily care and her physical and emotional well-being throughout her life must rest with an adult.

If you love your dog, you will enjoy spending time with her. But she's not a book or video game that you can stick on a shelf for a week when you're busy. She needs you every day, several times a day. When you first bring your adopted dog home, she may need an extra hour or two a day sharing walks and other one-on-one activities to help you bond. If you don't have enough time to give to a dog right now, postpone your adoption plans until you do.

Family Matters

The final decision about whether to adopt a dog should be made by the adult who will ultimately be responsible for the dog's care. If the head caretaker doesn't want the dog and the extra work and responsibility the dog brings with her, you're asking for trouble. At best, family relations will be strained. At worst, the dog will be neglected. For an adopted dog who has already experienced abandonment, neglect, or abuse, an environment filled with tension can exacerbate health and behavior problems, making the reluctant caretaker even more resentful. Whether she stays in such an unhealthy environment or loses her home again, the dog is the ultimate loser.

While the final decision will be up to the main caretaker, all members of your household should be included in the decision to adopt a dog. Not everyone must be committed to the dog's care, but no one should be so opposed that the dog herself will suffer. If you cannot reach a compromise that ensures your dog's physical and emotional well-being, postpone the adoption until your living arrangements are more conducive to successful dog parenting. If your child is pleading for a dog you really don't want and will resent, stick to your guns, explain to your children that you cannot take on the extra responsibility, and ask them to keep the dog's welfare in mind. Every dog deserves to be cared for by someone who wants the job as part of a loving relationship.

Dogs and children can make wonderful companions.

A Pooch to Fit Your Life and Lifestyle

It's easy to see a dog as a link to a happy time in life—perhaps a return to childhood and that wonderful pup you grew up with, or a reminder of your own children's childhood with a playful pooch. Unfortunately, it's also easy to ignore how differently we live at different stages of our lives. If you haven't had a dog for a while, or if your situation has changed, be sure that a dog will fit the way you live now, and the way you want to live in the coming years. Your lifestyle directly affects whether you should adopt a dog. Here are some things to ask yourself before you adopt:

☼ **Is my current residence suited to life with a dog?** What sort of dog can live comfortably here? Taking care of potty breaks is very different in an apartment or condo than in a suburban home with a big fenced yard, and while some toy dogs can be trained to use a litter box, you wouldn't want to do that with a big dog. Your home will also affect how you exercise your dog. If you live in an apartment or other small home with little or no yard, a small dog may have room to run and play all she needs. Indeed, some large dogs, such as Mastiffs and most of the sight hounds, are quite sedate as adults and do fine in smaller homes or apartments. More active dogs may benefit from long leash walks or visits to a local off-leash dog park. If you're truly dedicated to meeting her exercise needs, you can live with any type of dog in a small home, but be honest with yourself and with the rescuers you contact. Even within specific breed groups or common mixes there can be wide variation, and if you take your time you may be able to find an individual of a breed you like who will fit into your life. If your dog has never lived in a human home before, she may need extra time to adjust. A house with carpets and furniture is quite a step up for a dog who has been a stray, or who has lived in a kennel or in someone's backyard all her life.

❀ **How will my travels affect my life as a dog owner?** Some people travel with their dogs, but if you travel frequently and can't or don't want to take your dog along, consider the challenges your decision will raise. Arranging for reliable care for your dog while you travel will be an added responsibility and expense. Whether or not you are home, your dog will need food, exercise, and attention. You may consider boarding her or hiring a pet-sitter to care for her in your home. An adopted dog in particular needs emotional reassurance, and your frequent absences could be very stressful for her.

❀ **How will my social life or work obligations affect my ability to care for a dog?** It's lovely to come home from a long, hectic day to find a warm, tail-wagging friend waiting at the door. But if that friend waits by herself for ten or more hours a day, day in and day out, you're sentencing her to a lonely life. One solution is to find ways to include your dog in some aspects of your life and work—dog sports in place of other sports, for instance, or dog-assisted therapy (if your dog is suited to it) to fulfill your philanthropic urges. Some employers even allow well-mannered dogs to come to work. However, if you know that your current situation means that your dog will spend all day most days and many evenings alone, adoption may not be the best idea right now.

❀ **How do the people I live with feel about having a dog in the house?** If you live with someone who doesn't like dogs, you're asking for trouble if you bring one home, and chances are the dog will be the one who suffers most. That's why responsible shelters and rescuers will try to ensure that the whole household will welcome the adoptee.

❀ **Am I (or is my spouse, partner, or roommate) intolerant of**

hair, dirt, and other realities of sharing our home with a dog? Some types of dogs may work in a situation like that, but even the cleanest dog can make messes. If this describes you, you definitely don't want a dog that sheds heavily, loves mud, or drools! And please don't isolate your dog outdoors, in the basement, or in a room by herself in an attempt to protect your clean home. Dogs are pack animals and need to live as a part of your family. Making a dog live in the garage or backyard, especially by herself, is like putting her in solitary confinement. Besides, what's the point of having a dog if she can't be with you?

✿ **How will my health, or the health of someone else in my household, affect me as a dog parent, and how will having a dog affect my health?** Research shows that pet parents tend to live longer and be less prone to problems like depression. However, be realistic about whether you can handle a lively puppy, a big, rowdy dog, or an energetic pooch who needs to walk an hour a day. If someone in your household suffers from allergies or a respiratory problem, you may need a dog that sheds minimally. (Grooming may help as well—see Chapter 11.) If anyone in the household has mobility problems, a rambunctious dog, especially a big one, could be a hazard.

✿ **How do my other pets affect my dog adoption plans?** If you already have a dog, you'll want to choose another who is likely to get along well with the first. The most important consideration is the temperaments (what people sometimes call *disposition*) of the two (or more) animals. If you already have a dog or two, or will be spending time with friends or relatives who do, you'll want to choose a dog who is likely to be social with other dogs. If you have children or spend time around other people's kids, you want a dog who is friendly, fairly confident in the midst of noise and activity, and adores children. Gender can be a consideration, and opposites (one male, one female) are often more compatible, although this isn't as big a consideration when they are all spayed or neutered. If there's a big difference in size, you must ensure that the small dog is safe from rough play, hunting behavior, or aggression displayed by the bigger dog. If you have a cat or other small pet, the same principle applies. A dog who plays rough can injure a more fragile pet without meaning to, and a dog with a strong prey drive may instinctively regard a smaller pet as a legitimate target, especially when he or she is moving. Tell the shelter or rescue workers about your other pets and let them help you in your adoption decision.

The key to a successful adoption is to be realistic about what you need from a dog and can offer to a dog. If you decide that you really do want a dog, and that you can provide the right home for the right dog, the next step is to find one who fits your personality and your life.

Describing Your Dream Dog

No other domestic animal varies in size, looks, and personality as much as *Canis familiaris*—the dog. If you are honestly ready for a dog, there's a type of dog for you, whether a purebred or a mixture of breeds. You may already know what you want, but be careful. Don't choose a dog because you grew up with one of that breed, or because your friend or co-worker loves hers. Remember, all dogs (like all people) are individuals, and you're the one who will live with this dog. Take the time to learn about different breeds (see Chapter 3 for more) so that you can choose wisely. And remember, a mixed-breed dog can show any of the traits of any of the breeds that make up her ancestry.

If you think you don't have time to do all that research, it may be that you really don't have time to add a dog into your life right now. Consider this: A reasonably well-cared-for dog will probably live to be ten to fifteen years old. That's a long time to live with the wrong dog, and not the best life for either of you. After all, if she's not right for you, you're probably not right for her, either.

Whose Dog *Is* This?

One person's perfect pup is another's canine catastrophe. Listen to people's suggestions, but choose a dog who suits *you*, not someone else.

Your chances of finding the right dog will be much better if you are honest and realistic with yourself and with shelter or rescue staff and volunteers about what you do and do not want in a dog. Let's look at some factors that will increase the odds of finding the perfect dog for *you* to adopt.

Your Dog's Role in Your Life

The most important questions you need to ask yourself are:

- ❋ What do you expect your dog to contribute to your life?
- ❋ Do you want a running and hiking buddy, or is your idea of exercise a slow stroll around the block?
- ❋ Do you want a happy-go-lucky friend to everyone, or a highly alert alarm barker?
- ❋ Can you train and handle a bold, dominant dog, or do you need one who won't challenge your authority?
- ❋ Do you need a dog who will be reliable with children? Or one you can take with you when you travel?
- ❋ Do you want a dog who follows you all around the house, or would you prefer a less clingy, more independent character?

As you think about how your dog will fit into your life, identify the traits that will contribute to a good fit. Are you a jogger? You need a dog with enough size and energy to keep up. Frequent flyer? Maybe you need a dog small enough to fit into a carry-on airline carrier. Live cheek-by-jowl with your neighbors? A big-time barker won't do. And so on. Be clear about how specific traits will help or hinder a dog in the role you envision for her.

Purebred or Mixed?

Purebred and mixed-breed dogs are all terrific companions. If you want to participate with your dog in a specific sport or activity—say hunting, sheep-herding, or obedience competition—that will affect your choice. Many very successful competition dogs, therapy dogs, search-and-rescue dogs, and other "performance" dogs have been adopted from shelters and rescue programs. If you choose a dog who appears to be purebred, you'll have some idea of her potential natural talents. But mixed-breed dogs can also excel in many fields, because they have inherited the traits of their purebred ancestors. (For more on breeds and mixes, see Chapter 3.)

Be aware that dogs in shelters, and sometimes in rescue organizations, may be misidentified, especially if they are less commonly seen breeds. If

Mixed-up Crosses

A *cross-bred* dog is the offspring of two pure-breds of different breeds. A *mixed-breed* is a dog with more than two breeds in her background (in other words, one or both of her parents is not a purebred).

you really want a dog of a particular breed, learn as much as possible about how dogs of that breed look and especially how they behave before you begin meeting candidates for adoption. If you are open to a mixed-breed, you will still benefit from figuring out as well as you can the breeds that make up a given dog's ancestry. Not only will you know more about what to expect in personality and other behavioral traits, but you can learn more about special health concerns that may affect your new friend.

But wait, you say—aren't mixed-breeds healthier than purebreds? Sometimes. The term "hybrid vigor" with regard to dogs stems from the observation that mixed-breed dogs may seem heartier than their purebred counterparts. However, all puppies inherit genes from both parents. If the parents pass along the genes for a hereditary disease, the pups stand a good chance of having that disease. Suppose, for example, that you cross two breeds that are both prone to canine hip dysplasia, an inherited crippling disease of the hip joint. If both parents carry the genes for hip dysplasia and pass them to their offspring, the puppies may be affected by the disease, even though they are mixed-breeds (or labeled with a "designer dog" name by unscrupulous sellers).

Does this mean that all adoptable dogs have health issues? Absolutely not. What it does mean is that, regardless of where you get your dog, you should educate yourself about potential health concerns in your dog's breed or breeds so that you can take preventative steps where possible, and can recognize symptoms and understand your options if they occur.

Temperament and behavioral traits are also more predictable with purebreds and mixed-breeds of obvious ancestry than with dogs whose heritage is harder to determine. Remember, however, that every dog is an individual. Just as the members of your human family are alike in some ways and different in others, dogs of any breed (or specific combination of breeds) vary in terms of individual personality, energy level, behavior, and looks. If you speak to rescuers or read the listings for individual dogs on purebred rescue websites, you will get a feel for how these traits may vary within a specific breed.

If you plan to adopt a mixed-breed, you can also get an idea of what to expect by learning about the breeds that appear to be in her ancestry. If the breeds have similar traits, a mix of those breeds will very likely have those traits as well. For instance, a cross of Golden Retriever and Standard Poodle will likely be big, intelligent, very energetic, fond of swimming, and inclined to retrieve things, because both Goldens and Poodles tend to have those traits. A mix of dissimilar breeds, on the other hand, will be a bit trickier, and could show any of the traits of her ancestors in any combination. If you understand that and learn as much as possible about the breeds that seem to make up your mixed-breed buddy, her temperament, behavior, and other characteristics will make more sense, and the variables can certainly make life interesting.

Wall-Bouncer or Couch Potato

All dogs need some exercise, but some dogs need lots and lots of it every single day. A high-energy dog who doesn't get sufficient exercise will not be a pleasant companion. You can expect her to be wildly playful and hard to handle; the term "out of control" comes to mind. She'll have trouble settling down or paying attention, and she may develop destructive behaviors like digging, chewing, chasing things, running off, and barking just because she has to do *something*. In fact, all too many dogs are available for adoption because their people failed to understand and anticipate the dogs' need for daily exercise. Many dogs labeled "hyper" (hyperactive) are perfectly normal representatives of their breeds who simply haven't been given enough exercise and haven't been trained, and consequently, they have far too much excess energy and no idea what to do with it. So before you adopt, be realistic about how much canine energy you can manage responsibly (see also "Tiny, Medium, Big, or Beastly" on page 29).

And before you decide that you'll turn your dog loose in the backyard for an hour while you sit in front of the TV, you need to know two things. First, most dogs do not self-exercise—they want a playmate to walk or run with them or throw a ball. Even two or more dogs together may not exercise

If you lead a less active lifestyle, stick with a couch potato.

without some human direction; they're more likely to press their wet noses against the back door and wonder what you're doing in there. Second, those dogs who do self-exercise don't usually run simple laps around the yard. They're more likely to redo your landscaping, get into things, or jump the fence and take off.

The best things you can do to be sure you and the dog you adopt will be exercise compatible are to learn about the breeds and mixes that interest you and ask rescue or shelter personnel to help you choose the right individual. Keep in mind that there is no direct correlation between size and exercise needs. Some big dogs need lots of exercise, and some are content with a couple of daily walks around the block. Similarly, some smaller dogs, particularly some of the Toy breeds that were developed to be strictly companions, don't require much exercise. But other small dogs, including many terriers, need to run off an hour or more of energy a day. And remember, individuals' needs vary within breeds. Keep in mind that while you may think Australian Shepherds are the most beautiful dogs on earth, if several knowledgeable breed rescuers suggest that you won't be able to manage an Aussie's need for exercise, you will want to heed their warning. Bottom line: Be sure that you choose a dog whose exercise needs you can meet. You'll both be happier if you do.

Never Met a Stranger or a One-Person Pooch

Your dog's temperament is another critical trait to consider when choosing a dog. No matter how beautiful you find a dog, if her approach to the world doesn't fit yours or isn't compatible with the environment in which you will live together, neither of you will get the best benefit from a human-canine relationship. Your research on breeds will help you make a choice because members of a given breed tend to be similar in temperament. The temperaments and personalities of mixed-breed dogs are a bit more difficult to predict, though you will find plenty of information on mixed-breeds in Chapter 3, so it will be important to discuss individual dogs with their shelter caretakers or foster homes.

Keep in mind, though, normal temperament will vary among the members of any breed. In addition, sometimes an individual has a personality that is atypical for her breed. Each individual dog's personality and behavior have been shaped by her genetic makeup, by her experiences, and occasionally by a medical issue. Depending on her background, an adopted dog may lack the training, exercise, socialization, or even nutrition that help puppies grow into well-adjusted adults. Fortunately, most can overcome their histories and blossom when put in the right environment. The best way to find an individual whose temperament will suit you and your situation is to work with a knowledgeable adoption counselor who can help you find the right dog. And while we don't want to cast a cloud over the exciting prospect of adopting a new companion, it is important to keep in mind that some dogs have temperament or behavioral issues which will make them unsuitable to join your home. For more information on behavioral assessments and how to choose a dog you can live happily with, see Chapter 5.

Tiny, Medium, Big, or Beastly

Size may be a factor in your choice of a dog. If you adopt an adult dog, you know how big she is. How big a puppy will be can be hard to predict. Even purebred dogs of a single breed vary in size, although you can anticipate within a few inches how big a healthy dog of a particular breed will be at maturity. A "small" Great Dane will still be enormous next to a "big" Chihuahua. The adult size of a mixed-breed puppy, though, can be a surprise, especially if you don't know her ancestry or if there are dogs of widely varied sizes in her family tree. The biggest puppy in the litter at eight weeks does not necessarily grow up to be the biggest dog. And forget the "big feet" approach to predicting adult size by the size of a puppy's feet—it doesn't work. I adopted Kona when he was 6 weeks old and the adoption counselor warned me that he would probably grow to be 85 or 90 pounds. I was ready for a dog that size, but I was not disappointed when Kona failed to grow into his feet and topped out at 55 pounds. If adult size is a critical factor for you, consider adopting a fully grown dog, a purebred puppy, or a puppy whose parents are known and are of similar-size breeds.

Adopted dogs come in all shapes and sizes!

Here are some questions to ask yourself if you're not sure how important size is to you:

1. **Can my home accommodate a bigger dog?** A giant breed like a St. Bernard or Mastiff can take up a lot of space in a small home. On the other hand, a large but sedate dog might be a better fit than a smaller but very active dog.

2. **Can I manage a bigger dog physically?** Remember, you have to walk this dog, trim her nails, brush her, and, if she's ever injured or ill, lift her. Even with human help and canine cooperation, handling a ninety-pound dog can be a major job.

3. **How big of a dog can I afford to care for properly?** (See "Can You Afford a Dog." on page 17.)

4. **What size dog would suit the other people who live in or visit my home regularly?** Tiny dogs can be injured easily and don't fit most homes with young children, or with people with any condition that could endanger the dog or the person. A large, rambunctious dog, especially a young one, can accidentally knock over a young child or an infirm adult.

5. **Do I have another pet to consider when choosing the size of my next dog?** Big and small animals can certainly live together, but a large dog can injure or kill a smaller pet, either accidentally or intentionally. Before you introduce a new dog who is significantly bigger or smaller than the dog or other pets you already have, be sure everyone in your household understands the risk and can commit to keeping the smaller animals safe.

6. **How big of a dog can I travel with comfortably?** A big dog will take up more room in your vehicle. Her crate and other equipment will be bigger and heavier to load and unload. Some accommodations—as well as friends and relatives!—have size limits

Petfinder.com: The Adopted Dog Bible

for dogs they welcome. If you plan to travel frequently by air with your dog, bear in mind that only very small pets can ride inside the cabin. All others must travel in cargo (see Chapter 19).

As you consider what size dog you want and can manage, remember that there is no direct correlation between size and energy level (see "Wall-Bouncer or Couch Potato" on page 27), and some larger breeds are actually easier to manage than some smaller breeds.

Wash-and-Wear or Daily Grooming

Dogs don't end up with gorgeous coats by accident. All coats require some care, and some coats require a lot of care to stay healthy and attractive. Regardless of your dog's size, temperament, and exercise needs, she'll rely on you to keep her well-groomed (see Chapter 11 for more on coat types and grooming). Here are the most important considerations regarding canine coats:

- How much shed hair can you stand? There is no correlation between the length of the coat and the amount of shedding, so do your homework if you prefer a breed that sheds less. And don't believe the hype about some so-called "designer breeds" not shedding. Many of them do—remember, they inherit traits from both parents.
- How frequently are you willing to bathe your dog? Some dogs have oily coats designed to repel water and keep the dog dry when hunting or working. Oily coats tend to develop a "doggy smell" more quickly than less oily coats, so if you choose an oily-coat breed, expect to give more baths (or take her to a groomer more often).
- How well will you maintain this dog's coat? Poodles, terriers, and dogs with long, silky coats need regular, time-consuming grooming to keep their coats and skin clean and healthy. You must learn to or be able to afford to take your dog to a groomer every four to six weeks.

Pups Versus Older Dogs

One choice you'll need to make is whether to adopt a puppy, an adolescent, or an adult. It's not always an easy decision, so let's take a look at the advantages and disadvantages of adopting dogs of different ages.

Puppies are enchanting little beings. They're funny and cute and full of promise. But puppies, like all babies, need a lot of care and attention if they are to fulfill that promise. Your puppy will need to be trained so that she knows what you want her to do and not do. She will need lots of safe exercise and play so that her body develops properly, and she will need you to socialize her with other people and animals so that she feels comfortable in the world. As she learns and grows, she'll get into things, chew, make messes, and have accidents in the house. All in all, a puppy is a tremendous amount of work—much more than many unsuspecting adopters realize.

Puppies who are available for adoption through shelters and rescue organizations sometimes offer additional challenges because they come from less-than-ideal situations. Chances are good that their parents were not screened for inherited health or temperament problems, or that optimum pre-natal or post-natal care was provided for mama dog and her pups. Shelter and rescue puppies may have been taken from their mothers at too young an age for optimal emotional development. Veterinary attention may have been lacking prior to the pup's coming into the shelter or rescue group. Responsible shelters and rescue groups provide medical care, treatment for parasites, and vaccinations against infectious disease when appropriate; however, sometimes adopted puppies don't show signs of illness until they move to their new home.

Does this mean you shouldn't adopt a puppy from a shelter or rescue group? Not at all—many wonderful dogs grow from puppies who didn't have the best start in life. But you do need to be aware that even a young puppy has a history, and you may need to give her some extra care to make up for it. Realize, too, that you can't always predict how the puppy you adopt will mature, especially if she's a mixed-breed. If you adopt a puppy, make sure you're ready to accept her as an adult, even if she's thirty pounds bigger and six inches shaggier than you expected.

Petfinder.com: The Adopted Dog Bible

Puppies turn into adolescents at lightning speed. That babyish furball you bring home will turn all legs, ears, nose, and energy in another four months. Adolescence in dogs begins at six months and lasts until anywhere from eighteen months up to thirty-six months, depending on the breed. Small dogs tend to mature physically more quickly than big dogs do, but all dogs are quite immature mentally and emotionally until they are at least two or three years old. They continue to need training, lots of exercise, and ongoing socialization throughout this developmental period.

If this is your first dog, or if you cannot devote the time necessary to train, socialize, and exercise a young or adolescent puppy properly, an adult dog could be a better option for you. If you're not sure, talk to people who are currently raising puppies or have done so recently to get a realistic picture of what it's like. If dealing with puppy pee on the carpet and needle-sharp teeth in your toes for months on end sounds like too much chaos for your taste, adopt an adult.

Make sure you can handle a high-energy dog if you bring home a puppy!

When you choose an adult dog, you have a pretty good idea what you're getting. You can see her physical traits and get some idea of her basic temperament, even though dogs in shelters and dogs newly in rescue foster homes may not always show their true personality right away. Still, with the guidelines we offer you later in this book (see Chapter 5), you can select a behaviorally sound dog who will improve and blossom once settled into your loving home.

If you are concerned that an older dog won't bond to you, don't be. Dogs are remarkably resilient and open-hearted. Some completely overcome their pasts in a matter of days; others may take a few weeks or months, and a few will carry a little baggage for even longer than that. Working with your adopted dog to help her overcome any hurdles necessary to enjoy her new life can be an incredibly rewarding experience—and result in a long-term, loving relationship.

How Old Are You?

It can often be difficult for shelters or rescue groups to pinpoint a dog's precise age, but here are some guidelines to help you out.

Dogs are generally considered to be puppies—the equivalent of human infants, toddlers, and young children—for their first five or six months. Smaller dogs often mature physically more quickly than medium-sized and large dogs, but mentally most dogs can be considered adolescents (teen-agers—eek!) from five or six months until about eighteen months. Medium-sized dogs stop growing when they reach about fourteen months, but do not usually attain mature muscular development until they are two years old. Large and giant breeds often continue to grow until they are two, and by two years of age, most dogs are beginning to behave like adults, although for many medium-sized to large dogs, complete mental and emotional maturity doesn't arrive until the third year, at which time they are true adults. As a caveat, I will tell you that although Mojo has reached his third year and may officially be an adult, we are still waiting for complete emotional maturity!

Dogs are considered elderly or geriatric when they have reached the last 25 percent of their expected life span. In other words, if you anticipate that your dog will live for ten years, she is considered elderly at 7.5 years of age. This is directly related to a dog's size and breed, as well as to the quality of care she receives during her lifetime. For instance, most small-breed dogs are considered elderly when they reach twelve years of age, medium breed dogs at ten, large breed dogs at nine, and giant breed dogs at seven.

Easy to Train or Free Spirit

Some breeds tend be labeled as more or less "intelligent." What exactly does that mean to you as a dog owner? If you're like most people, you want a dog who learns quickly and obeys you willingly. A "smart" dog is more likely to do both, right?

Not exactly. The truth is that extremely smart dogs are typically very challenging pets because they learn not just what you want them to learn, but all sorts of other things as well. They are very observant, and they quickly come to understand our behavior patterns, which is why they sometimes seem to read our minds. Smart dogs watch carefully, experiment, and figure out things like how to open the back door or the dog-food container. They anticipate things they don't like and try to avoid them—you open the cabinet containing the doggy toothpaste or shampoo and spend the next half hour coaxing your dog out from under the couch. They also anticipate things they like, of course, and aren't ashamed to show how happy they are when you pick up their leash or head for the treat jar. Some brilliant dogs are easy to train and extremely obedient. Others are easily bored, happy to find their own entertainment, and not all that concerned about making people happy. Some dogs who take a little longer to learn things are also very obedient and less inclined be "creative" in their pursuit of fun.

Once again, you need to research the breed or breeds that interest you. If you already have your dog, learning about the breed or breeds in her ancestry will help you understand her and her training needs. Each dog is, of course, an individual, but in general, breeds that traditionally work independently of their handlers tend to be smart, self-motivated problem solvers who need more patient, persistent, and motivational training. Many of the Hounds, Terriers, and northern working breeds (such as Malamutes and Huskies) fall into this category. Breeds that traditionally work closely with people and under their direction tend to be more willing to listen and obey, and are therefore easier to train. That would include most of the sporting and herding breeds, although they also tend to be very energetic, making them a handful, especially when they are young.

Oh Boy, Oh Girl

Who will make a better pet: a male (dog) or a female (bitch)? The answer is they both will. Males in many breeds tend to be larger than females, which may be a consideration (although a big girl may be taller and heavier than a small male). But neither sex can claim to be better at the job of best friend.

Some people prefer one sex over the other due to concerns for lawns and shrubs. It's true that males often (although not always) lift their legs to urinate, anointing upright plants and objects, whereas females usually squat (although some also "hike" their legs to mark vertical surfaces). Those brown circles in the lawn, though, are likely caused not by urine but by fungi that grow on feces that's allowed to stay too long, and shrubs are more likely to be damaged by insects and other diseases than by urine. If your landscaping is a concern, you can train your dog, regardless of sex, to do his or her business in a designated area.

Some people also worry that male dogs will mark the inside of the house with urine and will mount people and other animals. In fact, some females engage in those behaviors, too, as expressions of dominance. Regardless of sex, such inappropriate behaviors are training issues more than gender issues. Many dogs of both sexes live as well-mannered pets. In the end, the important thing is the individual's personality, especially after spaying or neutering removes the sex drive and accompanying behaviors.

Dogs with Special Needs

Some dogs arrive in shelters and rescue organizations with conditions that create special needs and require special adopters. Some of these conditions require very little accommodation, while others demand ongoing medication, therapy, nursing care, or veterinary support. Among the pooches who have special needs are the following:

- Amputees
- Blind dogs
- Deaf dogs
- Dogs with seizure disorders or other neurological issues
- Dogs with chronic problems such as diabetes
- Dogs with chronic disease of the heart, kidneys, liver, or other organs
- Dogs with heartworm disease
- Dogs with chronic allergies or autoimmune problems
- Senior dogs (who may have no problems other than their age)

This list is not exhaustive, but it gives an idea of the sorts of issues some dogs face.

Petfinder.com: The Adopted Dog Bible

Adopting a dog with special needs can be extremely rewarding—these dogs are still able to love, after all. The key to a successful adoption is to be certain that you understand how those needs affect the dog's ability to function, and how they will affect you and your family as her caretakers. Some problems require only minimal adjustments—for instance, many canine amputees get around extremely well. Other conditions will require you to give more of your time and money—perhaps daily injections or other special care, or frequent trips to the vet. Adoption fees for special-needs dogs are sometimes reduced or waived alto-

Dogs with special needs do not have impaired abilities to love.

gether to help compensate for the extra expense, although often a shelter or rescue group has expended a great deal of precious resources on such a dog and would be grateful for a donation to help them continue helping others.

In some cases, you will have to accept that your time with this dog will be short. If you can believe that a relationship's depth is more important than its length, and if you can provide for the dog's needs while she's with you, she will repay you with love and gratitude, and the peace of knowing that she was well cared for and loved at the end of her life.

Clearly, there are many things to consider before you add a dog—or another dog—to your family. People who fail to plan responsibly are one reason so many dogs are in need of adoption. You can rectify the situation for at least one dog by making a well-informed choice and finding just the right dog to whom you can give a permanent home.

Pledge For New Adopters

- I pledge to make a reasonable commitment of time and effort, and to effect scheduling and lifestyle changes to make this relationship work.
- I pledge to make sure my dog is not exposed to the elements of weather without proper shelter, shade cover, dry ground, access to fresh water, and at least one hour of loving companionship and play a day (I understand this is a minimum and will strive to keep the dog with me as much as possible and treat him or her as an important member of my family).
- I pledge to provide appropriate and timely veterinary care for the life of my dog.
- I pledge to provide my dog with the proper nutrition for optimum health, and to keep my dog the proper weight, neither obese nor emaciated.
- I pledge to keep my dog indoors at night, and to include him or her in the activities of the household while we are home, as much as possible.
- I pledge to keep my dog groomed and free of external parasites and matting (particularly behind my dog's ears, under his elbows, his tail, and his thighs).
- I pledge to spay or neuter my dog, if he or she is not already altered.
- I pledge to give my dog ample aerobic exercise daily, and make sure that at least three times a week he or she gets to run and play and get tired out.
- I pledge to provide my dog with mental stimulation in the form of either play, interactive toys, training, or off-territory leash walks, DAILY.
- I pledge to provide my dog with enough training and/or behavioral management so as to enable him or her to be a welcome part of my community, or managed safely.
- I pledge to provide ample outlets for my dog's instincts (such as off-territory leash walks/running, opportunities to sniff and explore

continued

the natural world, agility training, trick training, fun and rewarding obedience training, play with other dogs, etc.), so that he or she does not feel constantly frustrated, or develop behavioral problems as a result of being neglected or under-stimulated.

- I pledge to provide a home in which my dog clearly knows there are certain rules that I will insist on and he or she can count on.
- I pledge to provide enough toys to satisfy my dog's urge to chew.
- I pledge to get professional help if my dog has or develops behavior or temperament problems, and, if safe, to manage my dog carefully so as not to endanger the people and other pets in my community.
- I pledge to do everything I can to keep my dog from becoming a nuisance in my community.
- I will not allow my dog to run free or out of my control, or to chase cars, bicycles, children, etc.
- I will seek professional help to get my dog to be quiet, or keep my dog quiet both when I am home and away, so as not to disturb my neighbors.
- I pledge to "scoop poop" when off my property, so that my dog and other dogs will always be welcome in public.
- I pledge that if I have to move residences for any reason, I am aware that finding housing that accepts pets can take longer than average, but I commit to moving with my dog, as I would move with a member of my family.
- I pledge that if, for any reason, I can no longer keep this dog, I will not abandon this dog, and
- I will return the dog to the shelter (if required) or allow ample time to find a new, appropriate home, tell the new owners truthfully all the dog's behaviors, good and bad, and follow up occasionally to make sure the dog is safe and content.

From Sue Sternberg, dog behaviorist, trainer, and shelter expert

Dog Biscuits for the Soul: Boomer

Boomer

I have two children: Zachary, who is two, and Samuel, who is four. Samuel has autism. I began to notice that when Samuel was around dogs, he became very calm and his speech took off. It was like the dog opened the door to the world for Samuel. We decided to look for a dog we could train to watch Samuel and be his best friend. We were searching on Petfinder.com when we came across a white German Shepherd. We applied at Echo Dogs White Shepherd Rescue and were approved. They said it usually takes a few months to find the right match, but God was with us because the day we were approved they found us the perfect dog. His name is Boomer. He is three years old and is unbelievably gentle, smart, and beautiful! He loves Samuel and all the rest of us. We are so happy to have him as part of our family.

Kimberly Turcott, Nashua, New Hampshire
Boomer was adopted from Echo Dogs White Shepherd Rescue in Londonderry, New Hampshire

Resources

Benjamin, Carol Lea: *Second Hand Dog.* Hungry Minds, 1994
Boneham, Sheila Webster, PhD: *Training Your Dog for Life.* T.F.H. Publications, 2008
Walkowicz, Chris: *Perfect Match: a Dog Buyer's Guide.* Howell Book House, 1996

3

Breed All About It

Here's help in sorting through the rich assortment of more than one hundred and fifty breeds, plus an infinite number of appealing breed mixtures. This chapter gives you the lowdown on what's to love about any dog, no matter his pedigree (or lack thereof). For more specifics on the characteristics of a given breed, visit the comprehensive Petfinder Dog Breed Directory at www.petfinder.com/dog-breeds. You also can consult breed rescue groups who can give you a better understanding of the breeds you're considering. In addition, many shelters have breed-specific waiting lists. If you are completely set on a particular breed, see if your local shelter has such an option. Many people are surprised to learn that roughly 25 percent of dogs available for adoption are purebred.

Doggie Group-Think

If you've ever watched any of the dog shows televised by *Animal Planet*, you've heard about breed groups. Breeds are often divided into seven main groups: the Sporting Group, the Hound Group, the Terrier Group, the Toy Group, the Working Group, the Herding Group, and the Non-Sporting Group. An eighth group, the Miscellaneous Class, consists of breeds that are generally quite rare.

You'd be surprised how many pure-bred dogs are available for adoption.

Not surprisingly, the breeds in each group may have similar temperaments and exercise requirements. But within each group there's also considerable variety in size (except for the Toy Group), behavior, grooming needs, and health issues. The rest of this chapter summarizes what breeds of each group have in common and where they diverge, as well as listing the breeds that belong to each group.

Looking for a mixed-breed? Not to worry: This chapter saves the best for last by describing the advantages and disadvantages of adopting these one-of-a-kind dogs. In addition, each breed group profile includes information about what to expect when adopting a dog who's a mix of one or more breeds from that group.

Good Sports: The Sporting Group

The dogs in this group were bred to help their human companions hunt birds and other game. The Retrievers do exactly what their name implies; they fetch fallen fowl and small animals and bring them back to the hunter. Spaniels find game that is hiding in grass, bushes, and shrubs, and flush it out for the hunter to shoot. Pointers search for animals that stay on land, and they freeze into position when they find one. The Setters do it all: retrieve, flush, and point.

Sporting dogs can lead perfectly happy lives even if they never find any animals for their human companions, but because they were developed to work outdoors all day, these dogs do need plenty of vigorous exercise. If they get that exercise as well as proper training, these dogs are generally sociable, good-natured, and wonderful companions. They do best in active households, as long as they're included in the activities of those households. If you want a canine couch potato or live in a tiny apartment, most sporting dogs are probably not for you, although seniors have much lower energy needs and could do well in a small, calm home.

The larger dogs in this group may be prone to hip and/or elbow dysplasia, which means the hip or elbow joints don't fit together properly. Such conditions can be very painful for the dog, and if severe, may require corrective surgery. Some, such as the Golden Retriever, are subject to hypothyroidism, a condition in which the thyroid gland doesn't secrete sufficient hormones, which can easily be corrected with medication. The Spaniels, especially Cockers, may suffer from eye problems later in life.

Grooming requirements for sporting dogs vary. Some, like the Labrador Retriever, have short, thick coats that need just a quick weekly brushing. Others, like the Golden Retriever, need to be thoroughly brushed twice a week or more to keep shedding under control. For the wirehaired or curly coated, weekly brushings will keep them looking their best. The high-maintenance dogs in this group include the Spaniels and the Gordon

Golden Retriever— Sporting Group

Setter. These dogs need frequent brushing and trimming to keep them comfortable and good-looking. Owners of these dogs often look to a grooming pro to do the trimming.

Mixes that include one or more sporting breeds in their family trees can make wonderfully loyal, affectionate pets. However, such dogs are also likely to be highly energetic, which makes vigorous daily exercise a must for them to live happily in human households. That high energy level may result in a dog who is too exuberant to be a good playmate for toddlers and preschoolers, although a senior can be a mellow and understanding companion for young children, as long as there's adult supervision. An older child, however, may discover that a sporting breed mix will become his new best friend.

Medium: 20 to 60 pounds
- American Water Spaniel
- Brittany
- Cocker Spaniel
- English Cocker Spaniel
- English Springer Spaniel
- Field Spaniel

- Nova Scotia Duck Tolling Retriever
- Sussex Spaniel
- Welsh Springer Spaniel
- Wirehaired Pointing Griffon

Large: over 60 pounds
- Clumber Spaniel
- Pointer
- German Shorthaired Pointer
- German Wirehaired Pointer
- Chesapeake Bay Retriever
- Curly-Coated Retriever
- Flat-Coated Retriever
- Golden Retriever
- Labrador Retriever
- English Setter
- Gordon Setter
- Irish Setter
- Irish Water Spaniel (females may be medium-sized)
- Spinone Italiano
- Vizsla
- Weimaraner

Elvis's Favorites: The Hound Group

Adults of a certain age may remember hearing Elvis Presley singing about hound dogs and the truth of the matter is that the members of the Hound Group are really something special. Like their cousins in the Sporting Group, hounds were bred to hunt. Their quarry of choice is small mammals, though some, like the Ridgeback and the Wolfhound, were bred to hunt larger animals, like lions and wolves. Some of these dogs, such as the Dachshund and the Beagle, are called *scent hounds,* because they depend on their noses to find their quarry. Others, such as the Greyhound and Scottish Deerhound, rely on their keen eyesight to do their jobs, which is why they're known as *sight hounds.*

Dogs in this group have a variety of temperaments. The sight hounds

Petfinder.com: The Adopted Dog Bible

tend to be more docile than the scent hounds, who are often so busy following their noses that they may be labeled "stubborn." But all hounds are relatively independent. They make good companions, but they may not be as tolerant of children (especially very young children) as dogs in other groups. That said, with good training and socializing, along with monitoring the behavior of children, hound dogs can become devoted family companions.

Many hounds are enthusiastic yodelers. Whether you consider hound howling to be endearing or annoying may depend largely on your living situation. If you live in a single-family home (where no one will hear the hound but you), this can be a lovable quirk, but if you live in an apartment it could be a big problem. I fostered a litter of beagle mix puppies once and I can still hear the "woo-wooing" in my dreams.

The chief health problem for the larger dogs in this group is hip and elbow dysplasia. The Beagle and Dachshund

Beagle puppy—
Hound Group

may be prone to invertebral disc disease, a condition in which one or more discs between the spinal vertebrae rupture, causing pain and lameness. Surgery is usually needed to treat this condition.

Grooming requirements vary for hound dogs. The smooth-coated hounds, such as the Beagle, smooth-haired Dachshund, and Rhodesian Ridgeback, need little more than a quick weekly brushing. Breeds with longer locks, such as the long-haired Dachshund, Afghan Hound, and Saluki, need thorough biweekly brushings, with perhaps some help from a grooming pro to keep those tresses trimmed. Hounds with folds in their skins, such as Basset Hounds and Bloodhounds, should be kept especially clean to avoid skin infections.

The temperaments of hound mixes depend in part on whether the dog is a scent hound mix or a sight hound mix. A scent hound mix may behave like a nose on four legs. Once this dog picks up an interesting scent, he can become extremely single-minded in his effort to track it. These dogs may also engage in howling. A sight hound mix may share a purebred sight hound's propensity to chase small "prey" and ability to sprint.

Small: under 20 pounds
- Dachshund (miniature)

Medium: 20 to 60 pounds
- Basenji
- Basset Hound
- Beagle
- Dachshund (standard)
- Foxhound (American)
- Foxhound (English)
- Harrier
- Petit Basset Griffon Vendeen
- Pharaoh Hound
- Plott Hound
- Whippet

Large: over 60 pounds
- Afghan Hound
- Black and Tan Coonhound
- Bloodhound
- Borzoi
- Greyhound
- Ibizan Hound
- Irish Wolfhound
- Norwegian Elkhound
- Otterhound
- Rhodesian Ridgeback
- Saluki
- Scottish Deerhound

Petfinder.com: The Adopted Dog Bible

Busy, Busy, Busy: The Terrier Group

Remember Toto in *The Wizard of Oz?* He was a spunky, confident little dog who would stop at nothing to defend Dorothy from all sorts of dangers, even the Wicked Witch of the West. Toto epitomized the spirit of the dogs in the Terrier Group: feisty, lively dogs with hearts of a not-so-cowardly lion.

The first terriers were bred to hunt and kill vermin, otters, badgers, foxes, etc. Today's terriers haven't lost the spunk and energy needed to get that job done. But don't think you need to open your home to mice to make a Terrier happy. He'll do just fine alerting you to the presence of strangers, accompanying you on brisk walks, and being a part of your daily activities. These lively, tenacious, confident dogs pack a whole lot of attitude within their compact bodies. They do best with experienced dog owners who have plenty of time to spend with them and who make sure that the person, not the Terrier, provides the leadership in the family.

Depending on the breed, a Terrier's grooming needs can be considerable. For example, a properly groomed Bedlington Terrier is combed and trimmed to resemble a lamb with down-drooping ears. However, some of the shorter-haired Terrier breeds do just fine with a weekly brushing.

Three breeds in this group, the American Staffordshire Terrier, the Bull Terrier, and the Staffordshire Bull Terrier, have the distinction of descending from bull-and-terrier crosses bred for bull-baiting and dogfighting before those cruel activities were outlawed. These breeds, as well as the American Pit Bull Terrier (a breed that is not recognized by the AKC), are what most people refer to as "Pit Bulls." Adopting one of these dogs requires a special understanding of the breed. (See "Pit Bulls: The Myths, the Legends, the Reality" on page 49 for things to keep in mind if you want to add one of these loving dogs to your household.)

Terrier mixes are quite common, and they do best with experienced owners who know how to be kind, benevolent leaders. That said, positive reinforcement training and socialization can help a Terrier mix remain a great companion. Terrier mixes sometimes need to be the only dogs in their families, due to the predisposition of some such mixes to be intolerant or even aggressive toward other dogs.

Airedale Terrier—
Terrier Group

Small: under 20 pounds
- Australian Terrier
- Bedlington Terrier
- Border Terrier
- Cairn Terrier
- Dandie Dinmont Terrier
- Fox Terrier (Smooth)
- Fox Terrier (Wire)
- Lakeland Terrier
- Manchester Terrier (Standard)
- Miniature Schnauzer
- Norfolk Terrier
- Norwich Terrier
- Parson Russell Terrier (formerly known as Jack Russell Terrier)
- Scottish Terrier
- Welsh Terrier
- West Highland White Terrier

Medium: 20 to 60 pounds
- American Staffordshire Terrier
- Bull Terrier
- Glen of Imaal Terrier
- Irish Terrier
- Kerry Blue Terrier
- Manchester Terrier
- Miniature Bull Terrier
- Sealyham Terrier
- Skye Terrier
- Soft Coated Wheaten Terrier
- Staffordshire Bull Terrier

Large: over 60 pounds
- Airedale Terrier (females may be smaller)
- American Staffordshire Terrier

Petfinder.com: The Adopted Dog Bible

Pit Bulls: The Myths, the Legends, the Reality

My Pit Bull Mojo is the sweetest dog ever.

Mention the words "Pit Bull," and an intense debate will almost inevitably follow. Unscrupulous breeding by less-than-upstanding citizens, negatively sensationalized (and often false) media accounts, and long-standing myths surrounding these types of dogs have led to their vilification. Some people, in response to misperceptions about the breed, believe that all Pit Bull-type dogs are to be feared and promote banning those breeds. Pit Bull advocates, deeply dedicated to protecting dogs they know to be friendly, loyal, loving family companions, can be as tenacious as the dogs to whom they are dedicated.

The general term "Pit Bull" refers to a number of breeds and mixes, including American Pit Bull Terriers, American Staffordshire Terriers, Staffordshire Bull Terriers, Bull Terriers, American Bulldogs, and any dogs made up of or resembling these breeds. Pit Bulls are physically powerful, strong, agile, and energetic dogs with an unrivaled *joie de vivre*. They are also known for the determination they bring to any task. These traits can

continued

sometimes combine to make the Pit Bull "too much dog" for an inexperienced pet parent or a family with small children, but that certainly doesn't mean that they can't be loving, wonderful dogs in the right homes.

Let's take a look at some common Pit Bull myths and the corresponding realities.

Myth: Pit Bulls have locking jaws and a higher biting power than other breeds.

Reality: There are no unique mechanisms in the jaws of Pit Bulls, and these dogs *cannot* lock their jaws. Additionally, in a test of biting pressure that included a German Shepherd Dog, a Rottweiler, and an American Pit Bull Terrier, the American Pit Bull Terrier had the least amount of bite pressure.

Myth: Pit Bulls are vicious to people or more dangerous than other dogs.

Reality: There is no room for human aggression in a behaviorally sound Pit Bull, and the reality is that most Pit Bulls are not aggressive toward people; many are extremely sociable and adore children. A Pit Bull who passes a behavioral evaluation poses no more of a threat to people than any other large dog. The American Temperament Test (see The American Temperament Society at www.atts.org) shows that Pit Bulls consistently score above the average for all breeds tested over the years. As of December 2007, American Pit Bull Terriers had a pass rate of 84.3 percent compared to a pass rate for all breeds tested of 81.6 percent.

Myth: Adopting a Pit Bull is the same as adding any other type of dog to your family.

Reality: While behaviorally sound Pit Bulls make excellent family companions, the reality is that adopting a Pit Bull does require some special considerations:

* Dog-to-dog aggression can be an issue with these dogs, and despite your best socialization efforts, a Pit Bull may become dog aggressive upon reaching maturity (roughly two years old). This will affect your ability to have other pets in your home as well as your

continued

responsibility for ensuring that your dog never has the opportunity to injure someone else's beloved pet.

❋ Pit Bulls face misunderstanding and prejudice from many people who do not know much about them, so adopting one requires a willingness to consider your friends' and neighbors' concerns and to educate them about Pit Bulls in general and your dog in particular.

Prejudice and discrimination can extend beyond individuals, and in some places can include local legislation banning Pit Bulls from the community. Be sure to check local laws before adopting and before moving with your Pit Bull. Securing homeowners' insurance can also be more of a challenge if you live with a Pit Bull, but there are insurance companies that do not discriminate based on the breed of dog.

The reality is that, as with all breeds, there are great Pit Bulls and Pit Bulls who—due to poor breeding, handling, or socialization—are not suitable as pets. While we urge shelters and rescue groups to perform a behavioral assessment on all dogs who enter their programs, it is particularly important to be sure that this has been done with the Pit Bull you are going to adopt. While a mistake in judgment with even a small dog can have serious consequences, a similar mistake with a large, strong breed such as a Pit Bull (or Akita, Rottweiler, Mastiff, Labrador Retriever, etc.) can be deadly.

If you are prepared, know your local laws, and have decided that a Pit Bull is a good fit for your family, do consider adopting one from a shelter or rescue group who carefully evaluates their dogs. My adopted dog Mojo, possesses the characteristic Pit Bull enthusiasm, determination, energy, love of life, and smile that the breed is known for. His stubbornness is sometimes a challenge for my other dogs and me. At times they have difficulty convincing him that they really don't want to play tug *again*. Likewise, I often cannot convince him that having him sit on my lap and lick my face is not my favorite thing in the whole world (but, truth be told, it's not far from it!).

Great Big Dogs in Very Little Packages: The Toy Group

The dogs in the Toy Group may be small in stature, but more than a few have big-dog attitudes. These plucky little dogs know how to make their presence known, and they may not want to limit themselves to being mere lap dogs. The dogs in this group can be great choices for people who live in small apartments and for those with mobility issues because many owners of Toy dogs will train them to do their business indoors, which can be a real boon if you live on the top floor of a high-rise apartment building or have trouble getting outdoors quickly enough for the pup to potty.

However, the dogs in this group are not for everyone. Households with children under the age of six might want to bypass these little guys (and gals), as young children may have trouble understanding that while these dogs are indeed part of the Toy Group, they are not animated playthings. Also, toy dogs are notorious for having bad bathroom manners, perhaps because overindulgent owners don't see the need to teach them where and when to potty. And even if the dog becomes a house-training ace, he is more than capable of training his people to cater to him. Such overindulgence can result in a tiny tyrant.

All of the dogs in this group are well under twenty pounds; most don't weigh more than ten. Their coats range from the no-nonsense crew-cut of a smooth coated Chihuahua to the glamorous show coat of a Maltese or Shih Tzu. Many pet parents choose to forgo the care and upkeep of a show dog's elaborate coif, and instead opt to have their dogs' coats styled in a puppy cut or other low-maintenance doggie 'do. But even those who opt for show dog looks may find that their dogs' small sizes can make grooming relatively easy, or at least command a smaller fee from a grooming pro.

Toy dog pet parents need to be careful that their dogs don't hurt themselves by jumping off furniture or performing other foolhardy feats. Toy dogs who persist in testing their limits may find themselves dealing with broken legs or dislocated kneecaps. That said, exercise is as important for these pooches as for their bigger counterparts. People just need to use common sense and limit physical exertions to those in which the Toy dog is less likely to get hurt.

Common Toy dog mixes include those who are bred to Poodles, resulting in such combos as the Malti-Poo and Yorkie-Poo, or those who are bred with Pugs, such as Puggles. Such dogs may be a little bigger than a purebred Toy dog, but may still be small enough to fit nicely into the lives of sedentary or apartment-dwelling owners.

Small: under 20 pounds
- Affenpinscher
- Brussels Griffon
- Cavalier King Charles Spaniel
- Chihuahua
- Chinese Crested
- English Toy Spaniel
- Havanese
- Italian Greyhound
- Japanese Chin
- Maltese
- Manchester Terrier
- Miniature Pinscher
- Papillion
- Pekingese
- Pomeranian
- Poodle (Toy)
- Pug
- Shih Tzu
- Silky Terrier
- Toy Fox Terrier
- Toy Manchester Terrier
- Yorkshire Terrier

Pug—Toy Group

Take This Job and Fetch It: The Working Group

The breeds in this group were all bred to perform various types of jobs for people. For example, Portuguese Water Dogs were bred to help fishermen retrieve their catches, while the Anatolian Shepherd Dog was developed to guard (but not herd) flocks of sheep. Other jobs performed by dogs in this group include rescuing people and pulling carts or sleds. Almost all of these jobs require dogs with considerable strength and stamina, certainly more than

*Saint Bernard—
Working Group*

almost any small or medium-sized breed would have. That's why all but two of the breeds in this group weigh sixty pounds or more.

A big dog's size, strength, and strong-mindedness could be challenging for an inexperienced pet parent. Such individuals often do better with smaller, more docile breeds. No matter how experienced someone is, training is crucial to succeeding with any dog in this group. Since these dogs are bred to work, they (and their families) will benefit from their having a job—even if that job is simply learning new tricks.

Working Group breeds have higher risks for hip dysplasia than smaller breeds do. Ordinarily, experts urge a person interested in acquiring a dog from this group to make sure that the parents of any puppy have had their hips assessed by X-ray and determined to be in good shape. However, dogs who end up in shelters or rescue groups generally don't come with such information. Consequently, those who acquire Working dogs or any other reasonably large pup need to be prepared to address hip or elbow problems that the dog may develop later in life.

Because of the way they're built, with deep, barrel chests, many Working Group breeds are also prone to a potentially fatal condition called *bloat,* in which the stomach swells abnormally and may twist upon itself. Chapter 17 describes this and other conditions in detail.

Mixed-breeds with roots in the Working Group are likely to be large, prone to joint problems, and at greater risk for developing bloat. They may also retain the strong-mindedness that requires equally strong-minded people. But they're also likely to retain the loyalty and devotion to family that have made these breeds beloved by so many people.

Medium: 20 to 60 pounds
- German Pinscher
- Standard Schnauzer

Large: over 60 pounds

- Akita
- Alaskan Malamute
- Anatolian Shepherd Dog
- Bernese Mountain Dog
- Black Russian Terrier
- Boxer
- Bullmastiff
- Doberman Pinscher
- Giant Schnauzer
- Great Dane
- Great Pyrenees
- Greater Swiss Mountain Dog
- Komondor
- Kuvasz
- Mastiff
- Neapolitan Mastiff
- Newfoundland
- Portuguese Water Dog
- Rottweiler
- Samoyed
- Siberian Husky
- Saint Bernard
- Tibetan Mastiff

Movers (But Not Shakers): The Herding Group

Not so long ago, the AKC didn't have a Herding Group; instead, the Herders were lumped in with the Working Group. Unlike the Working Group members, however, Herding dogs have a common talent: the ability to control the movements of other creatures, human and non-human alike. That Herding dog will be "on the job" to make sure that you and the rest of the "flock" remain together.

Unlike the dogs in the Working Group, size doesn't matter when it comes to herding. The compact Sheltie or short-legged Welsh Corgi can do just as good a job of directing sheep or cattle as an Australian Shepherd or Australian

Cattle Dog can. But don't make the mistake of thinking that members of this group are one-trick ponies! These dogs are multi-talented. Shelties are often whizzes on the agility course, while Border Collies defy gravity every time they leap into the air to catch a Frisbee. More than a few Collies have found good jobs portraying Lassie on stage, screen, and television, while German Shepherd Dogs often excel in law enforcement.

Herding Group coat colors and types are quite diverse, in part because such diversity abounds not only within the group but within individual breeds as well. Sheltie and Collie coat colors can be sable and white; black and white; black, tan, and white; or blue merle. Collies also come with one of two coat lengths: the Lassie-type Collie has long hair, but Collies can also have short hair (known as Smooth Collies).

Dogs in this group are typically highly intelligent and fiercely devoted to their people. Some, like the Sheltie, can be rather reserved toward strangers; others, such as the Collie, may be more outgoing. These versatile dogs generally do well in almost any household setting, as long as they get a decent amount of daily exercise (especially Border Collies) and a job to do (ditto). Some herding dogs may need training so that they don't try to "herd" small children. I am always impressed by families who share their lives with these dogs as I know that I am no match for a true herding dog's energy level.

Most mixes from this group seem to involve German Shepherd Dogs. Such dogs are likely to be highly intelligent, energetic, and lively. They provide great joy to owners committed to giving them sufficient training and frequent exercise, but they can create mayhem if left to their own devices too often or for too long. My adopted dog Kona, who introduced me to the world of animal welfare, includes German Shepherds in his very mixed lineage. While he matured into the best companion I ever could have hoped for, his intelligence and energy made him an extremely challenging puppy. He learned quickly and excelled at puppy kindergarten and subsequent training classes; however, he was often selective as to when he would choose to "remember" that training.

Medium: 20 to 60 pounds
- Australian Cattle Dog
- Australian Shepherd
- Bearded Collie

Petfinder.com: The Adopted Dog Bible

- Border Collie
- Canaan Dog
- Polish Lowland Sheepdog
- Puli
- Shetland Sheepdog
- Welsh Corgi (Cardigan)
- Welsh Corgi (Pembroke)

Large: over 60 pounds
- Beauceron
- Belgian Sheepdog (females may be smaller)
- Belgian Malinois (females may be smaller)
- Belgian Tervuren
- Bouvier des Flandres
- Briard
- Collie (females may be smaller)
- German Shepherd Dog
- Old English Sheepdog

*German
Shepherd Dog—
Herding Group*

Odds and Ends: The Non-Sporting Group

These dogs are really a group only because they are simply all the dogs that don't fit into the other breed groups. Consequently, the breeds in this group bear little resemblance to each other.

Sizes in this group range from the under-twenty-pound Lhasa Apso to the over-sixty-pound Chow Chow. Coats range widely, too, from the wash-and-wear Boston Terrier to the meticulously coiffed Poodle. And there's no standard Non-Sporting temperament: the Chow Chow typically does well with expert handling to offset his independent nature, while the happy go lucky Bichon Frise is usually just fine with doing whatever you want, whether he's your first dog or your fortieth.

For these reasons, it's tough to attribute any overall characteristics to this group. If any breeds in this group interest you, contact experts such as those who volunteer for rescue groups of the breeds you're considering. The same principle applies to mixes.

English Bulldog—
Non-Sporting Group

Small: under 20 pounds
- American Eskimo Dog
- Bichon Frise
- Boston Terrier
- Lhasa Apso
- Löwchen
- Poodle (Miniature)
- Schipperke
- Tibetan Spaniel

Medium: 20 to 60 pounds
- Bulldog (commonly referred to as the English Bulldog)
- Chinese Shar Pei
- Dalmatian
- Finnish Spitz
- French Bulldog
- Keeshond
- Poodle (Standard)
- Shiba Inu (females may be smaller)
- Tibetan Terrier

Large: over 60 pounds
- Chow Chow (females may be smaller)

A Little of This and a Little of That: Mixing It Up

The most common breed, of course, is a non-breed (or, more accurately, a variety of many breeds)—the mixed-breed or mutt. These canine combos offer plenty of advantages to adopters, including availability—they comprise the majority of available dogs at most shelters. Mixed-breed dogs are often said to be healthier, and have more stable personalities, than some pure-breds.

The downside to choosing a mixed-breed, especially if the dog is a puppy, is a lack of predictability about his size and personality once he's all grown up. You can look at a purebred Golden Retriever puppy and know that a year or so later, that dog probably will be somewhere between 21 and 25 inches tall at the shoulder and will weigh anywhere between 55 and 75 pounds. Unfortunately, you can make no such assumptions with a mixed-breed puppy. That sweet little bundle of fur nes-

Labrador Retriever + Basset Hound = Adorable!

tled in your lap today may grow up into a feisty little Terrier type, or morph into a big Lab look-alike. For that reason, you should try to gather as much information about a mixed-breed puppy's background as you can before you decide whether he's the right dog for you. An adult dog of unknown ancestry won't be such a surprise: if he's a year or older, he's likely as tall as he's going to get. By the same token, an adult mixed-breed's personality is probably already formed, giving you a better chance of knowing what that dog will be like than would be the case with any puppy, whether pure or mixed-breed.

A Golden Retriever-German Shepherd mix may be ecstatic at the sight of any and all humans (a typical Golden trait), but quick to protect you if he believes you're being threatened (a common German Shepherd trait). And because both breeds shed quite a bit, you may want to invest in a top-of-the-line vacuum cleaner before adopting this particular mix.

Looking at a Parson Russell Terrier-Corgi mix? You are likely to find an energetic, mischievous little dog who may try to herd your kids into a tight circle.

The most important information you can gain about a dog is what you discover when you spend some time with him. Hop on over to Chapter 5 for suggestions on how to assess the sociability of any dog, mixed-breed or purebred, who interests you.

The Truth About Designer Dogs

Over the past few years, dog lovers have been introduced to dogs who look different from any others they've seen. These dogs are the product of planned cross-breedings. They are usually small, have clever names, and are publicized as hip and trendy. The puppies that result from breeding a Labrador Retriever to a Poodle are called Labradoodles; a Poodle-Golden Retriever mix is called a Goldendoodle; Pug-Beagle mixes have been dubbed Puggles. Other planned breedings of two purebred dogs have resulted in mixes like the Cockapoo (a Cocker Spaniel and a Poodle); the Peke-a-Poo (a Pekingese and a Poodle), and the Malti-Poo (a Maltese and a Poodle).

Purveyors of these mixed-breed dogs call their creations "designer dogs," and many charge designer prices, such as $1,000 for a Labradoodle puppy.

Are these dogs worth that kind of money?

No one wants to say that a living creature is over-priced. And breeders of so-called "designer dogs" are counting on pet lovers to think that their particular hybrid has more cachet than a mere mutt. But that's just not so.

Much like unscrupulous or irresponsible breeders of purebred dogs, many breeders of designer dogs don't make any effort to have their breeding pairs checked for common inherited ailments such as hip dysplasia or progressive retinal atrophy. They generally don't try to determine whether a particular breeding will result in puppies that combine the best of both dogs—or the worst. When you buy a designer dog, you face the same uncertainties that you encounter with any mixed-breed—except that the designer dog costs several times as much as a mixed-breed in a shelter or rescue group would cost. Plus, you miss out on the satisfaction that comes from knowing you are saving a life when you adopt a shelter or rescue dog. Of course, if you adopt one of these breeds from a rescue group or shelter, you're saving a life, too.

Many of these hybrids are being produced by greedy breeders who care more about profits than puppies. Truly discerning dog lovers who really want a one-of-a-kind pooch should pass up deliberately and generally inhumanely bred designer dogs in favor of one of the hundreds of thousands of unique, deserving dogs who populate Petfinder and can be adopted from rescue groups and animal shelters.

Dog Biscuits for the Soul: Feebee and Rosie

Feebee & Rosie

Once a month I was going to local shelters to drop off treats, chews, and toys. I never really went inside because it was so incredibly sad for me to leave behind a dog I looked in the eyes; I always feel I am able to see their "heart." One day I was looking on Petfinder.com and saw a picture of two Pit Bull pups, about four months old, so skinny, huddled in the corner of their cage. I went to their shelter the next day with my bag of treats and toys. The person at the counter suggested I walk through and give the treats to the dogs. I did, with those two pups in mind. I came to their cage. They were still huddled in the corner. The one with the black patch stayed in the corner, shaking, but the other one came over to me, got a treat, and then took it back to her sister and dropped it in front of her. That was it for me. I did not want them to feel pain or hurt or hunger ever again. I filled out the application for both and took them home three days later. We walk five miles a day—and my granddog, who is also a Pit Bull, comes too. They are happy, healthy dogs, my friends and companions.

Paula Smith, Burlington, New Jersey
Feebee and Rosie were adopted from Burlington County Animal Shelter in New Jersey.

Resources

McCullough, Susan. *Housetraining for Dummies*. Wiley, 2002

McCullough, Susan: *Your New Dog: An Expert Answers Your Every Question*. Capital Books, 2003

Pet finder Dog Breed Directory www.petfinder.com/dog-breeds

Pit Bull Rescue Central: www.pbrc.net

Schultz, Jacque Lynn: "The Pit Pendulum." *ASPCA Animal Watch*. Fall, 2000

Walkowicz, Chris: *Choosing a Dog for Dummies*. Wiley, 2001

4

Getting Prepped for Parenthood

You may visit many adoptable dogs before you find just the right one, or the first dog you see might grab your heart in her paws. That's why you should begin to prepare for the arrival of your new best friend as soon as you've made the decision to adopt. Make sure that your home and yard are completely safe for a canine companion, and that you have everything she'll need. That way, when you do find the right dog, you'll be ready to welcome her.

Checklist of Supplies

Your new adopted dog will need some basic supplies. Here we'll review all the things you need to make your adopted dog feel right at home.

One quick note: Some of these supplies—such as food and water bowls or collars and harnesses—depend upon the size dog you will be adopting. If you are completely committed to a certain size, breed, or mix, you can buy these supplies in advance. However, it is probably wiser to wait until you find your new dog before you shop for these particular items. You may be totally set on a little short-haired dog, but find yourself falling in love with a shaggy Shepherd mix when you get to the shelter.

Food and Water Bowls

Don't plan on using bowls from your cupboard for your dog's food and water; dogs often play with their bowls, and a cereal or soup bowl won't stand up to the wear and tear. Instead, purchase bowls made specifically for feeding dogs, either metal, such as stainless steel (easy to clean) or ceramic (too heavy for the dog to pick up or move around the floor).

Smaller breed dogs and those with shorter muzzles will need wider bowls with shallow sides so they can reach the bottom. For any sized dog, the food bowl should be large enough to easily hold a meal with room to spare. If the food is heaped above the sides of the bowl, your dog will push it out as she's eating and make a mess.

The best water bowls are those that are spill-proof. A heavy, wide bowl that will be difficult for your dog to tip over will work well in the house, but outside you may want to use a metal bucket that can hold more water. It is very important that you make sure your dog always has access to clean drinking water, whether she is in the house or in the yard. If you're going to be bringing home a small-breed dog or a puppy, make sure the outside bucket is low enough for her to drink from easily. Wide, comparatively shallow galvanized tubs work well for many dogs.

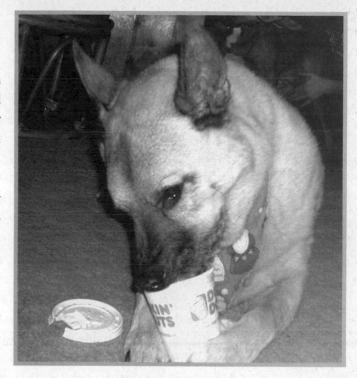

I told you no more coffee, Kona!

Dog Food

One thing you should *not* buy before adopting your new best friend is dog food. You'll need to find out from the shelter, rescue, or former owner what she has been eating, and continue feeding her that for the first few days, otherwise she could get an upset stomach. If you intend to feed her something else later, that's fine, but you will need to switch her over gradually. See Chapter 9 to learn how.

Every dog needs a buckle collar. This can be nylon or leather with either a safety quick-release plastic clip or a metal buckle. The collar should be strong, secure, and well-made. You will need to know how big your dog is before selecting her collar.

Buy a couple of leashes of different lengths. One should be four to six feet long—this is the length recommended by most trainers and is a nice length for everyday walking. A second leash that's about twenty feet long will allow your dog more room to move around when you take her to the park or beach for recreation.

There are two kinds of leashes: retractable and non-retractable. We don't recommend retractable leashes for several reasons. First, these leashes encourage bad leash manners, because dogs are rewarded for pulling by getting more lead. (See more information on proper leash behavior in Chapter 7.) Second, if a retractable leash should break, it's likely that your dog will be several feet away from you when it does, which will give her more time to bolt, should she see something worth chasing. Some dogs have been injured when the retractable function failed to engage and they were able to run into the street and in front of a car. Finally, retractable leashes have been the cause of many human injuries when the cord gets wrapped around a finger, arm, or leg, causing cuts, burns, and in the most severe cases, even amputations.

Leash material is a personal choice, and you will see leashes made from nylon, cotton web, soft rope, and leather. Choose a leash that is soft on your hands and comfortable to use. Like the collar, it should be very well-made; check the clip and stitching for flaws. After all, this leash is one of the most important tools for keeping your dog safe.

You can clip the leash to your dog's collar for walks, but many people choose to use a harness instead. This way, if your adopted dog is a puller, she won't be choking herself as she learns proper leash habits. Harnesses are made of the same materials as leashes, so you can decide what type you prefer. As with leashes and collars, it is imperative that the harness be strong, secure, and well-made.

A clicker and training stick are some of the most common tools that you can use to train basic behaviors. You can ask for these at your local pet supply store, but you can successfully train your dog without these items as well. If you plan to enroll your dog in a training class, your instructor may recommend additional training tools. If so, he will explain the purpose of those tools and show you how to fit and use them. In addition, you will find plenty of information on training and training tools in Chapter 7.

Every dog needs a leash and collar.

Identification

Far too many dogs end up in shelters because they were found wandering around with no tags. With proper identification, many of those dogs would have been reunited with their people. We hope your dog will never get lost, but it is essential that she have proper identification in case she does.

You can get an identification tag for your new best friend even before you adopt her. Go to a pet supply store and have an identification tag made that has your cell phone and home phone numbers on it. This can be attached to your new dog's collar as soon as you pick her up. Later, when you've decided on her name, you can have new tags made that include it.

Many rescue groups and shelters implant in the dogs they foster an identifying microchip that contains information on the dog.. The chip is the size of a grain of rice and is imbedded under the skin covering the dog's shoulder blades. When read using a microchip scanner, the chip provides information about the dog and where she lives. If your dog already has a chip, the shelter or rescue group will give you the relevant paperwork, which includes details about registration. Make sure you contact the registry to change your dog's information right away so that if she gets lost, the registry will be able to get in touch with you. If your dog doesn't have a microchip, ask your veterinarian about putting one in. This is an important safety measure that should be done right away. Most vets do this for a very minimal charge.

Crate, Exercise Pens, and Baby Gates

Crates, exercise pens (foldable, portable fencing), and baby gates can help you restrict your dog's freedom in the house, giving her access to only certain rooms or parts of rooms. Many behavioral problems that an adopted dog may exhibit—destructive chewing and house-training accidents, for example—can be prevented by restraining her. Preventing unwanted behavior is far easier than retraining it, and will allow you time to teach your dog the behaviors you want her to learn.

Crates have a variety of uses. While in the crate, your dog cannot chew up your shoes or tear up the curtains. She is less likely to have messy house-training accidents. A crate can also be used as your dog's bed at night and will quickly become a place of refuge for those times when she's tired or stressed. Either a plastic travel cage or a foldable metal crate work best, and you can line it initially with old, comfy towels or blankets. Don't buy an expensive bed until you're sure your new dog won't chew it up. The size of the crate you need will depend upon the size of your dog, so you may want to wait to purchase one until you know how big she'll be. You want a crate that is roomy enough for your dog to comfortably sit, stand, and turn around. You don't want it to be large enough for your dog to feel comfortable pottying in one corner and sleeping in another. However, if you do intend to use a crate, confirm your dog's size and make sure you get it prior to bringing home your new dog. It will be of immediate use. You should also bring the crate with you to the shelter or adoption location so you can bring your dog home in it. (There's more on this in Chapter 6.)

Baby gates and exercise pens are primarily used for restraining your dog. These are available at pet supply stores (and, in the case of baby gates, at baby supply stores as well), and can be used with any size dog, although larger breeds may need to be taught not to jump over them, and heavy breeds must be taught to not knock them down.

Grooming Supplies

Grooming requirements vary widely from dog to dog, so you may need to wait to purchase some of these items until you know what kind of dog you will be adopting. But every dog needs a few basics. You will need a means of bathing your dog, either outside under a hose in warm weather or inside (in the sink or tub, depending on the size of your dog) when it's cold. You may also be able to find a do-it-yourself dog washing center where towels, shampoo, tubs, and dryers are all provided for a minimal fee. I am a huge fan of these; spending $15 for the luxury of bathing my dog and leaving behind the wet towels and dirty, hair-covered tub is a bargain!

Other grooming essentials include:

- Shampoo and conditioner that are specially formulated for dogs (do not use products made for humans)
- Dog nail clippers (these come in different sizes, so don't buy them until you have a good idea how big your new dog will be)
- Canine toothbrush and toothpaste (again, do not use human products. Ask your veterinarian or local pet supply store for help)
- A brush or comb (see Chapter 11)

Clean-up Supplies

Bringing home a new dog will definitely result in some additional cleaning. It seems dogs will drag in every interesting leaf and stick from the backyard or street. They will track in mud and rain. They will bury toys and then find them again, bringing them inside covered with dirt. House-training accidents will happen, even with older dogs, as they adjust to their new home. So be sure to stock up on cleaning supplies.

You will need lots of paper towels (buy them by the case)—the super-absorbent kind—and a sponge and scrub brush to use only for dog clean-ups. White vinegar is a terrific cleaner that can be used on many surfaces without causing harm or discoloration. (Always test first—in a spot that can't easily be seen—to make sure the vinegar won't damage the item.) After cleaning up house-training accidents, rinse the area with white vinegar to remove the smell. You can also get an enzymatic odor neutralizer such as Nature's Miracle (available at pet supply stores), which will eliminate the smell of urine or feces, greatly reducing the likelihood of your dog soiling the same place again. A bucket is good to have, too, both for carrying water with cleaner added to it, and as a place to keep all your cleaning supplies organized and stored.

When selecting cleaning products, read the label and make sure the products you choose are safe for use around pets. There are many products specifically made for this purpose, and most contain enzymes that break down wastes, including urine and feces. You can find these at your local pet supply store. However, many other cleaners are not pet-friendly. If the product's label contains warnings that it should not touch skin or eyes, and that fumes should not be inhaled, then this is a potentially dangerous product to pets. If you have any doubts, call the manufacturer or the ASPCA poison control hotline.

A good vacuum cleaner is an excellent investment for all dog owners. It should have brushes that are easy to clean so you don't have trouble extracting hair. You will need to empty your vacuum often, so find a model that allows for quick, fuss-free disposal. Attachments that will help you clean the furniture are also important.

You will also want to have a supply of towels (old ones are fine) for wiping off a wet dog and cleaning muddy paws. A small washable rug is also a great idea. Place it at the doorway where the dog will go in and out of the house to cut down on some of the dirt that would otherwise be tracked inside. I've trained Mojo to sit on the rug when he comes in so I can decide whether or not his feet need wiping.

Pooper Scoopers and Bags

One of the less glamorous aspects of dog ownership is cleaning up after your dog relieves herself. However, it is an important task for responsible pet parents. If left in the yard or on the street, feces attract flies, which can carry disease, and can also harbor parasites, which are dangerous for your dog, cat, and children. In addition, of course, feces smell! If you have a backyard and are planning to let your dog potty there, you will need a bucket, a roll of trash bags, and a pooper scooper, which is usually a shovel-and-rake combination. To clean up, line the bucket with a trash bag, then pick up the feces with the pooper scooper and empty them into the bucket. When it's full, tie the bag off and put it in an outside trash can.

Pooper scoopers, which you can find at pet supply stores, come in a variety of types and sizes. One popular model has a bent shovel that lies flat on the ground, which is attached to a rake that you use to sweep the feces into the shovel. There are also models that are connected in the middle (like a pair of scissors) that pick up the feces between two small shovel-type appendages. Look at the different pooper scoopers available to decide which will work for you.

You will also need a means of picking up after your dog during walks. *Never* leave feces behind; it's your responsibility to pick up after your dog. If too many dog owners ignore their responsibility, dogs may be banned from public areas, parks, and other open spaces. In addition, many areas levy size-able fines on dog parents who do not clean up after their pets, which can be as high as $1,000 for a single incident!

While there are many commercially available systems for picking up and disposing of feces, most people prefer the simpler method of clean-up—plastic bags. There are a variety of bags and systems available, from rolls of bags to tiny carriers that attach to the leash, and even biodegrad-able bags if you're environmentally conscious. You can find all of these at your local pet supply store. To pick up waste, invert the bag over your hand, scoop up the feces, and pull the bag back down to wrap them up. You can then tie off the bag and dispose of it in a public trash can, or bring it home to put in your own.

If you are going to be adopting a small or Toy breed dog, you may want to train your dog to use a litter box. Depending upon the size of your dog, you can use a cat litter box or even a mortar pan from the hardware store. There are even types of litter made specifically for dogs.

Even if your adopted dog was previously house-trained (and many adopted dogs never were), accidents are likely to happen as she adjusts to her new environment. When my adopted girl Mocha first came to live with me, she insisted on urinating in front of the closet door, presumably because she thought that was the way outside. With patience and consistency, I was able to help her understand that when she needed "to go," she needed to go outdoors. See Chapter 8 for more detailed information on house-training.

Toys

All dogs deserve some toys, especially adopted dogs, who may never have had any. They're fun (of course) and will also help keep your dog occupied. If your dog is playing with a toy, she won't be chewing on inappropriate items (such as your shoes) or roaming around the house, getting into things she

Toys Galore!

There are almost as many toys available for dogs today as there are for children. Choosing the right toys is a bit challenging at first, because you won't know your dog well enough to have a good idea of what she likes until she's lived with you for a few months. So don't go crazy and buy a whole boxful of toys; get a few different types and then see what makes her tail wag.

- **Retrieving toys.** This includes all the toys made to be thrown, from a humble tennis ball to fancier balls made of different materials of various sizes. There are also toys made to help you throw the ball farther so your dog can run longer and faster to get it. (Make sure you play with these in a fenced yard or park!)
- **Chew toys.** These are made strong and tough so your dog can chew on them. Chewing is a natural activity for all dogs. When they chew, they relieve stress, get some exercise, and potentially even clean their teeth. Chew toys should be chosen with your dog's size in mind; a chew toy for a Papillion is obviously going to be much smaller than one for a Siberian Husky. Don't leave your dog alone with these toys until you know she won't chew them up and swallow the pieces.
- **Squeaky toys.** Squeaky toys all have a noisemaker inside. They may be soft rubber or stuffed fabric that the dog can squeeze to cause the sound. Some come in animal shapes that make the accompanying sound of that animal—the sheep-shaped toy *baaaas*, for example. These can be great fun, but if your dog plays rough, she may disembowel these toys very rapidly. Don't leave your dog unsupervised with these toys because the parts could be hazardous if they are swallowed.
- **Indestructible toys.** These toys are made with the toughest chewers in mind. If your new dog is a power chewer, this is the type of toy that you want to look for. Among Mojo's favorites are the Tuffies toys and the indestructible Nylabone big chew dino bones.

continued

- **Interactive toys.** These toys are made for you and your dog to play with together. Most are toys that fit within other toys, like small squirrels that all fit inside a little tree. You put the squirrels inside the tree and your dog has to figure out how to get them out. These are wonderful to facilitate bonding between you and your new pooch.
- **Food-dispensing toys.** These toys, such as the Buster Cube, can be loaded with a handful of treats or dry kibble. As the dog sniffs the toy and moves it around, it dispenses small amounts of food. These are great for distracting a newly adopted dog who is afraid to be left home alone. These are also good for the bored dog who might be destructive if left unoccupied.

shouldn't (such as the garbage). Playing fetch or tug with a ball or rope is also great exercise for your dog.

Playing with your dog is also a wonderful way for the two of you to develop a relationship. This process, called *bonding,* doesn't happen automatically—it takes time to develop trust—so the two of you should spend time together, interacting in a positive way, on a regular basis. When you're playing with your dog, you will touch her, pet her, talk to her, smile and laugh. What a wonderful way to form a new relationship!

When choosing toys, make sure they are appropriate for the size of your new dog, and when in doubt, choose the bigger or stronger toys. Many people underestimate the power of a dog's jaws, and you want these toys to withstand hard chewing. If a toy is too small, a dog could potentially choke on it or swallow it. If it is too flimsy, she could destroy it and perhaps swallow pieces of it.

Treats

Treats are more than just snacks. Some small, tasty treats can help with your dog's training, as they work both as a lure and a reward. (Chapter 7 discusses the use of treats in training in more detail.) Treats that are larger and take longer to chew can distract your dog from potentially bad behaviors (like destructive chewing), and many types also help clean her teeth. As with toys, though, you won't know what kinds of treats your dog prefers until you bring her home. Some pet supply stores have a "treats bar" (like a salad bar in a grocery store) that lets you select among a variety of treats. If you don't have that option, you should pick up a bag of small treats for training, and some larger, more exciting treats or chews to give your dog when you want to make her really happy. (See Chapter 9 for a discussion of the nutritional value of different types of treats.)

First Aid

We certainly hope your adopted dog will never have any emergencies or injuries, but of course, it's always better to be prepared. Make a list of emergency numbers to keep in a visible place in your home, including:

- Your veterinarian
- An additional vet in case you can't get hold of yours in a pinch
- An animal hospital (one that is open twenty-four hours)
- Poison control center

You will also need to assemble a canine first aid kit, to help you handle everything from a snake bite to a broken bone to a disaster. It's a good idea to keep a spare leash and a few cans of dog food with your first aid kit as well, in case of an emergency. See Chapter 14 for a complete list of what should be in your first aid kit, along with instructions on when and how to use each of the items.

And More . . .

Once you bring your dog home, you'll probably find that you need additional items. You might want a second crate so your dog can ride more safely in the car, or you may want to get some portable fencing to protect your garden. Items like these don't need to be purchased ahead of time. Start with the basics we've just discussed, and take inventory once your dog has started to settle in.

Shopping Checklist

Here is a list of all the items we've discussed in this chapter. You can copy this checklist and bring it with you when you're shopping for supplies.

Necessary Items

- Food and water bowls
- Dog food (see Chapter 9)
- Collar
- Four- to six-foot leash
- Temporary ID tag with your phone number
- Hard plastic or foldable metal crate
- Doggy shampoo and conditioner
- Nail clippers
- Canine toothbrush and toothpaste
- Brush or comb
- Super-absorbent paper towels
- Sponge and scrub brush
- Non-toxic cleanser
- Enzymatic odor neutralizer
- Plastic baggies (biodegradable ones are best)
- Absorbent house-training pads
- Variety of toys (a ball, a rope, a chew toy, and a puzzle toy is a good start)
- Variety of treats (some small cookies, some larger rawhides, etc.)
- First aid supplies

Optional Additional Items

- Twenty-foot leash
- Clicker and target stick
- Doggie bed
- Baby gate(s)
- Exercise pen
- White vinegar
- Vacuum cleaner
- Small washable rug(s) for entranceways
- Pooper-scooper
- Litter box (if you are adopting a small or Toy breed)

Dog-proofing Your Home, Inside and Out

Dog-proofing your home is the first step in keeping your newly adopted dog safe. Before you bring her home, you must make sure that your house, garage, and yard are free of as many dangers as possible. Your dog may never have been exposed to many of the things we take for granted, such as landscaping plants, children's toys, sprinkler systems, a pool, or a variety of other things that might be in and around your home. It can be difficult to determine what your dog might take an interest in and what might pose a danger, but it is your responsibility to make sure your home is as safe as possible. We'll show you how to make sure that her innocent curiosity doesn't put her in danger.

Inside

Almost all dogs like to chew. Chewing can be soothing to puppies who are teething, and dogs who are bored, lonely, or anxious may chew to relieve stress. Adopted dogs may arrive with a chewing problem—they may be anxious in a new environment and chew to relieve stress, or they may have developed the habit in their previous situation if they were neglected or lonely. They may even have been surrendered because of a chewing problem that easily could have been addressed with attention, training, or exercise.

No matter why she does it, if your adopted dog chews, there are two ways to alleviate the problem: Make sure your dog has plenty of things around the house that she can chew on safely, such as chew bones and toys, and keep unsafe items and things she shouldn't chew on out of her reach.

You never know what tastes or scents will appeal to your dog. Some poisonous chemicals (like antifreeze) have a taste that dogs find sweet. Personal items, like dirty underwear or tissues, may be enticing to your dog. She may be driven wild by the smell of the rotten food in the trash can. She may even be a little too interested in the contents of the cat's litter box. Any of these things you may find disgusting, and they could be very dangerous to your dog. Be extremely vigilant about keeping anything remotely harmful safely secured in a locked cupboard or out of your dog's reach. All electrical cords and cables need to be tucked away or protected inside cable protectors (available at electronic supply stores). You don't want your dog to trip on a loose cord and either hurt herself or knock over a lamp—or both! If there are cords you can't get out of reach, you can spray them with a bittering agent, to discourage chewing. And don't forget that dogs can jump!

The following items should be kept out of reach or put away in a cupboard or pantry with a childproof latch:

- Shoes, socks, dirty clothes and towels, and other personal items
- Purses, wallets, keys, cell phones, and other small personal items
- Electronics, including remote controls and video game controllers
- All cords, including computer cords, electrical cords, and cables
- Knickknacks and decorative objects
- Magazines and books
- Oven cleaners, floor cleaners, insect sprays and traps, carpet cleaners
- Medicines, vitamins and mineral supplements
- Shampoos and conditioners, hair care products, makeup, nail polish and remover
- Bathroom cleaners, toilet bowl cleaners, and mold or mildew cleaners.
- Knives, cooking utensils, and hanging pots and pans
- Laundry soap and bleach

Teach children to put away their toys when they're done playing and keep the smaller kids' toys away from the dog at all times.

If you have designated certain rooms as off-limits to the dog, instruct family members and roommates to keep those doors closed.

In the kitchen, use safety latches on lower cupboard doors. and securely put away all cleaners and other caustic substances. *Never* put rodent or insect poison anywhere your dog could get to it. Put garbage cans away, and don't leave food on low shelves or in open pantries where a dog could chew through the packaging.

In the rest of the house, pick up and put away all cigarettes, pencils, pens, and felt tips, as well as all craft, sewing, and art supplies, and trash cans. Thoroughly vacuum all carpets, especially those with thick pile, to remove any tiny dropped items, like pills, pins, earrings, rubber bands, etc.

Place covers over electrical outlets to discourage your dog from licking or biting them.

Secure windows, window screens, and doors. A dog may be able to chew through a screen or push open a door and disappear outside. Make sure there are no hanging drawstrings for the curtains or blinds, as a dog could find those very attractive and pull the whole thing down.

Finally, go through the house and look at everything again from a dog's-eye view. Crawl on your hands and knees if you can. Bend over and look underneath tables, beds, chairs, and other furniture. The world looks very different from down there, and you may find more things that need to be cleaned, removed, or secured.

It is critical that the entire household understand how important it is to keep your dog safe. If one person works hard to dog-proof the house and teach the dog what is right or wrong to play with, but another member of the household leaves doors open and unsafe items out in the open, your dog will not be safe.

The Garage

If you have a garage that your dog will have access to, it will need to be thoroughly dog-proofed as well. There are many very dangerous items in garages, all of which must be locked in secure cupboards or kept on very high shelves.

- All car repair and maintenance products, including car washes and waxes, oils, gasoline, and antifreeze, which is deadly to dogs, yet has a sweet taste that many find appealing
- All snail and slug baits, insecticides, herbicides, rodent baits and traps, fertilizers, and any other chemicals or hazardous substances
- Paints, paint removers, stains, spray paints, and other home maintenance supplies
- Check for electrical cords and put them away

If you want to allow your dog access to one portion of the garage only, use a tall, sturdy exercise pen or wooden lattice panels to seal off the dog-free zone. Make sure the fencing is sturdy and well anchored. This way you can keep the remaining portion of the garage available for its normal use without endangering your dog.

Petfinder.com: The Adopted Dog Bible

Fencing

If you have a yard and plan to let your dog outside, it is imperative that you have a sufficiently tall, sturdy fence. This is especially true for adopted dogs, some of whom may have been surrendered because they were escape artists. If your new dog does get away through a crack in the fence or by jumping over it, she probably will not be familiar enough with the area to find her way back. So do a very

Do fence me in!

thorough check of your fence. Make sure there are no gaps between boards or in the fence itself, and check for any holes underneath it. If you're going to adopt a puppy or a small breed dog, these little guys can squeeze through very small spaces, so examine the fence carefully and seal off any openings.

A clever dog can climb even a tall fence if things are piled up against it, so be sure that a stack of firewood, trash cans, or other debris doesn't make a potential doggy staircase. Athletic dogs can also jump a fence, especially one that is only a few feet tall. If the fence is tall but the gate is shorter, the dog may try jumping the gate. If you have made some modifications, but are still unsure whether your fence is completely secure, call a dog trainer or a fencing expert for help.

Outside

Dogs and backyards go together; your backyard can be a great place for your dog to chase butterflies, bask in the sun, or play with her toys. Although no dog should be left in the yard alone all day, the backyard is a great playground, so it should also be a safe place.

Unfortunately, your yard may be full of hazards for your dog. Just as in the house, look for potentially attractive but dangerous items and put them away.

Buried Electronic Fencing

In some neighborhoods, particularly those with restrictions on standard fencing, buried electronic fencing (also called *invisible fencing*) is very popular. With these systems, a wire is buried underneath the perimeter of the otherwise unfenced yard and the dog wears a special collar that will give her an audible alarm when she approaches the boundary. If she continues, she will receive an electric shock.

There are several downsides to this kind of arrangement. Your neighbor's pets or stray dogs can trespass into your yard because they are not wearing the collar. Predators and other wild animals will also be able to get in. In addition, some dogs who wear the collar learn to charge through the shock, and once out of the yard will not return because they do not want to get shocked again. Many dog trainers also report behavior problems—including extreme fearfulness, aggression, excessive barking, and other destructive behaviors—in dogs confined by electronic fences. After all, the dog is being warned away from (and punished by) something she cannot see. Finally, some dogs have suffered pain and injury resulting from burns caused by the shock-producing collar.

Keeping your dog safely contained should be a primary concern. However, we strongly encourage you to use means other than electric fencing whenever possible.

* Teach your children not to leave their toys in the yard.
* Put stuffed cushions for lawn chairs away when they're not being used.
* Remove gardening tools, fertilizers, insecticides, and other chemicals.
* Remove pool supplies.

If you have a garden, it's a good idea to put a fence around it to keep your dog out. If you grow vegetables, remember that just because these things are edible to humans, some are poisonous to dogs. In addition, your dog could poop or dig in the garden, causing a mess or ruined plants. Stop using all toxic pesticides and insecticides on your lawn or garden. Your dog could absorb them into her skin or lick them off of her paws. If you have a pool, keep it covered or fenced off to restrict access.

Take a look at the rest of your yard; what is there that is hazardous? A birdfeeder will spill seeds which normally aren't a problem for your dog, but the bird feces can contain parasites, bacteria, and disease. A barbecue can have meat drippings which could invite your dog to chew. Remove anything that could attract your dog's attention and cause her harm.

Many common landscaping plants and decorative flowers can be toxic to your dog, and some can be fatal. If your yard contains any of these plants, either remove them or make sure they are fenced off so your dog cannot chew on them or ingest them.

- Bulbs and tubers: Amaryllis, calla lily, crocus, daffodil, hyacinth, iris, and tulips
- Flowering plants: Anemone, azalea, buttercup, Christmas cactus, cyclamen, foxglove, impatiens, jasmine, lily of the valley, sweet pea, and verbena.
- Vegetables and fruits: Avocado leaves and pit, potato leaves, tomato leaves, peach pit, cherry seeds, rhubarb, and mushrooms.
- Trees and shrubs: common privet, hemlock, holly, horse chestnut, ivy, mistletoe, morning glory, oleander, pennyroyal, poinsettia, poison ivy, poison sumac, poison oak, wisteria, and yew.

Make sure your backyard plants are safe for your dog.

Marijuana also is harmful to your dog. It can depress the central nervous system, and cause incoordination, vomiting, diarrhea, drooling, increased heart rate, and even seizures and coma. Call the ASPCA's Animal Poison Control Hotline at (888) 426-4435 or visit www.aspca.org to learn more about indoor and outdoor plants and substances that may be poisonous to your dog.

For video tips on how to make sure your home is safe for your new pup, go to www.petfinder.com/dog-bible.

Dog Biscuits for the Soul: Pinny

Pinny and her mom, Evelyn.

I had just bought my first house, and the time seemed right to complete it with a little one. When I was house hunting, one house stood above all the rest, and I knew it was for me. I was just as certain with Pinwheel: When I saw her photo on Petfinder.com, I knew she was the one. She is my first dog ever. Pinny had been taken to a shelter with her two puppies. One was adopted, and one had to be put down because of a spinal injury. Pinny was slated to be put down, too, but was taken into foster care. How could I turn away from this adorable, abandoned single mom? When I first brought her home, she wouldn't eat or play, and I put my friends on standby for panic calls. But Pinny quickly adapted to her new lifestyle. Now we go on long walks and visits to cafés, galleries, and shops that allow dogs. At night she settles into my nice warm feather bed. I'm trying really hard to make a good life for Pinny—some of my friends say it's *too* good, because she is absolutely my precious angel and I spoil her rotten. But I feel much more fortunate to have her than she could ever feel to have me. She has completely changed my life. That little face just makes me so happy!

Evelyn Creekmore, Atlanta, Georgia
Pinny was adopted from the Georgia Humane Society.

Resources

Palika, Liz: *The KISS Guide to Raising a Puppy.* DK, 2002
ASPCA Poison Control Hotline: 1-888-426-4435

5

Choosing the Right Dog for You

Now that you've developed a pretty good idea of what sort of dog you want and you've matched that wish list with a realistic assessment of what sort of dog will do best in your home, you're ready to undertake your search, starting with trips to the animal shelters and rescue groups you identified in Chapter 1.

Before You Go

Here are some practical tips to assist you in finding and choosing your true dream dog.

Prepare Yourself

As eager as you are to find your new dog today, take your time. Choosing a dog is much too important a task to be conducted in haste. The dog you select could be with you for ten years or more (let's hope so!). You owe it to yourself, your family, and the dog to make sure that the choice you make is the best one for all concerned. Chances are you won't find "your" dog on the first trip. Maintaining that perspective is crucial to your effort to hold out against pleas by other members of your family, or even by shelter workers and rescue volunteers (yes, it could happen), to choose a dog with whom you

There are so many wonderful dogs in shelters! You'll want to take them all home.

don't feel a connection, or who for some other reason isn't right for you and your family. That said, sometimes miracles do happen; you could find your dream dog right away. So while you should not *expect* to find a dog during your first (or even second or third) trip to a shelter, it is still a good idea to plan any shelter trip for a day when bringing a new canine buddy home would be possible.

Go Alone the First Time

If you question your ability to withstand your children's inevitable pleading for a particular pup, go to the shelter or foster home on your own. Pick a couple of dogs who interest you, and ask the shelter staff or rescue volunteer about them (see "What to Ask the Shelter Staff" on page 84). If you like what you hear, ask if you can bring the rest of your family to meet the pets you're considering for adoption.

Prepare Your Kids

If you have children and you are taking them with you to the shelter or rescue group, make sure they understand that you almost certainly won't be going home with a dog today. Telling your children that "today we're just going to look" will help them understand that you're going to hold out for the right dog. A shelter dog who could be suitable for an adult may not be suitable for a family with children, especially if those children are under seven years of age. As a parent, you need to look for a dog who more than just tolerates children; you need a dog who *adores* children. Unfortunately, not all dogs will match that description. Even if you are lucky enough to find the dog you want on your very first trip, the shelter or rescue group may ask that

Petfinder.com: The Adopted Dog Bible

you wait a few days to give everyone time to make sure that you and your home are the right match for the dog you want. And sometimes the dog will need to be spayed or neutered prior to coming home with you, which may take a few days.

Set Some Rules

Make sure you all agree on some ground rules so that your effort to select carefully isn't sabotaged by an overeager family member. For example, consider telling your kids that the minute they start whining or pleading, you'll all be out of there—and keep your word. Other rules might be that the kids should not pet or otherwise engage a dog without your permission, and that they should use "inside voices" at all times. Horsing around or other rough play with dogs or siblings should be strictly forbidden.

Be Open-Minded

Even if you're sure about what sort of dog you want, don't be afraid to change your mind if you fall in love with a dog who doesn't fit all your criteria. If you wanted a mid-sized, mellow dog but find yourself falling in love with a small, higher-energy terrier mix, review why you wanted a larger, more easygoing dog. You may find that you can revise your specifications without upsetting your life too much. However, be realistic, and if you're feeling drawn to a dog who you know isn't right for you, don't let sentiment push you into making a bad decision.

Make a Checklist

To ensure that you find out all you can about a dog who interests you, make a list of the questions you'll want to ask and write down the answers that the staff or volunteers give you. When you're making your decision to choose a particular dog, those notes can help you make the right choice. See the next section "What to Ask the Shelter Staff" to learn what questions you need to ask and the answers you need to hear.

What to Ask the Shelter Staff

When faced with so many dogs, it can be hard to be discerning. Bring a small notepad with some prepared questions already written, and take notes on the responses. Here's what you need to ask, and the replies you should listen for:

How old is the dog? If this information isn't already included on the dog's cage card or in his file, someone at the shelter or rescue group should still be able to give you an informed estimate of the dog's age. In Chapter 2 we reviewed the pros and cons of puppies vs. young adult or older dogs, so you probably already have a good idea of the age you're looking for.

What kind of dog is he? If you're working with a purebred rescue group, the answer will be obvious! However, if you're working with an animal shelter or an all-breed rescue group, figuring out a dog's lineage can be tricky. Chapter 3 offered some information about breeds and breed groups to help you understand the differences among breeds. Shelter staff and volunteers should be able to give you some guidance as well.

What's his background? Shelter staff or rescue volunteers may or may not be able to tell you what this dog's life was like before he came under their care. If you can, find out how many homes he lived in, why he was relinquished, and how he's been behaving since. Of course, if the dog was a stray, information about his pre-shelter or rescue group life won't be available, but you should still be able to find out how he's behaved at the shelter or rescue. Keep in mind that many foster parents report that how a dog behaved while in the shelter is not at all how he behaves at home, where he feels more secure and comfortable. It is especially important to find out (if you can) whether the dog has a history of aggression or has been abused; such dogs can make poor choices for inexperienced owners and for families with children. While many dogs are returned through no fault of their own, it is possible that dogs who have had multiple homes could have more challenging behavior problems, including aggression. Carefully consider a dog who has a history of being returned, particularly if you have young children.

Petfinder.com: The Adopted Dog Bible

Sometimes adopters returning a problem dog refrain from openly sharing their experience for fear that the dog will suffer as a result.

Has his behavior been formally evaluated? More and more shelters and rescue groups are performing formal behavioral assessments on incoming dogs to determine whether those dogs should be made available for adoption and what a suitable home will be like. These tests are controversial and some question their validity, but others feel they are a valuable tool to predict behavior. Ask the shelter staff whether they've performed an assessment on the dog you're interested in. If they have, ask them to describe the test and if written documentation of the test results are available.

If the shelter doesn't do a formal evaluation on the dogs they place up for adoption, this chapter offers guidelines for general assessment of a dog. The information you gain from evaluating a dog you just met may not be conclusive, but it may help you identify certain behavioral tendencies. Of course, adopting from another facility where testing is more extensive is another option.

How does he behave with children? If you've got kids, plan on having any, or anticipate having children come to visit you regularly, you must ask this question in addition to checking to see whether the dog has had a behavioral evaluation. Any information that the staff can provide about how the dog reacts to children (as we mentioned, he should not just tolerate them; ideally he should adore them) and whether he's possessive of toys and food (a family pet should be okay with "sharing") can help you decide whether the rest of your family should see that particular dog, or if you should look for a dog who is better suited for life with children.

Does he have any health issues? If the answer to this question is "yes," don't automatically bypass the dog. Many dogs enter a rescue program or are brought to a shelter because their former owners wouldn't or couldn't give them the care they needed, and they may well have a couple of health problems. Most of those problems, however, are likely to be pretty minor and easy to manage. For example, even an inexperienced pet parent can deal with a dog who has intestinal parasites but otherwise is healthy. All that's needed is a trip or two to the vet for an exam and deworming meds—not a big deal. The same is true of a dog who is coughing. He could just have kennel cough, which is a mild respiratory infection that's extremely common among dogs in group settings and usually resolves on its own pretty quickly. On the other hand, a dog with multiple health problems or one very serious problem should prompt you to consider whether you have the money and patience to handle it. If you do, the satisfaction of bringing your new family member back to good health can be very rewarding.

At the Shelter: Guidelines for Making the Right Match

So here you are at the shelter, expectations in check and checklist in hand. Your goal is to find a social dog: one who's outwardly friendly, sweet, and seeks human companionship. Sociability is the most important factor for finding the right dog. We asked shelter and behavior expert Sue Sternberg for information to help you evaluate the behavior of a dog who interests you. The guidelines below, formulated from Sternberg's recommendations, focus primarily on adopting a dog from a shelter, but later in this chapter we'll show how to apply them if you're adopting from a rescue group. Before we move on, however, we must reiterate that finding the right match is not a science. In fact, the guidelines below are our field's best attempt to predict what may be unknowable. Approach these guidelines strictly if you are looking for a perfectly plug-and-play pooch (we hope you'll consider the slightly flawed ones, too). But, prepare yourself to be surprised and to find that the dog you met at the shelter provided only a tiny peek into his wonderfully complex personality. Even with these guidelines, it is best to be open-minded about training classes, lifestyle adjustments, and other compromises inherent with adding a new family member. After all, compromise and lifestyle adjustments are part of any healthy relationship!

Make a First Pass

Start by making a pass through the kennels without talking to the dogs. Stand upright in front of each kennel, facing the dog inside. Keep your eyes wide open, try not to smile, and make neutral eye contact with the dog for at least five full seconds. A dog who blinks less than once every two seconds, growls, barks, raises his hackles (puts his back hair up), backs away from the kennel door, or lunges may present behavioral challenges and is likely not a plug-and-play family member for first-time pet parents or those with children. Dogs who don't return direct eye contact, and/or are wiggling their bodies while trying to get your attention at the kennel door are the best choice for families with children. Note these dogs; you'll return to them during the next step.

Schmooze the Second Time Around

Make a second pass through the kennels, and stop to visit with each dog you noted on your first trip. When you reach one, offer your fist, knuckles forward, toward the dog, at

How to test for a social, people-oriented dog.

his head-height or lower, so that he doesn't have to jump up to investigate your hand. Then, at two-second intervals, slide your fist over four inches, down four inches, and back over four inches. The friendliest, most sociable dogs are those who go directly to your fist, lick or nuzzle the entire time, and follow your hand all four times. Dogs who follow your fist but only sniff the entire time are not necessarily being sociable. Dogs who jump at your face or lunge at you should raise concern, as should those who retreat to the back of the kennel.

Get to Know Some Dogs

When you've narrowed your list down to the very social dogs, you're ready to take a closer look and to try to see how sociable they really are. Ask the staff to take them out of their kennels one at a time to a quiet room if possible, or at least to a quiet corner. For a full sixty seconds, stand with the dog and totally ignore him (it's tough to do, but be patient). The dog should try to worm his way into your affections by nuzzling you, licking you, trying to cuddle, or jumping up—*gently*—in a way that contours to your body. (Don't be concerned about the jumping, which will be easy to retrain later. A dog who continues to jump up to get your attention is very likely to be a sociable dog.) The physical contact should last at least two seconds.

If a shelter employee is with you and the dog seeks attention from her, that's okay (and pretty typical); it just means the dog has already formed a bond with that person. Ask the shelter person to ignore the dog, and give the dog an extra sixty seconds to show some interest in you. If he doesn't, it could be a sign of unsociability that may present challenges for an inexperienced pet parent. If he does, move on to the next step.

Give Him Some Strokes

If the dog has shown that he is truly sociable and that he's interested in you, you're ready to see how he responds to your touch. Pet him slowly and gently down his back, starting at the base of his neck and traveling along the grain of his hair to the base of his tail. Pause after the first stroke, stand up, and count to two. Repeat this sequence twice. The most sociable dogs will move closer to you in between at least one out of the three strokes. He'll show that he enjoys your touch by standing still and leaning into you, seeking more contact. A dog who shakes you off or moves away from your touch may be telling you that he doesn't like being petted or being around you. Keep looking until you find a dog who does.

Test Resource Guarding Behavior

If the dog is still with you, you've come to the point in your assessment where you need some help. You need to check for resource guarding, the dog's tendency to protect things considered to be valuable—treats, food, toys, etc.—even to the point of causing harm to those he may view as a threat to such resources. Unless you're an expert trainer or behaviorist, it is *not* safe for you to perform these tests on your own. Instead, ask a shelter staffer to work with you, or team up with the expert volunteer (e.g., a professional dog trainer) who's accompanied you to the shelter.

This information is important to give you a full picture of the dog's personality and behavior. This is not about teasing a dog while he is eating or having a bone; it is about learning what his response will be when he has something that he really likes and wants to keep. While resource guarders can sometimes be successfully managed by willing adults, this is an issue you should be aware of before deciding to go ahead with the adoption. Families with small children should not adopt dogs with resource guarding issues, as children cannot be expected to manage this behavior and are at risk of being seriously injured. There is no definitive information on how much resource guarding in shelter dogs is acceptable. In other words, we don't know what levels of resource guarding in shelter dogs corresponds to what level of manageable or unmanageable (and dangerous) levels of resource guarding in the home after adoption.

Offer a High-Value Chewable Treat

Together with your helper, bring the dog to a quiet indoor room. The helper should be holding the dog's leash. Hand a high-value chewable treat such as a pig ear or rawhide to your helper, and ask her to offer it to the dog. As she does, watch to see how the dog reacts. You would like to see the dog settle down next to the helper to chew the pig ear without adjusting his position, settle down to chew it but occasionally look up at the helper while putting his ears back, squinting his eyes and wagging his tail, or toss the treat to the helper to get him to play. However, if the dog has trouble settling down or snatches the pig ear from the helper and begins to chew it voraciously, he may be showing signs of possessiveness (or resource guarding), which has the potential to escalate into a dangerous behavior problem. More uncommon, but very serious signs of resource guarding can be: if he snatches the treat but still can't settle down, if he gives furtive glances to the helper as soon as he acquires the treat, or if he lies down facing the helper and freezes, growls or stares at the helper. If you observe these behaviors, move on to another dog candidate.

Get Him Excited

If the dog is still with you, you're ready to assess whether he plays safely. Take out the toy you brought and see if he will play a game, such as fetch or tug-of-war. Play the game long enough to get him excited, probably for one or two minutes. Then stop abruptly and put the toy out of his reach, but where he can still see it. See how long the dog takes to settle down. The best pet dogs calm down and settle within sixty seconds. A dog who stays aroused longer than that, starts barking or leaping to get the toy, or can't disengage and forget the toy, may be a dog who doesn't deal well with frustration. This behavior may be associated with problems such as destructiveness when left alone or behaving in an out-of-control manner when he's around stimulating objects such as squirrels, moving cars, lawn mowers, or vacuum cleaners.

Such a dog may not make a good companion for a first-time pet parent looking for an easy-to-manage companion. If you are not interested in doing extensive training with your new dog and cannot offer him a high-energy outlet such as running, playing with another dog (think doggie daycare!), agility, herding, or field work, think twice about adopting him.

Take a Walk

With the shelter staff's permission, attach a leash to the dog and take a quick walk. Don't worry if he pulls or is very distracted, especially at first, or if he reacts to other dogs barking at him while you and he are clearing the kennel gauntlet. Remember, he's been in a kennel all day. But once you're outside, be wary if you can't get his attention at all, or if he pulls you off your feet, drags you everywhere, and does not turn back even once to look at you. Other red flags: if you can't get his attention at all while you're outdoors, or if he lunges at other people while you're outside. Dogs who engage in such behaviors are likely to present big training challenges.

Test with Strangers

If the dog is still with you, have a staff person put him back in his kennel. Then watch to see how he reacts when other strangers pass by, especially children, big men, and anyone who moves or dresses oddly. Avoid a dog who barks or lunges at everyone he sees: this is a sign of potential fear or territorial aggression. Such a dog may not want to let any of your friends, guests, or visitors come in the house. Look instead for a dog who's holding his tail lower than the level of his back (unless it is a tail designed to point up), is wagging that tail in a relaxed manner, and walks to the door of his kennel, showing friendly interest.

Ask for Time

If you still have one or more candidates in the running, ask the shelter staff if you can put them on temporary hold while you arrange to return with your kids, spouse, and (if applicable) your current dog or other pets. The staff may tell you that they can't put a dog on hold, because if someone else wants to adopt him in the meantime and you don't return for some reason, he might miss out on his best chance for a home. That's a reasonable explanation—but the staff may be willing to note your interest on the dog's records and give you a day or so to return with your crew. When you do return, ask the staff to help you make a final decision about which dog on your short list (if you still haven't narrowed it down to one) is the best choice for living happily ever after with you and your family.

If you're returning with your children—particularly if any of those children are under the age of seven—consider bringing one other person along: a professional dog trainer. The Association for Pet Dog Trainers provides information on how to choose an appropriately skilled and professional trainer and find one near you on their website at apdt.com. A trainer can evaluate the dog with greater objectivity than you can, especially if you've already fallen in love with a dog. A trainer can also help you differentiate between behavior issues you are willing to take on and work to modify or manage and those that are too dangerous or simply beyond your willingness or ability to handle.

At a Foster Home or Adoption Event

If you're checking out dogs at a shelter or rescue group's adoption event or visiting a foster home, you may not be able to perform all of the above suggestions in exactly the same way. Adoption events are usually held outdoors or inside pet superstores with noisy, stimulating conditions. However, you should still be able to generally assess a dog's behavior using the guidelines given earlier.

Do keep in mind that most dogs will be at least somewhat inhibited at an adoption event, or even a little overwhelmed. In particular, the sensitive, slightly insecure dog may appear calmer and/or more inhibited, and less playful than he'd generally be in a familiar environment. A dog with serious shyness problems may shut down completely, staying in the back of his crate and refusing to come out to meet potential adopters. This could simply be situational due to the stress and uncertainty of a new situation.

Some dogs, however, actually seem better behaved at an adoption event than they do in a more familiar environment. These dogs generally are supremely confident, bold, and relatively less sensitive than most of their canine peers. They may tend to be dominant and, in extreme cases, could even

Many dogs in shelters and foster homes already know basic obedience commands.

be aggressive. The inhibiting effects of the adoption event may cause these dogs to appear to be well behaved—but when they get more comfortable, they might lose some of those inhibitions and become mouthy, nippy, or overbearing.

Foster homes are generally private residences, and the people who live there may be fostering only one or two dogs at a time, thus limiting your ability to differentiate among a large group of adoptable dogs or see how the dog reacts to strangers.

When looking for a great dog at an adoption event or at a foster home, consider these steps:

Go online. Most rescue groups and shelters provide detailed descriptions on Petfinder.com of the dogs available for adoption—chances are, this is how you found your potential canine companion to begin with. Read the descriptions carefully, and jot down any questions you have in addition to those suggested in "Before You Go" on page 81.

Attend an adoption event. As with a shelter visit, you may be able to do a lot of interacting with the dogs at these events and take a close look at those who interest you. Don't hesitate to ask the event staff or volunteers to move away from the hustle of the event to give you the opportunity to evaluate the dog's behavior using the guidelines given earlier. Let the dog's foster care provider or other person in charge of him know you're interested in learning more about him, and agree on a time to visit the dog at the shelter or foster home if you feel that you would like another opportunity to evaluate the dog in a calmer setting.

Visit the shelter or foster home. When you visit, take your time evaluating the dog(s) you're interested in. While your opportunity to see the dog's reaction to a variety of people and other animals is limited in a foster home, you are able to see how he behaves in a more normal home situation. Ask as many questions as you need to get a sense of what the dog will be like to live with—and consider any doubts honestly and carefully before making the decision to adopt. Be prepared, too, to answer the foster caregiver's questions, which should be designed to help you

Pushing Paper

Once you've agreed to adopt a dog and the shelter or rescue group gives you a thumbs-up, you'll need to take one last step before you take your new pooch home: review and sign an adoption contract. Relax—you won't need to sign your life away, but you *will* be asked to commit yourself to the long-term well-being of the dog you've chosen to adopt. And rightly so! These dogs have already been surrendered once, and while everyone involved wants to see this dog live with you for the rest of his life, a contract provides a safety net for him in the event that you have an unforeseeable change in circumstances or tragedy occurs. Chapter 21 describes in detail what you should do if an unforeseen circumstance or problem you're having with the dog prompts you to decide that you must give up the dog.

Contracts differ from shelter to shelter and rescue group to rescue group, but generally all adoption contracts require you do the following:

- Spay or neuter your new dog within a designated time frame (often thirty days), if that procedure hasn't been performed already. Some groups will ask that you pay a refundable spay/neuter deposit at the time of the adoption. Others will offer you a spay/neuter voucher, which gives you a discounted rate on the procedure if you have it done by a certain veterinarian.
- Keep the dog indoors as a pet or companion. That means you promise to not chain him outside, make him sleep in a dog house, breed him, or use him for dog fights.
- Return the dog to the shelter or rescue group from which you adopted him if you're no longer able or willing to care for him.
- Assume full responsibility for the dog's health and behavior, including taking him for a veterinary health exam at least once per year for the rest of his life.

determine if this dog is right for you. Foster parents want what is best for these dogs, who have temporarily become members of their families. To that end, they should want to make sure that potential adopters know the whole truth about a given dog, and that adopters honestly consider whether that dog will be a good match for their family.

Know Your Rights

Your own research and prep work will go a long way toward ensuring that you choose the right dog for you and your family—but like any customer, you have certain rights when you deal with a shelter or rescue group. Here's what behavior and shelter expert Sue Sternberg says you should expect from any organization that offers dogs for adoption.

You have the right to:

- Adopt the best dog you have ever met.
- Adopt a dog who has not bitten and broken the skin of a human.
- Adopt a dog who will be safe with children.
- Adopt a dog who has not killed another dog.
- Not be blamed if the dog you adopt turns out to be aggressive.
- Not be blamed or made to feel guilty for not adopting a dog who has been at the shelter for too long.
- Not be pressured to adopt an incompatible dog or a dog you don't readily connect with, even if the dog is slated to be euthanized if he is not adopted.
- Know why a shelter or rescue group refuses to allow you to adopt one of its dogs, so that you can make the changes needed to become a conscientious dog parent.
- Be treated with respect, courtesy, and professionalism.
- Inquire about and receive as much behavioral and medical history on the dog as is currently available.
- Be told a dog's actual age or, if the actual age is not known, to receive the best guess of the dog's age from a shelter professional.
- Be informed of the dog's actual breed or breed mix, and if it is not known, to receive the best guess from a shelter professional, with no euphemisms or avoidance of breed names that conjure up public fear (e.g. Pit Bull or Rottweiler).
- Expect the shelter to stand behind its dogs/puppies, and accept them back at any time, for any reason, should the need ever arise in the dog's lifetime.

Dog Biscuits for the Soul: Spike

Spike

I'd been looking for a puppy for a long time, but I wasn't sure which breed was right for me. I live in a city apartment, and I wanted a smallish dog who would enjoy walks as well as a lot of cuddling time. After visiting Best Friends Animal Sanctuary in Kanab, Utah, I became interested in adopting a homeless pet. I searched Petfinder.com, and the moment I saw Spike's photo, that was it. I was hooked. I completed an application and visited him about a week later. Spike is a four-year-old, purebred, long-haired Chihuahua. He grew up in an apartment with an elderly woman and three other small dogs. When her landlord discovered her collecting animals, he gave her an ultimatum: get rid of the pack or be evicted. Thus, the four tinies ended up at the Lend-a-Paw Animal Rescue and the Garden State Vet Hospital in North Bergen, New Jersey. Though he was a bit timid at first, I could tell Spike was a sweet little guy and decided to give him a chance. I ended up with the most adorable, charming, and loving companion a girl could want! Spike wants nothing but to be a little, furry member of a family. Within hours, he had bonded to me as if he'd never had another owner in his life. If I'm home, he's either following close behind me as I go about my business or relaxing in his bed or on a pile of laundry nearby, watching the action.

Spike is already house-trained and enjoys going on jaunts around town. He loves meeting other dogs and even cats, and he's friendly but polite to every person he meets—and there are a lot of people! He attracts tons of attention when we're out and about, especially in his turtleneck sweaters. He loves being carried around, but best of all, he is beyond content when wedged next to me on the sofa, watching television or snoozing. Spike is a gem. I couldn't have asked for a better dog or a better little friend! He is eager to please and unconditionally loving. He causes me no trouble at all; something a puppy could never have promised. I've heard that shelter dogs know that they've been rescued and love their rescuers all the more for it, but I didn't believe it until I brought my little Spikey home. I urge everyone who is

Continued

in search of a pet: Before you go to a pet store supplied by cruel puppy mills . . . before you go to a breeder and spend hundreds of dollars on a puppy . . . before anything, check Petfinder.com, and find it in your heart to give these wonderful animals a second chance.

Sarah Hudson, New Jersey

Spike was adopted from Lend-a-Paw Animal Rescue and the Garden State Vet Hospital in North Bergen, New Jersey.

Resources

McCullough, Susan: *Your New Dog: An Expert Answers Your Every Question.* Capital Books, 2003

Pelar, Colleen, CPDT: *Living with Kids and Dogs . . . Without Losing Your Mind: A Guide to Controlling the Chaos.* C&R Publishing, 2005

Robertson, Barbara: "Dog is in the Details." *The Bark* www.thebark.com/ezine/features_specialFeatures/specialFeatures_04.html

Sternberg, Sue: "Bill of Rights for Adopters." www.petfinder.com/journal/index.cgi?article=691

Sternberg, Sue: *Successful Dog Adoption.* Wiley, 2003

6

Bringing Your New Hound Home

Today is the day you've been eagerly anticipating: you're bringing home your new adopted canine companion! Adding a four-legged family member to your life is certainly cause for celebration, but when the dog is adopted from an animal shelter or rescue organization, it's particularly special because you are helping to save a life. You will be repaid many times over with the love, loyalty, and trust of your new best friend.

Like many rescued animals, your new dog may have had an unpredictable and stressful life before she met you. She might have faced neglect, abuse, and abandonment, and these experiences could have a lasting effect on her. Your new dog will need time to adjust to her new surroundings—the place, the people, the routine, the rules. You can help make the transition smoother for everyone by knowing what to expect and planning ahead.

Before the big day, review Chapter 4 to make sure your home is properly puppy-proofed, and that you have all the things you'll need. This way you can focus all your attention on welcoming your new friend.

Picking Up Your Pup

The time has finally arrived for you to pick up your new dog. But wait—there are some important things to consider before your pup ever sets a paw outside of the shelter's facility.

First, make sure you bring a collar (with a current identification tag) and a leash. While some shelters and rescue groups provide these items or allow you to borrow them, it's better to bring your own. You also need to determine how your dog will travel on the way home. We strongly recommend bringing her home in a car. If you don't have a car and can't borrow one or get a ride, you can possibly use public transportation, but check ahead of time to make sure the bus, taxi, train, or subway allows dogs (many don't).

Assuming you're using a car, the best ways to safely transport your new pup are in a crate or wearing a safety harness (a doggy seat belt, which is secured to your vehicle's passenger seat belt). A crate should be large enough for your dog to sit and lie down in comfortably, and lined with a blanket or soft towel. If you will be using a safety harness, place your dog in the backseat to avoid injury in the event that the airbag deploys during a crash. (Some newer model cars and SUVs do have a feature that automatically disables the front passenger airbag when a small- to medium-sized object—such as a dog—is detected in the seat.) The safest place for your dog to sit is in the middle of the backseat, as she is less likely to sustain injuries in the event of a side-impact collision. Some safety harnesses, however, only work with a car's shoulder seat belt; in this case, your dog can sit on either side of the car. The exception is pickup trucks, which normally don't have a backseat. If this is your mode of transportation, have your new dog ride in the front passenger seat. *Never* allow her to ride in the bed of the truck.

At the shelter, rescue group, or foster home, ask the volunteers for a copy of your dog's adoption paperwork and any medical records she may have (including proof of vaccinations and spay/neuter surgery). If your dog is taking medication of any kind, ask for a prescription or supply of the medicine, and be sure you know how to administer it correctly. Ask for a telephone number that you can call if you have any questions during or after regular business hours. Also, have a supply of the food your new dog has been eating ready at home (some shelters will give you two or three days' worth). Even if you change your dog's diet later on, you should continue giving her the same food for a few weeks to avoid gastrointestinal problems (more on this in Chapter

9). Last but not least, bring some yummy treats to encourage your new pup to jump into the car and sit quietly while you buckle her safety harness or secure her in the crate.

The Drive Home

While some dogs will happily bound away from the shelter without a backward glance, others might be a little nervous the first time you clip a leash onto their collar and say, "Let's go home!" After all, she has no idea that you're about to become her new caretaker. Take things slowly and if your dog appears uneasy, stop and pet her and talk to her in a reassuring voice. If she's reluctant to get into the car, sit down with her next to the car and give her a few treats until she appears calmer. Understand that she might be nervous—after all, for many dogs, cars can be strongly associated with bad things, like going to the vet. In fact, it's likely that your dog was brought in a car to the shelter to be surrendered. So speak kindly to her, be patient, and if she still seems anxious, ask a shelter volunteer who is familiar with your dog to accompany you to the car and encourage her to hop in.

Make sure that your dog's leash is fastened before you open the car door.

Once your dog is safely inside, start the car and drive slowly away. Try not to make any sudden stops or turns, as some dogs will experience nausea and may even vomit during the trip. In fact, it's a good idea to spread a blanket over your backseat (if that's where she will be riding) and have some absorbent towels nearby for easy clean-up. Panting and dilated pupils are tell-tale signs of queasiness. If your dog exhibits these symptoms, try opening the windows partway or turning on the air conditioning, as the cool air may help her feel better. As with humans, gingersnaps have been known to settle a queasy canine stomach, so if you have been forewarned that your new dog is prone to carsickness, consider bringing a few along.

What to Expect During the First Twenty-Four Hours

If possible, bring your new dog home at the beginning of the weekend, or take a couple days off from work or school so you can stay home and help her get adjusted. Don't choose a weekend when you're having company, or during the rush of the holidays. Confusion and excitement in the house can cause stress for both of you and can make her transition more difficult. The first few days should be peaceful for your pup; there will be plenty of time later on to introduce her to friends and family.

When you arrive home, let your dog out of the car (clip on a leash first, please!) and give her a few minutes to stretch her legs. She may need to relieve herself, so have a plastic bag ready to clean up after her. After a brief stroll in the yard or around the block, take her inside and let her spend some time exploring her new surroundings. Take off her leash and introduce her to your other family members or roommates—slowly and quietly. Remember, she doesn't know yet that this is her new family, and meeting a lot of new people at once could be overwhelming for some dogs. For others, however, it will be great fun! Show her where to find her food and water dishes and let her see where she will sleep. Take her to these important spots several times during the first day to remind her where everything is.

Watch for signs that she needs to go to the bathroom, such as sniffing the floor, turning in circles, or squatting. Many shelter dogs were house-trained in their previous homes. While at the shelter, however, their regular routine may have been disrupted, weakening their house-training habits. Other dogs may have been left outside all day or never house-trained at all. You will find plenty of information on house-training and proper leash walking in Chapter 7, but for now, take your dog outside every couple of hours, or even more frequently. Praise her profusely when she does her business where you want her to, and *always* pick up after her when she poops. Keep your dog leashed whenever she is outside the house. This is especially important during the initial adjustment period, as new dogs have a tendency to roam, and if she does wander off, she's not likely to be able to find her way back home.

By now, your dog has had time to meet her new family members and explore her new surroundings. After all this excitement, you may both be ready for a nap! If so, take your dog to her bed (or crate), but don't be surprised if she's too nervous to sleep. Remember, everything is brand new to her. If she doesn't settle down after a few minutes, get up and take her for another walk or, depending on the time of day, give her a meal. (We'll discuss mealtime in detail in Chapter 9.) If you have some chews or toys, now is a great time to give her some. You want your dog's first associations with her new home to be as positive as they can be.

Petfinder.com: The Adopted Dog Bible

The first day with your new pup should be a time to get acquainted with one another and begin the bonding process. Go about your regular routine and keep your dog nearby (see "Getting Hitched" at right for information on a technique called *umbilical cording*). Most important, relax and allow your dog to do the same. You'll find that by spending this special time together, you and your new canine companion will begin to form a close relationship that will last a lifetime.

Sweet Dreams: Sleeping Arrangements

In the wild, a canine pack sleeps curled up together. This makes them feel safe from predators and gives them a sense of belonging. Domestic dogs are no different. While your dog may not need to worry about predators, she needs to feel connected to her family, and this means sleeping with you. That's not to say that you and your dog need to sleep tush to tail in the same bed (though mine do and I wouldn't have it any other way), but it does mean that she should sleep in your bedroom with you. From the first night onward, you can provide her with her own bed. However, if you are concerned that she may be destructive or not house-trained, you might consider using a crate lined with some soft blankets until you become more familiar with her habits. Crate training will be covered in Chapter 7. (If you would like your dog to sleep on the bed with you but she has arthritis or hip problems, you can purchase a carpeted ramp or stairs to help her climb onto the bed.)

An adopted dog in particular needs to feel loved and included right from the start, which is a message she may not get if she is forced to be away from you all night long. However, if you have allergies, you might need to choose another location in the house for her to sleep, such as the kitchen, laundry

Getting Hitched

You should closely supervise your newly adopted dog's activities during the first several days of living together. An excellent way to do this is by using a method called *umbilical cording*. Attach one end of a leash to your waistband or belt and another to your dog's collar. Now, she'll be able to follow you wherever you go and will quickly learn that you're her friend and leader. Umbilical cording is also a good way to monitor any undesirable behaviors (such as piddling).

Umbilical cording is *not* the same as tethering, which is chaining or tying your dog to a stationary object and leaving her alone for several hours. Tethering is inhumane, and several municipalities around the country have outlawed this practice.

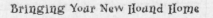

I may be a party animal, but let me settle in first.

room, or den. If you must go this route, place her bed or crate in a familiar area and be sure her food and water dishes are nearby. Never force your dog to sleep outdoors or in a damp, dark basement, garage, or other non-family area. She will be miserable, and will likely let you know by crying, barking, chewing, or scratching to get out.

Dogs generally sleep for about fourteen hours a day, although some of the larger breeds can sleep up to twenty hours a day. The amount of time spent sleeping varies from dog to dog and depends on age, personality, and overall health. Though they sleep more than we do, they're generally able to wake up more easily and fully. If your dog is a bit fidgety at night, give her a chew toy to keep her occupied when she's not asleep. Most dogs will eventually adjust to your sleep schedule.

Puppies and older dogs usually urinate more frequently, so if you've adopted a baby or an elder, be prepared to get up for middle-of-the-night walks. If the weather is cold or you must get your beauty rest, you can try training your senior dog to use "puppy pads" at night once she's settled in. These absorbent pads, available at pet supply stores, allow your dog to relieve herself when needed and afford you a restful night's sleep. We don't recommend puppy pads for puppies who are being trained to potty outside, as it sends them a mixed signal. Instead, invest the time to take your puppy outside frequently in the beginning and you will soon reap the benefits (and the full-night's sleep) that come from a fully house-trained pup. If you have a Toy breed, you may choose to train her to use a litter box, as discussed in the next chapter.

What to Expect During the First Week

If you adopted your dog from a rescue group or an animal shelter, you may not know much about her past. One thing is certain though: Regardless of the circumstances, your dog may feel that she has been abandoned in the past by people she trusted, so it may take her a while to begin to trust you. Your home may also be full of rules she's never experienced and doesn't understand, so give her time to learn what's expected. Of course, that is not to say she should be given carte blanche from the beginning. Having rules and sticking to them will actually help your dog feel more secure in her new environment, so set rules and enforce them—in a gentle, firm manner. *Never* yell at or hit your dog. The resulting fear will only thwart your efforts in fostering a well-socialized, happy companion.

If you're lucky, your new dog will be well-mannered and calm right from the start, but be aware that the first week or so with a new dog can sometimes be a bit of a "honeymoon"—your dog is putting her best paw forward and is focused on getting adjusted and pleasing you. As she settles in, she may begin revealing some less-than-desirable habits—shyness, anxiety, restlessness, overexcitement, whimpering, and excessive barking are all typical. At first, she may also pee in the house, threaten your other pets, or simply remain indifferent and hang out alone in her crate or away from the family. In addition, she could lose her appetite, drink water excessively, urinate frequently, or get diarrhea. These are all normal ways for dogs to express their anxiety at being in a totally unfamiliar place, but if any of these symptoms lasts more than a few days, call your veterinarian.

Most likely your dog is just nervous and needs some time to adjust to her new home. Bear in mind, too, that some adopted dogs have never had the benefit of training, and most shelters and rescue facilities simply do not have the necessary staff or resources to fill in the gaps. You can teach your dog basic obedience skills at home (you'll find plenty of advice in the next chapter), or join a private or group class in your community. Private instruction will obviously be more expensive, but may be helpful for dogs who don't get along with other animals or have severe behavioral issues. If your dog is outgoing and enjoys the company of other dogs, you might consider enrolling her in agility or flyball classes (more on that in Chapter 10). She will not only enjoy the camaraderie and physical exercise, but she will build confidence and learn basic obedience skills as well. Ask your shelter or rescue staff or volunteers, dog-loving friends, family members, or veterinarian for recommendations of trainers and classes in your area.

Bringing home a new dog is akin to bringing home a child—everyone has a lot of adjustments to make before things start to run smoothly. If you're like most new pet parents, you want to do everything "right." You may have read several books, perused countless websites, and sought advice from other people with adopted dogs. In the end, however, there's just you and your dog figuring out how to become buddies. You may make some mistakes along the way, but as with anything new, think of the missteps as learning experiences. The nice thing about dogs is that they are infinitely forgiving, and they love unconditionally. Together, you'll find what works for both of you.

Your Behavior: Managing Stress

Adding a new four-legged family member to a busy household is both exciting and stressful. And stress, as we all know, can be detrimental to our health. When we're under stress, some of us eat too much, drink to excess, or engage in other self-destructive behaviors. Like us, dogs can pick up some bad habits—barking, digging, or chewing on inappropriate items—when they're stressed. One of the best ways for you and your new pal to shake off some stress and get to know one another better is to engage in some good old-fashioned exercise. There's nothing quite like a game of fetch with a Frisbee or a slobbery tennis ball to help melt away tension (at least that's probably what your dog is thinking!). You may settle for a nice long walk at a nearby park or beach, but the point is to spend some time together in a constructive, healthy, and energy-expending way.

Full House: Introducing the New Arrival to Your Other Pets

While most dogs are eager to meet new friends, some won't be too keen on the idea of sharing their family with a newcomer. Then again, if your current pet is the only one in the home, she may like having a buddy to keep her company when you're away. In either case, it's important to properly introduce new pets to one another to help them start off on the right paw. There is an in-depth look at dog-to-dog introductions in Chapter 10, so here we will just cover the basics. For a brief video tutorial on dog introductions, visit www.petfinder.com/dog-bible.

You probably know whether your current dog is friendly or aggressive toward others. After all, she has most likely interacted with fellow canines at the beach, park, groomer, or veterinary office. However, these meetings occurred in neutral territory; bringing a new dog into your current dog's home can elicit a far different reaction. She may feel threatened or territorial, and may bark, snarl, lunge, or bite at a new dog.

Ideally, introductions should be made on neutral ground, such as a park or at the animal shelter (many shelters now offer areas at the facility where dogs can get to know one another). If possible, bring along a friend or family member to help you manage the dogs, should a tussle

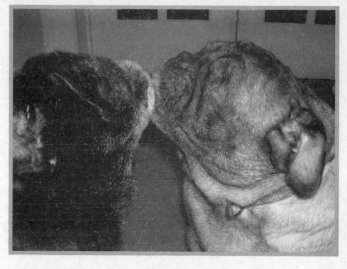

With a proper introduction, your pups will be fast friends.

break out. Be sure both dogs are leashed before allowing introductions to take place. Let them get acquainted by sniffing each other, which is the universal canine greeting. If you're outdoors and one dog urinates, let the other sniff the puddle, since urine tells dogs a lot about one another.

Wagging tails and playful behavior are good signs. If one dog appears tense (hair standing up, teeth bared, growling), separate the dogs until she calms down, and then bring them back together again. Keep the first encounter short. If possible, allow the dogs to meet on more than one occasion before bringing your new dog home full-time. If you have more than one resident dog, introduce each one to the new dog individually, starting with the friendliest, so that the new gal's not overwhelmed.

If you don't have the luxury of a slow introduction—if you bring home a stray dog on the spur of the moment, for instance—there are still ways to gradually introduce your dogs to one another. Start by keeping them in adjoining rooms, if possible, separated by a baby gate, so they can get accustomed to one another's presence and smell. You can also pet one dog, then let the other sniff your hand, to further familiarize each with the other's scent. Eventually, you can proceed to on-leash introductions in a park or yard.

Each of your dogs should have his or her own set of food and water dishes, toys, and beds. In time they may learn to share these items, but for now, let everyone have his or her own possessions to help reduce jealousy and confrontations. Since so much attention will be focused on the new arrival, make sure to spend some extra time with your resident pets so they don't feel left out. Once everyone has settled into a regular routine, you should still take some precautions until you are certain your pets won't harm one another. When you leave the house, separate the dogs by placing them in separate rooms or by crating one or all of them, making sure each has access to his or her own bed, water, and toys.

The Truth About Cats and Dogs

It's no secret that cats and dogs sometimes fight like, well, cats and dogs. Conversely, stories abound of canines and felines who are the best of friends. If you have a cat in your home and are bringing a new dog into the family, the following tips will help you make sure your pets become buddies.

Before your new dog comes home, ask the shelter or rescue workers if she has been "cat tested" or is known to be cat friendly. Many organizations will introduce an adoptable dog to a friendly and tolerant cat to gauge her reaction. If the dog lunges or bares her teeth, she shouldn't go into a home with cats. If she starts wagging her tail and seems interested in getting to know the cat (or ignores the cat altogether), chances are good she will do fine in a home that includes cats.

Even if your dog has been cat tested, go slowly with introductions at home. The worst thing you can do is open the front door and let your new dog loose into the house to start chasing your cat. One swipe of your cat's paw can cause serious injury to the dog, especially if she is scratched in the eye. Instead, begin by putting your new dog in a crate and allowing your cat to come up and sniff her. Alternately, use a baby gate to confine your dog to one room and allow the dog and cat to get acquainted through the security of this barrier. You may wish to keep them separated like this for a few days (or even a few weeks) until everyone becomes accustomed to one another. When you decide they're ready to meet face-to-face, leash your dog and bring her into the room with your cat. Give them some time to view each other from across the room. If your cat is outgoing, she may walk right up to your dog as if to say, "Let's be friends!" Other cats may be wary until they know the dog means no harm.

For your cat's safety, make sure she has some "safe spots" throughout your home to which she can escape if she feels threatened. Be sure to place her litter box in an area that is not accessible to your dog, who may be a little too interested in snacking on the contents. It is also important to keep feeding stations separate. Placing a slightly raised baby gate across the doorway of the room holding the litter box and/or cat food will allow your cat easy access (underneath or over the top of the gate) while keeping your new pup from munching on either delicacy.

Keep in mind that every situation is different, and you will have to experiment a little to see what works best for you and your pets. With proper introductions and patience, your four-legged pals may soon become fast friends—or at least learn to tolerate each other.

Courting Disaster

Because their ancestors were bred and trained to hunt rodents, some dogs (such as those in the Terrier Group) can be downright dangerous with cats or other small animals. Similarly, retired racing Greyhounds have been trained to chase small furry objects and may view the family cat as prey. With that said, there are plenty of terriers and Greyhounds who co-exist peacefully with cats, but you will need to take precautions when bringing any new dog into your home. Your cat depends on you for her safety.

Doctor, Doctor! The First Vet Visit

While some shelters and rescue organizations ensure that their adoptable dogs have been vaccinated, screened for major diseases, and spayed or neutered prior to adoption, many do not have the resources and the personnel to do all that. Even if the shelter has taken care of these things, you should still make an appointment with a veterinarian with whom you will want to form a strong and long-lasting relationship. If possible, take your dog for her first veterinary appointment within the first week of her arrival. The vet can examine your new dog for any pre-existing conditions, perform a spay or neuter surgery (if needed), administer any necessary shots, and advise you on proper diet and other needs. Some adoption organizations will give you a spay/neuter voucher, which allows you to have your dog altered at low or no cost at participating veterinary clinics or humane societies. For more on spaying and neutering, see Chapter 12.

If you don't know anything about your dog's medical history, you may need to have her vaccinated, but to avoid the possibility of over-vaccination, ask your veterinarian about titer testing. This test, which is discussed further in Chapter 14, checks for the presence of immunity to disease already in a dog's blood. Be aware, though, that in many municipalities, you can't obtain a license for your dog without showing proof of rabies vaccination. Many boarding kennels and doggie day-care facilities also require vaccinations, but more and more are accepting titer results, so be sure to find one that does if you choose to avoid overvaccinating your dog.

At the initial vet visit, bring any medical records you have for your dog, along with a stool sample (see Chapter 17 for instructions), which your vet will check to make sure your dog doesn't have any parasites. Be sure to ask questions! Your vet will be your partner in your dog's medical care for some time, possibly the rest of her life, so you need to make sure you trust and understand what he says. Here are some important questions for the first visit:

- **If my dog is not already spayed or neutered, when can we schedule that procedure?** Sometimes the shelter may not know if your female dog has already been spayed. In these cases, particularly if there is evidence of a scar on your dog's abdomen, many veterinarians advise waiting to see if your dog goes into heat. If you are advised to wait, make certain your vet explains the signs of heat and checks to make sure your new companion is not in the early stages of pregnancy. (Gestation is about sixty-three days and is not easy to detect in the first thirty days. Don't be angry if the shelter didn't warn you; they may not have known.) Also, if there are any intact male dogs around, make sure she is confined so she cannot get pregnant if she does come into heat.
- **What vaccinations should my dog have?** (See Chapter 14 for more information on vaccinations.)
- **Should my dog have a fecal and urine test as well as a basic blood panel test?** These tests are often conducted the first time you bring a dog in to a veterinary clinic, so that you will have a baseline to measure test results against in the future.
- **Should my dog be tested for heartworm, or given preventative medication?** Many heartworm preventatives also kill a variety of worms and other parasites.
- **What type and amount of food should I be feeding my dog?**
- **How much exercise should my dog get each day?**

Petfinder.com: The Adopted Dog Bible

- ☼ **How often should my dog come in for check-ups?** Most dogs see a veterinarian once a year, but some need to go more often for treatment of an ongoing problem.
- ☼ **If my dog is taking medication, how often and for how long should the medication be administered? Are there any side effects to be aware of?**
- ☼ **Is there anything special I should know about this breed, mix, or type of dog?** Many breeds have particular health concerns to watch out for—for example, German Shepherd Dogs are prone to hip dysplasia, some deep-chested dogs are at risk of bloat, Cocker Spaniels and Poodles get ear infections—so you may need to learn about special measures you can take to reduce the likelihood of encountering these and other breed-specific problems.

Making Checkups Less Stressful

Some dogs view a visit to the vet as an opportunity to meet new friends, while others are terrified. You can help ease your dog's tension if you stop by your veterinarian's office at a time when you don't have an actual appointment, though you may want to call ahead to make sure the vet doesn't mind. Once there, allow your dog to get acquainted with the veterinarian and staff and explore the office. Bring along treats and have the vet and staff give a few to your dog. This should help make your dog less anxious about coming back. One of my dogs, Mojo, thinks that a visit to the vet's office is the best thing that could happen to him. His joy at visiting with his friends there makes appointments much less stressful for all of us.

What to Expect During the First, Second, and Third Months

By now, your adopted dog has probably begun to settle into your household's daily routine. But remember, it can take her anywhere from a few weeks to a few months to feel totally safe and relaxed in her new environment. It's common for a dog who has been neglected or abused to need additional time before she fully trusts that you won't hurt or abandon her. So spend time with her every day, whether while training, exercising, or just lounging together on the couch. Treat her well, and she will do the same for you.

From Fido to Freddie—Changing Your Adopted Dog's Name

It's not uncommon for an adopted dog to come with a name you don't particularly like. If this is the case, don't worry. Your dog can easily learn a new name. Experiment with a few names that you like and see which one seems to suit her best. Call her name often and give her a treat when she responds. What's most important is the tone you use when saying her name; your dog will react to your calm, upbeat voice. Many trainers suggest avoiding very long names, or those that sound like basic obedience commands. For instance, you might want to avoid a name like Seth, as it sounds too much like "Sit!"

Petfinder.com's Top Ten Most Popular Names for Adopted Dogs in 2007
1. Buddy
2. Max
3. Sadie
4. Jack
5. Daisy
6. Lucy
7. Lady
8. Charlie
9. Rocky
10. Duke

Petfinder's Top Ten Most Unusual Pet Names in 2007
1. Not Pants
2. Zhivago
3. Fat Alice
4. Barney Google
5. Cinderella Cookiedough
6. Ditto Dippin' Dots
7. Fizzleboom
8. Miss Booty-Q
9. Bubba Big Foot
10. Partly Cloudy

Petfinder.com: The Adopted Dog Bible

Dog Biscuits for the Soul: Mia

Mia

We had been looking for a young female dog or puppy to add to our home. We had three rescued cats and one lively eighteen-month-old dog, Pofi, who loved the company of other dogs. The timing seemed perfect when my husband spotted Meeka (now known as Mia) on Petfinder.com and was quite smitten with her pretty face. We got to the adoption event early and I brought Pofi in a separate car. They met and all went well. We took them home in separate cars and went to a dog park (neutral territory) to let them get to know each other a bit more. Pofi was surprised when he got home and Meeka was there again, but it was mere minutes before he started offering her his toys to play with, and they have been best friends ever since. Watching them romp and play makes us really happy, and we know they make each other happy, too.

Lisa Pasquale, Minneapolis, Minnesota
Mia was adopted from Pet Haven Inc. of Minnesota.

Resources

Fogle, Bruce, DVM: *ASPCA Complete Dog Care Manual: The Ultimate Illustrated Guide to Caring for Your Dog.* DK, 1992

Kalina, Shari and Eliza Rubenstein: *The Adoption Option: Choosing and Raising the Shelter Dog for You.* Howell Books, 1996

McKinney, Barbara and John Ross: *Adoptable Dog: Teaching Your Adopted Pet to Obey, Trust, and Love You.* W. W. Norton & Company, 2003

7

Basic Re-Training

All dogs need training, but adopted dogs perhaps more than others. Your adopted dog may have gotten away with a few undesirable behaviors or been "trained" by getting smacked with a rolled-up newspaper or a stick. But don't despair! This can be corrected with kindness, patience, and the right kind of reward-based training.

Some dogs remain gentle souls even if their start in life has not been so favorable. Others may seem quiet and reserved at first, but change into juvenile delinquents as they settle in. That change may come as a surprise, but it can be modified. And don't assume your dog was physically abused because he squints and cowers if you raise a hand. It's true that he might have been hit, but it's also possible that your dog is just shy—some dogs, just like some people, are more reserved than others. Either way, you'll have to do some remedial work to change his opinion of people—and in the meantime try to keep voices down in the house and temper your gestures.

This chapter will teach you how to build your dog's confidence as you train some useful behaviors, and the next chapter will help you deal in a positive manner with his unwanted habits. Equip yourself with a good attitude and a large helping of patience, and you'll both do just fine.

How Dogs Operate

Dogs do what works. It's that simple. So if you want to stop a behavior, you have to figure out why the behavior is rewarding to your dog. Then either take away the reward or make some other, desired behavior more rewarding. By rewarding the behaviors we want, we make them more and more likely to happen, eventually eliciting them on cue. Sometimes this is obvious and sometimes it's not. For example, a dog who jumps up on people generally gets attention. Some people will yell and push the dog away and some will pet the dog. While yelling and pushing away may seem like punishment to you, it is still attention to him—so in your dog's eyes, his tactic worked. To help make jumping less rewarding for your dog, take away what he wants the most—your attention. Immediately stop all interaction with your leaping dog. That means no pushing or scolding; you should even remove eye contact. Instead, step toward your dog with your hip as you turn your back. By the end of this motion you should be facing away from your dog. To make another behavior more rewarding, you can teach him that sitting to greet people will result in receiving a lot of praise and petting. We'll talk a lot more about teaching "sit" in the next chapter.

One other note before we begin—nearly everything that we view as a "problem behavior" is actually a normal canine behavior that is occurring at the wrong time or in the wrong place for us humans. Your dog is not a demon because he steals food off the counter. All dogs are scavengers and hunters, and gaining nourishment with the least work makes good evolutionary sense. Digging, barking, eliminating, chewing on things—these are all normal dog behaviors that simply have to be redirected to acceptable times and places. We will return to this idea in the next chapter, but it is important for you to keep it in mind during training.

Becoming a Benevolent Dictator

Canine society has often been framed as a dominance hierarchy. This has led to some foolish advice and the view that dogs are dangerous subversives just waiting for an opportunity to ascend to leadership. While there *are* a handful of dogs who seem intent on having their own way at all times, most are not interested in world (or even household) domination. They are happy to have you assume a leadership position, as long as you demonstrate that you will take care of their needs for food, shelter, and entertainment.

When you adopt a dog, your first days and weeks are a time of exploration, when you will learn what your dog already knows (both good and bad). During this period of getting acquainted, don't endanger yourself and your dog by indulging in unthinking behavior that could bring an unwelcome response from your dog. As much as you may love him, don't grab your dog and give him a bear hug—being confined in this way might panic or anger him, and you are placing your face dangerously close to his powerful jaws. Don't try to kiss your dog on the nose for the same reason. These all-too-human gestures of affection may become acceptable as your dog comes to understand that you are trustworthy, but they are unacceptable, and possibly even dangerous, at the start of your relationship.

You will be working to gain your dog's trust through consistency of kindness and rewarding training sessions. Don't be in a hurry. Unfortunately, some dogs have had difficult pasts and may think that humans are not to be trusted. It can take months to repair that damage.

During your getting acquainted period, explore what your dog already knows. He may have had some training, and some of it may have stuck. Try saying the most common cues, such as "sit," "down," "come," and "heel." If any of them get the appropriate reaction, you'll know you're ahead of the game. If any get a bad reaction—the dog appearing distressed or moving away from you—make a mental note not to use those cues in your training, and choose a different word to attach to those behaviors. Pick any word, really—remember that, to your dog, it's just a word. Also try some hand signals, as some people never successfully attach a verbal cue. (If you don't know what the typical hand signals are, see "Training Some Basic Behaviors" on page 121.)

Dogs, especially adopted dogs, appreciate routine. To help your dog settle in, make everything in your life fairly predictable. While it isn't necessary to schedule events like clockwork, having a general time of day for mealtimes, walks, bedtime, and those all-important training sessions will help both of you find your groove.

Basic Equipment and Management Tools

Some tools can help you manage your dog's behavior while you learn what to do to train more appropriate behaviors. Other tools are useful for training itself. Here is a quick rundown of equipment you may want to use.

Crate

Crates are excellent containment devices, as long as they aren't overused. For an adult dog, it is optimal if you can make arrangements for him to leave his crate to stretch and relieve himself every four to six hours. While adult dogs can be crated for eight hours while you're at work, you should not expect your dog to sit in a crate all day unless you make the time to provide him with plenty of exercise and enrichment before and after.

Crates are especially handy for house training, and most dogs adjust easily to one. If your dog is resistant to entering the crate, don't panic. He may not have been exposed to a crate previously or he may have had a bad experience with one. We'll provide instructions on how to gently accustom your dog to a crate later in this chapter. With time and patience, most dogs learn to happily accept their crates; some dogs really love them. In the meantime, if you need to confine your dog, either use baby gates to block off a doggy-safe area or use an exercise pen.

Exercise Pen

An exercise pen is a set of panels hinged together. They can fold flat for storage or can be opened to form a rough square or circle. In times past, they were all made of heavy-gauge metal wire, but now you can also find pens made of heavy-duty plastic. Most form an enclosure of roughly four feet by four feet. This gives you enough room to create a designated "potty area," a sleeping area, and an area for food and water for all but the largest dogs.

Collar, Harness, and Leash

For outdoor excursions, you can choose a collar and leash or a harness and leash, but if your dog arrived with a habit of pulling on his leash, you

A well-trained dog makes a better companion than an untrained dog.

may want the control assistance of a head halter or a no-pull harness. There is an overview of collars, harnesses, and leashes in Chapter 4, and you can also talk to the staff at your local PETCO or other pet supply store if you have more specific questions.

Treats and Rewards

For training sessions, you'll need a good assortment of rewards. Treats are easy to use and most dogs are eager to earn them, but you don't want to use so many that you unbalance your dog's diet. Typically, no more than 10 percent of your dog's diet should be treats. At the start of training a new behavior, since you are likely to use quite a few treats, it's best to find a healthier way to reward your dog. Not all dogs will work for their regular daily kibble, but if yours will, you're set; just remember to decrease his meals accordingly. You can set aside his daily food portion in the morning and let him earn it as treats all day long. Then at the end of the day, you can hand-feed whatever is left to your dog. His dinner need not only come in a bowl, and hand feeding is a great way to further your bond and establish yourself in a leadership role.

If your dog isn't interested in kibble as a reward, try healthier treat options such as green beans, broccoli, carrots, and apples. Or, make a treat mix. Combine a handful of your dog's dry food (if that's what you choose to feed) in a plastic bag with some nutritious dog treats and some smelly, tasty human food such as cooked hot dog slices, roast beef, smoked turkey, or even bacon bits. The human food will impart its odor and flavor to the dry food, and you can give your pooch a piece of the human food when you want to offer an especially good reward.

Don't ignore non-food forms of reward. Toys are good, too. If your dog is ball crazy, a couple of quick tosses can be more rewarding than a whole handful of kibble. Most police dogs, bomb-sniffing dogs, and other working dogs do all they do just for the reward of being able to play with their ball. Other dogs may prefer to engage in a quick session of tug. Experiment to see what turns your pup on. And, of course, you should always offer plenty of praise.

Clicker and Target Stick

Though you can work without them, a clicker and a target stick are very useful tools, especially if you want to train beyond the basics. A clicker is a small box with a flexible piece of metal inside. When you depress and release the metal strip, it makes a distinctive *click-clack* sound. You use this sound to "mark" a behavior, and follow it up with a reward (typically a food reward). Your dog will quickly develop an association between the behavior that you mark with the clicker and the reward.

Another tool that works as a good complement for a clicker is a target stick. This can be as simple as a length of dowel with an eraser stuck on the end or as fancy as a telescoping metal rod with a clicker box built into the handle. This tool is essentially used as an extension of your arm, and is typically used to help your dog "target" for a position, like heeling at your side. Both are useful tools that work well together but can be used independent of each other as well. We'll talk more about clickers and target sticks in "Training Techniques" on page 119.

What Good Trainers Know

Training is a mechanical skill. Good trainers can make it look easy, but that's because they have had a lot of practice and know how to make any situation work for them. Consider these two factors good trainers know:

Consistency: Dogs are masters at reading each others' body language, and they extend that talent to observing their humans. Consistency in your hand signals is very important. For example, if you raise your hand in an upward motion for the signal to sit, you will want to be sure that you use a very different signal for come, down, or anything else. Think of your hand signal like sign language—communicating to your dog exactly what you want—and be sure to use distinct hand signals for specific behaviors to avoid confusion.

Voice: Humans seem to fall into one of two bad habits when giving dogs verbal cues—they either become quite militant and harsh, or they adopt a whiny, "please do it for me?" tone. Neither works particularly well. Instead, use the same sort of voice you'd use if you were leading a group of co-workers down a forest trail—"follow me . . . left turn . . . watch that root!"—clear and firm, but also upbeat and kind.

It's been scientifically proven that your voice and general attitude can energize your dog or calm him down. To excite your pup, raise the pitch of your voice higher and use three short, choppy words or sounds in rapid succession, with the last one ending in an "e" sound. Make yourself a soprano (or as close as you can get) and say something along the lines of "pup, pup, puppy!"

To calm him down, you want to do pretty much the opposite. Speak a little lower than normal and use long drawn-out sounds in a near-monotone, as if you were trying to put a group of people to sleep or in a trance. You should even feel your own breathing slow down as you do this.

Also consider that people tend to use their voice too much. It won't do you any good to keep repeating "sit" if you haven't shown your dog what "sit" means. So don't confuse "Buster, sit!" with "Buster, I said sit, sit, sit, no sit, sit, sit! Buster please SIT!" (By the way, saying it louder won't help him understand you better, either!) Dogs aren't born understanding English. The good news is you can assign any word you want to a particular behavior. As mentioned, if your adopted dog cringes when someone says "down," just use another word, like "lay" or "ground" or any other word that comes to mind. Some people choose to train in a foreign language, some just use words they like. It doesn't matter to the dog. None of them mean anything to your dog until, through training, he associates them with a behavior.

Finally, once your dog associates a word with a behavior, only that behavior is linked to that word. You can't use "down" to mean lie down, get off the couch, and don't jump up on people. It won't work. One action should be "down" and perhaps another should be "off," or any other word you choose. Just make sure you're consistent.

Whenever you train, have a plan, but "plan" to be flexible and patient. You can't expect to have a really good training session if you're feeling stressed, in a bad mood, or worried about the time. Your dog will pick up on your demeanor and body language. If your training sessions are positive and rewarding, you'll both be successful.

Petfinder.com: The Adopted Dog Bible

Training Techniques

Three basic techniques successful trainers use to teach their dogs are (1) lure and reward—for quick results in training simple behaviors such as "sit" and "down," (2) clickers, and (3) target sticks—both used for more complex behaviors, such as "heel" or "go to your crate." Understanding each technique will give you a variety of ways to communicate with your dog.

Lure and Reward

The simplest way to train is to use a piece of food as a lure to coax your dog into performing the behavior you want. If you're in the safety of your own home, you don't even need a collar or leash.

Some dogs are a bit grabby about taking treats. If yours is one of them, drop the treat on the floor rather than handing it to your dog.

If you start training a new behavior using a lure, you'll want to fade out the lure as quickly as possible. Remember, the behavior should produce the treat; you shouldn't need the treat to produce the behavior. So, begin with a few repetitions using your lure. Then repeat a few more times using the lure to get the behavior, *but* give your dog a treat from your other hand—don't give him the lure! Then repeat the same hand motion without a lure, and make sure that he gets a reward for doing his new behavior. Congratulations, you just faded out your lure.

Clicker Training

Clicker training can be used to train a spectrum of behaviors, from basic skills like "sit" and "stay" to complex behaviors requiring precision and timing as would be needed for many dog sports. You do not need a clicker to teach the basics, but it can be a helpful tool.

Some dogs are afraid of the clicker. This doesn't necessarily mean your adopted dog has had a bad experience with a clicker in the past—he may just be sensitive to sound. If you want to use a clicker but encounter this problem, there are plenty of tactics to try.

Charging the Clicker

The point of "charging" the clicker is to make your dog see it as a wonderful object that causes rewards to come his way. You don't have to hold the clicker near the dog, or point it like a TV remote. In fact, you want to be sure the clicker isn't too close to his ears. The routine for charging the clicker is:

- As long as your dog is not doing anything objectionable (jumping up, barking), click the clicker and give him a treat.
- Pause just a second, then click and treat him again. By now you should have his undivided attention—provided your treats are really valuable to him.
- Now, click and treat your dog ten times in the next fifteen to twenty seconds.
- By the time you finish, you should have a dog who is focused on you and ready to begin a training session.

Charging your clicker is a great way to kick off your training sessions during the first week or two that you are introducing him to clicker training. It will also give you a chance to warm up and practice your own skill in handling this tool.

- Get a different clicker—they have different tones, and some are specially made to be quieter.
- Put several layers of tape on the metal strip of your clicker to muffle the sound.
- Hold the clicker in your pocket.
- Use a retractable click pen or a bottle cap from a juice bottle instead of a clicker.
- Use a verbal mark like "yes!" instead of a clicker.

Target Training

When training certain behaviors, such as "heel," you can use a target stick or the palm of your hand to help your dog find the correct position. To get started, you'll first need to teach your dog to touch his nose to the tip of the stick or to your palm. Start by holding the stick (or your palm) about five or six inches in front of your dog's nose. Resist the temptation to push the target right into his face—that will only cause him to back away from it. Dogs are generally curious, so when your dog touches his nose to the stick, say "Yes!" (or click) and immediately give him a treat. If he doesn't touch the target at first, take a treat in your other hand and close your fist over it. Place your treat-filled hand just behind the tip of the stick or behind your empty palm. When your dog leans forward to sniff the treat, say "Yes!" and give your reward. After a few tries, your dog will get the idea.

If you find your adopted dog is skittish about the target stick, start with the stick lying on the floor. Click and treat when he looks at it, then when he moves toward it, and again when he touches it, before you begin to pick up

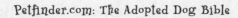

one end. Take your time with this. You can only teach your dog to target if you are patient. If he is biting at the stick, you are late with your click or verbal mark. This behavior is easier to nip in the bud than to try to eliminate after you've let your dog practice it for days, so start clicking or saying your verbal mark just before your dog touches the target. Then work back toward having him actually touch it, with a closed mouth.

For more useful information on clicker training and target training visit www.clickertraining.com.

With training, your dog will be able to greet other dogs peacefully.

Training Some Basic Behaviors

Be flexible and patient. Training is a learning and bonding experience for both of you, so if you find yourself becoming frustrated, or if it appears your dog is, end the session and try again tomorrow.

Sit

"Sit" is a great first behavior to train. Many dogs offer the first behavior they learned when they aren't sure what to do, and a sitting dog can't be running away, jumping up on people, or doing any number of other potentially troublesome things.

Start by holding a treat directly in front of your dog's nose, then move it up and back slightly, as if you're trying to put it between his ears. You will not use a verbal cue at this time. If your dog raises his nose to follow the treat, he will automatically fold himself into a sit. Give him the treat and tell him what a good dog he is.

Now to troubleshoot. . . . If your dog jumps up rather than sit, you're holding the treat too high. Lower it and try again. If he looks up at the treat but doesn't sit, you're not moving the treat back over his head far enough. If he backs up rather than sit, work in a corner of a room or against a wall so he has less space to maneuver. If he doesn't follow the treat at all, choose a more enticing treat.

As soon as your dog is following the lure and sitting readily, start mixing in some repetitions without the treat in your hand. Be sure to keep everything else exactly the same. If you hold the treat in your fist when luring, continue to make your hand into a fist, and make the same motion as when you were holding a treat.

When your dog is sitting in response to your hand signal four out of five times, you're ready to add your verbal cue "Sit!" Just as his rear moves down toward the floor, say "Sit!" and then immediately reward. Repeat this four or five times, and then begin to fade your lure as described earlier. For a visual guide on training your dog to sit, see www.petfinder.com/dog-bible.

Once he is responding to your verbal cue reliably, start to mix it up a little bit more. Trying teaching him to sit on your left side and then on your right. See if you can get him to sit while you sit in a chair, or even with your back turned. Keep a pocketful of treats, and throughout the day, regardless of where you are, try asking him to sit. When he does it, give him a treat and lots of praise.

For instructions on how to develop a sit-stay, see the instructions in the "Stay" section on page 123.

Down

Start with your dog in a sit. Hold a treat in front of his nose, then lower it straight to the floor. If his nose follows the treat down, move the treat along the floor a short distance—directly away from him—and hold it there. When he lies down, praise him and give him the treat. If he pops up, don't worry, just try it again.

Experiment with moving the treat at different speeds. Some dogs respond better to quick movement, while others follow better if you move slowly. Also try moving the treat along the floor for a shorter or longer distance. The goal is to find a combination that works well for your dog.

If your dog won't follow the treat into a "down" position, don't despair. There are other ways to get this behavior. Try sitting on the floor with your

Petfinder.com: The Adopted Dog Bible

legs out in front of you, and bend your knees to create space under them. If your dog is on your left side, use your right hand to offer a treat under your legs. Try to lure him under your legs with it. If it works, give him the treat. Some adopted dogs will not feel secure enough to travel under your legs at first. Try bending your legs more to create a bigger space or put your feet up on a stool or ottoman, especially if your dog is large. You might even try luring your dog under a coffee table.

Once he is comfortable lying down for a treat, use the steps outlined previously to add your cue and fade your lure.

Stay

When teaching "stay," you'll be working on the three Ds: Distance, Duration, and Distractions. Before you start, you need to think of a "release" cue. After all, you can't expect your dog to stay put forever, and you certainly don't want to let him decide how long is long enough! Many common choice for release cues include "release," "break," or "free."

When you first start working on "stay," begin inside your home in a small room with minimal distractions. As the days progress, so will the distraction factor. When you are ready to graduate to the outdoors, start in an enclosed, safe area. You may also want to keep your dog on a leash at all times for added control.

Consider investing in a long leash to practice staying for long distances of ten to fifty feet, and for when you leave the enclosed areas outdoors.

First, just try getting your dog to sit and wait for three seconds. After each successful sit, calmly use your verbal marker "Yes!" or your clicker, and reward him with a treat. Now mix things up and try different ways to increase his ability to stay in the sit position.

Okay? Okay!

People tend to use "okay" as their release word. That's, well, okay—except that, as the previous sentence illustrates, "okay" tends to come up in conversation quite often. Picture this: You've told your dog to "stay" in the car as you open the hatch or door to load some purchases. A friend walks by and says "See you at the party tonight." If you reply with "Okay," you have just released your dog from his stay. Now he could jump out of the car into an unsafe situation, with cars zipping past. The choice of the release word is yours, but we recommend that you either pick another word, or work to wipe "okay" out of your casual vocabulary.

- Sit while you take a step back
- Sit while you take two steps back
- Sit while you take a step to the right
- Sit while you take a step to the left
- Sit for five seconds, then ten seconds, and so on

Each time he is successful, make sure you say "Yes!" immediately followed by a reward.

If you find that any of these steps are "too much" for your dog, simply break them down into smaller steps. For example, if sitting for five seconds is too long, try three seconds. After you have success with three seconds at least twice, try five seconds again. When working on distance, start with just one step. If that's too much and your dog is already popping up, try just lifting your foot off the ground. Work your way up to walking a few feet away. Set your dog up for success: start small and advance from there.

Over the next several days, slowly increase the space between you and your dog, increase the length of time of the stay, and add some distractions, too. Following these guidelines, by the end of the week you may be able to walk twenty steps away from your dog while clapping your hands and walking toward a door—or better. Be creative and enthusiastic, and always keep these exercises fun for you and your dog.

For a visual guide on training your dog to stay, see www.petfinder.com/dog-bible.

Come

It's easy to teach your dog to come to you, but it's hard to make that behavior nearly foolproof in challenging conditions. How hard you want to work at this is up to you, but if you plan to let your dog offleash in uncontrolled circumstances, you need to have a pretty solid recall in place.

Because a recall could literally be a lifesaving cue, and because in many instances the dog is free to respond or not, "come" has a few more rules and guidelines than other cues.

First, you want as few cue failures as humanly (or caninely) possible, so you need to set up the circumstances to favor an appropriate outcome.

Second, you want coming when called to be an *extremely* rewarding behavior. That means that you cannot call the dog to you for anything he

Petfinder.com: The Adopted Dog Bible

might consider negative. No calling him in from the yard to be locked in a crate, no calling him to you for nail clipping or a bath, no calling him away from rolling happily in some horrible smelly stuff. Instead, in such circumstances, you must go and get your dog. That's hard for humans. Many of us would much rather stand still and call our dog than walk across the yard and snap on a leash. But remember—*consequences drive behavior*. If you want a recall that works, you must keep it rewarding.

Now, you know there are certain times when your dog is going to eagerly come to you—when you're filling his dinner bowl, jingling the car keys, or taking his leash down from its hook. You know what makes your dog appear out of nowhere. Each time one of these occasions arises, say "come," even if your dog is already on his way to you. Take a couple of steps away from him, and when he follows you, reward him by putting down his food bowl or clipping on his leash for a walk.

You can also set up circumstances where you are almost certain your dog will come to you. Station people at opposite ends of a short hallway and call your dog back and forth between you. Have someone hold your dog while you go hide behind a door or around a corner. When you call, have the other person release the dog to come and find you. When he finds you, lavish him with rewards in the form of treats or praise.

The hard part is making the cue work when circumstances become more challenging. A good group class can help by setting up careful distractions while still making sure you succeed. On your own, this will be more difficult, as you must keep your dog safe while practicing. You can use a long leash, either standing on the end and letting your dog wander away from you, or tethering the line to an immovable object. You can also use a fenced yard, or a fenced dog park if you find a time when it is deserted.

If at any point you make a mistake, and your dog does not respond to your call, you have to gently make it happen. Remember, this is a behavior that you want to be as "no fail" as possible, just in case you ever need it in an emergency. If your dog is on a long leash, do not pull him to you. Instead, walk up the line, taking in slack as you go. When you get to your dog, use an especially good treat to lure him with you back to where you were when you called. Once you get there, give him the treat and praise him like crazy, just as if he had come when you called . . . even if what you'd most like to do at the moment is strangle him. If you give in to your emotions and yell at him, you'll only make it more likely that the next call won't work, either. If your dog isn't on a long line when your recall fails, you'll need to follow him until you can manage to get hold of him, at which point the same holds true—lure him back to where you were when you called, and then reward him lavishly.

Place

In this behavior, you send your dog to a designated place, such as on a mat or rug. If you make it a strong behavior, you can use it during distractions, like when someone is at the door or when you're cooking dinner and don't want the dog underfoot. The instructions here will include a clicker or verbal marker, as they can be useful in teaching this behavior.

Start by standing close to your designated place, with your dog hungry and ready to work. When he puts a foot on the mat, mark (or click) and drop a treat. If he happens to stay on the mat, mark and treat again. Do this for a maximum of five repetitions, then say your release word and walk away from the mat. Wait a few seconds, then come back and start again.

If your dog doesn't touch the mat, move yourself slightly to try and maneuver him onto the mat. Mark and drop a treat when he gets there.

When you have practiced standing close to the mat for several sessions, move a little distance away. Now toss a treat onto the mat, making sure your dog is watching. When he goes to the mat to get the treat, mark and toss another treat. After several repetitions, say your release word and stop tossing treats onto the mat.

After a couple of sessions of tossing treats, make the same motion but without actually throwing a treat (using the throwing motion as a new hand signal). If your dog goes to the mat, mark and throw a treat as a reward. If he doesn't go to the mat, resume throwing a treat for another session or two before you try again with just the hand signal.

Gradually extend your distance from the mat, remembering to mix up shorter distances with longer ones. By the time you can be about six or seven feet away, you should be ready to add your verbal cue. Say it first, then make your tossing motion.

At about the same time, you can start training your dog to perform other behaviors, such as sit and down, on the mat. Decrease your distance at first, because you're making the behavior more complex. Gradually work back up to being farther away.

"Come" in an Emergency Situation

Having a reliable "come" command can save your dog's life—if it works. There are situations, though, when even a well-trained dog will be too distracted to obey commands that he knows in a quiet yard. We've explained that if your dog does not respond when you tell him to "come," you must go and get him, then bring him back to where you were when the command was issued. In an emergency situation, however, your response will be very different.

If your dog somehow gets out of the car or slips his collar and you're near traffic, or if you know that he is about to plunge into that rushing river without a second thought, try calling "come," and hope that he remembers his training. If your command doesn't work, however, *do not run toward your dog*. Run in the opposite direction, away from him, and whoop it up like crazy while you go. If you give chase, your dog is likely to think you're playing and run away, probably right into the danger you're trying to save him from. If *you* run away, your dog will probably chase after you. Use anything enticing that is available to you. If your dog loves car rides, run to the car, open the door. Throw yourself on the ground and wail and beat your fists if you have to. It shouldn't take much acting under the circumstances, and dogs tend to approach novel sights.

If nothing is working to lure him away from the danger, you could try walking (not running) on a curving path that will eventually intersect with where the dog is, without going directly toward him. This of course assumes that you've got the time to do that, which you may not.

We certainly hope you will never need this advice, but if this happens to you and you manage to get your dog back safely, vow that it will never happen again. Get a new collar fitted, always attach his leash before opening a car door, and don't let your dog offleash in unfenced surroundings. Your dog is your responsibility. Do everything in your power to keep him safe.

Eventually you can add a stay to the sit or down (always being sure to release your dog afterward), then gradually add distractions, such as dropping something in the kitchen or having someone knock on the front door. The more you work at this, the better and more dependable the behavior will be.

Crate

Related to the "place" command is the command for "crate" or "kennel up," that is, training your dog to go into his crate. For this specific application, be especially careful to take it slow and to present the reward *inside* the crate, even if it's just inside the doorway. You want to reward your dog for being *in* the crate, not for exiting it. An early crate training session may look like this:

- Toss a treat (make it a good one) a short distance into the crate
- Click when your dog reaches in to get the treat and drop another treat into the crate
- Click again while the dog is still partially in the crate, and drop another treat
- Repeat five or six times

When you stop clicking and treating and your dog exits the crate, be neutral toward him, but keep watching. If he voluntarily puts his head back into the crate without your offering a treat, you want to be ready to click and toss another treat into the crate.

As you continue the training session, toss or drop the treat a little farther into the crate, so your dog has to put more of his body inside to retrieve the treat. Don't rush things. Keep it a fun, highly rewarding game. Once your dog will actually go all the way into the crate, you're ready to add your verbal cue. Say it first, then make your tossing motion in the same way you did with the "place" command above.

Don't be in a hurry to close the crate door. Let your dog gain a considerable history of receiving many rewards and being able to enter and exit at will before taking this big step. It's important to get it right.

Wait for your dog to be relaxed and tired. Start a crate-training session. After he has eaten a couple of treats, close the crate door, while continuing to click and treat him for being in the crate. After you have delivered your last treat, wait a brief time (three to five seconds), then open the door. If he comes out of the crate, be neutral, but if he chooses to remain inside, offer some quiet, soothing praise.

As you practice, start increasing the time between clicks and treats, just a bit at a time, so your dog will stay in the crate with the door closed for a longer time while still being rewarded regularly. As the time period lengthens, he will be more and more used to the crate and less and less reliant on the clicks and treats. Congratulations, you're well on your way to having a crate-trained dog who will enter his crate at your request!

Changing from a Pez Dispenser to a Slot Machine

A lot of people sneer at using treats as rewards, saying things like, "That dog will never behave if you aren't carrying cookies," or "I want my dog to obey because he wants to please me." I am a firm proponent of using treats in training—because it works. If you follow the directions in this chapter, your dog will never know when or how you might produce a reward, so he'll be willing to gamble that something good will be forthcoming soon . . . just like all the people pulling the handles on slot machines in casinos. Think about this: While you may want to perform your job well, you probably wouldn't care as much about pleasing your boss if there weren't a paycheck involved. Why would you expect your dog to work with no hope of a reward?

But as you and your adopted dog become accustomed to each other, and once most of these basic behaviors have been trained, you do need to change from the constant reward system you use while teaching a new behavior to a maintenance schedule of more sporadic rewards. Start by waiting for multiple repetitions of a given behavior before giving a reward—perhaps three sits for one cookie. You might give the treat for the first, last, or middle sit—it's up to you. Also, remove the food from your body. Before a training session, put some treats on the counter, or a windowsill, or on top of the refrigerator, wherever you can run with the dog and grab a reward to give. The more you practice this, the more you will convince your dog that you can pull treats out of thin air. And that means you *might* produce a reward at any second, even if there doesn't seem to be one around.

Never stop offering rewards entirely. You probably wouldn't continue going to your job every day if you didn't get paid at intervals, so why would you expect your dog to continue working for you if it becomes clear that payment has dried up? Give fewer rewards, but continue to give rewards your dog likes, either at random intervals or for an especially quick response or an extra-precise performance.

Make Your Dog a Good Canine Citizen

The Canine Good Citizen (CGC) program is the only AKC event open to adopted dogs, mixed-breed dogs, and any dog-and-handler team who can perform the requirements. The point of the CGC test is to encourage responsible dog ownership and, as such, all dogs are welcome. There are ten "tests" involved in the CGC.

Test 1. Accepting a Friendly Stranger

Your dog must sit at your side and remain in a sit as a person approaches, talks to you, and shakes hands, while completely ignoring your dog.

Test 2. Sitting Politely for Petting

Your dog sits at your side. A person approaches and asks if he or she may pet your dog, then pets your dog's head and body. The dog does not have to remain sitting, but he can't pull away or jump on the person.

Test 3. Appearance and Grooming

Your dog must appear clean, healthy, and alert. You will bring his comb or brush with you, and the evaluator will use it to gently groom your dog for a moment. The evaluator will also look in your dog's ears and pick up each front foot.

Test 4. Walking on a Loose Lead

You and your dog must walk a short course as laid out by the evaluator. It will include left and right turns, an about-face (180-degree) turn, and a stop somewhere along the course and at the end. Your dog does not have to sit when you stop, and does not have to be in heel position, but he does have to be attentive and respond to your changes in direction. The dog can be on either side of you when you walk the course.

Test 5. Walking Through a Crowd

You and your dog will walk across an area, with other people standing and talking, or also walking through the area. You will pass close by at least three people, and your dog must remain under control, not shying away from, rushing at, or jumping on anyone.

Test 6. Sit, Down, and Stay

You will be asked to have your dog sit and down. You can then choose either position to have your dog stay in, while you walk about twenty feet away, come back, and release your dog.

Test 7. Come When Called

You can tell your dog to stay or you can just walk away, while the tester or a helper holds your dog. You will walk ten feet away, turn, and call your dog. You may use more than one cue.

Test 8. Reaction to Another Dog

Two handlers and their dogs will walk toward each other from about fifteen feet, with the dogs on the outside. When abreast of each other, the handlers will stop, shake hands, and talk for a moment, then continue on. The dogs must not try to contact one another before, during, or after the greeting.

Test 9. Reaction to Distraction

You and your dog will be presented with two distractions, one visual and one auditory. Some evaluators will do this in combination with *Test 5, Walking Through a Crowd;* others will do it separately as you simply stand with your dog.

Test 10. Supervised Separation

You will leave your dog with another person holding the leash, and go out of sight for three minutes. Your dog may be mildly nervous, but cannot pace, bark, or whine constantly.

With your guidance, your dog will ace every command, just like this proud graduate!

During the CGC test, you may talk to and praise your dog as much as you like, and you may repeat cues if necessary. However, you are not permitted to carry any treats or toys. Dogs are not allowed to wear head halter collars and may not eliminate (go to the bathroom) during the test.

If you pass nine out of the ten tests, you will be given a second opportunity to pass whichever test you failed, but you need to pass all ten tests to earn the CGC. Once you do, your dog can add the letters "CGC" after his name, and you can get a special collar tag or a certificate to display your accomplishment. Now you have even more reassurance that your adopted dog is an upstanding member of canine society, as well as the reward (for you both) of a job well done.

Many kennel clubs, obedience clubs, and training centers offer CGC tests several times a year. Watch for listings of events in your local newspaper, and look for fliers at pet supply stores and veterinary offices.

Dog Biscuits for the Soul: Gizmo

Gizmo

Gizmo, a three-year-old Klee Kai, found his way to the shelter because his last mother chose to abandon him when she moved to a smaller house. How anyone could give away their baby is beyond our imagination. We think Giz may have been abused in his last home; he is afraid of cameras and flashlights, and the slightest sound makes him jump. He used to growl at all dogs and people, but was always very loving toward us. We did several training classes and socialized Giz at the dog park. Now, one year later, he is cautious but no longer terrified of every human or dog he meets. He's starting to learn to play. Gizmo changed our lives immensely and now I couldn't imagine not waking up to him snuggled beside me.

Lisa Lafleur, Seattle, Washington
Gizmo was adopted from NW Pom Rescue in Portland, Oregon

Resources for this chapter can be found following Chapter 8.

8

Modifying Undesirable Behaviors

This chapter describes ways to humanely help your adopted pup overcome common problems. If you find that these methods just aren't working, turn to the last section on how to consult a behavior specialist or trainer experienced in dealing with behavioral issues.

Scary Sounds

You probably don't ordinarily give much thought to the sounds in and around your household, but try hearing them from the vantage point of your adopted dog, who may have never encountered a doorbell or heard fireworks explode. Even dogs who grew up in settled households have problems with some of these things, so show your adopted dog a little extra understanding.

Doorbells and Knocking

Doorbells and knocking on the door are common triggers for noisy reactions, even for dogs without a disadvantaged start in life. It's up to you how much you want to work on counter-conditioning this. A dog who announces her presence isn't a bad thing when you don't know who's at the door, but you probably want to be able to stop the noise once you know it's a friend or a

Petfinder.com: The Adopted Dog Bible

delivery-person. To work on this, you will need to enlist the help of family or friends to do the knocking or ringing.

The object is to get your dog to stop barking when requested. Have a supply of high-value treats at hand. (It helps if the treats are something the dog has to chew a bit—so a bigger biscuit than you would ordinarily use for training, a smear of peanut butter, or some squeeze cheese straight out of the can all could work well.) Instruct your helper to knock or ring the bell, then stand quietly on the other side of the closed door, without reacting to the dog. Leave your dog off-leash, both because that will be the normal situation and so you won't be tempted to use the leash to drag her around. Let her bark a few times in response to the knock or ring, then go to the door with your treats.

Wait for your dog to take a breath in between barks. In that moment of silence, say "Thank you," or whatever your cue for quiet is going to be, and immediately give her the special treat. Do this as quickly as you can, because it *must* happen while she is quiet. You *do not* want to reward barking, which would defeat the whole point. If she stays quiet to eat the treat, you can let your helper in, provided that your dog will welcome the appearance of this person, and he too can give the pooch some love.

With practice, your dog will start responding to the cue to get the double reward of the treat and the visitor more quickly.

This training is fairly demanding, requiring good timing from you and self-control from your dog. Don't hesitate to seek professional help if it isn't working.

Thunderstorms, Sirens, Gunfire

These are harder sound triggers to deal with because they aren't under your control. For most, your best option is desensitization. You can purchase CDs of these sounds, which you can then play extremely low, increasing the volume slightly as your dog becomes comfortable with the sounds. It is important to never increase the volume so much that your dog reacts.

Fireworks

Families across America love to celebrate with fireworks. For many dogs, however, fireworks can be a source of extreme fear and stress. Some signs of stress from fireworks include: shaking or trembling, excessive barking, howling, drooling, trying to hide or escape, refusing to eat food or treats, scratching, chewing, or other destructive behaviors, even loss of bladder or bowel control. While some of these are rather extreme symptoms, here are some tips that should help:

Take your dog for a long walk and plan to return home about an hour before the festivities start. This will allow her to potty outside, and the exercise may help wear her out a bit, too.

During fireworks displays, keep your dog indoors in a confined and secure area with the shades closed. You might also try adding some white noise by turning on an oscillating fan. Turn up the volume on the television or radio for an added distraction.

If your dog does become stressed, try not to comfort her too much. Instead, try to make the fireworks a cue for fun time to begin. Play a fun game with her and act a bit silly (don't worry—nobody will be watching!). Your calm, happy behavior and body language can help distract her from the noise outside.

You can also try a pheromone product like Comfort Zone with D.A.P., which is available in both a plug-in diffuser and a spray. This can help relax your dog. Start exposing her to the pheromones at least a couple of weeks ahead of time.

We recommend that you not take your dog to a fireworks display. However, if you do, keep her on a leash and check her collar beforehand to make sure that it's properly fitted so she won't slip out of it.

Ideally, you should stay home with your dog during fireworks events, or consider arranging for someone to stay with her. If she is extremely sensitive, consider talking to your veterinarian about a mild sedative or tranquilizer to help keep your dog calm. There are also herbal remedies that can sometimes help. Review the options with your vet.

Can I See Some ID?

As a precaution, a week or so before any festivity that is likely to include fireworks, make sure your dog is microchipped and that her ID tags are current, in case she does escape. July 5th is one of the busiest days of the year for local animal shelters. Dogs end up miles from home, confused, disoriented, and exhausted. Having an up-to-date ID tag and microchip can help expedite your reunion, should this happen to your pup.

A Touching Problem

Many adopted dogs are sensitive about being touched on some area of their body. Perhaps they don't want anyone to touch their feet or their tail. This behavior might be the result of some prior unpleasant experience, or it could just be a lack of any experience. In the long run, the origin of the problem is not as important as your patience in working to improve the situation.

Let's say your dog is hand shy (overly concerned about human hands approaching), a common occurrence with adopted dogs. This makes it hard to attach a leash, perform any sort of grooming and brushing, and may even make it difficult to pet your dog. It also means you have to caution other people not to reach quickly toward her. It's a major management issue, but one you can improve over time. Here are some do's and don'ts.

First the don'ts.

- Don't—and don't let anyone else—pat your dog on the top of the head. (It's annoying. Try it on yourself and see.)
- Don't let anyone attempt to hug your dog. In general, dogs don't naturally like being hugged, although some tolerate it, and some even learn to like it. Your hand-shy adopted dog will most certainly not like it, and if you were to lose control, the hugger's face is very close to your dog's mouth.
- Don't let anyone slap at your dog, even "in play."

Head-patting, hugs, and sudden movements can make your dog feel even less secure about human hands, and could even result in a bite, so do not be shy about telling people to keep their distance and mind their manners.

Now for the dos. Slowly and carefully, you need to build up your dog's history of kind touch. You can start by smearing some peanut butter or cream cheese on your fingertip, holding it out, and letting your dog lick it off. Don't push your hand right into her face; let her come to you. At first, let that be enough. After a few tries (maybe even a few days), either tickle your dog under the chin with the other fingers of the same hand, or use your other hand to gently scratch her chest. The chest is generally one of the more pleasurable, least threatening places to offer a scratch.

When your dog seems to be accepting this well, slightly extend the area you scratch. Stay low rather than high; reaching over a dog can be seen as a threatening gesture. Once your dog seems to be able to relax and enjoy the scratching, try it without the treat. If all goes well, have another person start the same procedure.

Eventually, you will want to be able to touch your dog anywhere, but take it slowly. If attaching a leash is a problem, you may find it easier to use an all-in-one martingale or another type of slip collar with a leash attached. The whole thing slides over the dog's head, so you won't have to grab her collar to get the leash attached.

Once your dog calmly accepts your touching her body, gently move to her head, legs and feet, and tail. Some dogs will be more sensitive about being touched in particular areas. If your dog moves away from you, you will have to take the time to slowly work on having her accept handling of all body parts. If you get a bad reaction—your dog reaching around to put her mouth on you, snapping at the air, or attempting to bite you—or if you are otherwise alarmed at your dog's response, enlist the help of a professional to work through the problem with you.

House-training

It's important that you understand at the onset that your dog has no idea where she should go to the bathroom, only that she needs to go. For many pet parents, house-training can be a frustrating and challenging experience. The good news is, it doesn't have to be. The key to successful house-training is really pretty simple. First, you will need to create an environment designed to prevent house-training accidents. Next, set up a consistent schedule. Finally, reward your dog every time she goes to the bathroom in the right place.

Start by developing a general schedule for taking your dog out to go to the bathroom. Here are some times your dog will likely need to go potty:

- First thing in the morning
- Last thing at night
- Immediately after being confined in her crate or doggie-safe area
- After naps
- About five to ten minutes after meals and after drinking water

Petfinder.com: The Adopted Dog Bible

- After playtime or after chewing on toys or a bone
- After long walks (because she may be so distracted by everything going on that she forgets to go)

Feeding your dog high-quality food will help her digestion, meaning that she'll go to the bathroom less frequently and there will be less "output" when she does.

One way to reward your dog for good behavior is to let her play in the yard.

If you combine high-quality food with a regular feeding schedule, you'll be better able to predict when your dog will need to go out. So put your dog's food bowl down for ten minutes and if she doesn't finish, don't worry. Just pick it up and she'll get a chance to eat it at her next mealtime. (This is discussed further in Chapter 9.)

As you begin the house-training process, your dog will have two living environments. One is in her crate, for those times when you're not able to supervise her or when you have to leave home. The other is under your *close* supervision when she's not in her crate. It is important, in the early stages of house-training, that you know where your dog is at all times. To do so, you can limit your dog's access to a small portion of your home—essentially, only areas where you're able to keep a really close eye on her.

If you have hallways or other rooms without doors, baby gates are a great solution. Your dog will earn the freedom to venture into other areas of your home with time. If you really want to keep a close eye on your dog, keep her on leash even while you're inside, and attach the other end to your waist. (This process is called *umbilical cording* and it is discussed more thoroughly in "Getting Hitched" on page 101 in Chapter 6.) By doing this, you can always keep one eye on your dog and the other on the TV, dishes, computer, etc. Be sure to watch for telltale "I've gotta go to the bathroom" signals, such as:

House-training with a Crate

A crate can be a very effective tool for house-training. Think of a crate as you would a playpen for a baby. You'll be using it at times when you can't actively supervise your dog. Of course, you need to make sure you never leave your dog in her crate longer than she can hold her bladder. To figure out how many hours a young puppy can be expected to hold it, simply take the age of your dog in months and add 1. So, a four-month-old puppy can hold it for about five hours. However, you shouldn't expect a dog of any age to able to hold her bladder for more than eight or nine hours. (This is also discussed in Chapter 6.) If you're going to be away from home longer than your dog can wait, or if you're consistently gone for long periods of time, consider doggie day care, hiring a pet-sitter, or asking a neighbor to let her out so she can relieve herself without stress.

Using a crate is an effective way to train your dog through some critical behaviors. However, if you simply cannot or will not use a crate, setting up a doggy-safe area is the next best thing. To do this, gate off a small area of your home that has easy-to-clean floors, such as your laundry room, kitchen, or bathroom. These harder floor surfaces are good because dogs generally like to eliminate on absorbent surfaces, which means they are less likely to have accidents on concrete or tile floors. Don't make the area too large; you want a small, den-like space to encourage your dog to keep it clean. Provide a designated potty place using newspaper, house-training pads, or even a tray filled with sod. Be aware that this will probably set back your house-training process a bit, because you will miss some opportunities to reward her for going to the bathroom outside.

- ☼ Pacing
- ☼ Whining
- ☼ Circling
- ☼ Sniffing
- ☼ Staring at you
- ☼ Trying to wander off to another room

Now, here's something every dog owner must realize: *accidents happen.*

No matter how well the house-training is going, there will almost surely be some mistakes. If your dog has an accident, simply roll up a newspaper and give yourself a whack on the head while saying, "I will supervise my dog more closely next time!" since the likeliest reason for the accident was that you missed her signal.

Clean up the mistake by first blotting the area to pick up any excess fluid. Follow up with an enzymatic cleaner designed for pet messes. This type of cleaner removes the odors that you and your dog can smell, and will prevent her from returning to that same spot. Do not clean with ammonia products, because they can actually encourage your dog to return to the spot.

Accidents Happen

If you catch your dog in the act, try to distract her while you quickly hurry her outside to finish. Don't scream at her. Never yell, rub her nose in her mess, or spank her. Punishment will only make her anxious and afraid to go potty in front of you. Your dog may then start to seek out hidden places to go, like behind the couch, or she may wait until you leave the room to relieve herself. You could also find yourself waiting longer outside if your dog is thinking: "Do not potty in front of him! He completely freaks out when I do." So when accidents happen, keep your cool, clean up the mess, and supervise your dog more closely.

Now you need to teach your dog where you *do* want her to go potty. You're going to reward your dog every time she goes potty in the appropriate place. First, choose a place outdoors to be your dog's bathroom area. You'll only need an area that's about five square feet. Because dogs get distracted easily, do your best to pick a quiet place that's away from busy areas like the road or sidewalk.

Now, leash up your dog, grab some treats, and walk her out to the bathroom area you've selected. During the beginning stages of house-training, you'll want to keep her on leash, even if you have a fenced-in yard. All dogs should learn to potty while on a leash, at the very least for when you go on vacation, to the vet, or to a friend's house. The leash sends a clear signal to your dog that you are in control of the situation and won't allow her to wander away while she should be taking care of business. Keeping your dog on leash may also alert you to any possible medical problems, like intestinal parasites or an upset stomach. You'll see her business when she eliminates.

Sticking "close to the action" also means you'll know if your dog actually went potty. This is especially important during bad weather, because your dog may be reluctant to go when it's cold or raining outside. You don't want to just assume that your dog pottied, or she might have accidents later.

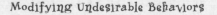

Modifying Undesirable Behaviors

Training the Tiny Ones

The smaller members of the canine world present some special problems when it comes to house-training. First, their smaller size makes them more susceptible to becoming chilled, so they may be extra-reluctant to potty outside in cold or wet weather. Second, these little guys typically require even closer supervision indoors than larger dogs, since they pee in such small amounts that it's easy to miss a puddle if you aren't watching. If you've adopted a little dog, you will need to be extremely vigilant with your house-training, as well as your cleanup of accidents, until you are absolutely certain she understands what to do. And if the cold is the problem, consider a cute sweater for winter walks.

When you get to the bathroom area, stand still, wait, and be patient. As your dog starts going to the bathroom, use a phrase such as "Go potty" to help teach her a future potty cue. (This will be incredibly helpful later on, especially on frigid winter nights.) As soon as she finishes, say "Good job!" and immediately reward her with a couple of treats and lots of praise (maybe even some playtime with you outside).

If after a few minutes of waiting your dog does not go potty, take her back inside and put her in her crate to prevent an accident. Wait about ten minutes, then take her back out to the same spot. This time there's a good chance your dog will go, or at least give you a courtesy tinkle. Be sure to reward her as soon as she finishes. It won't take long for her to get the idea that going potty outside is a really good thing.

Soon you will have rewarded your dog for good potty behavior so often that she'll actually begin to let you know when she needs to go outside. If your dog begins to stare at you, bark at you, or even paw at you to make it clear to you when she wants to go out, you will be able to give her much more freedom, without the worry.

You are probably wondering just how long house-training will take. Well, we've all heard stories about dogs that are totally house-trained in two days, but that's far from typical—and is likely an exaggeration. A critical factor in house-training success is how reliable you are at preventing accidents and rewarding your dog when she successfully goes potty outside. Unfortunately, there is no standard time frame for reliable house-training. Some dogs simply house-train more easily than others. Large breed dogs are typically faster to house-train than smaller breeds, but that isn't true in every case. The age that dogs become completely reliable in your home can be anywhere between four months to a year after house-training has begun.

Modifying Problem Behaviors

First, a quick word about "problem" behaviors—as we mentioned in the previous chapter, these are nearly always normal canine behaviors that occur in places or ways that we humans find unacceptable. As *we* are the ones who object to these behaviors, it's up to us to explain to our canine companions where they can and can't occur.

Keep in mind that it's much easier—and sometimes essential—to provide a place where the dog can engage in most of these behaviors, rather than trying to get rid of them completely. You could forbid your dog to dig, but if that's an ingrained instinctual behavior, as it is for many Terriers and Dachshunds, the result can be a frustrated dog who will redirect her energy into some other, even more objectionable behavior. Find a way to make these behaviors work for both of you, and you'll both be happier.

Submissive Urination

It is very important to note that submissive wetting or excitement wetting are *not* house-training problems. If your dog only has "accidents" when greeting family members or when someone approaches to interact with her, this is almost certainly not a house-training problem, but rather a case of submissive urination. Many young dogs will outgrow this behavior, and some adopted dogs will get over this as they settle in and gain more assurance. Owners can help by being low-key and calming around the dog, and by having greetings take place outdoors whenever possible.

Chewing

For most dogs, chewing on something can be a way to release stress, so it shouldn't come as a surprise that a lot of adopted dogs come with a chewing problem. If your dog is chewing on your possessions, do two things:

1. provide acceptable chewing options
2. eliminate as many chewing misadventures as possible

If your dog is chewing on small portable items such as shoes, the remote control, or kids' toys, the first part of the solution should be obvious—keep those things out of her reach. You may have trouble driving that point home to some of your family members or roommates, but if you hold them responsible and don't rush to replace items that were left out for the dog to chew, you may find their cooperation increasing.

The human members of the family aren't the only ones who may suffer in this scenario. A dog who chews on whatever she can get into her mouth runs the risk of ingesting a great variety of harmful things. Many medicines, some foods, and even chocolate can be toxic to dogs. Socks, stockings, underwire bras, and bathing suits can wrap around and cut into parts of a dog's digestive tract. More solid objects can cause intestinal blockages. Any of these will likely result in veterinary expense and upset for everyone, and could even be fatal if not caught in time.

So the other part of the equation is, once again, supervision. While you can enlist the aid of taste deterrents such as Bitter Apple or Yuck!, they are not always successful, and there really is no substitute for keeping an eye on your dog to keep her out of trouble. If you see her chewing on something she shouldn't, take the object away, or, if it's something large, like furniture, move the dog away from the object. Then be sure to give her an appropriate chew object instead, and keep a closer eye on her.

Your dog should always have a selection of good, safe chew toys. That doesn't mean an old pair of shoes you no longer want, because being allowed to chew those shoes but not others will just be confusing to your dog. Stock up on Kongs, Busy Buddies (both meant to be stuffed with food to make them more enticing), Nylabones, Orbees, and Bullie sticks. You might be amazed at the variety available. Try several types to see what appeals most to your dog. (For a rundown of available treats and chews, see Chapter 9.)

Mouthing

Have you ever closely watched two dogs playing together? They wrestle back and forth using their whole bodies—including their mouths. However, if one gets too rough, the other will let out a quick squeal. Play stops for a brief moment, and then resumes at a lower intensity level. These dogs are teaching each other how gentle they need to be when using their mouths, and setting their play rules. In this case they learn, "Okay, I can't bite down that hard or play will stop."

You can teach your dog that same lesson for human interactions, but you will make it clear that there can never be *any* contact between her

Petfinder.com: The Adopted Dog Bible

teeth and your skin. As soon as she mouths or bites, you will withdraw all your attention, and play will stop. Eventually, your dog will learn not to let her teeth come into contact with your skin at all. If you are consistent with this message, it won't take long for her to learn what level of play is acceptable. You can find excellent video tips on dealing with mouthing at www.petfinder.com/dog-bible.

Start by playing in an enclosed area with your dog tethered to a heavy object (if you don't have a tether, you can use her leash). Using a tether will give you better control of the situation. Have some of her toys nearby so there are appropriate things for her to chew on.

While you're playing, if your dog's mouth makes contact with your skin, say "Ouch!" in a high-pitched, yelping way, even if it didn't hurt. You don't want to frighten her, you just want to get her attention. Then immediately take a ten-second break from giving your dog any attention by standing up and turning away from her. If she follows around to your other side, just continue to ignore her until her time out is over. Once the ten seconds is up, go back to playing with her as though nothing happened. Give her one of her toys, and reward her with lots of praise when she takes the toy.

Every time your dog mouths or bites you, repeat the time out, and soon she'll understand that if she places her mouth on you, the fun ends.

If your dog will not calm down despite the time outs and continues to play too roughly, give her a short time out in her crate, or walk out of the room for several minutes. By doing this, you're removing what your dog wants most of all—your attention. This will also keep her from getting carried away. Be sure to do this immediately after her teeth touch your hand, so it's clear what action led to the withdrawal of your attention.

One good way to avoid mouthing altogether is to try to avoid getting your dog overly excited during playtime. For example, if you know that after ten minutes of play she starts to get worked up and mouthy, keep your play sessions to five minutes. Eventually, once your dog learns what is acceptable, you should be able to play with her for longer periods of time.

Finally, you need to be clear that this "no mouth" rule applies to everyone. Any excessive roughhousing or mouthy behavior, even if it's just with one person, will teach your dog that it's okay to play that way. It's not fair to expect your dog to understand different play rules for you, your kids, or Grandma. The rule must be that no teeth ever touch human skin.

Jumping on the Furniture

Dogs get into trouble both for jumping up on people and for jumping onto the furniture. For the former, see "Meet and Greet" on page 193 in Chapter 10. Practice the "turn and walk away" procedure with as many people as you can enlist to help. The more consistent you are, the better your dog's response.

Now we come to jumping on the furniture. Especially for adopted dogs who aren't used to being inside a house, furniture may just be elevated parts of the floor in your dog's eyes, and she will have no idea that those lumps are objects with special rules. A little kind direction is all that's needed to keep her paws off your nice couches, if that's important to you.

Be sure to get all of your family members or roommates on board with the program. If some people invite the dog onto the couch while others shove her off, your training will be set back a lot, and may never fully work. When people are out of the home and the dog is unsupervised, baby gate her in a doggy-safe area, such as the kitchen, away from furniture, or confine her in an exercise pen or crate. When family members are present, it's essential that they pay attention to the dog while she is on the floor and not trying to jump on furniture. Otherwise, jumping up can easily become an attention-seeking behavior.

Working on this behavior with an adopted dog is a balancing act. You don't want to upset the trust you're trying to establish, so you don't want to be constantly dragging her off the furniture, yet you may not want her on the furniture. Don't worry, there are ways to do this right. You can have your dog tethered to you and you can sit on the floor with her. You can help make the floor more attractive by littering it with chew toys and hard chew treats. You can sit in a chair just big enough for you, with your dog on her leash on the floor. Do all that you can to keep the dog on the floor voluntarily.

If your dog still gets on the furniture and you need to get her off, see if you can lure her off with a treat. Only let her have the treat when she has all four paws on the floor. If she won't follow the treat, and the furniture she's on has seat cushions, rather than taking hold of the dog, take hold of the cushion and lift the back side so that you tip your dog off onto the floor. Make it seem as if the furniture did it, not you.

Begging

Some people think it's sweet to feed dogs tidbits from the table, but unless you want your dog to develop a begging habit, don't let anyone do this. Be firm with family members and roommates, and tell any dinner guests that for the good of everyone, the dog only gets fed in the kitchen (or whatever your particular rules may be). You can still give her some human food treats if you want . . . just not from the table. If your dog is never rewarded for bothering people when they are eating, the behavior will naturally decrease and eventually disappear. Remember, dogs do what works, so if begging at the table doesn't get her any yummy scraps, she'll see no point in continuing the behavior.

If your adopted dog arrives with an ingrained begging habit from a previous household, you have more work to do. If she is a real pest and can't be ignored, you will have to restrain her away from the table (but within sight). Perhaps you could baby gate her in the kitchen or tie her leash to a solid piece of furniture. You want her to be able to see your family sitting and eating, and you want to be able to see when she is being calm and settled.

Be vigilant; don't ever reward your dog for begging.

If possible, give your dog her dinner before you sit down to eat, so that you know she isn't ravenously hungry and you won't feel sorry for her. Feeding your dog first will not make her think she ranks above you—that's a myth. It should make it easier for family members to ignore her begging behavior.

Sit down and enjoy your meal, keeping one eye on the dog. When she is settled quietly, give her some praise or even get up and give her a treat if you like. Ignore any fussing. Eventually the rewarded behavior—waiting calmly—will increase and the fussing and begging will decrease.

For this training to work, *everyone* must stay firm in their resolve, all the time. One person slipping the dog a treat from the table will derail the entire program, as random rewards will keep the dog working hard at begging for days or weeks. Consider again the power of slot machines, and you'll have some idea of the allure that begging for even the occasional table tidbit holds for your pooch.

Digging

If you live in a city and your dog spends most of her time in your apartment, digging isn't likely to be a problem. But for suburban and rural dogs who spend a lot of time in the yard, seeing your new dog digging up your freshly planted petunias is behavior you're going to want to retrain. For some dogs, digging is a favorite recreation. For others, it's a way to reach cool earth to lie down in. The rich loose soil of your garden or lawn probably proves attractive to a digger, but you can make another area just as attractive, with a little work and training.

Choose a location where digging *will* be allowed, even encouraged, and build your dog a sandbox there. It doesn't have to be fancy—cinder block walls with rebar pounded through them into the ground will work fine—but you can make it as elaborate as you like. Just make sure it's big enough for your dog to have room to sprawl out in several different spots. Fill it with builders' sand or a mix of builders' sand and dirt, at least a foot deep for small dogs and considerably more for bigger dogs.

Now comes the training. Bury some treats and a favorite toy in the sandbox. Take your dog outside, run excitedly to the sandbox, dig up a treat, and give it to her. Scratch in the dirt a little and see if your dog will join in. Praise any movements toward digging in the sand. Dig up another toy, play with it with the dog for a little while, then let her watch you bury it again. Encourage her to get it.

Repeat this procedure each time you go out into the yard. If your adopted dog has been punished in the past for digging, it may take some time before she is willing to dig in front of you. If she starts digging anywhere other than the sandbox, run to the sandbox, encouraging her to come with you, and dig up some treats and toys to share.

Supervise your dog in the yard so you can be consistent with this training. Don't just put your dog outdoors and ignore her—or digging could become the least of your worries. Some dogs are surrendered because they have become escape artists, and you could find your dog missing. She could eat some mushrooms growing in the yard and poison herself. Or she could bark at adults and children passing by. A yard, even a totally fenced yard, is not a dog-sitter.

Coprophagia

Coprophagia is a fancy scientific word for eating poop. Humans find it disgusting, but believe it or not, it's actually normal behavior for a variety of animals. And yet, regardless of how normal it may be, this behavior is unacceptable for most people. Furthermore, it can contribute to the spread of parasites and disease if a dog consumes another animal's excrement. So let's talk about how to deal with this issue.

First, if your dog hasn't had a veterinary checkup recently, schedule a visit. You want to confirm her good health and ensure that she doesn't have any dietary deficiencies. A veterinary checkup becomes even more critical if your dog is losing weight. If for some reason your dog isn't digesting her food very well, there may be enough nourishment in her excrement to make it a worthwhile food source.

Once you've determined that your dog is healthy, you may want to try one of the variety of products that you can purchase over the counter which are supposed to make the poop taste bad. (Yes, I understand the irony of that sentence!) Products like For-Bid and Dis-Taste are two such items you can add to your dog's food. There are also home remedies, such as adding a sprinkle of meat tenderizer to your dog's food, giving a Fig Newton to your dog each day, or feeding her pineapple chunks or pineapple juice. These may work for some dogs but not for others.

The most obvious solution, which is also 100 percent effective, is to keep your dog away from poop. That means you have to go out with your dog every time she eliminates, and clean up after her immediately. This could get to be quite a chore if yours is a multi-dog household, but it will really help, since the more opportunities your dog has to practice poop eating behavior, the harder it will be to conquer.

Unfortunately, there is no quick or easy solution to this behavior. It's more a management problem, and you will need to pick up any poop that she could come into contact with, so that that your dog won't get a chance to indulge in it in the first place.

Resource Guarding

Resource guarding is a fairly common behavior issue that pet parents encounter: A dog bares her teeth, growls, raises her hackles, lunges, or even bites when food, toys, specific locations, or other things the dog regards as "hers" are approached by people or other pets. Punishment and scolding will *not* solve this problem. Often, people who use punishment in an attempt to "fix" this behavior do little more than extinguish the warning cue, which is freezing and growling. Without that warning, you could wind up with a dog who no longer growls, but instead goes right to snapping or, worse, biting.

Resource guarding is a complex issue and not one that can be simplified enough to provide you with a quick and easy solution here. If your dog does not have extreme resource guarding tendencies (and you do not have children in the home), you may choose to live with it, knowing you will just leave her alone when she is chewing on a bone or eating dinner. On the other hand, your dog's resource guarding may be severe enough that physical harm to you or a family member is likely to result without a training and management program. To help you decide how to handle this situation, we urge you to seek the assistance of a professional dog trainer. If you choose to embark on a program of training and management with the help of a professional, you may also want to check out *Mine!* by Jean Donaldson. This book provides a program for teaching your dog to give things up willingly, and even enjoy having people approach while she has the object that she covets.

Enlisting Professional Help

While this book will answer many of your questions about living a long and happy life with your adopted dog, problems can arise that require a more personal, one-on-one solution. You have plenty of places to go for help, should you decide that you and your dog need some professional assistance. Here are the steps you should take when looking for a trainer.

Find some trainers. There are likely to be at least a few dog trainers in your area. A good resource is the website for the Association of Pet Dog Trainers (APDT), www.apdt.com. This site provides a "trainer

Petfinder.com: The Adopted Dog Bible

search" that only requires your zip code to help you find local trainers. Another good source is the International Association of Animal Behavior Consultants (IAABC). Their website, www.iaabc.org, also has a consultant locator.

Conduct interviews. Ask prospective trainers about their training philosophy and about their experience with whatever problem or problems you are facing. Progressive trainers use reward-based training methods (like those described in this book), which involve motivating your dog with treats, toys, and praise to achieve the desired results. Ask the trainer what educational organizations they belong to. Organizations such as the above-mentioned APDT and IAABC, as well as the National Organization of Dog Obedience Instructors (NADOI) and the Certification Council for Professional Dog Trainers (CCPDT) strongly encourage or even require continuing education for their trainers, so people who belong to these organizations are most likely keeping their training skills and knowledge current. If you are attending group training, find out what they will do to ensure that your pet's health is protected during training. Most trainers will require a health certificate or proof of vaccinations before you bring your dog to class.

Go for a visit. Ask the trainer if you can observe a class. While there, look for a few things:

1. **Are the class area and surroundings secure and clean?**
   There shouldn't be open gates and doors, there should be clean water available for the dogs, and there should be supplies for fast cleanup of potty accidents.
2. **Is there a good ratio of people to dogs?**
   Most classes should have one trainer for about six dogs.
3. **Are the dogs happy?**
   The dogs should look like they are enjoying the class—remember, training should be fun!
4. **Are the people enjoying themselves?**
   Look for a class that encourages all family members to participate.
5. **What kinds of tools are used in the class?**
   Good tools to look for in general training classes include leashes, flat collars, head halters, clickers, bite-sized treats, toys, harnesses, and lots of praise (for the dogs and the people).

Veterinary Behaviorists

If you have already tried, unsuccessfully, to work with a professional dog trainer, or if you are dealing with an extreme behavior issue like aggression or severe separation anxiety, consider working with a veterinary behaviorist. Veterinary behaviorists are the most academically qualified professionals. These veterinarians have gone beyond their medical training and passed courses specifically on companion animal behavior, both normal and abnormal. Unfortunately, there aren't many of them, and they are generally quite expensive. But if you feel that that's the type of help you and your dog need, you can find them all listed on the American College of Veterinary Behaviorists' website, www.dacvb.org.

6. **Does the trainer use negative reinforcement or any type of punishment?**
Avoid trainers who use physical punishment. Training should never include hitting or kicking, jerking, popping the leash, stringing the dog up, or hanging the dog.

If you feel that this person isn't right for you or your dog, keep looking. But if you're satisfied that the trainer meets all of the above criteria, discuss whether you should consider private training or if group classes will suffice. Provide as much information as you can and don't minimize any concerns. Your trainer should provide you with a plan for management and/or behavior modification, hands-on instruction for any techniques to be used, and follow-up. You should expect to pay considerably more for private training than for group classes that are more general. But with a good expert on your side, many of the behavior issues that seemed so dreadful can be resolved successfully, helping your adopted dog become the fine companion and family member you know she can be.

Dog Biscuits for the Soul: Nike

Nike

I contacted the Safe Harbor Prison Dog program, looking for a small dog to compete in the canine sport Dock Diving. They did not have any small dogs that liked water but suggested a rather large dog that was crazy about water and asked if I would I give him a chance. I really wasn't looking for a large dog at the time, but said okay after they said they really needed to find him a good home with a job. He had been in the prison program for most of his young life and had been passed over for adoption many, many times. He had a very bad problem of jumping up on people, and with potential adopters that is not a good selling point. They brought him over for a trial evaluation, and I agreed to keep him to see if he would work out. I figured training him for a job that *required* him to jump up would be perfect. So we started training for Dock Dogs diving competitions, and within six weeks I entered him in his first competition. He did very well there and went on that first year to finish second in the Novice division at the Dock Dogs National Championship. Then he started his Extreme Vertical training and has done very well, with a 4th place win in Big Air and a 4th place in Extreme Vertical at the Dock Dogs National Championships in Rogers, Minnesota. He has come a long way with his training and has become an extremely awesome dog. Thanks to the Safe Harbor Prison Dog Program for sending me this incredible dog. Their program is very important and wonderful for helping homeless pets get a chance at a normal, happy life.

Beth Todd, Leavenworth, Kansas
Nike was adopted from Safe Harbor for Pets, Kansas City, Kansas

Resources

Training Equipment
Busy Buddy: www.busybuddytoys.com
Comfort Zone with D.A.P. www.farnampet.com/products (pheromone product to help alleviate stress and fear)
Kong Company: www.kongcompany.com
K-V Vet Supply: www.kvvet.com
Legacy Canine: www.legacycanine.com (store includes sound desensitization CDs)
PETCO: Local retail stores or www.petco.com
SitStay Dog Supplies: www.sitstay.com

Training Books
Anderson, Teoti: *Your Outta Control Puppy: How to Turn Your Precocious Pup Into a Perfect Pet*. TFH Publications, 2003
Book, Mady and Cheryl S. Smith: *Quick Clicks*. Dogwise Publishing, 2001
Donaldson, Jean: *Mine!* Kinship Communications, 2002
Dunbar, Ian, DVM: *Before & After You Get Your Puppy*. New World Library, 2004
McConnell, Patricia, PhD: *The Other End of the Leash*. Ballantine Books, 2003
Miller, Pat: *The Power of Positive Dog Training*. Howell Book House, 2001
Nelson, Leslie: *The Really Reliable Recall*. Tails-U-Win, 2002
Pryor, Karen: *Don't Shoot the Dog: The New Art of Teaching and Training*. Bantam, 1999
Smith, Cheryl S.: *Dogs in the Yard: Dog Friendly Gardens, Garden Friendly Dogs*. Dogwise Publishing, 2003

Dog Training Organizations / Professional Consultants
American College of Veterinary Behaviorists: www.dacvb.org
The Association of Pet Dog Trainers: www.apdt.com
The Certification Council for Professional Dog Trainers: www.ccpdt.org
International Association of Animal Behavior Consultants: www.iaabc.org

Petfinder.com: The Adopted Dog Bible

9

Dinner's On

Proper nutrition is one of the most important components of health—for humans as well as dogs. Unfortunately, many dogs don't receive the necessary nutrition that will help them enjoy vibrant health. You will likely not know your adopted dog's feeding history, but there is a good chance it included poor-quality food, being fed sporadically, or otherwise not having the benefit of a nutritional, balanced, healthy diet. An inadequate diet can contribute to many health issues, such as poor body condition and weight loss, bad breath and dental problems, impaired immune function, and nutrient deficiencies and imbalances. In some scenarios, a dog may even be surrendered to a shelter because of diet-related behavioral problems.

In this chapter, we'll help take the guesswork out of what to feed your adopted dog by comparing commercially prepared dog food and home-cooked meals, examining the pros and cons of raw food diets, and providing insight into how to read pet food labels so you can select the best food for your dog's age, size, and activity level. In addition, we'll tell you how much and how often to feed your pooch, offer advice for vegetarians, and share some recipes from devoted Petfinder members.

Where Should You Feed Your Dog?

For most dogs, mealtime is one of the high points of the day. It's not only a time to receive nourishment, but also a chance to bond with their favorite human companion. While it's true that dogs are pack animals and enjoy being close to their families—both human and canine—that doesn't necessarily mean they want their food bowl plopped down in the middle of the kitchen floor, amid the hustle and bustle of daily life. This could cause your dog to become anxious and gulp his meal, which can lead to digestive problems. He may also become protective of his food and snap at a family member who tries to pet him while he's eating. If your adopted dog has resource guarding issues like these, see Chapter 8 for help in training him to be less protective of his food. Generally, though, you can avoid such problems by keeping food and water dishes in an out-of-the-way spot that is reserved just for doggy dining. There, your pup can relax and savor his meal without interruption.

Pick a spot (probably uncarpeted) that will be easy to clean. Dogs can be very messy eaters, spilling food all around the floor and even on the walls, so make sure there's nothing near your pup's eating area that can be damaged. We recommend putting his food bowl near his water bowl, which should always be there, cleaned often and filled with fresh water. A caution: If you have wood floors, you may want to put the water bowl on a waterproof mat, because dogs are not tidy drinkers, and you don't want the constant drip of spilled water to ruin the floors.

How Often Should You Feed Your Dog?

Most experts recommend feeding your dog twice a day—once in the morning and once in the evening—though puppies under five months of age should be fed three to four times a day, or as directed by your veterinarian. While most dogs will dig in the moment you place the bowl on the floor, you may find that your adopted dog is a finicky eater, at least at first. After all, he's been thrust into a new home with new people, and he may be too nervous to eat. If this is the case, you will need to teach him to eat on a sched-

The Best Dishes to Use

Use ceramic, pyrex, or stainless steel bowls to feed your dog, and make sure they're heavy enough that they won't tip or spill while he's eating. Don't use plastic bowls, because plastic is a breeding ground for germs, and it can retain the smell of cleaning products and previous meals, which may discourage your dog from eating. Do not use strong detergents or bleach to clean your dog's food and water dishes, as these products can be toxic. Instead, wash bowls between feedings with a mild dishwashing detergent, and always rinse thoroughly.

Many older dogs suffer from arthritis or other health problems that can make eating difficult. Try elevating the dishes off the floor so your dog can reach the food more easily. You can find several different varieties of dishes at your local pet supply store or from an online retailer.

ule. Leave the bowl on the floor for ten minutes and then pick it up, regardless of whether he has eaten. (If your dog is a slow eater, this period can be extended to twenty minutes, but only if he is still eating during that time and hasn't gone off in search of other entertainment.) At the next scheduled feeding time, put the bowl back down, again for only ten minutes. Pretty soon your dog will learn that he needs to eat when the food is offered.

Having regularly-scheduled feeding times not only establishes a routine, it also allows you to monitor your dog's health. If he picks at his food throughout the day, you may not notice right away if he's not eating well. But if he normally eats heartily as soon as you put the bowl down, you will immediately see a sudden lack of appetite, which is often an indication that he's not feeling well. If your dog's appetite doesn't improve in a few days, have him checked by your veterinarian.

Another benefit of set feedings is that a dog who eats on a schedule poops on a schedule. In addition, if you live in an urban area, leaving a bowl of kibble on the ground all day can attract unwanted houseguests, like cockroaches and mice. It is to everyone's advantage to keep feeding times regular.

Changing Your New Dog's Diet

As we discussed in Chapter 6, when you adopt a dog from a shelter, it's important to ask about his previous feeding schedule and what type of food he was eating. You'll want to keep his feeding times and types of food consistent for a few days, and then gradually switch to any new food or schedule. Here is the transition process to use when changing your dog's food:

- Week 1: all old food
- Week 2: 75% old food, 25% new food
- Week 3: 50-50 split
- Week 4: 25% old food, 75% new food
- Week 5: all new food

If at any point in the future you change your dog's diet to a new brand or type of food, you should follow a similar transition process. While there are appropriate times to change a dog's diet, most veterinarians don't recommend frequent changes, as this can contribute to finicky eating habits and increase the potential for stomach upsets. However, some experts believe that you *should* routinely change your dog's food (particularly if he's eating a commercial dog food) so that any nutritional deficiencies in one brand of food can be addressed in another brand. Whichever route you choose (consistency or variety), always watch your dog carefully when he first begins eating a new kind of food, so you will be able to determine whether it's giving him any problems.

How Much Should You Feed Your Dog?

The amount you feed your adopted dog will vary greatly depending on his age, size, and activity level, as well as on the type of food he's eating. As a general rule, puppies and young dogs burn more calories, so they need a greater quantity of food that is higher in protein and fat. Older, less active dogs require fewer calories to remain healthy.

Richard H. Pitcairn, DVM, PhD, author of *Dr. Pitcairn's Complete Guide to Natural Health for Dogs and Cats*, believes the most reliable approach is to feed what seems to be a reasonable amount and monitor his body weight. "You should be able to feel your pet's ribs easily as you slide your hand over his sides," Pitcairn says. "If you can't, he's probably too heavy, so begin to feed a smaller quantity."

If you're using a commercial pet food, beware of the "feeding guidelines" on the bag or box. It lists different weights and the corresponding amount of food to feed your dog to maintain that weight, and should be used only as a rough guideline. Many dogs are overweight because their families closely followed the directions on the label, which often indicates portion sizes that are too large. After all, the sooner the bag is empty, the sooner you will need to buy more food. Starting at the low end of the suggested guidelines and then monitoring your dog for hunger and body condition is a good way to proceed.

Different Portions for Different Pooches

Though it may sound counterintuitive, as a general rule, large breed dogs require less food and small breed dogs require more food when expressed on a volume of food per pound of body weight. The food requirements of individual dogs vary according to their health, level of activity, and age. We will discuss the differences in the various types of food later in this chapter, but here are some guidelines for portion sizes at different stages of your dog's life.

Puppies. Puppies are typically introduced to solid food at three to four weeks of age and are completely weaned from their mother's milk by eight weeks. Puppies require a diet that is higher in protein and other nutrients to support normal growth and development. If you are feeding commercial pet food to your adopted puppy, select a brand that is specially formulated for puppies.

Young puppies should be fed at least three times a day—morning, noon, and early evening—until their food requirements per pound of body weight begin to level off as they mature. By the time the puppy is five or six months of age, his feeding schedule can be reduced to twice a day.

If you have a finicky puppy, you can add some warm water to dry food to encourage him to eat it. Cow's milk can act as a laxative and cause digestive problems for some puppies and adult dogs, so avoid giving this to your pup or only give very small amounts. If your puppy doesn't eat all his food within an hour, discard the uneaten portion.

The amount of food you feed your puppy will vary depending upon his size, activity, metabolism, and environment. Feeding too much can not only lead to a pudgy pup, but can also cause bone abnormalities and other health issues. If your puppy appears to be gaining too much weight, gradually decrease his food intake, but if his ribs are showing, increase his portions. If you are unsure about his proper weight or appearance, talk to your vet for guidance.

Adults. When the average dog is one year old, he has reached full maturity and enters a "maintenance period." This means that his nutritional requirements will stay about the same during his young adult life, assuming he is not ill or engaging in extreme physical exercise. His weight should remain stable and his body should be well-proportioned—he should have an observable waist and you should be able to feel his ribs with your fingertips, beneath a thin layer of fat.

If you are feeding your adopted adult dog a commercial pet food, select one that is specially formulated for adult dogs. As with humans, a dog's appetite may vary from day to day. This is not cause for alarm unless his loss of appetite persists for several days or he shows obvious signs of weight loss or illness. However, having no desire to eat can be the first sign of many illnesses, so monitor your dog's food intake carefully. You know your dog best, so if something seems amiss, don't hesitate to take him to his vet.

Active adults. Moderate exercise is essential for all dogs and helps them remain fit and trim throughout their lifetime. But some dogs, like some humans, will regularly do more intense exercising. If your adopted dog is particularly active (for instance, if he jogs or runs with you regularly, or is involved in sporting activities) his energy needs will be greater than those of his more sedentary counterparts. Be aware, though, when a typically active dog is less active (for instance, during the cold winter months or when he suffers an injury, such as a sprain or muscle pull), his food requirements decrease. In these instances, experts recommend gradually changing to a lower energy, less nutrient-dense dog food.

Very active dogs should not be fed immediately before or immediately after a strenuous workout. This can lead to digestion problems or discomfort (such as vomiting or loose stools) and may increase the risk of gastric bloat, a painful and often life-threatening condition caused by a twisting of the stomach. Although a small meal can be provided in the morning, hard-working dogs should receive the bulk of their daily calories one hour or more following their last exercise session each day. You can also feed your dog small snacks or treats during periods of increased activity to prevent hunger and fatigue. Allow him to rest intermittently and make sure he has access to fresh water at all times. (See Chapter 10 for more on this.)

Seniors. As with humans, the dietary requirements of dogs will change as they age. Elderly dogs have reduced energy requirements and therefore shouldn't consume the same quantity of food as they did when they were

Petfinder.com: The Adopted Dog Bible

younger. So, if you're feeding your adopted senior dog commercial pet food, look for brands that offer reduced calories while still including all the necessary nutrients (see the next section for more information on this). Senior dogs, like all dogs, should be fed according to their overall health and level of activity. A less active dog can quickly gain weight if you're not careful.

Feeding your dog a high-quality diet will keep him happy and healthy.

The Diet Dilemma: What Should You Feed Your Dog?

Commercial pet foods, home-cooked meals, or raw food diets—which is best for your dog? Premium commercial pet foods are specifically designed to be complete and balanced and are tested and guaranteed for consistent nutrient content and palatability. Home-cooked meals offer wholesome, fresh ingredients and variety, while raw food diets allow companion dogs to eat like their ancestors did. It's important that you research these diets and consider your dog's age, size, and activity level before you make a decision about what to serve your dog for dinner.

The Necessary Nutrients

Before you decide among commercial, home-cooked, and raw food for your pooch, it's important to have a basic understanding of the building blocks of a healthy canine diet.

Water. Your dog should always have access to fresh water, from a clean bowl. Some people limit a dog's water supply or take it away altogether in the evenings, to avoid late-night bathroom needs. This may be a helpful house-training tool, but it is not fair or healthy for your dog in the long-term.

Water helps the body to:

- Stay hydrated
- Regulate body temperature
- Aid digestion
- Lubricate muscle tissues
- Flush away bacteria that cause urinary tract infections

- ❉ Ease constipation by moving stools along more smoothly
- ❉ Transport oxygen and nutrients throughout the body

The quality of your dog's drinking water is also important. Most tap water contains chemical additives, such as chlorine and fluoride, as well as heavy metals such as lead and cadmium, which can be harmful to your dog's health. While it's true that dogs drink from ponds, puddles and—horrors—the toilet, these water sources are teeming with bacteria and parasites. You can reduce the risk of infection by providing your dog with only bottled or filtered water.

Proteins. Proteins build and maintain muscles, organs, bones, blood, body tissues, hair, nails, and the immune system. Many foods contain protein, but the best sources are beef, poultry, fish, eggs, dairy products, grains, and soy.

Adopted dogs with a history of poor nutrition may be at risk of developing a protein deficiency. Signs of a protein deficiency include:

- ❉ Dry, brittle fur
- ❉ Poor muscle development
- ❉ Anemia
- ❉ Growth problems
- ❉ Weakened immune system

If your adopted dog comes to you with some or all of these symptoms, talk to your vet.

Protein levels that exceed a dog's minimum requirement do not pose a problem to healthy dogs, unless your dog has impaired kidney or liver function (your veterinarian can monitor organ function with regular blood tests), or an allergy to a particular protein source. Recent research has shown that previous recommendations to reduce protein intake for senior dogs was not sound. In fact, healthy senior dogs may need significantly more protein than their younger counterparts because they metabolize the protein less efficiently.

Fats. Fats are the main source of dietary energy (or calories) in a dog's diet and provide the most concentrated source of energy in foods. One gram of fat contains more than twice the energy than one gram of protein or carbohydrate. They are needed for healthy skin, coat, eyes, brain, and other tissues.

Healthy fats come from sources such as:

Petfinder.com: The Adopted Dog Bible

- ❁ Chicken fat
- ❁ Lamb fat
- ❁ Sunflower oil
- ❁ Herring oil

Carbohydrates. Along with proteins and fats, carbohydrates are one of the three major nutrients in food and a major source of energy for a dog's body. Sedentary dogs have a lower energy requirement than their more active canine counterparts to produce the energy needed to fuel their brain and muscles. Most commercial dog foods contain as much as 30 to 60 percent carbohydrates because a minimum proportion of starch is needed in the formula for the commercial extrusion process, and, many believe, because carbohydrates are less expensive than proteins and fats.

Dogs can't digest uncooked grain as easily as meats, so if grains are fed, it is important to cook them to increase digestibility. Simmer rice or other grains until they are soft. To add a little extra flavor, cook them in chicken or beef broth.

Good sources of carbohydrates include:

- ❁ Rice
- ❁ Corn
- ❁ Potatoes
- ❁ Barley
- ❁ Whole grain breads and other grains

Vitamins and Minerals. One thing a dog's body can't do on its own is make vitamins (though vitamin C is an exception).

Vitamins and minerals such as calcium, iron, and magnesium are essential nutrients that can be found in the following foods:

- ❁ Bread
- ❁ Dairy products
- ❁ Fish
- ❁ Fruits and vegetables
- ❁ Grains
- ❁ Milk

While most commercial pet food manufacturers claim their products are "complete and balanced," (a claim they substantiate through feeding trials or by meeting certain requirements) these products may lose necessary vitamins and minerals, which may be destroyed by the heating process. There is some debate as to whether a dog's diet needs to be supplemented with vitamins and minerals so you may want to consult a holistic veterinarian before doing so. Holistic veterinarians have all the same training as a conventional veterinarian but incorporate alternative medicine (this might include homeopathy, acupuncture, chiropractic, herbs, etc.) in their practice, as well. See Chapter 18 for more on holistic and alternative treatments.

Fatty Acids. Dietary fatty acids can be classified as essential and nonessential. Nonessential fatty acids can be synthesized within a dog's body at a level that meets the pet's requirements, whereas essential fatty acids cannot be synthesized, so they must be supplied in the diet.

Dogs require one essential fatty acid (linoleic acid), which is a type of omega-6 fatty acid. Linoleic acid helps the body to:

- Regulate the blood flow to body tissues
- Clot blood after an injury
- Reproduce normally
- Respond to injury and infection by boosting the immune system
- Maintain a handsome coat and healthy skin

This fatty acid is found primarily in grains and animal fat, and is provided at appropriate levels in high-quality dog foods.

Commercial Dog Food

Most high-quality, complete and balanced dog foods are formulated to meet the nutritional requirements of normal, healthy dogs. Pet parents can look for a statement on the bag or can indicating that the product meets the nutritional requirements set by the Association of American Feed Control Officials (AAFCO), which allows the manufacturer to place the "complete and balanced for all life stages" claim on the label. The AAFCO, along with the Food and Drug Administration (FDA) and the Department of Agriculture (DOA), plays a role in regulating the pet food industry. The AAFCO is responsible for identifying ingredients that can legally be used in pet food, establishing nutrient profiles, providing protocols for feeding trials to ensure product safety, and enforcing the regulations, standards, and laws regarding the manufacture, distribution, and sale of pet food. Meeting AAFCO standards is one element a pet parent can take into consideration when determining that a brand or kind of dog food is healthy and safe; but even with these safeguards in place, problems do occur. (See "Pet Food Recalls" on page 167 for more information.)

In addition, many canine authorities believe that some commercial dog foods are loaded with unnecessary ingredients and potentially dangerous chemicals, fillers, and byproducts. It's important to take your time researching and reading about the different pet foods available and reading their ingredient lists carefully. (See "Reading Pet Food Labels" on page 168 for more information.) The *Whole Dog Journal,* a monthly publication full of information on natural dog care and training, publishes an annual review of dry and canned dog food, which is a great resource to consider when choosing what to feed your dog.

Let's start by looking at the three main types of commercial dog foods, which are wet, dry, and soft/moist. They differ in a number of characteristics, including moisture content, palatability, nutritional benefit, and cost.

Wet Food. All wet food, which is sold in cans, contains 75 to 80 percent water (look for "moisture content" on the label), 8 to 15 percent protein, and 2 to 15 percent fat. Because of the high moisture content, dogs can eat more of this type of food without gaining weight. Canned foods offer the highest palatability when compared to dry and soft/moist products (which is good for finicky eaters, toothless dogs, and for hiding medications), but wet food also has the highest cost per serving. Once a can is opened, it must be refrigerated to retain freshness, and many dogs will not eat their food very cold. To solve this problem, most people will warm subsequent meals.

Dry Food. Dry food comes in bags (as with most things, the larger the bag, the bigger the cost savings) and contains 18 to 40 percent protein, 7 to 22 percent fat, 12 to 50 percent carbohydrates, and about 10 percent moisture.

Dry dog food comes in different shapes, sizes, and colors, because dogs discern the texture, density, size and shape of the food, and the way a food feels in the mouth contributes to its relative palatability. One advantage of dry dog food is that it acts like a toothbrush, helping to remove plaque and tartar from a dog's teeth while he eats. In addition, it stays fresh longer than soft/moist and canned food once the package is opened.

Soft/Moist Food. This type of food is usually sold in boxes that contain single-serving pouches. Soft/moist dog food contains approximately 15 to 25 percent protein, 5 to 10 percent fat, 25 to 35 percent carbohydrates, and approximately 30 percent water. Soft/moist food is highly palatable and convenient to serve and store (perfect for travel), although it is more expensive than dry food. However, soft/moist food should not be fed as a substitute for dry or wet food, as it is high in sugar and salt.

Specialty, Premium, and Grocery Store Brand Foods

The major differences between premium foods and grocery store brand foods are the level of substantiation used to support label claims (calculation vs. feeding trials), the overall quality of ingredients that are used, and the amount of research that stands behind product claims. However, after the massive pet food recall initiated by Menu Foods in 2007, consumers were shocked to learn the same company that produces many grocery store brand dog foods (known as "private label") also manufactures the supposedly higher quality pet foods (referred to as "specialty" or "premium"). There is no national organization that regulates the use of words like "specialty" and "premium" on dog foods, so you should research the manufacturer of a given brand before deciding that it is safe and healthy for your dog. With this caveat in mind, here are the basic differences between specialty, premium, and grocery store brand dog foods.

- *Specialty foods* contain the highest quality ingredients and tend to be more digestible, therefore providing a higher proportion of essential nutrients (and energy) for your dog. There are also many specialty foods formulated for inactive and overweight dogs; these have reduced energy densities and do not contain higher levels of fat than comparable premium products. Specialty foods are sold in pet specialty stores and veterinary offices, and generally carry the highest price of the three types of products.
- *Premium foods* contain higher quality ingredients than grocery store brand foods. They are traditionally sold at pet supply and grocery stores and are moderately priced.
- *Grocery store brand foods* are sold under a store's own name as opposed to a national brand name, though they generally offer ingredients and nutritional guarantees similar to the nationally advertised

Petfinder.com: The Adopted Dog Bible

Pet Food Recalls

Since the early 1950s when commercial pet food became popular, many pet foods have been recalled after various contaminants were found in the foods. Two of the larger recalls in recent years involved dry pet foods contaminated with Aflatoxin B1, a fungus found in moldy grains. In 1999, the Doane Pet Care Center in Temple, Texas, recalled dozens of brands of dry food that were thought to contain the fungus, after reports of the deaths of about thirty dogs. Then, in late 2005 and early 2006, 34 million pounds of dog and cat food were recalled by Diamond Pet Food of Gaston, South Carolina. Again, the source of the contamination was Aflatoxin B1, and this time more than one hundred dogs were poisoned.

On March 16, 2007, Menu Foods (a Canadian-based company with plants in Emporia, Kansas, and Pennsauken, New Jersey) began what has become the largest pet food recall in the history of the industry. By April 1, 2007, 60 million containers of wet food (in cans and foil pouches) for dogs and cats were recalled.

While wheat gluten (a source of protein or filler in many pet foods) was initially identified as the contaminant, it was later believed that melamine (a plastic used in kitchen utensils or plates) was the main culprit. Two weeks later, aminopterin, a rat poison, was found in samples of wheat gluten that were imported from China. To this day, the FDA continues to search for other contaminants that sickened and killed dozens of companion pets.

Pet food recalls serve as a wake-up call for pet parents to educate themselves about what goes into the commercial food our canine companions consume. Read labels, research manufacturers, and buy only the highest-quality products from reputable companies. Even then, problems can occur, as seen in the most recent food recalls. Always monitor your dog's eating habits and health closely. And if your dog turns his nose up at his food, heed his concern and don't force it on him. Your dog's life depends on your diligence.

brands. Feed stores and warehouse-type outlets often carry grocery store brand foods, which are the least expensive of the three different types of products.

Reading Pet Food Labels

Pet food labels must list the minimum percentages of protein and fat and maximum percentages of fiber and water in the food. Ingredients are listed by weight, so if chicken is listed first, it is the largest ingredient in that product. It's important to note that some pet food manufacturers engage in a practice called *splitting,* which is a way to disguise the true contents of their food. For example, if a food is comprised mostly of corn products, but the manufacturer wants the consumer to believe it contains mostly meat, it will divide the corn into two small categories, such as ground corn and corn gluten meal, so they can list the meat first, making it appear that the food is mostly meat when, in fact, it's mostly corn.

The following list will help you decipher the ingredient list on a typical dog food label. Where possible, avoid foods that contain animal by-products, artificial colors, flavors, and preservatives, growth hormones, factory farmed and rendered meat, and meat from animals that have been treated with antibiotics.

Animal fat is a by-product of meat processing and is obtained from the tissues of mammals and/or poultry in the commercial process of rendering or extracting.

Animal meat (turkey, chicken, beef, fish, etc.) is the clean flesh derived from the slaughtered animal.

Animal meat meal and by-product meal is the clean, rendered remainder of a slaughtered animal once the meat has been removed. Often includes necks, feet, blood, bones, intestines, and tissue.

Animal meat by-products are the clean, nonrendered remains after the meat and meat by-product meal has been removed. Often includes bones, beaks, and viscera.

Artificial flavors and colors are used to enhance the look and taste of food. There is no nutritional quality in artificial flavors and, since they are not regulated by the FDA, many could actually be harmful to your dog's health.

Ascorbic acid (vitamin C), is an antioxidant good for normal metabolism.

Beef and bone meal is a by-product made from beef tissues, including bone, but exclusive of any blood, hair, hoof, horn, hide trimmings, manure, and entrails.

Beet pulp is the dried residue from sugar beet. It is added for fiber, but it is high in sugar.

BHA/BHT, or Butylated Hydroxyanisole (BHA) and Butylated Hydroxytoluene (BHT) respectively, are chemical preservatives which are used to protect dietary fats from rancidity. They are also included in human foods in the United States, though they have been banned from human consumption in many countries. Toxicity studies have shown that BHA and BHT at high levels can be detrimental to an animal's health in various ways, promoting or contributing to dry skin, dental disease, stomach and urinary carcinogenesis, and kidney and liver impairment.

Biotin is a water-soluble vitamin, nitrogen-containing acid essential for growth and well-being in animals and some microorganisms. Eggs are a common source of biotin.

Brewer's dried yeast is a by-product of the brewing of beer and ale. Although brewer's yeast is a good source of vitamin B, it is a potential allergen for some dogs.

Calcium pantothenate is a source of pantothenic acid, a B vitamin known as vitamin B3. It acts as a catalyst in the production of fats, cholesterol, bile, vitamin D, red blood cells, and some neurotransmitters and hormones.

Choline chloride is source of choline, a member of the B-complex group of water-soluble vitamins (vitamin B4).

Copper is an essential trace mineral. The metabolism and functions of copper are closely tied to those of iron. Copper is necessary for normal absorption and transport of dietary iron.

Corn bran is the outer coating of the corn kernel, with little or no nutritional value.

Corn gluten meal is the dried residue from corn after the removal of the larger part of the starch and germ. While small amounts can be used as a source of protein, corn gluten meal, like other protein sources, is a potential allergen for some dogs.

D-Activated animal sterol is a source of vitamin D3.

Dried whey is the product obtained by removing water from whey (the watery part of milk) and is a protein source.

Folic acid is a vitamin of the B-complex that is water-soluble and essential in animal metabolism.

It's easy to supplement your dog's commercial diet with homemade delights.

Gelatin is a colorless or slightly yellow substance that is nearly tasteless and odorless. It is created by prolonged boiling of animal skin, connective tissue, or bones.

Glucosamine hydrochloride is a compound that occurs naturally in the cartilage cushioning the joints and may play a role in preventing or treating osteoarthritis.

Inositol is a source of vitamin B8.

Iodine is an essential mineral element and is required by the body for the production of the hormones needed by the thyroid gland.

Lecithin is essential for normal fatty acid transport within cells.

Linoleic acid is an essential fatty acid found in fats and oils and helps promote healthy skin and a shiny coat.

Manganese is a micromineral and is necessary for normal bone development and reproduction.

Natural flavors are minimally processed flavor ingredients that do not contain artificial or synthetic components.

Potassium is an essential mineral that plays various roles in metabolism and body functions and assists in the regulation of the acid-base balance and water balance in the blood and the body tissue.

Rice gluten meal is the dried residue from rice after the removal of the larger part of the starch and germ. Rice gluten is an option for a dog who is allergic to wheat or corn.

Sodium selenite is an essential trace mineral and an important antioxidant nutrient.

Home-Cooked Diets

Preparing wholesome, healthy meals from scratch is an excellent way to be sure you know the health benefits of everything that goes into your dog's mouth. Many dogs with allergies, skin conditions, or frequent gastrointestinal upsets respond well to a home-cooked diet. Relieving such maladies can stop your dog from developing nuisance behaviors that would prevent you from enjoying his company. But remember, it's crucial to your adopted dog's health that he receive the proper nutrients in the proper quantities. If you decide to cook all of his meals at home, you are taking full responsibility for all of your dog's nutritional requirements. You will need to consult your veterinarian or a nutritionist to be certain that your home-cooked meals are giving your dog everything he needs to stay healthy and happy. Your conventional veterinarian may be concerned that your dog won't receive proper nutrition with a home-cooked diet; however, your quest for nutritional guidance should put her at ease and encourage her to assist you in learning all you need to know about monitoring your dog for ongoing good health.

What if you're a klutz in the kitchen? Not to worry. You can still add fresh, wholesome foods to your dog's commercial diet. A few nights a week, give your dog some leftover meat and vegetables from your own dinner, but avoid feeding him fast food or spicy dishes. (Remember to put these tidbits into his own food bowl, though, as opposed to slipping him scraps from the table—you don't want to encourage begging.)

Some terrific "people food" that your dog will love (and his body will find healthy as well) include:

- Lean chicken or turkey, skinless and boneless
- Beef, ground or cubed
- Liver, raw or cooked (no more than once a week to avoid a vitamin A toxicity build-up)
- Most fish, including tuna and salmon
- Whole (cooked) grains, like brown rice, wheat, couscous, oatmeal, and quinoa
- Boiled pasta (without sauce)
- Eggs in any form—scrambled, hardboiled, or poached—no more than a few times a week. You can even feed your dog the eggshells—bake them for ten or fifteen minutes to soften and then grind them up. Some veterinarians believe that you can safely feed raw eggs to your dog while others are concerned of risks of salmonella poisoning or biotin deficiency. (My own dogs only get the no-drug, no-hormone, free-range eggs that I eat, and I scramble them.)

- Nearly any raw or steamed vegetables—carrots, green beans, broccoli, cauliflower, peas, brussels sprouts, etc. (but no onions)
- Lettuce or other leafy greens
- Boiled potatoes: the more colorful the potato (like gold and purple), the healthier it is. Red and brown potatoes are harder for dogs to digest, but sweet potatoes, which are not true potatoes, but the root of a flowering plant, are a good source of vitamin A.
- Peanut butter (organic is better, as many commercial peanut butters are high in sugar and additives)
- Cheese (no pepperjack or other spicy or flavored cheeses, please)
- Milk, cottage cheese, or plain yogurt in small quantities
- Many fruits, including apples, pears, and bananas (but no grapes or raisins). Keep portions small, because too much fruit can cause an upset stomach and diarrhea.
- Organic apple cider vinegar can be added to your dog's drinking water (roughly one teaspoon in a quart of water) to aid digestion and deter fleas.

For some home-cooked recipes that will tantalize your dog's taste buds, see the "Favorite Recipes" section at the end of this chapter.

Food Allergies and Hypoallergenic Diets

Some dogs develop food allergies caused by many ingredients in dog food, including beef, pork, fish, dairy, eggs, corn, soy, and wheat, as well as preservatives and dyes.

A dog might become allergic to his food after just a few days or he may eat the same diet for years before developing allergies, so it's important to recognize the symptoms when they occur: persistent itching or licking, face rubbing (to alleviate itchy ears and eyes), excessive gas, or chronic vomiting and diarrhea. If you suspect your dog is suffering from food allergies, consult your veterinarian for diagnosis and treatment.

Testing for food allergies usually involves removing all suspected ingredients from a dog's diet (called an *elimination diet trial*) for a period of eight weeks, then gradually introducing ingredients back into the diet to see which ones triggers an allergic reaction. It's important to realize that an allergy isn't

Dangerous Foods

Sometimes it seems like dogs are little garbage disposals dressed in fur. Dogs are scavengers by nature, so they are likely to try to get their teeth into things they shouldn't. And they are omnivores, which means they will munch on just about anything—from roadkill to garbage to the contents of the cat's litterbox. Yuck! While some things will just leave a bad taste in your dog's mouth, there are other common foods that can be very dangerous, and even fatal, if ingested. These include:

- Alcohol
- Avocados
- Chocolate (all types)
- Coffee (all forms)
- Garlic
- Grapes and raisins
- Macadamia nuts
- Moldy or spoiled foods
- Onions or onion powder
- Salt
- Yeast dough
- Xylitol (sweetener)

In addition, avoid feeding your dog bones (especially small, soft bones such as those from chickens and pork chops) as they can splinter and cause injury to the mouth, throat, and intestines.

If your dog eats a chocolate chip cookie or a piece of moldy bread, chances are he will be perfectly fine (although he may need to go outside to vomit). However, if you discover he's eaten an entire chocolate cake, or even a smaller portion of unsweetened (baker's) chocolate, which contains a much higher concentration of the toxic component, theobromine, or any of the above listed foods in any significant quantities, get him to the vet right away. (See Chapter 14 for more information on how to treat medical emergencies.)

Organic Dog Food: What Is It?

The word *organic* refers to food that is produced without synthetic fertilizers and pesticides, preservatives, genetic engineering, growth hormones, irradiation, or antibiotics. Many people find that feeding their dog an organic diet (either a commercial pet food or home-cooked meals) reduces skin ailments and gives their dog more energy, fewer digestive disorders, a stronger immune system, and better overall health.

caused by the quality of the food, but by a specific ingredient. There isn't one food item that causes more allergies than another.

Some pet food companies have developed "hypoallergenic" diets in which the physical characteristics of protein molecules are altered, so they are more easily tolerated. Talk to your vet if you think this is something your dog needs.

Raw Food Diets

Proponents of the raw food movement contend that feeding dogs only uncooked foods is the closest we can get to the diet of dogs in the wild. Wolves eat their meat raw and ingest plants, berries, and other non-meat foods from the intestines of their prey. As repulsive as this may sound to you, raw diets are perceived as more natural than processed foods and, some feel, are quite healthy for dogs. In fact, many holistic veterinarians recommend them. As with home-cooked diets, feeding your dog only raw food requires a strong commitment from you, and it's important to do some research and consult a holistic veterinarian or naturopath before embarking on this type of meal plan for your dog.

You must exercise caution if you're going to feed your dog raw meat, which often contains harmful bacteria like E. coli and salmonella, as well as some parasites. These bacteria can cause illness and even death. For your dog's safety, when feeding a raw diet:

- Use only fresh meat and keep it refrigerated or frozen prior to feeding
- Never leave meat at room temperature, as bacteria can proliferate quickly
- Avoid feeding raw pork or fish, which frequently contain parasites
- Always wash your hands with soap and hot water after handling raw meat
- Clean cutting boards, dishes, and utensils thoroughly after use to reduce the risk of spreading food-borne illnesses

You can also rinse the meat with food-grade hydrogen peroxide—a teaspoon of peroxide diluted into a quart of water—or lightly steam or boil the meat (for about five minutes), keeping the pan covered to help keep nutrients intact. While some believe that cooking the meat destroys healthy enzymes that help the body to detoxify, cleanse, repair, and rebuild itself, it will also kill the harmful bacteria and parasites.

Finally, commercial raw food diets are readily available at pet specialty stores, making it a more realistic option for the average pet parent. By way of example, I have found that Mojo flourishes on a diet that includes Nature's Variety raw frozen foods. It is available in convenient patties or medallions in a variety of flavor formulas, and our veterinarian was relieved to learn that it meets AAFCO standards. The packaging also boldly suggests safe handling guidelines, much like those outlined above.

While feeding raw meat is controversial, almost everyone agrees that feeding a dog fresh fruits and vegetables (preferably organic) is a good idea. Foods such as broccoli, cauliflower, legumes, green beans, and apples are excellent sources of vitamins and minerals, and dogs love the way they taste. Large, raw (uncooked) bones are generally considered safe, and they also help keep your dog's teeth healthy by removing plaque and tartar.

The raw food movement is gaining popularity today. Below are brief descriptions of a few of the main types of raw food diets.

Biologically Appropriate Raw Food Diet (BARF)

The BARF—Biologically Appropriate Raw Food—diet, also known as the Bones and Raw Food diet, was developed by Ian Billinghurst, DVM Billinghurst believes that every living animal requires a biologically appropriate diet and that cooked foods do not allow them to thrive.

The BARF diet mimics the evolutionary diet of dogs. It consists of finely-ground bones mixed with proteins, vitamins, and minerals. Some people find that feeding this diet to their dog helps clear up skin problems and minimizes the need for dental visits. Opponents of the BARF diet believe that dogs (and cats) are at risk of infection by the many bacteria in raw meat, such as salmonella, Campylobactor, E.coli, and Listeria, and that this diet (and all raw food diets) does not allow dogs to get full, balanced nutrition.

To learn more about Dr. Ian Billinghurst and the BARF diet, visit www.barfworld.com and www.drianbillinghurst.com.

The Volhard Diet

The Volhard Diet, developed by Wendy Volhard, has strict requirements for mealtimes: the morning meal is made up of molasses, grains, yogurt, egg, oil, and vitamins. For dinner, dogs are fed raw muscle meat, liver, fresh greens, and herbs. Other supplementary ingredients include kelp, cod liver oil, vitamin C and fruit.

For more information, visit www.volhard.com

The Whole Prey Diet

The Whole Prey Diet is about as close as you can get to feeding your dog a "natural" diet. It is a model that simulates the portions of an actual prey animal. As the name implies, with this diet, a dog eats an entire animal, like a chicken, fish, or rabbit. If that's not practical, he can eat various parts of the animal, such as chunks of raw meat, organs, skin, fat, and edible bone. As a general rule, a dog eats 10 percent edible bone, 10 percent organs, and 80 percent meat, skin, and fat.

The Ultimate Raw Food Plan

Similar to the Volhard Diet, the Ultimate Raw Food Plan consists mostly of feeding your dog muscle meat, organs, raw eggs, bones, and vegetables, and supplementing these with kelp and alfalfa.

Obesity—Is My Dog Fat or Just at the Top of His Weight Class?

The statistics are sobering: Approximately 25 to 40 percent of adult dogs are overweight or obese. Obesity is associated with conditions such as heart disease, impaired breathing, decreased liver functions, diabetes, musculoskeletal diseases, respiratory problems, gastrointestinal disorders, and increased stress on bones, joints, and tendons. A study conducted by Nestlé Purina Pet care in 2004 found that dogs who maintained ideal body weights throughout their lives had a median life span of 15 percent longer than dogs who were consistently overweight (almost two years for the Labrador Retrievers in the

Petfinder.com: The Adopted Dog Bible

study). Potentially gaining up to two more years with our canine buddies is a strong incentive to keep them in shape.

As with humans, dogs will gain weight if they consume more calories than they burn. And as with human food, the lower the caloric density of a given dog food, the healthier it will be, and the more it will help your dog lose weight. Although pet food companies are not currently required to list the caloric density of their food on the container, most companies have this information on their website.

The causes of obesity generally fall into three categories: genetic predisposition, hormonal disorders, and an inappropriate diet and sedentary lifestyle. Certain breeds (such as Beagles, Basset Hounds, Dachshunds, and Labrador Retrievers) pack on the pounds more easily than others. Thyroid or pituitary gland dysfunction affects hormone balance in the body and may contribute to the development of obesity. Talk to your vet if you have concerns about either of these causes.

Inappropriate diet and sedentary lifestyle is by far the most common reason for obesity in dogs. A dog cannot decide to cut calories or hit the gym; it is our responsibility to make sure that our dogs don't become obese due to too many table scraps and not enough long walks. If your adopted dog is overweight when you get him, you'll need to do some maintenance work to get him to a more manageable size. If you notice that your once-svelte pooch has started to expand, you need to change your habits (and by extension, his). Reducing the amount of food he eats will obviously help, but don't forget about exercise. Unlike many of us, dogs don't view exercise as punishment; they think it's *fun*. See Chapter 10 for some ways that you and your pup can get fit together.

Weight Control Guidelines

Preventing your dog from gaining weight in the first place is the best approach. But anyone who has ever looked into their dog's eyes as he stares longingly at your pastrami sandwich knows that it's hard to say no. If you're having trouble keeping your pup fit and trim, the following suggestions will help:

1. Reduce or eliminate table scraps and treats. These are often high in fat and calories, which contribute to obesity. Alternatively, if you

feed a small amount of low-fat treats, reduce the amount of your dog's normal meal to balance those calories.

2. Reduce the amount fed at each meal. If you are feeding your dog a commercial pet food, you can easily calculate the proper amount of food by using a measuring cup or scoop. If your dog weighs forty pounds and his ideal weight is thirty pounds, feed him the suggested amount for a thirty-pound dog. When my adopted dog, Mocha, needed to take off some extra weight, I added green beans to her dinner daily while reducing the amount of other food she received. Doing this added bulk without adding many calories and helped her to feel fuller—important to me, as I am no match for her begging!

3. Increase the amount of exercise your dog receives. Walking and fetching are two favorite activities that not only burn calories, but also build muscle and endurance.

4. Consider switching to a commercially available low-calorie or "light" dog food. These products are typically lower in fat and higher in fiber. (Note: There is no such thing as fat-free dog food!)

Always consult a veterinarian before beginning any weight-reduction program. The veterinarian can design a weight-loss program specifically for your dog and help identify specific problems and suggest alternatives along the way. And don't forget to weigh your dog periodically to track his progress.

What if Your Dog Is Underweight?

It's common for adopted dogs to be underweight, and if a pup moves from shelter to shelter, frequent changes in food types and feeding schedules can often lead to diarrhea and other gastronomic distress. Unlike humans, who think that "thin is in," being underweight is not healthy for dogs and can compromise their long-term health and quality of life.

If your dog is underweight—have this verified by your vet—start feeding him either a calorically and nutrient dense food that is formulated for performance, or a veterinary diet that is formulated for weight gain in chronically ill pets. These foods are both energy/nutrient dense and highly digestible. If your dog does not begin to gain weight within a week or two, it's possible that he is suffering from an undiagnosed illness or parasites, or is nauseous from a medication he is taking. Again, talk with your vet about any concerns. Be sure that as your dog reaches his ideal weight, you adjust his diet accordingly, so he doesn't inadvertently become overweight.

As with any weight management program, the key is to go slowly to allow your dog time to adjust to his new meal plan. In the meantime, keep in mind that underweight dogs (especially those with less fur) can get colder than dogs of normal weight, especially during the winter months. Provide your dog with warm sleeping accommodations and don't be afraid to dress him in a chic canine coat!

Treats should make up no more than ten percent of your dog's daily diet.

That's a Good Boy! Finding the Right Treats

Dog treats come in many varieties—from all-natural snacks made from fresh, wholesome ingredients to discount bulk items you purchase by the scoop in many pet supply stores. Below is a rundown:

Commercial Treats

- ☼ **Biscuits and Cookies.** There are more types and flavors of biscuits and cookies in a typical pet food aisle than you can shake a stick at. Some are high in fat, and thus, high in calories. Because they are usually grain- or flour-based, biscuits and cookies can be potential allergens. In addition, they can cause plaque and tartar build-up.
- ☼ **Chews.** Chewy treats come in a variety of sizes and flavors. As the treat is chewed, it massages your dog's gums and helps reduce plaque and tarter build-up.
- ☼ **Nylabones.** Made from nylon, plastic polymer, or rubber, Nylabones are exceptionally strong, completely digestible, and made for

the enthusiastic chewer. A word of caution, however: If your dog is a particularly aggressive chewer, he may bite off small pieces of the bone, which can pose a choking hazard. The same goes for any bones that are too small (puppy-sized) for your dog: He may inadvertently swallow the bone, which could become lodged in his throat. The Nylabone website (www.nylabone.com) gives helpful hints for choosing the right type and size of bone for your dog.

❁ **Pig ears.** Pig ears, which are made from real, dried pig ears, have a high fat content and can lead to obesity if given in high quantities. They can also cause stomach upset in some dogs. Pig ears can also be a source of salmonella bacteria, so be sure you purchase the ears from only reputable companies. Imitation pig ears are available at most pet supply stores, and these are lower in calories and more easily digestible.

❁ **Rawhide bones.** All rawhide bones are not created equal. Check to make sure that the bones you purchase have been manufactured in accordance with the highest USDA specifications (bones made in other countries are often inferior). Consider size, shape, hardness, and flavor, and choose a bone that matches your dog's chewing rate and habits (some dogs won't touch a bone that is too large, but will chew for hours on a smaller bone). A dog who chews for short periods of time with a soft bite may find rawhide chips, sticks, or twists more enjoyable. Rawhide bones are low in calories and may prevent destructive chewing. As with chews, pig ears, and Nylabones, rawhide bones should only be given to your dog when you can supervise him to avoid possible choking. Once the treat is small enough that he could swallow it, take it away from him and throw it out.

Help, We're Kosher!

According to a recent survey conducted by the American Pet Products Manufacturers Association, one percent of dog guardians feed their dogs kosher foods. If you're interested in serving home-cooked kosher food to your dog, ask for it at your local deli. For commercially prepared kosher dog foods, see www.kosherpets.com or www.evangersdogfood.com.

Help, We're Vegetarians!

More and more people are foregoing meat, poultry, and fish in their diets and switching to vegetarianism for health or moral reasons. Can your dog do the same? Well, it will take a strong commitment to his nutritional wellness, but yes, dogs can not only survive, but thrive on a vegetarian or even vegan diet.

You can find many commercially prepared vegetarian and vegan dog foods at specialty pet supply shops or online. These use protein sources from plants instead of animals, and are formulated to be nutritionally balanced and healthy for dogs. Some companies to look for include Nature's Recipe (www.naturesrecipe.com), Pet Guard (www.petguard.com), and V-Dog (www.v-dogfood.com).

If you decide to prepare vegetarian meals for your dog yourself, you must be sure he is getting the right amounts of protein, fat, and carbohydrates. Run all your proposed dishes by a veterinarian to make sure that you haven't overlooked anything.

For the sake of full disclosure, while I have opted for a meat-free diet for myself, Kona, Mocha, and Mojo proudly embrace their status as omnivores.

Ready-Made Treats

For something a little healthier, give your dog fresh, ready-made treats such as small bites of meat, chunks of cheese, cantaloupe balls, celery sticks with peanut butter, apple slices, or carrots. These treats are not only delicious, but healthy, too!

Just like people, dogs need variety in the foods they eat, so alternate the type of treats you offer.

Dog Biscuits for the Soul: Kiki

Kiki

We adopted Kiki in August. A year before, we had adopted Bryce, a Beagle/Chihuahua mix, from the St. Louis Humane Society. Both Kiki and Bryce have been such wonderful additions to our family! Someone told me when we first were looking into adopting that there's nothing better than rescue dogs—and it's really true. Kiki was rescued from a backyard breeder and was neglected and malnourished. She has gained weight nicely and is now a very contented snuggler. Bryce was rescued from an animal hoarder who had over 200 animals. She is frightened of some dogs, but gets along very well with her "sister." Both girls are very happy and healthy! My fiancé and I feel very blessed to have these dogs in our lives.

Sara Trice, Fenton, Missouri

Kiki was adopted from Metro East Humane Society, Edwardsville, Illinois

CHEESE BALLS

Submitted by Kellyann Conway of Florida

1 cup cheddar cheese, grated
1 cup cottage cheese
1 tablespoon vegetable oil
1 teaspoon salt
1 teaspoon Worcestershire sauce
1 cup whole wheat flour
1/3 cup chopped nuts

Preheat oven to 400 degrees. In a bowl, mix the cheddar cheese and cottage cheese, then add the vegetable oil and Worcestershire sauce. Very slowly, mix in the flour. Mix until you see that the dough can easily be molded. Divide the dough into bite-sized balls about the size of a marble, then roll the balls in the chopped nuts. Arrange the balls on a cookie tray.

Bake for about 20 minutes or until cheese balls are golden brown. Make sure they are completely cool before giving them to your pooch, and store any leftovers in a covered container in the fridge.

SUPER SIMPLE YUM DROPS

Submitted by Kristi Simmons of Texas

An easy microwaveable treat for busy people who still want to cook for their furry companions!

3 jars baby food meat (or vegetables)
1-1/2 cup wheat germ (or cream of wheat)
1 egg

In a bowl, combine all ingredients and mix well.

For the microwave: Drop by spoonfuls on a wax paper covered plate and cover with wax paper. Cook on high in microwave for 5 to 8 minutes or until treats are formed and firm.

For the oven: Drop by spoonfuls on a nonstick cookie tray. Bake at 300 degrees for about 50 minutes.

Let cool completely before giving them to your pup.

Store in refrigerator in an airtight container.

Editor's Note: Read the label of the baby food jars to be sure the contents don't contain garlic, garlic powder, or onion powder, which can be toxic to dogs.

LIVER SNAPS
Submitted by Kellyann Conway of Florida

1 pound chicken livers
1 cup whole wheat flour
1 cup corn meal
1 egg

Preheat the oven to 400 degrees. Put the chicken livers in a blender and liquefy them. Add the egg and blend for another minute. Pour the mixture into a bowl. Add the flour and corn meal and mix well. Spray a cookie sheet with some non-stick cooking spray and pour the mixture onto it. Using the tip of a butter knife, lightly score the surface in a square pattern to make it easier to cut after baking.

Bake for 15 minutes. Cut into small squares while still warm. For safe storage, put them in a resealable container and keep them in the freezer.

SHREDDED ROAST CHICKEN WITH STUFFING
Submitted by Cary Moran of Pennsylvania

(1) 5 to 8 pound oven roaster chicken
1 sweet potato, cooked and mashed
1 cup oatmeal
6–8 egg shells, boiled, dried, and crushed (to provide bone meal)
1 cup cooked spinach
1 tablespoon rosemary
1 teaspoon sea salt (not table salt)
1 tablespoon dried parsley
1 cup water
(1) 12 ounce can low sodium chicken broth or vegetarian vegetable broth
4 tablespoons of unbleached flour

Preheat oven to 325 degrees. Rinse the chicken and pat dry.

To make stuffing: In a bowl, combine mashed sweet potato, oatmeal, dried egg shell, and spinach.

Combine rosemary, sea salt and parsley and rub on the chicken. Stuff chicken.

Place chicken in a shallow roasting pan with one cup of water and one cup of either low sodium chicken broth or vegetarian vegetable broth, saving 4 ounces to make a gravy.

Cover with aluminum foil and cook for 1 hour.

Petfinder.com: The Adopted Dog Bible

Remove foil and begin basting every 10 to 15 minutes. Using a cooking thermometer inserted at the thickest part of the chicken, cook until the internal temperature reaches 180 degrees and juices run clear.

Let chicken stand for 10 minutes and whisk remaining juices with flour to make a gravy. Scoop out stuffing and set aside. Once the chicken cools to a comfortable handling temperature, remove chicken from the bones and shred. Mix shredded chicken, stuffing, and gravy and refrigerate in an airtight container. Use it as a topping for dry food, or temporarily as a food replacement.

FRIED RICE (FOR YOU AND YOUR DOG!)
Submitted by: Eunice Peters of Kansas

2 to 3 cups cut up chunks of any meat (pork and chicken work best)
2 cups cold cooked rice (day-old, stored in refrigerator)
3 eggs
3 tablespoons soy sauce
2 tablespoons sunflower oil or safflower oil (for vitamin E)
1 tablespoon dried or fresh parsley
*Optional: Juiced carrots and other assorted veggies. Add 1 to 2 tablespoons before each serving that way the nutrients remain intact and are fresh.
*Optional: Dog vitamins pounded into a powder.

Beat eggs lightly in a bowl and set aside. Heat wok or large pan over medium heat. When oil is hot, add the meat. Cook until almost done (a little pink in middle). Add rice. Stir frequently to avoid food sticking to pan. When rice is warm, add the eggs, still stirring frequently. When the eggs are almost completely cooked, add soy sauce, parsley, and garlic powder. Stir frequently until dry and somewhat crispy. It should take up to 15 minutes to cook the entire dish.

Cool completely before serving. Put mixture in your dog's dish, add the juiced vegetables and vitamins.

"PEAMUTT" BUTTER AND PUMPKIN "PUPCAKES"
Submitted by Gina Moultrie of Nevada

2-1/2 cups water
1/2 cup canned pumpkin
1 egg (slightly beaten)
1/2 teaspoon vanilla extract
1/4 cup peanut butter (chunky)
3-1/2 cups whole wheat flour

½ cup oats
1 tablespoon baking powder
½ teaspoon nutmeg
½ teaspoon cinnamon

Preheat oven to 350 degrees. In a medium bowl, thoroughly mix water, pumpkin, egg, vanilla, and peanut butter. In a large bowl, combine flour, oats, baking powder, nutmeg, and cinnamon. Mix wet and dry ingredients together and stir well. Spoon into a greased mini-muffin pan, making sure each cup is filled completely and piled high. Bake for 35 to 40 minutes or until firm (but not too brown). Cool completely and store in an open container or paper bag in the refrigerator. Makes 30 mini pupcakes.

DOGGONE BIRTHDAY CAKE
Submitted by Jennifer Latshaw of Pennsylvania

1 ½ cups all-purpose flour
1 ½ teaspoons baking powder
¼ cup margarine, softened
¼ cup corn oil
(1) 3.5 ounce jar strained beef (baby food) or strained chicken
1 cup shredded carrots
3 eggs
2 strips bacon, fried and crumbled, or dog beef jerky
Plain yogurt or cottage cheese for icing.

Preheat oven to 325 degrees. Grease and flour an 8-inch round pan. Cream butter until smooth. Add corn oil, baby food, eggs, and carrots. Mix until smooth. Gradually add flour and baking powder, mixing until smooth. Fold in crumbled bacon (or beef jerky). Pour batter into cake pan. Bake 60 to 70 minutes, depending on your oven—surface of the cake should be springy to the touch. Let cool. Top with plain yogurt or cottage cheese. Refrigerate any remaining portions.

Editor's Note: Read the label of the baby food jars to be sure the contents don't contain garlic, garlic powder, or onion powder, which can be toxic to dogs.

PB & CHEESE BISCUITS
Submitted by Kellyann Conway of Florida

1 cup flour
1 cup milk
2 tablespoons peanut butter

Petfinder.com: The Adopted Dog Bible

2 tablespoons grated parmesan cheese (organic, natural, or sugar-free are best for your pup)

1 teaspoon baking powder

1 egg white

1 tablespoon of water

Preheat the oven to 350 degrees.

In a bowl, mix the flour and milk until lumpy, then add the peanut butter and water. Mix in the parmesan cheese and then add the egg white. The mixture should have the consistency of pancake batter. Add the baking powder.

Spray a cookie sheet with non-stick cooking spray and spoon the batter onto it in approximately 2" blobs. Bake for about 20 minutes or until biscuits are golden brown. Let them cool and serve 'em up!

Resources

Association of American Feed Control Officials (AAFCO): www.aafco.org

Brown, Andi: *The Whole Pet Diet: Eight Weeks to Great Health for Dogs and Cats.* Celestial Arts, 2006

Case, Linda P.: *The Dog: Its Behavior, Nutrition and Health.* Wiley-Blackwell, 2005

Martin, Ann M.: *Food Pets Die For: Shocking Facts about Pet Food.* NewSage Press; Third edition edition, 2007

The Pet Food Institute (PFI), a non-governmental organization that oversees the pet food industry in the United States: www.petfoodinstitute.org

Pitcairn, Richard H., DVM, PhD and Susan Hubble Pitcairn: *Dr. Pitcairn's Complete Guide to Natural Health for Dogs & Cats.* Rodale, 2005

Shojai, Amy D. and the Editors of *Prevention for Pets: New Choices in Natural Healing for Dogs & Cats.* Rodale, 2001

The Whole Dog Journal: A monthly guide to natural dog care and training. Available Online: www.Whole-dog-journal.com

10

Walks, Workouts, and Play

One of the best things about having a canine companion is that she's not just willing but eager to get out there and exercise. A dog makes a fitness program more palatable, giving you the perfect workout buddy. The exercise will benefit both of you, both physically and mentally. And while walking is great, there are plenty of other activities you can do together as well.

Walking Basics

For dogs, walks serve two basic purposes: potty breaks and exercise (and possibly socialization). The first starts out as vitally important and diminishes in urgency as the dog grows older and learns the rules. The second remains a necessity, increasing and decreasing in duration, through the stages of the dog's life.

Let's look first at house-training outings, with the big question being: How Often Should I Walk My Dog? The answer is: It varies. A lot depends on the age of your adopted dog. As mentioned earlier, up to about six months, the dog's age in months plus one roughly equals the number of hours she can "hold it" between potty breaks. So a three-month-old dog could wait about four hours before needing to relieve herself, a four-month-old about five hours, etc. That doesn't necessarily mean she *will* wait that long, but she should be physically capable of it. Once the dog is older than six months, trips outdoors every four or five hours should be sufficient.

Trips outside for the purpose of house-training aren't really walks, they're training. You're only going as far as your chosen area for elimination, and you're doing so with your dog onleash. You don't want her scampering off to chase butterflies when you're trying to accomplish some serious training.

If you have a house with a yard, that's the destination for your house-training ventures. Initially, and until your dog is completely house-trained, it is important to accompany your dog into the yard. This allows you the opportunity to ensure your dog is eliminating in the right place—and to go wild praising her success. These steps will prevent your dog from "forgetting" to potty when outside alone and coming back in to have an accident. Your efforts early on will prevent problems later. Once your dog is trained—and provided the yard is safely fenced—you can just open the door for her when she needs to use the facilities. If, however, you live in an apartment or condo without a yard of your own, you'll have to choose a walking route to a nearby, acceptable potty area. You'll always have to take your dog out for daily potty breaks if these are your living conditions, but the trips won't need to be as frequent once your dog is trained. And always, always, *always* clean up after your dog.

Immediately after a successful potty break is a great time to take your dog for an actual walk. You won't have to worry so much about where she eliminated, and the walk serves as a reward for doing her business in the proper place.

The frequency, duration, and strenuousness of your exercise walks will depend on your dog's age, breed or mix of breeds, and health status. Young dogs or dogs who have led a sedentary life won't be ready for long walks or jogs. You may not know your adopted dog's background, so you'll need to start slow and assess as you go along.

Map out some short walks and try them out with your dog. If she's still bouncing eagerly along at the end, you'll know you can do more. But if she's slowing down, panting, or sitting down and refusing to move, you will need to make future outings easier. Most dogs will improve their endurance through regular exercise, but some dogs—Pekingese and Bulldogs, for example—are just not built for a lot of it. If your dog isn't a short-faced or heavy-bodied type, yet she still doesn't tolerate exercise well, check with your

Finding a Dog Walker

If all the humans go off to their occupations and schooling during the day, the dog still needs a potty break and some exercise. So you might need a little outside help. When it comes to hiring a dog walker, you can look to professionals or right in your own neighborhood. Perhaps there's a responsible teenager nearby who gets along with your dog and would like to earn a little extra cash. You could hire him to take your dog out for a walk as soon as he gets home from school, but this may be too late in the day if you have to leave early for work and there's no one else to take the dog out in the afternoon.

Perhaps there's a retired person nearby who would enjoy a canine walking companion. He or she could likely provide a more accommodating schedule, but you'll have to gently ascertain whether this person can handle your dog. If you're still working on loose leash walking with your big, boisterous adopted dog, you don't want her pulling your older dog walker down the street or breaking free.

Professional dog walkers tend to be more widely available in cities, but these services are springing up in other areas as well. There is no official accrediting organization for dog walkers, so you'll need to do your own checking. Find out how many dogs are taken out at one time—three may be okay, two is better. Ask for references. Check that the person is bonded. After all, you will be trusting them in your home and, more importantly, with your dog.

Ask about where they walk, and how they manage cleaning up after multiple dogs. Be clear about whether you want your dog taken to a dog park. If your dog has any issues with children, cats, loud noises, or anything else, make that clear and be sure your dog walker will not take your dog into a situation where something bad could happen.

Introduce the potential dog walker to your dog and watch your dog's reaction—if they don't get along, this is not the right person to walk your dog, no matter how terrific their credentials. If another dog is going to be walked with yours, ask to be there when the dogs are first introduced, to be sure they are also compatible. Once you have chosen a dog walker, ask for reports on outings.

You can also see Chapter 19 for information about choosing a pet-sitter. Much of the criteria for selecting a walker and a sitter is the same.

veterinarian to make sure she's healthy. See "Workouts" on page 203 for more on how to safely exercise your dog.

Loose Leash Walking

To make your exercise outings more enjoyable for both of you, some leash manners will help. If your adopted dog seems to be completely unacquainted with the concept of a leash, you may have to start out by letting her drag the leash around the confines of your home when you are there to ensure she doesn't get stuck on furniture or household items. When you do start walking, just follow your leashed dog wherever she goes on your first few walks. Wait until she is comfortable enough to walk freely on a leash before beginning any type of training.

Because your adopted dog probably doesn't have a reliable "stay" or "wait" cue yet, attach your leash before you open the door to go outside. Block the door with your body and take a firm hold on the leash before you let your dog out. Brace yourself to withstand any initial lunge. Make her wait while you lock the door and get yourself ready to walk.

Once you begin walking, you should have one simple initial goal: to reward the behavior you want (calm walking without pulling) and discourage the behavior you don't want (pulling and jerking). This requires dedication and patience to put into practice . . . not to mention the strength to be physically able to restrain your dog. If you're slight of build and you've adopted an adolescent Retriever or other large, exuberant dog, you may need a management tool such as an EZ Walk harness or Gentle Leader to assist you.

Otherwise, use a regular sturdy nylon or leather leash, not a retractable lead (this rewards the dog for pulling by gaining more leash). Hold the leash in both hands and hold your hands against your waist. This not only keeps the leash a set length so your dog can learn how much distance she can move away from you, it also gives you a better chance of stopping her when necessary. Use the handle at the end of the leash rather than wrapping the leash around your hand—wrapping changes the length of the leash and can lead to finger injuries if the dog gives a mighty yank.

Once you're ready, start walking! Continue to move forward as long as there is any slack in the leash. The dog doesn't have to be heeling directly by your side, just staying within the confines of the leash. As long as that's the case, have a nice brisk walk. But the second your dog hits the end of the leash and you have to resist having your arms pulled away from your body, you have several options to encourage your dog to return to a loose leash.

The first option is to stop and stand still. You don't have to say anything—just wait. Sooner or later, your dog will turn her head to look at you or take a step back toward you. When she does, the tension will leave the leash. You must then move forward again in response.

This start-and-stop may not get you anywhere very quickly (in fact, in the beginning, you may not make it to the end of your own walkway), but it will work to reward the behavior you want—walking without pulling. You may need to use other strategies, such as playing fetch in a fenced area or in a dog run, to provide the exercise your dog needs while you're working on loose leash walking. To see an excellent video tutorial on the "start-and-stop" method to loose leash walking, check out www.petfinder.com/dog-bible.

Another option to help reform dedicated puller-jerker dogs involves walking backward when the leash gets tight. This will cause your dog to look back at you to see what is happening. At that time and once the leash is loose, you may proceed forward again.

In a third method, when the leash tightens, you abruptly and silently execute an "about turn." Once facing away from your dog, you walk boldly in the new direction and your dog will quickly seek to catch up to you. Continue walking until once again the leash tightens and then repeat, heading back the other way. With the consistent use of any of these methods, your dog can learn to associate a loose leash with progress toward the walk they enjoy—and one that you can enjoy, as well.

A Walk in the Park

Once you and your dog have had some time to get accustomed to one another's walking habits, you can plan your first trip to the park. The park is a great place to do a lot of socializing of your new adopted dog. She will meet other people of all shapes and sizes, other dogs, and other animals as well. Keep in mind, though, that all this can be overwhelming, so choose the time and location to minimize distractions. You don't want to start at the park with the most popular playground, or on a jogging path so busy it should have police directing traffic. In fact, even if the park is totally deserted, your dog can still smell all the people, dogs, squirrels, deer, and anyone else who has been there recently. That alone could be enough for her to attempt to drag you along as she follows all those enticing scents. You never know: this might be your adopted dog's first visit ever to a park! Thinking about how overwhelmed *you* would be in such circumstances will help you be more understanding. At the same time, you need to have a plan. It's best if you can present your dog with new experiences gradually rather than all at once, and be willing to cut your outing short if you find your dog becoming overwhelmed. Carry plenty of treats, and offer praise and a treat or two whenever your dog is behaving calmly. You can also use treats to help her learn to greet other people.

Of course, people and dogs aren't the only things your dog might encounter in the park. You may also see lawnmowers, bicycles, strollers, horseback riders, skateboarders, and who knows what else. It's not unusual for dogs to be frightened by lawnmowers, leaf blowers, and other noisy equipment. Many dogs, especially herding dogs and sight hounds, might be enticed to chase the rapid movement of bicycles or skateboards. Be prepared for your dog's reaction to anything new you may encounter.

Meet and Greet

A big part of socialization is meeting new people and dogs. But not all dogs automatically do this well. If her early upbringing lacked socialization opportunities, you will have to work to remedy that. Take it slow—don't force crowds of people on your dog. And take special care with children.

Human–Dog Interactions

First, always remember that *you* control interactions. Don't be shy about telling people to keep their distance. Keep in mind that if your dog were to bite someone, you would be held responsible—even if the other person was at fault. So use your voice and be proactive. Stop children while they are still some distance from you and your dog. If you're going to allow a greeting, instruct the other person in how you would like it to take place, keeping the safety of everyone in mind. Tell people your dog is newly adopted, and you are trying to make sure she will be an excellent canine member of society, but you don't know each other all that well yet.

What to Wear?

Some dogs will need a little assistance in adverse weather conditions. Small dogs have more surface area for their weight than their larger cousins, so they tend to lose heat more easily. Small dogs without a thick double coat, like Chihuahuas, are especially vulnerable and need clothing to help

Some pups need a little extra warmth in cool weather.

them keep warm outdoors when temperatures dip. In dry weather, a sweater or coat is fine, but in wet weather the covering should be waterproof.

Larger dogs without a lot of body fat or hair coat, such as Greyhounds, also need outer coverings in colder weather. If your adopted dog becomes reluctant to go out as the weather becomes frosty, try some outerwear. A coat that buckles or is secured with Velcro under the dog's belly is usually easier to get on and off than a sweater and may be accepted more easily by your dog.

If you find that ice balls build in your dog's pads on winter walks, you may need some booties. But as mentioned earlier, be aware that you will have to accustom your dog to wearing them. It is the rare dog indeed who will accept footwear without some training work. Before the weather turns frosty, have daily sessions where you reward your dog just for wearing booties at first, then for walking in them.

If you have a heavily coated hunting-type dog (like a Cocker Spaniel or even a Cavalier) and you walk in the woods, you can have your dog wear a tighter-fitting jacket to protect against cuts and scratches from thorns and brambles. It can also help keep debris out of her coat.

For completely different circumstances—boating with your dog—don't forget the life vest. It's as much a safety device for your dog as for the humans onboard.

By now you should have some idea of your adopted dog's personality. Most dogs, when confronted with new situations, will either be very shy and nervous, or will get excited. First we'll discuss how to help your under-socialized, nervous pup become more comfortable with people, and then we'll talk about what to do if your dog is boisterous and overly friendly.

Let's start with your scared pup. When an adult approaches, give the adult a few of your treats. Ask him to come close enough that your dog can reach him without pulling on her leash, but not to come right up to your dog. If your dog backs away, ask the person to stand still and talk to you, without looking directly at the dog. Have him drop a treat on the ground near his feet. If your dog approaches to take the treat, he can drop another, still without looking at or reaching toward your dog. Keep one eye on your dog, watching for any signs of increasing stress or arousal. Break off the interaction if you think it's making your dog too nervous.

If your dog is fairly calm and has been willing to eat the treats dropped by the other person, you can ask him to hold out a treat on his palm, with his hand flat. (Offering the treat this way, the same way you would present a treat to a horse, prevents fingers from being nipped by an anxious dog. Nervous dogs tend to be grabbier when taking food, and no one should blame an adopted dog for being nervous in new situations.) The person should still ignore your dog, other than perhaps talking quietly to her. It's your dog's choice to take the treat. Be sure that the person has enough treats so that he will not run out. You want your nervous dog to believe that the stranger has unending treats and you want to end the encounter with your dog wanting more interaction with the stranger.

If you have a variety of people adopt this routine, your insecure dog should start to connect strangers with food raining from the sky. This is bound to improve her attitude toward friendly new humans, and she should start approaching people more willingly. Once that change takes place, you can ask people to scratch your dog gently behind her ears or on her chest. Do *not* let them reach over your dog's head or stare into her eyes—these can be seen as threatening gestures. Also be sure your dog can move away if she wants to. By taking it slow and easy, you can help your under-socialized adopted dog realize that other humans aren't so scary.

Now let's discuss the dogs on the other end of the spectrum, who are more than willing to jump up exuberantly on any human who comes within range. For these social but unrefined canines, you'll provide a different set of instructions for any humans who want to greet your dog.

Again, supply the person with some treats. Ask him to walk toward you and your dog. If your dog tries to leap at the person or jump up on them, he should turn and walk out of range. He should not push the dog away, yell, or interact with her in any manner, but simply remove himself. You should not jerk on the leash or yell at your dog if this occurs. After a few seconds, have the person approach again. If your dog is still too rambunctious, the person should move away once more. Usually, after a few approaches and withdrawals, the dog will change her behavior. If she stands without jumping up or, even better, sits, the person should give her a treat (offered on a flat hand) and a calm scratch behind the ears. If your dog loses control and jumps up again, the person should immediately move out of reach.

By practicing this with a variety of people, your dog will figure out that showing some self-control gets her the interaction she wants, while jumping on people makes them go away. Really exuberant dogs may have to be reminded of this many times, but with practice and some maturing, they will learn. Remember, the dog is seeking attention, so if you yell and push her (or let others do the same), you're giving her what she wants, even though it may seem like "punishment" to you. Punishment is in the eyes of the beholder—or in this case, the punishee. If what the dog wants is attention, even "bad" attention is better than no attention. So stick to the plan: ignore the bad behavior and reward the good with the attention the dog craves.

If you don't have willing helpers, you can work on eliminating the overly boisterous behavior yourself. Simply tether your dog outside your door or to a tree in your yard. Walk away and then re-approach your dog. As with the instructions for strangers above, only approach your dog when her behavior is such that you want to reward. If you work on this on your own with your dog, she will likely offer appropriate behavior toward approaching strangers that much sooner.

These instructions have been based on encounters with *adult* humans. Children are another matter. Although parents these days seem to be fairly good at telling children they have to ask before they pet a dog, they are woefully bad at instructing their offspring not to run toward you, shrieking the question. Because an adopted dogs's history with children is usually unknown, and because children are the victims of dog bites more often than adults, be especially cautious. First, put a stop to any children running toward you and your dog. Begin in a polite tone while there's still plenty of

Petfinder.com: The Adopted Dog Bible

distance between you, but get more forceful if necessary. A parent may get upset about your "yelling" at their child, but that's far preferable to a bite incident.

If the child and parent are cooperative, you can ask the child to stand still and drop treats while you and your dog approach. Keep a loose leash and allow your dog to avoid the encounter if she chooses. Never force a dog to meet a child. Watch your dog's body language. Any bristling of the hair or stiffness in posture are clear warnings to break off the greeting. If your dog exhibits these warning signs, seek help from a behaviorist or a trainer experienced in behavior modification. Most problems are based in fear, and if your adopted dog has had no experience (or negative experience) with children, she is likely to be afraid. It may be something she can overcome, but it requires face-to-face help, not a book.

Dog–Dog Interactions

As with humans, some dogs are loners and some are social butterflies. You shouldn't try to change that, but you probably do want your dog to be able to be around other dogs without problems.

First you need to assess where you stand. If you had other dogs at home when you adopted this dog, you've already seen some interactions and probably have an idea about whether your new dog is the life of the party or wants to be by herself. But if not, you'll need to arrange some meetings to get an idea of her behavior around other dogs. Look to your friends with dogs first. If someone you know has a pleasantly social dog, you can let your dog meet that one offleash in a safely fenced yard.

A "normal" dog-to-dog greeting goes something like this:

- Dogs approach each other, usually in a curve, and go head to tail, sniffing butts.
- One or both dogs turn so they are side by side or face to face. One dog may lick the other's mouth or they may just stand that way.
- One dog may attempt to initiate play with a play bow, bouncing up and down, or darting toward and away from the other dog.
- The dogs play, or choose to go their separate ways.

A paw or chin on another dog's back can be a sign of play—or something more serious.

Behaviors you do not want to see include:

☼ Very stiff upright postures
☼ Lips pushed forward and/or wrinkles on the muzzle
☼ Ears flattened back and tail tucked

Some body postures are less clear-cut. Watch for other signs to clarify things, such as:

☼ Tail held above back level and wagging slowly—often indicates that the dog is willing to be friends, though cautious, but this attitude can change quickly into a low-level challenge.
☼ Putting a paw or chin over another dog's back—can be part of play, but may also indicate a dog who wants to be in charge.
☼ Air snapping (an exaggerated biting at the air)—can be part of play or a warning to back off.
☼ Erect hair over the shoulders and/or at the base of the tail—this indicates arousal, which might just be excitement over play or could be more serious.

With all of this in mind, watch your dog's interactions with other dogs. If they sniff and then go their separate ways, that's fine. It just means they aren't interested in playing right now.

If your dog will not allow herself to be sniffed, that's a little more troublesome. Sniffing is a normal part of canine interactions, and refusing to do it could signal a fairly high level of insecurity, or a total lack of early socialization with dogs. Give your dog a chance to be around a friendly dog for several visits and see if anything changes. If she allows the other dog to sniff her (even only briefly) after a more extended get-acquainted time, then it's likely that she is just insecure about meeting other dogs. Enlist all your friends with dogs and let your dog have plenty of safe one-on-one experiences with a variety of other dogs. The more she sees that other dogs aren't automatically a threat, the better she will feel around them. Do not take your dog anyplace where she will be forced to deal with other un-

Petfinder.com: The Adopted Dog Bible

known dogs (such as a dog park) while you are working to bolster her courage.

Should your dog exhibit more worrisome behavior when you try to introduce her to other dogs—growling, snapping, running away in panic—you need an assessment from a professional who can watch your dog's reaction and coach you through a behavior modification program.

For those lucky enough to adopt dogs who are happy around other dogs, you can go ahead and let your dog meet others you may encounter on your walks. Always ask first if the other person wants to let the dogs say hello—they may have an adopted dog of their own who isn't ready to meet and greet! Meetings can be a little tricky onleash. You want to keep the leashes slack, because being restrained on a tight leash can force a dog into an artificially upright posture that can be read by the other dog as a challenge, or can create a form of *barrier frustration*. Being restrained from turning around to face each other, being held in certain proximity to the other dog, or having any movement interference from a tight leash can corrupt greeting behavior and result in tension that wouldn't occur if the dogs were free to move about at will. These restraints can change a friendly meeting into a tense one. To avoid this, stand near the other dog's human, and be prepared to maneuver leashes to keep them untangled.

Remain relaxed but vigilant. Don't let sniffing go on for too long. It's normal to sniff, but most dogs don't want an extended inspection. Call your dog away if sniffing continues for more than a few seconds. Wait a moment, then let them get together again.

Some trainers and training centers offer socialization classes, where dogs can romp and play in pairs or small groups under the watchful eye of an experienced trainer. This offers an excellent socialization opportunity, but if you ever feel your dog is being overwhelmed, even if the trainer tells you to "let them work it out," get yourself and your dog out of there. Remember, no one knows your dog better than you, so if you see signs of anything that you suspect might indicate problems, you always have the right to say good-bye and walk away.

Keep in mind that your dog does not have to be able to meet and greet strange dogs well to be the great dog you already think she is. In fact, some dogs simply won't be able to do so—and that is okay. To help your dog become and remain a good canine citizen, your goal is to help her learn to ignore passing dogs. This is not difficult to train and can be done by teaching your dog to heel with attention or to sit and stay with her attention on you.

Dog Parks

More and more communities have put in fenced-off areas specifically for dogs to be offleash, socializing, and running free. Like many aspects of caring for dogs, the dog park can be a double-edged sword. While it can offer excellent socialization and exercise possibilities, not everyone follows the rules, and common sense (among humans) sometimes appears to be in uncommonly short supply.

Don't take your adopted dog to a dog park before you've had a chance to develop a relationship of trust, do some basic training, and learn how she will react to other dogs and people. You could do a lot of damage by taking an insecure dog to a dog park and letting her feel overwhelmed. For one thing, you'll set back her confidence in your ability to keep her safe. Much worse outcomes are possible as well.

So put the dog park on the back burner until you and your adopted dog have spent a good amount of time getting to know and trust each other, and have met many strangers and dogs in controlled, one-on-one interactions. When you do decide you're both ready to pay a visit to a dog park, go with the firm resolution to leave the second your dog shows concern or isn't having a good time. It doesn't matter if you're having a good time being outdoors and talking with other dog owners. Your first responsibility is to your dog.

Choose a time when you know

Common Dog Park Rules

The details can vary from dog park to dog park, but this is the most common set of rules and regulations . . . all with good reasons behind them.

- Dogs must be supervised (some parks specify by owner)
- People must clean up after their dogs
- No more than two (or three) dogs per person
- No dogs with any history of aggression toward humans or other dogs
- No females in heat (some parks specify that dogs must be spayed/neutered)
- No puppies under six months old
- No children under twelve years old
- No people without dogs; no dogs without people
- No choke, prong, or shock collars
- No toys or treats
- Dogs must have current licenses
- Dogs must be current on vaccinations
- No smoking or eating in the dog park
- Dogs must be onleash outside the fence and offleash inside the fence
- Follow any size restrictions for a separate small dog area

the dog park is not likely to be crowded. Stop outside the fence and check out who's inside. If you know the dogs and know they aren't bullies and don't play too roughly, then wait until everyone is away from the gate and make your entrance. If you don't know the people and dogs who are already there, watch how everyone is getting along and how rough the dogs' play style is. If all looks good, enter when the gate area is clear.

In the gate area, take off your dog's leash, then bring her inside and walk around with her. The other dogs may continue playing on their own or they might rush over to meet the newcomer. If the others come over and your dog doesn't seem to welcome the attention, head for the gate at once. Ask the other folks to call their dogs away if necessary. Only stay if your dog appears willing to meet and interact with the other dogs, or if everyone stays away and your dog enjoys wandering the outskirts of the park with you.

Pretty soon, if all goes well, your dog will start interacting with the other dogs in the park. Keep an eye on her at all times, and make sure she's not acting aggressive or being bullied. If you've never seen a group of dogs interacting, you may be surprised at some of their behaviors. Dog play can look and sound pretty intense, but good play involves dogs running alongside each other, chasing or darting about without making contact, or wrestling on the ground. Be aware that dogs running and slamming into others can result in injuries or bad feelings. This is the play style of some dogs, but not others. Either match dogs of rowdy play style (if your dog happens to be one of them), or avoid them if your dog plays more sedately.

Playing dogs should reverse positions often. In chase games, the dog being chased should turn around and do the chasing after a few moments. If dogs are wrestling, the one on the bottom should take a turn at being on top. Dogs who do not reverse and assume the "inferior" position may be bullies. Avoid them. Dogs often call timeouts—suddenly stopping and standing still—and other dogs should respect them.

Remember, the dog park may be for the benefit of the dogs, but the humans are still in charge. If you see something you don't like, either talk to the other people or take yourself and your dog out of the situation. Obey all dog park rules and expect others to do likewise.

Especially important for adopted dogs: Stay only as long as all is going well and your dog is having a good time. To know that, of course, you'll have to be keeping a close eye on your dog. Always keep in mind that dog parks are only as good as the people and dogs who inhabit them.

Establishing a Dog Park

If you don't already have a dog park in your area and would like to, here are some tips for how to approach your local officials and build support for your idea.

Express your interest to other dog parents in your area. Post flyers announcing the formation of a pro-dog-park group—giving time and place of a meeting, or your contact info—in pet supply stores, veterinary offices, and grooming shops. Attend your local kennel club or other dog enthusiast group meetings and bring up the topic of dog parks.

At your first meeting, brainstorm where space may be available in your area for a dog park. Being able to present a realistic plan will help you to be taken more seriously. Develop the basic points of letters to be written to public officials, editorials to be sent to local newspapers, and a presentation to be made to officials.

Make a list of people who should be contacted and start a letter-writing campaign. Include benefits to the community and information about successful dog runs in other areas. (If people have a place to let their dogs off-leash, they'll be less likely to let the dog run through the park; well-exercised dogs are less likely to cause neighborhood problems such as barking, etc.) Note other park areas devoted to specific users, such as tennis courts, softball fields, skateboard parks, and children's playgrounds. You aren't asking for anything more than these other special-interest groups.

Seek endorsements from any high-profile dog parents or enthusiasts in your area, and from local veterinarians or trainers. Ask companies for commitments to donate or discount their products (such as fencing, benches, shade structures, and sewer pipe) that could be used for doggie playgrounds in return for recognition at the finished dog park.

Develop a presentation and present it, not just to city or county officials but to service groups and at other community meetings.

Hand out flyers and/or buttons with your pro-dog-park message in front of supermarkets. Have a petition for people to sign. Ask for time on a local radio station, if your area has one.

If your group is successful, don't disband once you have your dog park. Stay active and become the keepers of the dog park, ensuring that everyone follows the rules and that the dog park actually provides the benefits you promised. Otherwise, your space could be taken away more quickly than it was given.

Workouts

Now that you and your dog can walk together without a struggle, it's time to get out there and get going. Estimates of dogs who suffer from obesity range from one-half to three-quarters of our canine population! Studies show that obese dogs live shorter lives than their fit counterparts, so don't let your adopted dog be part of the overweight canine population. Exercise outings keep your dog pleasantly tired both physically and mentally, and that's a good state of affairs. A properly pooped pup is less likely to bark, chew on things, or otherwise get into trouble at home.

The canine guidelines for safe exercise are remarkably similar to those for humans:

- Don't exercise immediately before or after meals.
- Warm up before exercise.
- Cool down after exercise.
- Stick to a regular exercise schedule as much as possible.
- It doesn't have to hurt to be good for you.

Warm-ups and Stretching

Warm-ups stretch muscles and ligaments and prepare them for activity. So if you bike with your dog, do some walking together before you ask her to run alongside you. If you jog, start out at a walk until your dog is warmed up. Walking serves as a good general warm-up, but if you're really going to ask for a lot from your dog, some additional stretching would be good.

Your dog already knows how to stretch; you just need to get her to do it on cue. You know that lovely fore and aft stretch she does after getting up from a nap? You can put it on cue and then use it before workouts. Have a clicker and treats within reach at all times, and the next time your dog gets up and stretches, click and give her a treat. (See Chapter 7 for more on clicker training.) After you have done this several dozen times, use a vocal cue (like "stretch") as your dog is stretching, then click and treat. After more repetitions, start saying your cue as the dog gets up, before the stretch begins. Continue to click and treat.

This technique is called *capturing a behavior*. It requires a considerable number of repetitions to get the behavior on cue, but it lets you take advantage of behaviors that occur naturally.

If you'd prefer to train a behavior you can use, teach your dog to do figure eights through and around your legs. This tight turning in both directions will stretch her core muscles. To start, stand with your legs about shoulder width apart and your dog at your left side in heel position. Use a treat to lure her in front of your left leg and between your legs to behind your right leg. Some adopted dogs may be reluctant to go under you or between your legs at first. Take your time, and use plenty of treats and encouragement. Once she goes through a few times (and gets rewarded for it), it will stop being so scary to her. Next, lure her around your right leg to the front, and back between your legs again. Soon you should be able to have her make a complete figure eight circuit around your legs. Add a vocal cue. Keep practicing, and soon you'll have a great way for her to stretch those muscles out.

Exercising

Okay, so you're both warmed up, stretched out, and ready to go. But what is the appropriate type of exercise? And how much is too much?

The answers depend a lot on your dog. With an adopted dog, you probably won't have the advantage of a breed profile, but you can compare your dog's build and weight to pictures of purebreds. A dog who resembles a Spaniel or a Border Collie in size and shape is likely to need considerably more exercise than one who looks more like a Mastiff or Basset Hound.

A regular exercise schedule is a better idea than days of inactivity followed by bouts of high-energy activity. Dogs can suffer from "weekend warrior" syndrome just as humans can. My adopted dog, Mojo, and I learned this after he overexerted himself in lure coursing on our vacation at Camp Gone to the Dogs (see www.campgonetothedogs.com). His fatigue and clearly sore muscles were a reminder to me that he and I needed a more regular exercise regimen at home. It's okay to skip an outing now and then because of inclement weather or a crush of other responsibilities claiming your time, but do try to keep your exercise schedule as regular as possible.

If you've got a regular job, this might mean getting up a half hour earlier so that you'll have time for a run before leaving for work, or venturing out after dark when you get home in the winter. Of course, you should always take steps to keep you and your dog safe. Perhaps there's a well-lighted jogging path or public park nearby, or your neighborhood has wide sidewalks and good lighting. Maybe there's a group you could join, or start—maybe even a group of other dog people. However you work it out, put together an exercise plan and stick to it. And should you find that your dog's stamina outstrips your own, that you're finishing a walk or run exhausted while your dog seems to have just gotten started, you might need to hire some help. (See "Finding a Dog Walker" on page 190 for tips on this.) Even if you do turn over some of your dog exercising responsibilities, keep up your own walks with your dog, as well. It's a great bonding experience, and you just may find yourself getting into better shape as well!

On the other end of the spectrum, if you're already an athlete who trains for marathons or bikes a dozen miles at a time, you may need to slowly build up your dog's stamina before she'll be able to keep up with you. If you've adopted a particularly heavy-bodied or short-muzzled dog, she may not ever be capable of joining such a high-powered exercise routine. Here's hoping you made a better match, but part of anyone's responsibility when exercising with a dog is to ensure that exercise is beneficial, not detrimental, to both your health.

Don't forget to help your dog cool down after exercising. If all you do is walk together, when you're done, you're done. But if you bike or jog, slow down for the last ten minutes or so, giving your dog the opportunity to walk rather than trot or run. Some cool down time and a snack once you're back home can help prevent lactic acid buildup in your dog's muscles.

Safety Precautions

For dogs, not exercising after meals is particularly important. Exercising with a full stomach increases the chance of bloat, a life-threatening illness where the dog's stomach distends. Because the dog's stomach swings like a hammock, attached at both ends to other parts of the digestive tract, it can flip over during exercise, squeezing off its openings and trapping gas. Deep-chested dogs who gulp their food are at highest risk, but this could happen to any dog who is exercised on a full stomach. Don't risk it. Exercise first, eat later. If you take a morning run, bring your dog along, take a shower while she cools down, and then feed her breakfast.

During all exercise sessions, keep an eye on your dog. Many of our canine friends will do their utmost to keep up with us, and could sicken or injure themselves in the process. Know how your dog looks when she is moving freely. Watch for any change from that free and flowing movement—a shortening of stride, a limp, anything that looks like she is having to make a greater effort to keep up. Be especially watchful in hot weather, as dogs do not cool themselves as efficiently as humans. If your dog's tongue is hanging out and dripping saliva, this is an automatic body-cooling action, and indicates that she may be starting to overheat. Stop for a rest.

If you are a more active exerciser—biking or jogging rather than just walking—you should bring along water for you and your dog. Just like humans, dogs can get dehydrated from too little water, or cramp up if they drink too much. In addition, drinking too much water can contribute to bloat. So, if you have water available, take breaks to let her have a quick drink (but don't let her lap up a quart), and wet her feet and her belly to help her cool down if you think she needs it.

In colder temperatures there is less to worry about, as most dogs can withstand the cold better than humans, but some dogs require more protection. See "What to Wear?" on page 194 for tips on equipping your dog appropriately for the weather.

You also need to be aware of wear and tear to your dog's footpads. If she's used to playing on dirt and grass, running for miles on pavement can give her very sore feet. The pads need some time to toughen up. Pavement can be especially damaging to dogs' feet in warm weather because blacktop surfaces can become extremely hot. If you can't hold your hand flat on a paved surface for several seconds without feeling a burn starting, it's too hot to run your dog on pavement. Choose a jaunt on grass, dirt, or in the woods instead.

You could have your dog wear booties as her pads adjust, but most dogs don't readily accept footwear. You'll have to invest some time and plenty of encouragement to get your dog to exercise while wearing booties. And if she has serious foot issues (many adopted dogs do not like to have their feet handled at all), then booties are definitely not a good idea. Just take the time to gradually toughen up her footpads, starting out with short exercise sessions on pavement, and gradually increasing their length and difficulty.

Cold weather also brings some foot worries. Rock salt and the various chemicals used to de-ice roads are irritating to canine feet and can be toxic if swallowed while your dog is trying to lick her feet clean. Because of this,

Petfinder.com: The Adopted Dog Bible

always wash your dog's feet in warm water after returning from a winter walk or run. Warm water will also help to melt any ice balls that may have formed in her paws or on her legs. Keeping the hair between her pads trimmed will help keep ice balls from forming. If it's still a problem, you can smear some petroleum jelly into your dog's paws right before you start your walk. Just be sure to wash them when you get back home.

If you are careful, exercising your dog can be safe and happy for both of you.

Finally, your exercise regimen will need to change over time. If you start with a puppy or adolescent, or with a previously under-exercised dog, your exercise regimen will resemble a bell curve, starting with light exercise as she matures and develops stamina, rising to the optimum exercise program for your adult dog, and gradually decreasing again as she reaches her senior years.

Don't stop exercising because your dog is getting older. Just slow down or cut back as appropriate. Exercise is good for aging bodies, both canine and human, as long as it isn't pushed too far. You should be seeing your veterinarian more frequently for wellness checkups as your dog ages anyway, so while you're there, ask about any definite restrictions, such as jumping or running alongside a bike, and some warning signs to watch for. Swimming can take the place of more bone-jarring activities, for example, if you have a lake, pond, or pool available.

Play

When it comes to exercising and entertaining dogs, don't stop at just walking or jogging. There's a whole world of fun activities that you both can share. Some are organized sports, with competitions, titles, and trophies; others are for the sheer fun of it. Your dog will probably be a natural at some and not so enthusiastic about others. Try a variety and see what turns her (and you) on.

Go Fetch

Chasing and/or retrieving rank high on most dogs' list of things they love. This might involve tossing tennis balls, flinging a Frisbee, or kicking a soccer ball. Your dog might be inclined to return the object to you, or she may challenge you to a game of keep-away. Either works, though you can train her to retrieve if you would prefer not to have to do all the retrieving yourself. Just don't forget, these are interactive games. Your dog doesn't want to play by herself, she wants you there with her.

One word of caution: Once playtime is over, don't leave tennis balls around for your dog to chew on. She can likely break the ball into pieces, and those pieces can cause an obstruction if swallowed. Normal soccer balls can also be destroyed, but some balls of similar size or larger are specially made to withstand canine chewing (they were originally designed as horse toys).

If you're playing fetch with a ball, make sure you pick one that is a good size for your dog to hold in her mouth, but not so small that she risks swallowing it. For maximum throwing distance, you can use a tennis racquet or one of many innovative devices made specifically for tennis ball play with dogs. Some of these, available in pet supply stores or at dog supply sites online, helpfully pick up the ball so you don't have to touch it once it's covered in slobber.

Whereas tennis balls are usually picked up from the ground, Frisbees are usually caught. You may have seen high-flying performances at disc dog competitions, but for the safety of your dog, you should toss the Frisbee low enough that she can snatch it out of the air without having to leap. Many veterinarians also caution against using the traditional hard plastic disc, instead recommending one of the softer cloth or cloth and rope options made especially for dogs. These are easier on your pup's mouth and teeth.

Some dogs are more foot oriented and love the chance to bat a soccer ball or similar-sized ball around the yard. If you're going to play soccer with your dog, just be careful not to accidentally kick her as you tussle over the ball or trip over her as you move around together.

Dog Sport

You can take part in a whole world of dog sports with your adopted dog. From agility to tracking, there are many organizations that are more concerned with training than the pedigree, and they will welcome you and your canine partner. Learning how to scramble around an agility course or trigger a flyball box can be a great confidence-builder for less-than-secure adopted dogs.

Agility is undoubtedly the most popular dog sport. Dogs running an obstacle course under the direction of their owners are fast and fun! But you'll need to do some serious training. While you can do a lot of foundation work no matter how young your dog may be, wait to navigate the obstacles themselves until your dog is a year old. Too much jumping, climbing over A-frames, and bending through weave poles isn't good for immature bodies.

Find yourself a trainer who knows how to motivate and control a dog and who understands the demands of agility. Beginning classes should be all about teaching dogs to work close, work away, change directions, and work in different positions relative to you. You'll need all that and more on an agility course. By the time you and she have mastered those basics, your dog will be old enough for the equipment. Be sure that the training you choose allows you and your dog to have fun; trainers who take it all too seriously can lose track of the fact that having a good time with your dog is one of your motivators for doing agility. Mojo and I enjoy our agility classes with Purina Incredible Dog Challenge finalist and agility expert, Susan Rocco, because her main concerns are that Mojo is having a good time and is safe while he learns. She reminds me never to appear disappointed over a missed obstacle so as not to dampen Mojo's enthusiasm for what he considers a great game.

Dancing with dogs, or freestyle, is also gaining in popularity. If you like teaching your dog tricks, this may be the activity for you. You start by choosing a piece of music, then choreograph a routine to it—with your dog as your dance partner. Popular moves include the dog weaving between the human's legs, the dog spinning in circles, backing up, rolling over, or crawling. Pretty much anything goes, as long as it's safe for both partners. Once you and your dog have your routines down pat, you can do demonstrations or compete. The World Canine Freestyle Organization is devoted to the sport, and you can find trainers or other competitors in your area, as well as a list of the rules for competing, at www.worldcaninefreestyle.org.

Rally O is another choice. It's sort of "obedience lite," as it is much friendlier than traditional obedience competition. You follow numbered signs through a course, asking your dog to do such things as sit, down, heel in various patterns, stay, and come. It may be a little harder to find Rally O competitions that accept all dogs (the AKC is one of the major sponsors, and they permit registered purebreds only, though they are considering allowing mixed-breed dogs into a variety of performance events in the future, a change we look forward to seeing).

In response to the exclusion of mixed-breed companions from AKC and other purebred-only dog sports, the Mixed Breed Dog Club of America (MBDCA) was created in 1978. MBDCA is a national registry for spayed and neutered mixed-breed dogs, providing many of the same opportunities that the AKC offers for purebreds, including the ability to compete in obedience and conformation dog shows. It also provides rules for competition in tracking, lure coursing, and retriever instinct. There are smaller mixed-breed dog clubs in various regions across the country, including California, St. Louis, and Oregon. If you'd like to learn more, or see if there's a mixed-breed dog club in your area, go to mbdca.tripod.com.

This has only been a brief overview of the activities available to you and your adopted dog. There are many other ways you can play together, like herding, lure coursing, tracking, flyball, earthdog, and more. While many of the organizations devoted to dog sport accept purebred dogs only, if you and your adopted dog are interested in a specific activity, with a little effort, you can probably find a group to do it with. The United Kennel Club, renowned as a dog performance registry, will let you enroll your adopted dog, whether purebred or mixed-breed, and take part in its activities. Many clubs and organizations devoted to more breed-specific activities, such as herding, care only that the dog can do the job, not whether she has a pedigree, a position we applaud. It doesn't matter what you choose, as long as you get out there and have some fun and exercise with your dog.

Dog Biscuits for the Soul: Nestlé

Nestlé

In the Kitsap Humane Society in Washington, Nestlé was the most inactive dog I'd ever seen. He sat in his bare, tiny puppy run, staring into space. When I carried him to a get-acquainted room and put him down on a bench, he sat exactly where and how I'd placed him.

After a year of living together, he had gotten a lot better, but was still insecure. I started taking agility lessons with him, hoping to help boost his confidence. That went so well, we signed up for a seminar our agility instructor was hosting.

Each day started with dog/handler teams each running a speed circle, a series of jumps spaced around the perimeter of the ring. Nestlé was running his first circle well, but when we were halfway around and starting to come toward the end of the ring where everyone was sitting, Nestlé stopped cold. We had always had private lessons—he couldn't run toward all those people.

We progressed through the rest of the day all right, with lots of treats and encouragement. But when it came time to run our speed circle to start the second day, I was prepared to stop. Nestlé had other ideas. He not only ran his full speed circle, he put on a burst at the end, jumped up onto the rock wall directly in front of the seating area, and stood with his chest puffed out, tremendously proud of himself. Tears still well up even as I write this, thinking of that once spiritless pup and seeing how far he'd come.

Cheryl Smith, Seattle, Washington
Nestlé was adopted from the Kitsap Humane Society in Washington

Resources

McConnell, Patricia, PhD: *The Other End of the Leash*. Ballantine Books, 2003

McDevitt, Leslie: *Control Unleashed*. Clean Run Productions, 2007

Parsons, Emma: *Click to Calm*. Sunshine Books, 2004

Smith, Cheryl S.: *Visiting the Dog Park: Having Fun, Staying Safe*. Dogwise, 2007

www.dogpark.com

Zink, Christine: *Peak Performance*. Howell Book House, 1997

Agility Organizations

North American Dog Agility Council: http://nadac.com

United Kennel Club: www.ukcdogs.com

United States Dog Agility Association: www.usdaa.com

WFCO, The World Canine Freestyle Organization, Inc.: www.worldcaninefreestyle.org

11

Washing and Grooming for Good Looks and Good Health

One of the most loving things you can do for your adopted dog is to wash and groom him regularly. Doing so will keep him looking and smelling his best—big pluses in a companion. More importantly, good hygiene will help keep him feeling good, and may even help him live longer. Proper skin and coat care will help prevent sores, infections, and other potential health problems. Ear and eye care will keep those organs healthier. Regular dental care will promote oral health, which can affect overall well-being. Regular coat and skin care will also help reduce your housecleaning chores, and help prevent the dreaded doggy odor from permeating your home. That's a lot of benefits for a little time and effort. Sadly, lack of proper (or any) grooming lands all too many dogs in shelters and rescue organizations because, through no fault of their own, they have become little stinkers—literally! As an adopter, you can avoid that situation by picking a dog whose grooming needs you can meet, and by keeping your dog tidy and clean. If you'd like some additional tips, Petfinder has some videos that can help. Check out www.petfinder.com/dog-bible for some general washing grooming tips.

Grooming for Good Health

Regular grooming is an important part of a comprehensive health-maintenance and early-warning program for your dog. When you groom, watch for:

- Lumps, tender areas, cuts, sores, or other abnormalities on your dog's body
- Cuts, lumps, bleeding, or bad odor in your dog's mouth
- Excessive discharge, redness, tenderness, or strong odor in or around your dog's ears
- Redness, swelling, excessive tearing, or other abnormalities in or around your dog's eyes
- Fleas, ticks, or apparent bites or irritations on your dog's skin
- Flaky or scaly skin, bald spots or other abnormalities

If you see something that needs attention, don't put off a vet visit. Most problems are easier to cure or manage if caught early.

Grooming Essentials

All dogs need some grooming, and some dogs need lots of grooming. Even if you take your dog to a groomer for the big jobs (see next page), you still need to do some maintenance at home. Besides, grooming sessions are a wonderful time to interact one-on-one with your dog, and if you make it pleasant for him, he'll love to see the grooming gadgets in your hands.

How much grooming equipment you need depends on several factors that we'll discuss throughout this chapter. But no matter what kind of dog you have, you'll need to purchase nail clippers, at least one brush, and doggy dental-care products. If you hire a professional groomer to bathe and clip your dog, you probably won't need much more grooming equipment, unless your dog requires extra ear or eye care or special treatment of some sort. If you do all your dog's grooming at home, you will likely need a few other tools and products.

The fantastic variety of canine hair coats is one of the things that makes dogs so interesting (see Chapter 13 for more on this). It can also make grooming a little intimidating if you don't know what brush to buy or how to use it to make your dog look great. So let's begin with an overview of common grooming tools.

How to Choose a Professional Groomer

To find a good dog groomer, ask your veterinarian and friends for recommendations. Narrow it down to a potential groomer or two, but before you hand over your dog, ask questions and, if possible, pay an unscheduled visit during work hours. Here are some things to check out:

- What training does the groomer have? How long has she been grooming dogs? Does she know how to groom your type of dog?
- Is the shop clean?
- Will your dog be tranquilized? (Do not allow anyone other than your veterinarian to prescribe a tranquilizer for your dog. If your veterinarian does recommend a tranquilizer, ask what training the groomer has in proper use of tranquilizers and in first aid.) Do they have veterinary backup if something goes wrong?
- If they use a cage drier, which blows on your dog while he is in a cage, is someone always present when the dog is exposed to the drier? (If not, go elsewhere.)
- Which of the following services are included: bathing, drying, brushing, trimming, ear cleaning (including removing hair from ear canal, if appropriate for your breed)?
- Will they check the anal glands and express them if necessary? (If you don't know what that means, we'll define it later in this chapter.)
- How long will your dog be there? Will he be in a clean, comfortable, safe place when he's not being groomed? Will he have clean drinking water and be taken to potty in a safely fenced area?

How to Learn to Groom Your Own Dog

With more than two hundred breeds and a gazillion mixtures of those breeds, we can't cover the ins and outs of grooming every individual breed. Here are some ideas if you want to learn to groom your adopted purebred to look like what he is, or to groom your mixed-breed in a manner that suits his general appearance:

- If you adopted from a purebred rescue organization, ask your adoption counselor to show you or give you tips on grooming your dog.
- Contact your local kennel club or breed club and ask whether they have any grooming demonstrations scheduled that you can attend. To find a club, search the Internet for "your breed + club + location" (for instance, "Poodle + club + Indiana"), or ask your vet or local groomers for contact information.
- Contact a responsible breeder, or a groomer who knows how to groom your breed, and ask if you could watch her groom a dog or two so that you can learn to groom the dog you've saved. (Offer to pay for a lesson, or take her a small gift for her trouble.) You can locate a responsible local breeder through breed clubs or by asking the breed rescue group from whom you adopted.
- Check your library, book store, or online sources like DogWise.com for books, videos, CDs, or DVDs that explain how to groom your breed (or one that looks similar to your mixed-breed dog).
- Ask your veterinarian for advice on cleaning your dog's ears, eyes, and teeth, and on trimming your dog's nails.

Grooming Tools

Every pet parent needs a few basic grooming tools, including at least one of the following:

- ✿ Brush (see "How to Pick the Right Brush" on page 220)
- ✿ Nail clippers (see "Foot and Nail Care" on page 231)
- ✿ Dental care tools (see "Oral Health Care" on page 230)

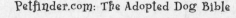

- Ear cleaner (see "Ear Care" on page 228)
- Mild dog shampoo (*do not* use shampoo for people on your dog—the pH is too acidic and will dry his skin and coat)

Rub-a-dub-dub, just relaxin' in the tub

You may also want to have:

- Additional brush(es) or comb(s)
- Flea comb
- Shedding tool
- Nail file or dremel tool
- Blow dryer with cool setting
- Eye-care products
- Electric clippers
- Scissors and/or thinning shears
- Ear powder
- Canine coat conditioner and/or detangler
- Spray bottle(s)
- Grooming table

Now that you have your supplies together, let's put them to use!

Caring for Canine Coats and Skin

Dogs relinquished to adoption programs often have coats that are in very bad condition. Healthy skin and coat begins with good nutrition, which your dog may have lacked before you got him. His coat may have been left dirty, tangled, and matted. If your adopted dog has been in a foster home, volunteers have probably done some remedial grooming to clean him up and relieve him of painful, ugly mats. Shelters usually try to provide basic clean ups as well, but many just don't have the resources for

full-scale grooming, and the real coat-rescue falls to the adopter. If your dog was a stray or you acquired him directly from someone who neglected his coat, you will need to hire a groomer or tackle the job yourself.

If your dog has short, non-matting fur, you might want to jump ahead to "Caring for Shorter Coats" (next page), but the rest of us are going to get rid of a few tangles and mats. Then we'll be able to brush, comb, and bathe these beautiful dogs without making mats worse.

How to Deal with Tangles and Mats

Even well-cared-for dogs sometimes get tangles or mats in their coats, and your adopted dog may come with more than his share. Mats are not only unattractive and painful as they pull against the skin; they are also a health threat. Matted hair traps moisture and dirt against the skin, creating a perfect environment for bacterial and fungal infections and for parasites. Mats often catch, or form around, plant matter and other foreign objects that can injure your dog. Here are some suggestions for defeating tangles and mats without hurting your dog.

Emmie BEFORE

Emmie AFTER

You'd be amazed what a haircut can do.

If you find tangled hair that hasn't yet formed a mat, spray it with conditioner or detangler and let the spray soak in for a minute or two. Then gently tease the tangle apart with your fingers, or with one tooth of a metal comb or pin brush. Work from the ends of the hairs toward the roots, a half inch or so at a time. Try not to pull—we all know how that hurts.

Mats are tougher than tangles. Don't try to pull a whole mat out—that will hurt like crazy, and won't help your dog learn to trust you or the grooming process. To loosen the mat, saturate it with detangler, coat conditioning oil, or baby oil and let it soak for a few minutes. When the mat is completely wet, begin teasing loose a few hairs at a time using your fingers or the end tooth of a metal comb. If the mat is big, you may have to work on it a little at a time to avoid overtaxing your dog (or yourself).

Some dogs who have been neglected for a long time are severely matted. If your dog has a lot of mats, or if the mats are tight to the skin or have caused sores or infections to form under them, it may be easier and kinder to clip off the whole hairy mess. If you do, be very careful. It's easy to cut into living flesh and cause your dog a serious injury. If you are inexperienced, hire an experienced groomer after having your dog examined by a veterinarian. It may be necessary to give him a mild tranquilizer to do the job safely and humanely.

How to Brush Your Dog

Regular brushing removes loose hair, dander, and debris from your dog's coat, stimulates circulation, and distributes skin oils that lubricate skin and hair. Different kinds of canine coats require different tools and techniques (see "How to Pick the Right Brush" on page 220). All require care and gentleness—you don't want to yank your dog's hair or scrape his skin with brushes or combs. During the spring and fall, most dogs shed more than at other times in preparation for the change in season, and a shedding rake will help pull out loose hair more quickly. Talk to your dog in a soothing voice as you brush, and stop once in a while just to give him a smooch. Make this a time you can both enjoy. When your dog behaves well during grooming, give him a small treat occasionally to reward him. Remember, too, that standing still to be brushed can be tiring, so go for frequent, short sessions rather than occasional grooming marathons.

Caring for Shorter Coats

Dogs with short, smooth coats are a snap to keep looking great—think Boxers, Pit Bulls, Greyhounds, Smooth Dachshunds, and dogs with similarly sleek coats. Rub the coat with a gentle, circular motion using a *rubber curry* (a rubber oval with a nubby surface) or a *grooming mitt* (a mitten with nubs in the palm). Finish by smoothing the hair in the direction of growth with a soft bristle brush or a chamois cloth. A daily rubdown is ideal, but even once a week will keep a slick coat in good condition.

Some dogs that we think of as short-haired, like the Labrador Retriever, actually have longer, thicker hair than the truly short, smooth coats. Labs, Lab mixes, and similar dogs have *double coats* in which a soft, dense, warm undercoat layer lies close the skin covered by a straight, coarse outer coat.

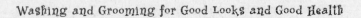

How to Pick the Right Brush

The right brush or comb can make the difference between a relatively easy grooming process with a good-looking result, or a serious struggle and a poorly groomed pup. This chart will help you choose.

TYPE OF COAT	EXAMPLES	BRUSHES AND/OR COMBS
Very short & slick	Boxer, Smooth Dachshund, Pit Bull	Natural bristle brush Rubber curry Grooming mitt Steel comb
Moderately short, single or double	Labrador Retriever, Chesapeake Bay Retriever, German Shepherd Dog	Wire slicker Steel comb
Curly	Poodle, Bichon Frise, many Terriers	Fine curved-wire Slicker brush
Moderately long, straight or wavy	Australian Shepherd, Golden Retriever (body hair)	Steel pin brush Wire slicker Steel comb
Long and flowing	Body coats on Maltese, Yorkshire Terrier, long feathers on legs and tails of Setters, Spaniels, and many other breeds and mixed-breeds	Steel pin brush Wire slicker Steel comb for finishing
Any, to use as needed		Flea comb Shedding tool

The undercoat grows denser in the fall and sheds out in the spring (with some shedding all year long). A slicker brush, which consists of wire pins set into a wooden or plastic base, works well on these coats for regular grooming. Use the slicker or rake only on the neck, body, and tail, where the thicker hair protects the skin below, and be careful not to push too hard. On the head and legs, where hair is thinner, use a stiff bristle brush or a comb to remove loose hair or dirt.

Caring for Medium and Longer Coats

Medium and longer coats come in many styles, and they require more grooming than short coats, although they don't necessarily shed more. This is particularly true with curly coats (think of Poodle-type coats) and some double coats (we see these on Collies, Shetland Sheepdogs, Australian Shepherds, and others). Long, silky coats (think Yorkshire Terriers or Maltese) tangle easily and must be brushed and combed daily, or trimmed to make them more manageable. Many dogs with short to moderately long body coats also have longer hair on the backs of their legs, behind their ears, and on their tails (think of Golden Retrievers or Australian Shepherds). Called *furnishings* or *feathers*, this longer hair tangles and mats easily and collects burrs and other debris, so it should be brushed out several times a week.

Proper brushing of medium to long coats is one activity where beauty really is skin deep. If you brush

What About Shedding?

"Do they shed?" For many people, that is a critical concern when deciding which pup to adopt. Here's the scoop on shedding.

- All dogs shed; some more than others. Some coats catch most of the unattached hairs and hold them until they are clipped or brushed out—we commonly think of these as "non-shedding." Most "non-shedding" breeds have to be clipped or hand stripped regularly. Many of the "doodles," touted as non-shedding, do in fact shed.
- There is no relationship between length of coat and shedding. Some short-coated dogs are notorious shedders, and some long-coated dogs drop very little hair.
- Indoor dogs usually shed year round (more in spring and fall) because of their exposure to artificial light.
- Excessive shedding (more than is normal for the breed or season) may indicate health problems or nutritional deficiencies.
- Regular grooming will reduce the amount of hair your dog leaves around your house.

through only the outer coat, you may leave tangles and mats deep in the fur. Here's how to brush these coats effectively:

1. Before you start to brush, spritz your dog lightly with water or diluted conditioner made for dogs. (Dilute one tablespoon conditioner in sixteen ounces of water in a spray bottle.) Don't drench him—you just want his coat slightly damp to prevent static electricity and hair breakage.
2. Begin at the front of your dog and work toward his tail.
3. Gently part the coat into a manageable section—you should see the skin where the hair is parted.
4. Brush or comb the hair in front of the part against the direction of growth, lifting the hair at skin level and pulling the brush through to the hair tips—in other words, brush each section toward the dog's front end.
5. If you hit a snag, (see the section "How to Deal with Tangles and Mats" on page 218.)
6. Work your way from front to back. Don't forget your dog's belly, groin, and neck.
7. When you have brushed your dog's entire body, begin at his rear end and brush each section of hair in the direction of growth, putting the coat back in place.
8. Finally, comb through your dog's coat with a steel comb to be sure you haven't missed any tangles or tiny mats.

If your dog has long hair behind his ears, legs, and fanny (I affectionately call this "fuzzybutt"), be sure to brush it out thoroughly, as this hair often mats easily. Use a slicker brush to brush small sections of hair in the direction of growth, then smooth the sections together. You can use thinning shears to thin and tidy this hair without making it look chopped off. Trimming away the long hair around your dog's anus and in his or her groin can also help prevent feces or urine from clinging (see "How to Learn to Groom Your Own Dog" on page 216).

If your dog has long, silky, flowing hair (such as a Yorkshire Terrier or Maltese) that you don't want to cut shorter, you'll have to brush or comb him at least every other day. Even a day or two without a good grooming can result in terrible tangles.

Curly and wirehaired dogs also require frequent brushing to undo tangles, prevent mats, stimulate circulation, and distribute oils. They also need more specialized coat care every so often or their coats will grow very long and bushy. Most pets with curly or wiry coats are clipped every month or two for easier coat care. Wire coats, such as those found on many Terriers, can be hand *stripped* to remove dead hairs rather than clipped. Whether stripped or clipped, wirehaired dogs usually need a little scissoring to keep their beards and eyebrows tidy.

Clipping and Trimming

The tools and methods used to clip different types of coats for different purposes are too diverse to cover here. If you want to learn to clip your dog's coat yourself, your best bet is to consult the experts on grooming that breed or a breed that your mixed-breed resembles (see "How to Learn to Groom Your Own Dog" on page 216).

Pet parents sometimes have their dogs' body coats cut short even though the breed is not conventionally clipped. Clipping may be a good choice if your dog has a long coat that you cannot keep free of tangles and mats. It may also give some relief to a dog who has health problems that make him more susceptible to overheating, or if he is elderly. Before you give your dog a buzz cut, though, keep in mind that without his coat your dog is susceptible to sunburn, bug bites, and skin injuries. And if you are motivated by housekeeping concerns, you need to know that clipping won't keep your dog from shedding—you'll just be vacuuming shorter hairs.

Some breeds do benefit from periodic trimming to tidy long, straggly hair on and behind their ears, feet, and tail or, in the case of dogs with docked or naturally short tails, like

How About a Shave?

People sometimes wonder if they should trim their dogs' whiskers—the long, stiff hairs that grow from the sides of the muzzle and under the chin, from points on the cheeks, and over the eyebrows. Whiskers can be trimmed, and often are on show dogs, but while lack of whiskers doesn't actually hurt your dog, it does deprive him of sensory organs and is not recommended. His whiskers are very sensitive, specialized hairs through which your dog experiences his world (much as we do through our fingertips). We can't really know what experiences dogs miss without their whiskers, but we can be sure they miss something. Besides, those stiff little hairs cut short will prickle you when you smooch your pooch!

What's that Smell (and How Do We Get Rid of It)?

Some dogs have a knack for getting themselves good and stinky. Here are tips for cleaning up three particularly offensive (to humans, at least) smells: skunk, dead fish, and "I don't even want to know what you rolled in." Be very careful not to get any of these cleansers in your dog's eyes or ears—if you do, flush thoroughly with water and call your vet.

Skunk: If your dog tangles with a skunk, here's a formula that works for many dog owners:

- 1 quart 3% hydrogen peroxide
- ¼ cup baking soda
- 1 teaspoon liquid soap

Use the mixture immediately (it cannot be stored in a container), while it's bubbly, and rinse thoroughly. It may discolor fabric as well as dark colored fur. Don't leave the mixture on your dog more than a few minutes. Bathe and condition afterward, if you like.

Dead fish: If you spend time with your dog by a pond, lake, or beach, he may anoint himself from time to time with eau de dead fish. Wash the worst of it off with dog shampoo and water, and rinse well. Then saturate the fishy area with lemon juice—freshly squeezed works best. Let it soak for five to ten minutes—a nice time to chat with your dog. (Don't scold him—he's just doing dog things that you could prevent with a leash.) Then rinse, shampoo, and rinse again, and apply conditioner according to directions to counteract the drying effect of the lemon juice.

Icky, greasy, who-knows-what gunk: If your dog rolls in foul-smelling things he finds in the yard or on a walk, a bath with Dawn® dishwashing liquid will probably remove it. Dawn® is often used to clean up wildlife that has been exposed to oil and other toxic substances.

Australian Shepherds or some Spaniels, to tidy up their tail "nubs." It's easy to make a raggedy mess of trimming a coat if you don't know what you're doing, so again, the best way to learn is to ask (or pay) a groomer or someone else who really knows how to handle scissors, thinning shears, and other tools safely, and how to make your dog look dapper.

Petfinder.com: The Adopted Dog Bible

Bath Time

Baths are an essential part of good skin and coat care for dogs. Some dogs rarely need to be bathed, while others need frequent baths to feel, look, and smell their best. Here are some factors that affect how often your dog will need to be bathed:

Condition of his skin and coat: Many dogs arrive in rescue situations with mild to severe skin and coat problems due to poor nutrition, dirty living conditions, parasites, lack of grooming, and other factors.

Genetics: Some breeds have oilier skin than others, and skin oil becomes rancid after a while. Many allergies and other skin conditions are inherited, and many rescued dogs were bred by people who paid no attention to these and other health problems in the dogs they used for breeding.

Lifestyle: If your dog gets wet and dirty fairly regularly, you'll no doubt want to bathe him more often.

Type of coat and other grooming needs: If you keep your dog's coat trimmed short, he will need a bath before every haircut.

Your personal preference: If you enjoy living with a spanking clean dog, or if someone in your household is allergic to canine dander or saliva (deposited on the hair when your dog licks himself), you will want to bathe your dog frequently.

Can you bathe your dog too often? Yes. If you use a mild shampoo formulated for dogs (or a special shampoo if recommended by your vet) and lukewarm water, you can bathe your dog frequently, but even the mildest shampoos can wash away the natural oils and cause dry skin problems if used too frequently. Harsh shampoos and too frequent exposure to a hot dryer will also damage your dog's skin and coat. While dogs' needs vary, you probably won't want to bathe your dog more than every 4 to 6 weeks.

Baths don't have to be traumatic for either of you. If he comes to you in desperate need of a bath, you won't have a choice, but if you can, introduce your dog to the tub or sink before you want to bathe him. Put a rubber mat or damp towel in the bottom of the tub for traction, and stand your dog on it. Praise him, give him a treat, and, if he's calm, let him out. If he struggles, hold him gently but firmly in the tub, talking quietly and stroking him until he calms down. When he stops fighting you, give him a small treat and then let him out. Remember: reward him in the tub, not after he gets out. If he needs extra motivation, try feeding him his meals in the tub for a few days.

When your dog is used to the dry tub, add a little lukewarm water and repeat the process. When he's relaxed about getting his feet wet, begin to wet his body using a gentle sprayer or an unbreakable container. When he's calm about getting wet, he's ready for a bath.

Gather your supplies before you start. Brush your dog to remove loose hair, tangles, and foreign matter. Water in the ear can be extremely annoying and may promote ear infections, so gently insert a cotton ball just inside the opening of each ear to protect the ear canal. We all know that shampoo in the eyes is no fun, and it can cause corneal ulcers, so be very careful to keep soap out of your dogs eyes or protect them with an application of bland ophthalmic ointment (available from your vet, groomer, or pet supply store).

Now for the bath. Here we go, step by step:

1. Put your dog in the tub or sink. Make sure his footing is secure (consider placing a towel in the tub for him to stand on), and that you have control. Remove his regular collar and tags, but you might want to put an old or inexpensive cloth collar on him (wet, soapy dogs are slippery and hard to hold).
2. Wet your dog thoroughly with lukewarm water, but do not place him in a tub full of water as you might do if you were taking a bath. Using a handheld shower head is very helpful.
3. Apply dog shampoo (avoid people shampoo, which may dry out your dog's skin and coat) and work it through his fur, beginning high on his neck and working toward his tail. Don't forget his belly, armpits, groin, and anal area. If you are using a special shampoo to treat a problem (with your vet's approval, please), follow the directions on the bottle. Be careful not to get shampoo in his eyes; if you do, flush them with clean water and call your vet if they seem bloodshot or excessively teary afterward.
4. Carefully use a washcloth with dog shampoo on it to wash his face.

Petfinder.com: The Adopted Dog Bible

5. Rinse your dog thoroughly. Soap residue can irritate his skin and make his coat sticky, and won't do his tummy any good when he licks it off. Check his armpits, groin, and the groove along his belly between his ribs. He should feel clean but not slimy or slippery.

6. Apply and rinse out doggy conditioner, if you wish.

7. Gently squeeze or scrape excess water from his coat with your hands. Your dog will want to shake himself—if he's in the tub, you might want to close the shower curtain to protect the walls and let him have at it. If not, chances are good that he will let you have it!

8. Pat your dog all over with a towel. If he has long hair, don't rub—you'll create tangles that will be hard to comb or brush out.

9. If your dog has medium to long hair, a leave-in conditioner will make brushing easier and reduce static (unless you used a rinse-out conditioner already). Apply conditioner according to directions, and work it carefully through his coat, especially his legs and tail since they're prone to drying out.

10. If you want to blow dry your dog's coat, use a dryer made for dogs or your own hair dryer set on cool—hot hair will dry out his skin, and in warm weather it may cause him to overheat. Don't aim the dryer at any one spot for more than a few seconds—keep it moving to avoid burning or irritating his skin.

11. Keep your dog warm and out of drafts until he is completely dry. You will no doubt also want to keep him off your carpets and furniture.

12. Be sure to replace your dog's collar and ID tags.

13. Most dogs need to piddle after a bath. Take your dog out on a leash—freshly shampooed dogs love to roll in dirt!

To keep your dog clean and healthy between baths, brush him as needed. Some dogs also need a little spot cleaning on occasion—muddy feet at the door, for example, or urine or feces caught in the hair. Clumps of mud or feces should be carefully wiped off with tissue or paper towel before you wash his fur.

To wash small areas, try a dab of dog shampoo on a washcloth, or one part dog shampoo to three parts water in a spray bottle. (Do not spray your dog's face or ears.) Rinse thoroughly with plain water, either on a cloth (rinse, wring, re-wet, wipe, and repeat until all shampoo residue is gone) or in a spray bottle. You can also purchase no-rinse shampoo formulated for dogs

Skin Care for Hairless Dogs

A hairless dog needs grooming, too. His skin is susceptible to sunburn, so you need to apply sunscreen when he goes outdoors. He needs moisturizing lotion and weekly baths to keep his skin healthy, and if he has hair on parts of his body, that needs to be combed or brushed. Finally, he needs his nails clipped, teeth cleaned, and ears and eyes cared for like any other dog.

which, true to its name, does not need to be rinsed out.

If you think you need a visual guide, Petfinder has you covered. Go to www.petfinder.com/dog-bible for a video on canine bath time.

Ear Care

Check your dog's ears every day. The skin lining the ear leather, which is the proper name for the fleshy appendage that we commonly call the ear, and the opening to the internal ear should be clean and pink or flesh colored. Sniff the ear. A mild, musky smell is normal, but a strong, objectionable odor is not. This may be the sign of an ear infection (see Chapter 16 for more information). A little wax on the skin is also normal, but a lot of dirty-looking gunk indicates a problem. If you suspect that your dog has something wrong with his ear, take him to your vet.

If your dog's ears are healthy, you may or may not need to clean them. If they produce a lot of wax (without infection), or if your dog has hanging ear leathers or gets wet frequently, clean them regularly with a cleaner designed to keep the ear canal free of excess moisture, yeast, and bacteria. A lot of recipes circulate for homemade ear cleaners, but some of them are not suited to dogs with a history of infections or other medical problems. Good commercial ear cleaners are also available. Ask your vet or groomer for recommendations on the frequency of cleaning and products to use.

Ear cleaning can be messy. Your dog will shake his head when you release him, so clean his ears where flying cleaner and ear wax won't be a problem. Tie your dog or have someone hold him so he can't walk away mid-cleaning. Follow directions on commercial cleaners. Generally, you squirt the cleaner into the internal ear, then press the ear leather over the opening and massage for a few seconds to move the cleaner around and loosen wax and debris. Then stand back and let your dog shake. When he's finished shaking, wipe the underside of his leathers and the opening to the internal ears gently with a tissue or cotton ball or pad.

Never insert anything into your dog's ears. Doing so can damage delicate organs and impact wax.

Hair inside the ear leather and the opening to the ear canal can be a problem as it holds moisture and can harbor fleas and other pests. Hair in the opening to the canal can be plucked out, though this may irritate the skin and open a path for bacteria. If you or your groomer pluck hair from your dog's ears, check them frequently for signs of redness or irritation and if you see signs of either, don't repeat the process. Apply ear powder (available from pet supply stores) to the hair, especially around the base. Wait a few minutes for the powder to dry the hair, then grasp a few hairs at a time (never a large clump) in your fingers, or with a hemostat (a type of surgical clamp) or tweezers, and pluck them out. If the insides of your dog's ear leathers are covered with long hair, it can be removed with electric clippers or scissors. Test your dog's reaction to the sound of the clippers or scissors before you put sharp blades near enough to cut him. Good-quality dog clippers are made to be relatively quiet but are still terrifying to some dogs, and for a dog who is extremely sound sensitive, even the *snick snick* sound of scissors can be frightening. If your dog tolerates the sound, be careful not to cut your dog's skin, and don't let any hair fall into the ear canal.

Eye Care

Eye injuries and infections, as well as inherited eye problems, are not unusual in dogs who haven't had the best care. In this section, we'll talk primarily about grooming around the eye, routine protection for the eye, and signs of trouble you may notice when grooming (report them to your vet).

It is normal to see some mucous in the inner corners of the eyes. It's not very attractive, though, and it can harbor bacteria that may cause eye infections, so it should be removed once or twice a day by gently wiping it off with a moist tissue or soft, moist cloth. If the mucous or tearing around your dog's eyes seems excessive, or if you notice any swelling, redness, tenderness, or squinting, a quick trip to the vet is in order. (For a more detailed discussion of possible eye problems, see Chapter 16.)

Some dogs, especially those with white or light-colored hair around their eyes, are prone to reddish-brown staining from the proteins in their tears. Keeping the corners of the eyes as free of mucous as possible will help. You can

DIY Tearstain Remover

Note: Always be extremely careful when cleaning near your dog's eyes.

Thoroughly mix equal parts corn starch, milk of magnesia, and hydrogen peroxide to make a creamy paste. The amount you will need depends on the size of your dog, but about a teaspoon each should be enough to get you started. Apply this mixture carefully to the stained area, taking precautions not to get it in your dog's eyes, nose, or mouth. Do not let him lick it off.

Keep your dog's head still, and let the paste stay on his fur for ten to twenty minutes, then wash it out thoroughly. You may want to condition the bleached fur after this process, as it may be brittle. You can repeat this process as necessary every couple of days until the stains are removed.

If you cannot easily keep your dog still for the ten to twenty minutes needed for the solution to work, do not risk this method as the solution could get in your dog's eyes.

also clean eye stains with special commercial cleaners made for that purpose or try the homemade tearstain remover here. Always follow the directions carefully.

Oral Health Care

The good news is that cavities are rare in dogs. The really bad news is that more than 80 percent of dogs over the age of three have gum disease, and among dogs adopted from shelters and rescue groups the percentage is closer to one hundred. Even young dogs who have had poor care often have gum disease, broken or missing teeth, and other oral problems.

Your adopted dog may come to you needing dental care. At the very least, he could probably benefit from a professional teeth cleaning by your vet. If he has other problems that need attention, they could be addressed at the same time. Although relatively expensive, regular professional dental care will make your dog feel better and keep his breath more pleasant for you to be near. Most important, good dental hygiene may prolong your dog's life, because infected gums release bacteria into the bloodstream that can attack organs throughout the body.

Teeth cleaning is done under general anesthesia to give your vet free access to your dog's mouth. Your vet, or her assistant, will remove tartar and plaque, and then polish your dog's teeth. She will check for loose or damaged teeth, which may need to be removed or repaired, and for other signs of trouble. Different dogs need their teeth cleaned with varying frequencies, so be sure to talk to your vet about this.

There's more to doggy dental care than vet visits. Between professional

Desperately Seeking Single, Playful, Loving Companion?

You can find the dog of your dreams in a shelter or rescue group. Just check this wide variety of adopted pure and mixed breed dogs who are currently in committed relationships.

The Sporting Group

Cocker Spaniel–Golden Retriever Mix

Purebred Cocker Spaniel

Cocker Spaniel–Cavalier King Charles Spaniel Mix

Cocker Spaniel–Border Collie Mix

The Sporting Group

Labrador Retriever–Siberian Husky Mix

Purebred Labrador Retriever

Labrador Retriever–German Shepherd
Dog Mix

Labrador Retriever–Basenji Mix

The Hound Group

Bloodhound–Redbone Coonhound Mix

Purebred Bloodhound

Bloodhound–Treeing Walker Coonhound Mix

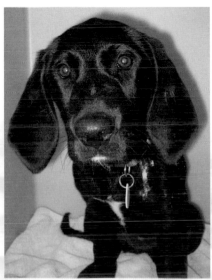

Bloodhound–Labrador Retriever Mix

Purebred Dachshund

Dachshund–Beagle Mix

Dachshund–Spaniel Mix

Dachshund–Terrier Mix

The Terrier Group

Cairn Terrier–Lhasa Apso Mix

Purebred Cairn Terrier

Cairn Terrier–Jack Russell Terrier Mix

Cairn Terrier–Yorkshire Terrier Mix

The Terrier Group

Purebred Wheaten Terrier

Wheaten Terrier–Schnauzer Mix

Wheaten Terrier–Havanese Mix

Wheaten Terrier–Fox Terrier Mix

The Toy Group

Purebred Pomeranian

Pomeranian–Spitz Mix

Pomeranian–Pekingese Mix

Pomeranian–Chihuahua Mix

The Toy Group

Purebred Chihuahua

Chihuahua–Jack Russell Terrier Mix

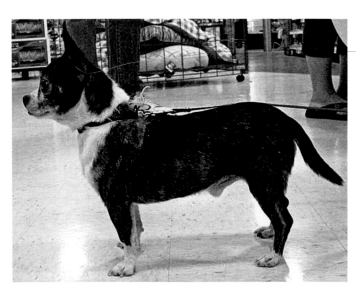

Chihuahua–Boston Terrier Mix

Chihuahua–Pug Mix

The Working Group

Boxer–American Staffordshire Terrier Mix

Purebred Boxer

Boxer–Greyhound Mix

Boxer–Labrador Retriever Mix

The Working Group

Rottweiler–Siberian Husky Mix

Purebred Rottweiler

Rottweiler–Labrador Retriever Mix

Rottweiler–German Shepherd Dog Mix

The Herding Group

Border Collie–Australian Shepherd Mix

Purebred Border Collie

Border Collie–German Shepherd Dog Mix

Border Collie–Labrador Retriever Mix

The Herding Group

Purebred Collie

Collie–German Shepherd Dog Mix

Collie–Border Collie Mix

Collie–Golden Retriever Mix

Chow Chow–Labrador Retriever Mix

Purebred Chow Chow

Chow Chow–Golden Retriever Mix

Chow Chow–German Shepherd Dog Mix

Purebred Bichon Frisés

Bichon Frisé–Shih Tzu Mix

Bichon Frisé–Poodle Mix

Bichon Frisé–Maltese Mix

A Buddy for Life and Every Lifestyle

Road Warrior

Handy Dog

Playground Monitor

Soccer Star

Frisbee Player

A Buddy for Life and Every Lifestyle

Dive Champion

Super Hero

Patriotic Pup

Horseback Rider

A Best Friend

cleanings, bacteria cluster along your dog's gum line. The bacteria form plaque, which hardens into tartar (calculus) if it's not removed. Tartar irritates the gums, causing gingivitis and periodontal (gum) disease characterized by abscesses, infections, and tooth and bone loss. To prevent or slow this destructive process, you need to brush your dog's teeth. Ideally, you should brush them every day, but every two or three days will go a long way toward preventing gum disease. Use toothpaste made for dogs—toothpaste for people can make your dog sick if he swallows it—and apply it with a brush designed for dogs, or a finger brush, or a small disposable dental sponge, whichever you find easiest.

Keep an eye out for signs of oral problems, including red, puffy gums; sudden or prolonged and copious drooling; swelling or lumps; ulcers and sores on the lips, gums, tongue, or other oral tissues; tenderness around the mouth; damaged teeth or tissues; inability to eat, or obvious discomfort when doing so; and foul breath. The sooner you catch a problem and bring it to your vet's attention, the better for your dog and, probably, your wallet.

In addition to a good dental care regimen, you can help keep your dog's mouth and teeth healthy by feeding him high-quality food, and by providing him with safe chew toys that help clean his teeth and gums (see Chapter 8 for more information). The more you can do to remove plaque and tartar from your dog's teeth between veterinary visits, the less frequently your dog will need to undergo a veterinary dental treatment. Since the procedure involves anesthesia—which is never without some risk—and can be costly, it's in your and your dog's best interests to follow a regular dental health regime at home.

Foot and Nail Care

Can you hear your dog's nails clicking when he walks on hard surfaces? Do his nails curl, or touch the floor when he's standing? A "yes" means his nails are too long. Overgrown nails, like poorly fitted shoes, can permanently distort your dog's feet, making walking painful. Long nails are also prone to splitting and tearing. As important as they are to his mobility and overall comfort, though, your dog can't care for his own feet and nails. He depends on you. Although some dogs who take long daily walks on concrete rarely need their nails trimmed, most dogs need regular maintenance.

To keep your dog's paws in good shape, you need to check them frequently,

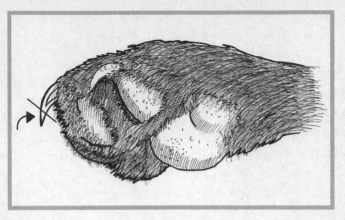

Don't cut too close!

keep his nails short, and, if he has hairy feet, keep them trimmed. Many dogs in rescue situations have never had good foot care, and they often arrive with grossly overgrown nails and other foot problems. Unfortunately, even good pet parents often let foot care slide, often because they're afraid of hurting the dog. But you can learn to trim your dog's nails without drawing blood, and your dog can learn to tolerate the process without being afraid.

The first thing you want to do is accustom your dog to having his feet handled. When he is calm and quiet, enjoying being petted, begin to handle his paws. If he's not used to this, you may have to begin by briefly handling one paw each session. Gently massage his foot and flex his toes lightly. If he tries to pull away, reassure him softly with your voice. Try not to let go of his paw until he stops pulling away from you, but don't hang on so tightly that you hurt or frighten him. Give him a little treat *while you are holding his foot.* If you release it and then give him a treat, he won't associate the treat with letting you handle his foot.

If your dog begins to panic, move your petting hand up his leg to his chest and continue to touch, massage, and scratch his chest. Over the course of several sessions, work your hand down his legs, a little further each time, until you are touching his paws again. Experiment to learn whether he will accept foot handling more willingly in one position than another. Some dogs seem more comfortable lying down for pedicures, while others do better standing up. If your dog prefers to stand, don't pull his foot forward or sideways. Fold it up and back, the way his legs bend naturally, so your dog can balance more easily and be careful not to squeeze his foot as you concentrate on the task at hand.

When your dog will let you handle his paws, begin trimming his nails. You don't have to trim all the nails on all four feet in one session. Your goal is to tidy his nails while teaching him to trust you. If he learns that having one nail at a time trimmed is okay, eventually he'll let you do two, then the whole foot, two feet, then all four in one sitting. If possible, continue to handle his

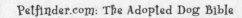

Petfinder.com: The Adopted Dog Bible

paw for a few seconds after you finish trimming, whether you do one nail or a foot-full, so that he doesn't learn to jerk his foot away as you snip.

If your dog's nails are light-colored, you will see a pink area inside—this is the *quick,* the living part of the nail. Blood flowing inside the quick gives it the pink look, and if you cut into the quick, it will bleed and sting, just like if you cut your own nails too short. If some or all of your dog's nails are dark, you won't be able to see the quick, but don't despair—there is a way to tell when you are close to it.

Gather your tools before you settle in—you need canine nail clippers, possibly a file or dremel (electric grinding tool), and styptic powder (available from drug stores) or cornstarch handy in case you cut into a quick. If necessary, have someone hold your dog and reassure him while you trim. Be sure you have good light so that you can see the nails clearly.

Now for the trimming itself. This part scares many people as much as it does their dogs, but it's really not difficult. Let's take it step by step. Talk to your dog in a calm, reassuring voice throughout the process—if his feet have been neglected in the past, or if he's been roughly handled or hurt during past pedicures, it will take him some time to learn to trust you and the process.

1. Pick up a paw and press gently against the foot pad to extend the nail.
2. Part-way down, the nail narrows and begins to curve downward. Position your clipper with the cutting blade on the underside of the nail, so that it will cut from the bottom upward.
3. Trim off the tip of the nail, below the start of the downward curve. Start small—you don't want to cut into the quick. You can always trim a little more if you need to.
4. Check the nail end-on. If you see a black dot at its center, you have reached the beginning of the quick, and it's time to stop. If not, trim a tiny bit more and check again. Do this until you see the black dot. While working to gain your dog's trust in handling his feet and nails, it is better to err on the side of caution and not risk causing your dog pain by cutting the quick by mistake.
5. If a nail bleeds, don't panic—styptic powder or a bit of cornstarch will stop most bleeding. Put a little in your palm or in a shallow dish and dip the nail into it. Reassure your dog, but don't reinforce any

fear he has by making a big deal of it. (If the bleeding doesn't stop in a minute or two, or if it's spurting, hold a clean cloth or tissue against it and call your vet.)

6. Be aware that clipping leaves rough edges that scratch and snag. You can smooth them with a file—the type made for use on acrylic nails work well. File each nail in the direction of growth until the edges are smooth. You can also use an electric dremel tool with a sandpaper head, but safe use of a dremel requires some practice, and the sound of the tool frightens some dogs. If you want to use a dremel, have a groomer or other knowledgeable person teach you how. There is an excellent online tutorial at www.DoberDawn.com.

Trim all your dog's nails, front and back, either in one session or several. Don't forget the *dewclaws*, the nails you find on the inside of the leg, above the foot. Most dogs have only front dewclaws, but some have them on the hind legs as well. Dewclaws are often removed at birth, so your dog may not have any.

Most dogs eventually learn to accept nail trimming without a struggle. However, if you dislike trimming your dog's nails, or if you don't feel you can physically manage the process with an individual dog, it may be worth paying your vet or a groomer a few dollars to do the job.

There are other things you can do to keep your dog's feet healthy. Check his feet frequently, especially if he has been in the great outdoors. Thorns, burrs, glass, and other sharp things can cut or become embedded in flesh or tangled in long hair. Remove them gently, clean cuts and abrasions, and treat them with a topical antibiotic.

Foreign substances, such as oil, tar, salt or other ice-melting chemicals, lawn-care products, and so on, can stick to your dog's feet, damaging his skin and hair. They can also poison him when he licks them off. If there's a chance that he has walked in any toxic substance, wash his paws with a mild detergent, rinse them thoroughly, and check for irritation.

Long hair on your dog's feet can collect debris or ice balls, and cause him to slip on smooth surfaces. To trim it, cut the hair short around the edges of the individual pads and between his toes using electric clippers or scissors. Be very careful not to cut or pinch his pads. Brush long hair on top of his paws against the growth so that it stands up. Lay your scissors along the top of the foot and snip. Brush the hair back down after you're finished.

Anal Gland Care

You know all that doggy butt-sniffing that we humans seem to find either appalling or hilarious? Ever ask yourself what that's all about? You may not think of that dog in your bed as a predator, but at heart, he is. And like all predators, your dog has *anal sacs* (anal glands) located on both sides and slightly below his anus. They produce fluid with a distinctive odor that identifies him and tells other dogs his sex, approximate age, health status, and other things.

Healthy anal glands *express*, or empty, this fluid when the dog has a bowel movement. Unfortunately, some anal glands don't work as they should because of inherited malformations, or because of a history of poor-quality foods that produce poor-quality bowel movements. If the anal glands don't empty properly, they can become impacted, making bowel movements difficult or painful, and potentially leading to infections or abscesses. It's not uncommon for a rescued dog to have a history of anal gland problems. Your dog may damage the delicate tissue around his anus in his attempts to relieve his own discomfort, so if you see him biting at his butt, or scooting it along the ground, take him to the vet.

Impacted anal glands can often be relieved by manually *expressing*, or squeezing out, the fluid they contain. This is a very smelly process, but if you're game you can have your vet or groomer teach you how to do it. Most people whose dogs need their anal glands expressed periodically prefer to pay to have it done.

If your dog's anal glands get impacted frequently, ask your vet to recommend a high-fiber diet to create bulkier stools. If that doesn't work, and if your dog has repeated infections or abscesses from impaction, the anal glands may need to be removed.

My Dog Has Fleas—NOT!

More than just being irritating pests, fleas carry disease and parasites. If your dog is allergic to flea saliva, even a single bite can send him into a frenzy of scratching, leaving his skin irritated, torn, and infected. Here's how to keep the little demons under control:

- When you groom your dog, part his hair and check for fleas or "flea dirt"—tiny black specks of flea feces that resemble black pepper. (If in doubt, add a drop of water. If the water turns red, it's flea dirt, which contains blood from the flea's victim.) Use a flea comb, which catches fleas in dense hair with its narrowly-spaced teeth.
- If you find fleas, you need to mount a comprehensive program to remove them from all your pets, your home, and your yard, and to kill the adult fleas, their eggs, and larvae. Clean everything thoroughly, whether by vacuuming, steam cleaning, or laundering beds, couches, and carpets in hot, soapy water. Make sure to empty or dispose of the vacuum bag, because the flea eggs you've vacuumed up could still hatch. Put everything you can into the dryer, on high heat.
- Ask your vet to recommend an effective topical product to use on your pup. Products such as Frontline Plus are applied topically between your dog's shoulder blades and not only kills fleas on your dog, but also kills flea eggs and larvae. These products are considered relatively safe if applied in accordance with the directions.
- Some products are dangerous if used together. Be sure the products you use are compatible, and follow directions.
- Flea collars do little to control fleas and they can be extremely dangerous for your dog. Don't waste your money.
- Dogs and people can become ill from exposure to some flea collars, powders, and other products, so consult your vet.
- If your dog and home are free of fleas, don't be suckered into continuous use of ingestible or external flea control products. You'll be wasting your money and exposing your dog to insecticides unnecessarily. However, if the problem recurs, consult your vet. Some once-a-month heartworm products also control fleas and ticks.

Natural Flea Remedies

There are also many natural flea remedies that you can use, both preventatively and during or after an outbreak of fleas. While they may not be scientifically proven, many pet parents swear by them. If you're concerned about exposing your pup to too many harsh chemicals, try some of these alternatives. However, it is always wise to talk with your vet before doing so. Simply because a remedy is natural does not mean that it cannot negatively impact your dog's health.

- Many people prefer not to use harsh insecticidal shampoo to kill fleas. As an alternative you can make a ring of regular dog-shampoo lather around your dog's neck right behind his ears to keep fleas from hiding on his head and ears. Lather his body, legs, and tail, and leave the lather on for ten minutes to drown the fleas on your dog's body while you hunt down any on his head with a flea comb. Remove any fleas you find with a flea comb; drop them into a container of soapy water and flush them when bath time is finished.
- Make a homemade repellant with a lemon and some water. Cut the lemon (including the peel) into thin slices, pour boiling water over it, and let it steep overnight. Sponge or spray it onto your dog (be careful not to get it in his eyes), and around your home.
- Make a natural flea collar using essential oils. Each week, put a few drops of eucalyptus oil, tea tree oil, citronella oil, or geranium oil on your dog's collar.
- Put a tablet of brewer's yeast into your pup's food or a spoonful of apple cider vinegar into his water. These will be excreted through his skin, making him less tasty to fleas. Brewer's yeast in powdered form can also be sprinkled on your dog's fur.
- Use essential oils as a topical repellent. Mix 10ml of almond oil with 10 drops of lavender oil and 5 drops of cedarwood oil and shake well. Put one or two drops on your dog's skin twice a week.
- If your dog is already infested, make an herbal flea dip. Steep two cups of fresh rosemary leaves in two pints of boiling water for a half hour (you can double or triple the quantities, depending on the size

continued

of your dog). Strain to remove the leaves, and add warm water until you have about a gallon of the dip. Saturate your dog with the mixture, and allow it to dry naturally.

- Cover a steel brush with a piece of thick rag or towel, pushed down so the tips of the bristles poke through. Put four drops of cedarwood oil or pine oil into a bowl of warm water and soak the brush in the mixture. Brush your dog thoroughly, rinsing the brush in the solution often as you go.

Petfinder.com: The Adopted Dog Bible

Dog Biscuits for the Soul: Louis

Louis

While on vacation, my daughter was checking out Petfinder.com and saw a classified ad about a one-and-a-half-year-old mixed-breed "sheep dog" that sounded perfect for us. The ad had just been listed that day, and it felt like an omen. We immediately contacted the family and expressed our interest in pursuing this after our return the following week. When we got back the family e-mailed us pictures, and it was love at first sight. Louis came to live with us before the end of that month and has been the cutest and funniest dog we have ever had. People at the dog park call him the movie dog. He is sixty pounds, pure white and shaggy, but not a sheep dog mix as originally described—perhaps part Briard and Wheaten. He loves to perform, but only at home or on the phone, and he takes this very seriously. He is bashful in public, so forget David Letterman! When dirty from outdoors, all we have to say is "rub-a-dub!" and he runs upstairs to the bathtub. He has brought so much love and happiness into our lives. With every dog we have owned (all rescued mixed-breeds) we say there could never be a better one, but this time we may be right.

Ellen Baron, Anne Arundel, Maryland
Louis was adopted through a classified ad on Petfinder.com.

Resources

Adamson, Eve and Sandy Roth: *Simple Guide to Grooming Your Dog.* TFH
    Publications, 2003
Webster, Sheila Boneham, PhD: *The Complete Idiot's Guide to Getting and Owning a Dog.*
    Alpha Books, 2002
See Fido.com
www.aspca.org/site/PageServer?pagename=pets_groomdog
www.caninenaturalcures.co.uk/
www.lacetoleather.com/safefleacure.html

12

Neutering Your Dog

Take a stroll through your local humane society or animal shelter and your heart breaks as you pass row after row of cages filled with dogs who desperately need homes. The fact is that we are not finding enough homes for all the animals being born each year. Consider these facts:

- Approximately 34,000 puppies are born in the United States *every day.*
- Millions of dogs are euthanized in our nation's shelters *every year.*
- Over one and a half million pets are adopted each year through Petfinder, and the total number of annual adoptions is even higher than that.

By spaying or neutering your dog, your positive impact is twofold: you will not be contributing to the pet overpopulation problem, and you won't be taking away potential homes from other dogs awaiting adoption.

What Does Neuter Mean?

Neutering refers to the surgical removal of the reproductive organs of a dog (either male or female) as a permanent means of birth control. The process is also known as *altering, castrating, fixing,* or *sterilizing.* Neutering a female dog is often referred to as *spaying*. Neuter surgeries are very common, safe surgeries, and the chances of complications are quite low. Your dog can be fully recovered in anywhere from one to ten days, depending on his or her age and health.

The Benefits of Neutering for Your Dog

Preventing unwanted litters from being born is the most obvious reason to neuter your dog. But did you know that neutering has other health and behavioral benefits as well? Neutered dogs live longer and remain healthier than their intact counterparts. Neutering a female dog before she reaches sexual maturity (at approximately five to six months of age for small- and medium-breed dogs, and eighteen to twenty-four months for some giant breeds) greatly reduces her chances of developing breast cancer, which is common in intact females.

Neutered male dogs are more likely to concentrate on their human families, while intact dogs are likelier to roam in search of a mate. In addition—and often embarrassingly—intact male dogs tend to mount furniture and people when aroused. Neutering a male dog also reduces the incidences of testicular cancer, perianal tumors, hernias, and prostate problems by stopping the production of testosterone. (Over 80 percent of all unneutered male dogs develop enlarged prostates.)

Neutering also diminishes the occurrence of "stud tail," a common condition in unneutered males that causes an accumulation of large amounts of greasy, waxy secretions from glands located on top of the tail. Stud tail can also cause thinning of the hair, black pigmentation of the skin, and bacterial infections. Although it's possible to remove the excess oil by shampooing or clipping the hair around the affected area, neutering your dog is still preferred, even though this doesn't always eliminate or cure the problems associated with stud tail.

Your dog will rebound quickly after being spayed or neutered.

The Benefits of Neutering for Your Community

While saving animals' lives is certainly the most important reason for neutering your dog, saving taxpayer dollars and making our communities safer is part of the picture as well. Every year, millions of dollars are spent on animal control agencies, whose dedicated and hardworking officers have the heartbreaking task of rounding up, housing, and ultimately euthanizing unwanted animals. A combination of research, education, community programs, and legislation need to be enacted to help control pet overpopulation.

Unneutered stray dogs are cause for alarm in many communities. Dog packs not only add to the burgeoning pet overpopulation problem by continuing to mate and reproduce, but they are also responsible for thousands of dog bite injuries each year. (Fatalities due to dog bites are far less common; for instance, in 2007, less than ten such deaths were reported in the United States.) Research has shown that unaltered dogs are three times more likely to bite humans than those who have been neutered, and children are the most common victims.

Is My Dog Too Young to Be Neutered?

For many years, the arbitrary age of six months was accepted as the appropriate time to neuter dogs. However, in response to the overwhelming pet overpopulation problem, veterinarians and animal shelters began offering pediatric neutering, also known as *early age neutering*. The American Veterinary Medical Association (AVMA) House of Delegates approved a resolution on early age neutering as a means of further reducing pet overpopulation. Many other organizations—such as the American Animal Hospital Association (AAHA), the American Society for the Prevention of Cruelty to Animals (ASPCA), the American Humane Association (AHA), American Kennel Club (AKC), The Humane Society of the United States (HSUS), and the California Veterinary Medical Association (CVMA)— endorsed pediatric neutering in the 1990s.

Development of new anesthetics and surgical procedures has made the surgery safe even for very young puppies. In addition, the incisions are smaller, surgery time is reduced, and younger patients recover faster and have no more complications than their older counterparts. Though the procedure has been deemed safe by many veterinarians and the organizations just mentioned, opponents claim that early age neutering will stunt the growth of a young puppy. In fact, the opposite is true. Studies show that early age neutering actually causes puppies' bones to grow a little longer because the growth plate closes later.

Years of research on the physical, behavioral, and long-term effects of early age neutering have proven it to be a relatively safe and effective way to prevent the birth of millions of unwanted animals. (We'll discuss ongoing research into alternatives to surgical neutering a little bit later.)

Some Common Myths About Neutering

Myth: Anesthesia and surgery are too risky.
Fact: Although there is always a risk involved with any type of surgery, neuter procedures are very common and safe, and the benefits outweigh the slight risk involved with anesthesia and surgery. In addition, advances in anesthesiology and surgical techniques have made the procedure safe, even for puppies and older dogs.

Myth: Neuter surgery is too expensive.
Fact: Many humane societies and veterinary clinics offer low-cost neuter services for dogs in their community. In addition, many humane societies and rescue organizations offer low-cost or no-cost surgery for dogs adopted from their facility.

Myth: A neutered dog won't be protective of his or her family.
Fact: Most dogs are naturally protective of their territory. A dog's breed and how he was raised have much more to do with determining his "protective" behavior than his hormones will.

Myth: My dog will gain weight after the surgery.
Fact: Contrary to popular belief, neutering a dog will not necessarily cause weight gain. While it's true that dogs may become less active once they're neutered, they don't automatically gain weight. Overfeeding and not enough exercise are usually the causes of a pudgy pooch. (See Chapter 9 for

more information on the right foods and amounts to feed your dog, and Chapter 10 for proper exercise regimens.)

Myth: My male dog's personality will change due to the hormonal difference.

Fact: Your male dog's personality might alter slightly, but it will actually be an improvement. He may be less aggressive toward other animals (especially other male dogs who are vying for a female's affection) and will be less likely to wander the neighborhood in search of a mate (something your neighbors will surely appreciate).

Myth: A male dog will suffer from low self-esteem after being neutered.

Fact: This myth is perpetuated by humans who believe that neutering diminishes a dog's masculinity. In reality, neutering doesn't cause a dog any emotional trauma, and it will not change basic personality traits. If you're concerned about the way your dog will look after surgery (the absence of testicles), consider "neuticles," a testicular implant procedure for pets (just remember, these are for your sake, not your dog's!). For more information, visit www.neuticles.com.

Myth: A female dog should have at least one litter before she is neutered.

Fact: This is an old notion that has been debunked in recent years. The truth is, the earlier you neuter your female dog, the better her health will be in the future. A female who is neutered before sexual maturity (approximately six months of age for most small- and medium-breed dogs) is much less likely to develop diseases like mammary cancer.

Myth: If we don't neuter our dog, we can breed her, and then sell the puppies to make extra money.

Fact: Even reputable breeders don't usually make oodles of money breeding puppies. The costs of raising a litter, which include health care costs and food for the mom as well as veterinary exams, vaccinations, neuter surgery, and worming for the pups, cuts into profits severely. Additional veterinary care to deal with unforeseen medical issues or emergencies can turn the whole prospect into a money loser very quickly. Finally, it can be extremely time-consuming to care for the little ones—if you think it's easy to clean up after a litter of non-house-trained puppies, think again!

Myth: We should breed our dog so our children can witness the miracle of birth.

Fact: Letting your dog have puppies when there is a huge pet overpopulation problem is irresponsible and sends the wrong message to your children. If you want your children to learn about the birth process, buy a book or DVD on the subject and then donate it to a local charity, so other people may become educated as well.

Myth: I can find homes for all the puppies my dog gives birth to.

Fact: Even if you are willing to find loving, responsible homes for every puppy and make sure they are subsequently neutered by their new families (a daunting task), remember that every puppy that is born takes away a home from a deserving dog in a shelter.

The Future of Sterilization

At the moment, surgically neutering companion animals is the best method we have to manage the pet overpopulation problem. But these procedures are only effective to those who use them, and since so many people don't or can't, there are still millions of animals being euthanized each year. In addition, an emerging body of research—which remains inconclusive as of this writing—has suggested that surgical sterilization can cause some adverse effects in female dogs, such as incontinence, vaginitis, and increased aggression. These findings have not been studied in a systematic way by the veterinary profession, but research like this, combined with the reality that the number of fertile dogs born each day far outweighs the number of dogs being neutered, clearly indicates a need to discover other methods of contraception and sterilization to solve the devastating issue of pet overpopulation in this country and all over the world.

The organization at the forefront of this movement is the Alliance for Contraception in Cats and Dogs (ACC&D), which was founded in 2000 by Drs. Henry Baker, Stephen Boyle, and Brenda Griffin. They are working to expedite the successful introduction of non-surgical methods of neutering companion animals and to support the distribution and promotion of these products to humanely control the pet population worldwide. Their major goal is to develop a drug, vaccine, or implant that is safe, inexpensive, and capable of rendering an animal permanently sterile after a one-time procedure. To learn more about the ACC&D, and the future of contraception for pets, visit their website, www.acc-d.org.

Dog Biscuits for the Soul: Buddy

Buddy

After a long time begging my boyfriend for a dog, he finally agreed! But there was a stipulation. My new friend had to be a Brittany Spaniel. I thought to myself: How am I ever going to find a Brittany in a shelter? I did an Internet search, and that is how I discovered Petfinder.com. What an amazing site! To my surprise, there were Brittany Spaniels in shelters across the United States. I used the great feature Petfinder.com has that updates when new dogs are posted that I am interested in. Finally, there he was! My new Buddy! He was so cute, and he needed me as badly as I needed him. He was not available for another week so that his owners would have time to reclaim him. I was afraid I would not get him, but I went ahead and got supplies for my new buddy anyway. I got him a harness, collar, leash, bed, food, shampoo, and a big comfy bed. I called the shelter to check on him daily, and finally he was released to me. We went straight to the vet for him to get his shots, heartworm and flea preventative, and to be neutered. People were amazed that I was getting this beautiful purebred dog neutered. My reply was that he ended up in the shelter, and I was not going to take a chance with his offspring. He follows me everywhere and listens to me so well. He is even house-trained. He loves my cats. They get along great! Imagine! This sweet boy could have been put to sleep, but now he is making my life much better. That bed I bought him—never used. He sleeps with me and my two cats and another Brittany I recently got from American Brittany Rescue, whom I now foster for.

Angie Sturm, Mullins, South Carolina
Buddy was adopted from Florence Area Humane Society, Florence, South Carolina

Note: The breed, formerly known as the Brittany Spaniel, has undergone a name change and is now called simply the Brittany.

Petfinder.com: The Adopted Dog Bible

We hope we've shown you the benefits of neutering your canine companion: better health and temperament and a longer life for your dog, a reduction in pet overpopulation, and millions of dollars in savings to taxpayers. If you're still unsure about the health benefits or the procedures themselves, discuss it with your veterinarian. If you're worried about the psychological ramifications, talk to a behaviorist. And if you really want more pups around, consider fostering a litter of shelter puppies or adopting another dog!

Resources

Alliance for Contraception in Cats and Dogs: www.acc-d.org

American Society for the Prevention of Cruelty to Animals: www.aspca.org

American Veterinary Medicine Association: www.avma.org

The Humane Society of the United States: www.hsus.org

Spay USA: www.spayusa.org

13

Anatomy 101

Your Dog, Her Body, and How It Functions

There is no species of mammal that exists in such a variety of shapes and sizes as do domesticated dogs. It's amazing that the giant, heavy-bodied, long-coated Newfoundland and the tiny, big-eyed, fragile Chihuahua are both dogs; both from the same species. Both *selective breeding* and *random breeding* have created these differences in size, body shape, coat types and colors, and other variations seen in dogs today.

Selective breeding is the process of planning a breeding program to emphasize certain traits or characteristics. This type of breeding program is what keeps a Greyhound looking like a Greyhound instead of a Rottweiler.

Random breeding is what produces mixed-breed dogs, and this can create as much variation as selective breeding. When dogs of very different breeds (or mixtures of breeds) are bred, on purpose or accidentally, the variations in their offspring can be immense. However, even with all of the different sizes, shapes, and builds of dogs; they are all dogs and share many common characteristics. In this chapter, we'll take a look at your dog's body, identifying the many different parts and seeing how they work.

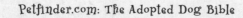

The Head

There are two basic head types, with several intermediate types. The head type that most resembles the dog's ancestor, the wolf, is a long skull with a broad head and a long muzzle. Some breeds with this type of head shape include:

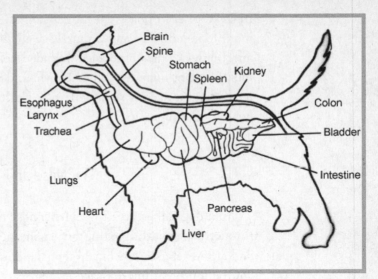

Overview of canine anatomy. See Chapters 13–17 for details.

- ✺ German Shepherd Dogs
- ✺ Siberian Huskies
- ✺ Alaskan Malamutes
- ✺ Belgian Shepherds

Mixed-breeds who have any of these breeds in their background tend to have this head type. A German Shepherd and Labrador Retriever mix, for example, will have a long muzzle with a broad head.

The second basic head type is a wide skull, often rounded, and a very short muzzle, which is called *brachycephalic*. Some of the breeds with this head shape include:

- ✺ Japanese Chins
- ✺ Pekingese
- ✺ Pugs
- ✺ Bulldogs

Mixed-breed dogs who can claim a brachycephalic breed as an ancestor usually have a longer muzzle than the purebred brachycephalic dogs, but still a much shorter muzzle than other dogs. Puggles, for example, a mix of Beagles and Pugs, tend to have a medium-length muzzle rather than an extremely short one, because Pugs are brachycephalic and have an extremely short muzzle while Beagles have a medium-length muzzle.

In between these two extremes are many other breeds which share some traits from each head type. American Cocker Spaniels, for example, have a more rounded head and a muzzle of medium length. Australian Shepherds and Border Collies have a less rounded head but also have a medium-length muzzle. Sight hounds such as Greyhounds, Borzoi, and Salukis, have a long muzzle but a narrow skull with less width between the ears. The variety of head types is immense!

The Nose and Mouth

Your dog will breathe through her nose normally, although she can breathe through her mouth (panting) when she needs more oxygen, such as during and after exercise. The brachycephalic dog breeds often have small, tight, or convoluted breathing passages which can cause breathing difficulties, and these dogs may pant even when breathing normally.

Your dog will also pant and breathe through her mouth when she's hot, either after exercise, or simply in response to the temperature of the air around her. A dog's tongue is relatively thin and thin-skinned, and as your dog pants and moves air over her tongue, the evaporation of moisture off the tongue helps cool her off.

Most dogs have forty-two teeth designed to catch, grab, and hold prey, and so are strong and well-rooted in the mouth. Some breeds have an inherited problem of missing teeth. Doberman Pinschers, for example, may be missing two or more teeth, often the premolars, and many of the hairless breeds have an inherited defect that can cause missing teeth. When a dog is only missing one or two teeth, there is usually little effect on her ability to eat; however, if she is missing several teeth, she may have eating difficulties.

Most dogs have an excellent sense of smell, although the brachycephalic breeds, because of their difficulty breathing and their shortened muzzle, do not scent as well as those breeds with a longer muzzle. Contrary to popular belief, a cold, wet nose is not necessarily a sign of good health. A dog's nose is damp to enhance her sense of smell.

Taste, however, isn't affected by muzzle length at all, and doesn't seem to be as important to dogs as it does to people. Most dogs eat their food by chewing once or twice and then gulping, so the food doesn't stay in the mouth long enough to be really tasted.

Petfinder.com: The Adopted Dog Bible

The Ears

Dogs' ears come in a variety of ear shapes and sizes. The common groupings are prick ears, bat ears, semi-prick ears, and dropped ears.

Wolves, coyotes, and many other wild dogs have upright ears, called *prick ears*. Domesticated dogs with prick ears include:

- German Shepherd Dogs
- Alaskan Malamutes
- Siberian Huskies
- Belgian Shepherds
- Dutch Shepherds

The bat ear is similar to the prick ear, but it is wider at the base and rounded at the tip. Breeds with bat ears include:

- Chihuahuas
- French Bulldogs

A semi-prick ear is upright, but the tip folds forward slightly. Breeds with this type of ear include:

- Shetland Sheepdogs
- Collies

Dropped ears hang naturally from the head. These ears can vary in size, from the Australian Shepherd's relatively small ears to a Basset Hound's huge, pendulous ones. Breeds with dropped ears include:

- Beagles
- Basset Hounds
- Foxhounds
- Coonhounds
- Australian Shepherds
- English Shepherds
- Border Collies

Cropped ears are ears that are cut to form a specific shape or to make ears stand upright that might normally hang. Although cropped ears used to be very common, they are losing popularity as more and more pet parents prefer the breed's natural ears and more veterinarians are refusing to do the surgery, finding it inhumane. The American Animal Hospital Association (AAHA) developed a position statement that ear cropping should not be performed unless medically necessary, and the AAHA encourages the elimination of the procedure from breed standards. Cropping a dog's ears is now illegal in many countries, and there are movements in the United States to make the unnecessary cosmetic procedure illegal in all fifty states. There are no proven health benefits regarding ear cropping. However, some breeds that may be subjected to ear cropping include:

- Doberman Pinschers
- American Pit Bull Terriers
- Great Danes
- Giant Schnauzers
- Standard Schnauzers
- Miniature Schnauzers

Regardless of the size or shape of the ears, your dog's ears enable her to hear—and she hears *very* well. Although ear shape generally doesn't affect ear health, many dogs with heavy, pendulous dropped ears may be more prone to ear infections than dogs with ears that get more air circulation (see Chapter 16 for more on this). In addition, those dogs with prick ears or cropped ears can sometimes be more prone to the bites of flies during hot weather.

The Eyes

Your dog's eyes are those of a predator; she will notice things that are moving before she registers those that are not. (This is why so many prey animals, such as rabbits, will freeze in place when they spot a predator.) How well a dog might see depends upon the breed's original occupation. Sight hounds, those breeds designed to hunt by sight (rather than scent), have a wider and longer field of vision than those bred for other purposes.

Some breeds, including Pugs, Pekingese, and Chihuahuas, have rounder, more protruding eyes, which are not protected by a bony brow ridge like many other breeds. This leaves the eyes potentially more vulnerable to injury (see Chapter 16 for more information).

The Neck and Body

Just like humans and other mammals, a dog's neck connects her head to her shoulders and body. Depending upon the length of the vertebrae, the neck may be long, such as on Greyhounds, or short, as on Pugs. The angle of the neck also depends upon the breed. Doberman Pinschers normally carry their heads high and have a more upright neck, whereas many herding breeds, such as Border Collies and Australian Shepherds, normally carry their heads forward and lower than Dobermans.

The dog's body is supported by her musculoskeletal system. The skeleton provides the internal support structure. Dogs have a similar skeleton to people, although many of the bones are shaped a little differently due to the difference in body posture. The dog's muscles, tendons, ligaments, and other support structures are also very similar to those of humans, but designed for the dog's skeletal structure.

The amount of bone and muscle mass a dog has is dependant upon the dog's breed and the breed's original occupation. Greyhounds and other sight hounds, for example, were designed to run very quickly, and they had to be able to turn on a dime to catch their prey. These breeds have deep chests for a runner's large heart and lungs, lean muscles, and fine yet strong bones. Mastiffs, on the other hand, were used as a property guard dogs. They had no need for speed but instead had to be strong, powerful, and visually imposing. Mastiffs have a broad head with strong jaws, are wide chested, heavy boned, and powerful. The Greyhound can be compared to a human marathon runner while the Mastiff is more like a heavyweight bodybuilder.

Many of the dog's body, organ, and other functions are very similar to those of humans as well:

* **The Circulatory System** is made up of the heart, arteries, veins, and smaller blood vessels. As blood is moved through the body, oxygen and nutrients are carried to the cells and waste products are removed.

- ☼ **The Digestive System.** After food is eaten, it moves through the digestive system, is broken down into its chemical parts, and is absorbed by the body. Wastes are then excreted.

- ☼ **The Urinary System.** The kidneys filter the blood, remove wastes, and send the waste on to the bladder, along with any excess water in the body. The bladder stores the water and wastes as urine, which is then excreted.

- ☼ **The Endocrine System**. This system includes a variety of glands (including the ovaries, testicles, thyroid, and pancreas) that produce hormones which affect and govern bodily processes.

- ☼ **The Respiratory System.** Air comes in through the nose or mouth and is brought into the lungs. In the lungs, oxygen is taken in by the body and exchanged with carbon dioxide, which is then exhaled. Because dogs do not sweat except for a small amount through the pads of their feet, the respiratory system also helps regulate the dog's body temperature.

- ☼ **The Nervous System.** The brain controls all the processes in the body, from breathing to muscle movements. The nerves and spinal cord carry messages from the brain throughout the rest of the body.

And there's more! The immune system works to keep the dog healthy, and the digestive system makes sure all the vitamins and minerals are absorbed in correct amounts, while the enzymes trigger all the needed chemical reactions throughout the body. The bone marrow in the bones creates blood cells while the lymphatic system supports the immune system and assists the cardiovascular system. Your dog has a complicated body and it's amazing it works as well as it does.

The Tail

Your dog's tail is much more than simply an appendage to be waved when she's happy, although her tail *can* help you read her body language and moods. A dog's tail aids in balance when she twists, turns, or jumps, and it can even work as a rudder to aid the dog when she's running fast and hard.

Petfinder.com: The Adopted Dog Bible

Tails, like ears, are found in a variety of shapes and sizes:

- **Saber:** The saber tail is very common, and is carried lower than the hips in a soft curve like a saber. The German Shepherd Dog and Belgian Shepherd have a saber-shaped tail.
- **Wheel:** The wheel tail is carried high over the back and is curved into a wheel shape. A Samoyed is one breed with this tail.
- **Corkscrew:** The corkscrew tail is relatively short and twisted. Pugs and Bulldogs have a corkscrew-shaped tail.
- **Gay:** A gay tail is carried very upright from the hips. Many terriers, including the Welsh, Norfolk, and Norwich Terriers, have a gay tail.
- **Plume:** A plume tail is carried out from the hips. It has a plume of coat that is long at the hips and tapers to a shorter length at the tip. Irish Setters, Gordon Setters, and Golden Retrievers have a plumed tail.
- **Otter:** This thickly-muscled tail is often used as a rudder by swimming dogs. Labrador Retrievers are the most common example of dogs with an otter tail.
- **Docked Tails:** Similar to ear cropping, tail docking is a process where the tail is cut, usually within a day or so of birth, to make it shorter. Although this dates back to the Roman Empire, where working dogs' tails were shortened to identify them as valuable, the practice today is purely cosmetic and is a subject of much debate. There is no proven health benefit to a docked tail; in fact, a tail that has been docked too close to the body can cause a number of serious problems, including hernias and urinary incontinence. As with ear cropping, the AAHA encourages veterinarians to counsel and educate pet parents that these procedures should not be performed unless medically necessary, and encourages the elimination of these procedures from breed standards. Tail docking is illegal in some countries, where it is considered inhumane, and many opponents would like to see this unnecessary cosmetic procedure made illegal in the United States as well.

The Legs and Feet

As predators, the ancestors of today's dogs had to be strong, fast, agile, and able to run and leap to catch and bring down prey. Although selective breeding has changed the body shape, leg length, and size of many breeds of dogs, just as selective breeding has changed ear and tail shapes, dogs still retain some characteristics of their ancestors.

Dogs' back legs are relatively rigid and strong. They have a joint, called the *hock*, about one-third to one-half of the way up the leg that allows the bottom half of the leg to bend forward. There is another joint, called the *knee*, where the leg meets the thigh. This allows the leg to be folded or drawn up under the body. The rear legs have another joint at the hip that allows the legs to swivel as they move.

The front legs are more agile than the back legs. Dogs do not have a collar bone between their front legs and body, as people do between their body and arms, thus allowing dogs a greater range of motion. The front legs bend at the *carpus* (often called the *wrist*) and elbow, and move from the shoulder. The front legs also have a tremendous reach for running, leaping, and climbing.

Dogs walk on their toes, and have claws that do not retract. These enable a dog to grip firmly when running hard or climbing. Most dogs also have a vestigial thumb called a *dewclaw* on the front legs. Some breeds have a dewclaw on each of the rear legs, and a few have several rear dewclaws. The dewclaws are often removed surgically to prevent them from getting caught on brush or other objects, and thereby causing injury to the dog.

The Skin

The skin is the largest organ on a dog's body, just as it is for people. A dog's skin protects her from loss of temperature as well as water loss, and it shields her body from infection or injury. Although some breeds have been bred to be hairless, most dogs have skin covered in hair. The hair is more than just cosmetic; it also serves to maintain the dog's body temperature and to protect the skin from injury.

Coat Types and Textures

Dogs have an immense variety of coat types and textures, from the curly coats seen on Poodles to the stiff fur of a Shar Pei. Although some breeds are advertised as being good for people with allergies to dog hair or dander, each person's allergic reactions are different. The different coat types are:

- **Single Coat:** This coat has only one type of hair and has no under-coat. Dalmatians have a single coat.
- **Double Coat:** This coat has a thick, warm undercoat close to the skin, and a coarser outer coat. The outer coat is usually made up of *guard hairs*. German Shepherd Dogs, Australian Shepherds, and Shibu Inus have a double coat.
- **Smooth Coat:** This coat lies close to the body and is smooth to the touch. Doberman Pinschers, Miniature Pinschers, and French Bull-dogs have smooth coats.
- **Wirehaired or Broken Coated:** This is a coarse outer coat that is harsh and well-suited for inclement weather. Border Terriers, Wire Fox Terriers, and Wirehaired Pointing Griffons all have this coat.
- **Medium-Length Coat:** A coat between one and five inches long is considered medium-length. Australian Shepherds and Border Collies have medium-length coats.
- **Long Coats:** Dogs with hair that is longer than five inches over most of their bodies are considered long-haired. All the Setters, many of the Spaniels, and Afghan Hounds are all long-haired dogs.
- **Corded Coats:** These coats form long, vertical tangles of fur that over time become quite solid. Although rarely seen this way, Poodles can have corded coats, as do Pulis and Komondors.

Besides being found in many textures, hair can also vary in its growth and whether it sheds. Poodles have coats that continue to grow, just like human hair, and must be cut at regular intervals. Other breeds, such as Siberian Huskies, have coats that will grow only to a specific length.

Dogs usually shed in the spring and fall, losing their winter coat in the spring and growing a heavier coat in the fall. Female dogs who haven't been spayed often shed during their twice-yearly season.

Most dogs shed, even many of those advertised to be non-shedding. What happens with many of these dogs is that instead of losing a lot of coat all at once as most dogs do, they lose a few hairs on a regular basis. Many of these hairs then get caught in the coat where they are pulled out during grooming rather than floating off to land on your furniture.

Coat Colors and Patterns

The great variety in dogs can also be seen in the numerous colors and patterns of their coats. Although some breeds are always one color, such as the white Samoyed, other breeds may be found in a variety of colors and color patterns. Some colors include:

- **White:** May be a pure white with no other colors, or may include shadings of cream, beige, or biscuit.
- **Black:** Usually reserved for dogs that are entirely black with no (or just a few) hairs of other colors. The coats of black dogs who spend a lot of time in the sun often bleach to a reddish-black.
- **Brown:** Ranges from a reddish-brown to a deep, dark brown that is almost black.
- **Red:** Any color that contains shades of red, from reddish-gold through liver or rust.
- **Yellow:** Any shade of beige, pale cream, biscuit, or gold.
- **Gray:** From pale silver gray to blue-black gray.

Common coat color patterns include:

- **Single Color:** Some examples include white Samoyeds, Kuvasz or Komondors, all-black German Shepherd Dogs, and gray Weimaraners.
- **Two-Color Coats:** Common examples include Dalmatians, Rottweilers, and Doberman Pinschers.
- **Classic Tri-Color:** The pattern on these dogs' coats has a base color, a marking color, and an accent color. Papillions, for example, can be prominently white, with black markings and tan accents on the legs, cheeks, and eyebrows. Bernese Mountain Dogs may be predominantly black, with white markings and rust or tan accents.
- **Tri-Color:** These dogs do not fit the classic tri-color pattern but have three distinct coat colors. Beagles, Basset Hounds, and Foxhounds are very commonly three colors.

- ❖ **Brindle:** A mixture of hairs of several colors, including brown, tan, gold and/or black; often in a striped or tiger pattern.
- ❖ **Merle:** A patched or marbled coat of related colors, such as a blue merle that has shades of gray, silver, and black.
- ❖ **Particolor:** Two distinct coat colors with patches of color.

Although the immediate genetic inheritance differs from breed to breed, the genes that determine coat color can also control or affect other aspects of a dog's development or health. Most coat colors have no effect on the dog's health, but that is not always so. Merle colored dogs (such as blue or red merle Australian Shepherds), for example, should never be bred to each other as their combined genetics can lead to puppies with hearing and vision defects. In many breeds—Boxers for example—individual dogs with a lot of white on the head, especially around the eyes or ears, may have vision or hearing defects. See Chapter 16 for more on this.

Now that you have a basic understanding of all the different parts of your dog's body, let's move on to the next chapter on ways to keep her healthy.

Dog Biscuits for the Soul: Bruno

Bruno

Bruno is a beautiful, seven-year-old Maltese. His previous owners dropped him off at the Columbia Animal Shelter. Fifteen days later, my family and I adopted him after finding his precious picture on Petfinder.com. Bruno looked as if he needed the love and care that we wanted to give. We called the shelter to find out a little more about him. He had just been neutered, he had kennel cough, and they had removed all but six teeth. Bruno's previous owners had allowed his hair to grow down around his teeth, causing major tooth decay. He was still healing from all his surgeries. After traveling an hour to go get our new baby, we anxiously awaited his arrival in the lobby area. We heard the clicking of his nails on the floor, and the assistant said, "Wait, Bruno!" He was so eager to greet us! Before he even rounded the corner, I knew he was exactly the dog I had been looking for. Thinking about our first meeting, I still get emotional. Although his situation was pitiful (he did not even know his own name, he had breathing problems, an enlarged heart, and a heart murmur), we have given him love, attention and medical treatment. Bruno has improved greatly in both his behavior and health. It is inspiring to watch his progression in learning how to love. He now knows his name, has learned a few commands, and has learned how to kiss. He is the perfect dog for us—a baby that needed our love and also our help. He was waiting for us to come get him.

Lauren Medlin, Chester, South Carolina
Bruno was adopted from Columbia Animal Shelter, Columbia, South Carolina

Resources

Bonham, Margaret and James M. Wingert, DVM: *The Complete Idiot's Guide to Dog Health and Nutrition*. Alpha, 2003

Goldstein, Robert VMD and Susan Goldstein: *The Goldsteins' Wellness & Longevity Program*. TFH, 2005

Messonnier, Shawn DVM: *Natural Health Bible for Dogs & Cats*. Prima, 2001

Palika, Liz: *The KISS Guide to Raising a Puppy*. DK, 2002

Thornton, Kim and Debra Eldredge, DVM.: *The Everything Dog Health Book*. Adams Media, 2005

Volhard, Wendy and Kerry Brown, DVM: *Holistic Guide for a Healthy Dog*. Howell, 2000

14

Health Basics for Your Adopted Dog

The primary challenge the family of an adopted dog faces is the lack of information about their dog's past, especially health information. If you can learn anything about your dog's health history from his previous family or from his shelter or foster caretakers, take advantage of the opportunity. However, if your dog has come to you with no information at all, that's okay, too. You can still care for him; but let your veterinarian know what you do and do not know.

There are several infectious diseases that can be potentially dangerous to your dog. While a few will only threaten his health, others are fatal. In this chapter you'll read about effective vaccinations that can prevent the onset of most of these diseases. As beneficial as vaccinations are, however, there can be problems with vaccination use, which we'll also discuss.

Infectious Diseases

The diseases that affect dogs (and all canines, wild and domestic) can be spread in many ways, through a viral or bacterial infection, parasites, funguses, and so on. Most are spread through direct contact with another dog, or contact with an infected dog's urine, feces, or droplets from a sneeze or

Your vet is your partner in your dog's good health.

cough. Some of these diseases are very serious; others are more of a nuisance. All should be taken seriously and treatment should be supervised by your veterinarian.

Canine Distemper (CDV). Canine distemper is a viral infection that is almost always fatal. It usually begins with a high fever, a discharge from the nose and eyes, and a dry cough. There is often appetite loss, vomiting, and diarrhea. The virus may then attack the nervous system, causing seizures. The disease can be spread through contact with an infected dog or the dog's urine or feces, or through contact with the clothing of someone who has been with an infected dog. There is no cure for CDV although your veterinarian can provide supportive care, and most dogs affected will die. CDV is not contagious to people.

Canine Influenza. This disease, which is also called the *dog flu,* is a highly contagious viral respiratory infection. The first symptom is usually a soft, moist cough that can last for ten days to a month. Mild cases—dogs with just a mild cough—are often mistakenly thought to be kennel cough. In severe cases, the cough progresses to secondary infections, including pneumonia with a high fever. Supportive care is necessary for most dogs, even those with milder cases, but is especially important for the dogs who develop secondary infections. Five to ten percent of dogs with the severe form of the disease die. This virus is spread through contact with an infected dog. It is not transmittable to people. Although researchers are working on a vaccine, as of this writing it is not yet available.

Infectious Canine Hepatitis (CA). Infectious canine hepatitis is a virus that can be fatal. The first symptoms include severe thirst, fever, vomiting, eye and nasal discharge, and diarrhea. Because this virus affects the liver, there will also be jaundice, a hunched back (because of liver discomfort), and blood in the stools. CA may also attack the kidneys, eyes, and blood vessels. The virus is spread through contact with an infected dog's urine, feces, or saliva. Treatment includes supportive therapy (including intravenous fluids) and antibiotics for secondary infections. This is not contagious to people.

Canine Parvovirus. This virus is also called *parvo* and is a relatively new virus that appeared in the United States in the late 1970s, destroying entire kennels full of dogs. This virus can be fatal, especially when it attacks puppies and older dogs. The first symptoms are usually fever, depression, severe bloody diarrhea with an odd, unusual odor, and vomiting. Puppies are most susceptible and most likely to die from this virus. Parvo is spread through contact with an infected dog's vomit or feces. The virus is extremely durable and can live in contaminated soil for up to one year. Treatment of infected dogs consists of supportive therapy (such as intravenous fluids), as well as treating the diarrhea and vomiting. Parvo is not contagious to people.

Rabies. This fatal disease is caused by a virus. Infected animals usually die within a few days of the onset of the disease. The virus attacks the brain and the first symptoms usually include drooling, loss of balance (staggering), and changes from normal behavior. Infected dogs may not be able to swallow. Dogs often get it when they catch, touch, or are bitten by an infected wild animal. Rabies is contagious to and from almost all warm-blooded animals, including people, and is transmitted through contact with an infected animal's saliva. Vaccination against Rabies is necessary to protect your dog and is required by law.

Leptospirosis. This is a bacterial infection that usually begins with a high fever. The dog will also urinate more frequently and may have diarrhea or vomit with blood in it, and will be depressed. The dog may stand with a hunched back because of abdominal discomfort. This virus is transmitted through contact with an infected dog or the dog's urine, from infected rodents, or contaminated water. Although leptospirosis can be fatal without treatment, antibiotic and supportive treatment are usually very effective. Leptospirosis can be transmitted to people and is very serious; if you suspect that your dog is infected, call your veterinarian right away.

Canine Adenovirus. This is one of several diseases often referred to as *kennel cough*. The primary symptom is a dry, gagging cough. It is rarely serious and most dogs will recover without treatment, though your veterinarian may recommend an over-the-counter cough suppressant so that you and your dog can both sleep easier. However, very young puppies and older dogs may need supportive treatment to prevent pneumonia. This is spread through droplets in the air when the dog coughs, so in a situation where many dogs are in close quarters—such as in a kennel—it can spread rapidly. It is not contagious to people.

Canine Parainfluenza. This is another virus often referred to as kennel cough and it is very similar to kennel cough in symptoms and treatment. The primary symptom is a dry cough. This virus is rarely serious and most dogs will recover without treatment. However, very young puppies and older dogs may need supportive treatment to prevent pneumonia. This virus is also spread through airborne droplets when the dog coughs, so in a situation where many dogs are in close quarters, such as in a kennel, it can spread rapidly. Like canine adenovirus, it is not contagious to people.

Bordetella. Bordetella is a third form of kennel cough, but one caused by a bacteria rather than a virus. The first symptom is a dry cough. Some dogs will cough as if they are gagging or have something caught in their throat. This virus is rarely serious and most dogs will recover without treatment. However, very young puppies and older dogs may need supportive treatment to prevent pneumonia. Like the previously mentioned diseases, this is spread through droplets in the air when the dog coughs, so in a kennel or shelter situation where many dogs are in close quarters, it can also spread rapidly. Like the other forms of kennel cough, it is not contagious to people.

Lyme Disease. This bacterial disease is transmitted by the bite of infected deer ticks. It is most prevalent along the East Coast and Upper Midwest in the United States, but it continues to spread. The first symptoms include fever, joint pain, loss of appetite, and depression. Treatment consists of antibiotics and often needs to continue for a long period of time. Although Lyme disease cannot be transmitted to people directly from an infected dog, people are just as susceptible should they be bitten by an infected tick.

Coronavirus. This virus is more serious in puppies than adult dogs, and can cause severe dehydration. The first symptoms include diarrhea and vomiting. It is rarely fatal, although the dehydration in puppies can certainly be dangerous. It is transmitted through contact with an infected dog, or the dog's urine or feces. It is not contagious to people.

Giardia. Giardia is a microscopic organism that lives in water. It originated in the Rocky Mountains but now has spread through many water systems across the country. Unfortunately, some pets contract Giardia from dog-friendly recreation and swimming areas. When your dog, or a wild animal, drinks infected water and consumes this organism, he may develop diarrhea and vomiting, and may lose weight. Giardia is usually treated with anti-protozoals but may need a long course as it can be tough to kill. It is also extremely important to clean up after your dog and treat the environment; preventing the accumulation of standing water or moisture and bathing the dog can help prevent reinfection. People are as susceptible to Giardia as dogs and other wild animals.

Vaccinations

When your dog is exposed to a disease, his immune system produces antibodies to help fight the disease, preferably before he becomes sick. But even if your dog does get sick, the antibodies will work to prevent a re-infection later.

Immunity to disease can also be created artificially by giving your dog vaccinations, which expose him to the disease in very small measured and treated doses, causing his body to produce antibodies. There are several types of vaccinations available for dogs:

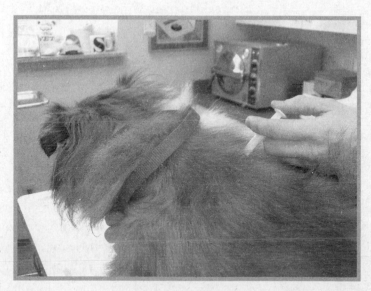

Ask your vet what schedule she recommends for boosters.

- **Modified Live Virus (MLV).** The vaccine is made by introducing the virus into a host that is not a dog (such as chicken eggs) or modifying the vaccine in tissue cultures. MLV vaccinations usually produce long-lasting results, although boosters (defined later in this chapter) are usually recommended.
- **Killed or Inactivated Virus.** These vaccines contain dead viruses that cannot replicate in the dog but can still stimulate the immune system.
- **Recombinant Vaccines**. This new technology in vaccinations uses gene-sized fragments of the virus or bacteria. These fragments are combined with a noninfectious virus, for example, and yet are still enough to stimulate the dog's body to create antibodies.

Core and Noncore Vaccines

Vaccines for dogs are divided into two categories. The *core* vaccines are those that most veterinarians consider necessary to protect a dog from a potentially life-threatening disease. Most veterinarians and the American Animal Hospital Association consider the following to be core vaccines:

- Canine Distemper
- Infectious Hepatitis
- Canine Parvovirus
- Adenovirus
- Rabies

Noncore vaccinations are those that may be a problem in a particular community or region. Obviously this can change; what threatens dogs in the Southeastern part of the United States is not necessarily a problem in the Northwestern regions. Noncore vaccinations may also be recommended if your dog is going to be traveling to a particular region or is going to be boarded in a kennel. These include:

- Leptospirosis
- Parainfluenza
- Bordetella
- Lyme disease

Petfinder.com: The Adopted Dog Bible

Other vaccinations, such as those for Giardia and Coronavirus, should be given only if your veterinarian recommends them. Also, see Chapter 18 for a discussion on nosodes, the homeopathic equivalent to vaccines.

Vaccination Schedules

Vaccination schedules vary as do the reasons for vaccinations. Some veterinarians prefer to give vaccinations separately (distemper only, or hepatitis only, for example) so that the dog's body can build individual antibodies to a single disease rather than being potentially overwhelmed with multiple diseases. Other veterinarians don't see a problem with combined vaccines (such as one that includes distemper, hepatitis, and parvovirus). While the norm may still be to give a combined vaccine, if you would prefer to vaccinate your dog to single diseases, your veterinarian can obtain individual vaccinations for you. You need to be your pet's health advocate and if you would prefer not to overwhelm your dog's immune system with multiple diseases at once, a concerned veterinary professional should be happy to work with you. The age at which puppies should begin their vaccinations varies, too, as does the need for boosters.

The following schedule is based upon one recommended by the American Animal Hospital Association's 2006 Vaccine Guidelines and is one followed by many veterinarians. However, if your veterinarian prefers to follow another set of guidelines, that's fine; just ask her to explain why she feels those might suit your dog better.

- Rabies (Core): 1 dose at 3 to 6 months of age.
- Canine Distemper (Core): 1 dose at 6 to 8 weeks of age, followed by another dose every 3 to 4 weeks until 12 to 14 weeks of age.
- Parvovirus (Core): 1 dose at 5 to 8 weeks of age, followed by another dose every 3 to 4 weeks until 12 to 14 weeks of age.
- Adenovirus (Core): 1 dose at 6 to 8 weeks of age, then every 3 to 4 weeks until 12 to 14 weeks of age.

Your veterinarian can also provide guidance regarding the noncore vaccinations, especially regarding whether those diseases are a problem in your area. If you plan on traveling with your dog, either to dog shows, performance events, or just to go camping, let your veterinarian know, as this can affect your dog's vaccination needs.

Reactions

Although adverse reactions to vaccinations are not common, they can happen. It's usually a good idea to wait in your veterinarian's office for fifteen to thirty minutes after a vaccination just to be sure no reaction will occur.

Sometimes a reaction may just be some redness or mild swelling at the injection site, but anaphylactic shock (paleness, shallow or rapid breathing, agitation followed by lack of response, vomiting and/or diarrhea, and more) can also occur. If this happens, your dog will need your vet's assistance right away.

Vaccination Boosters and Titer Testing

Natural exposure to a disease usually produces lifelong immunity to that disease; however, vaccinations do not always do the same. Booster vaccinations are given at a specified time after the initial vaccination so that the dog's body continues to produce antibodies.

When and if a booster is given is based on many factors, including the dog's age, his state of health, the disease involved, and whether the dog has actually been exposed to the disease. Many veterinarians (and dog parents) today are concerned about the dangers of giving too many vaccinations.

An over-abundance of vaccinations can stress the immune system and possibly even lead to other serious health problems. For these reasons, many veterinarians, at the request of their clients, are performing a blood test to check the titer, or level of antibodies, in a dog prior to administering booster shots. If the dog's titers are high and strong, there may be no need to re-vaccinate.

This issue is especially relevant for your adopted dog, as dogs in the rescue system can often be over-vaccinated. If a dog was vaccinated in his first home, but then ends up in a rescue group or a shelter with no health records, he will be vaccinated again. If the dog is then transferred to a foster home, he will most likely receive more vaccinations. When adopted, he will go to his new veterinarian, where in all likelihood, he will be vaccinated once more. All these vaccinations are given so that the dog will be protected against potentially dangerous diseases; however, the repetitive vaccinations can also threaten his health.

Most rescue groups and shelters survive on very limited budgets and do not have the funds to have blood titers for vaccinations run on every dog in

Petfinder.com: The Adopted Dog Bible

the system. However, as the parent of a newly adopted dog, it is very important for you to talk to your vet about running titers on your dog prior to giving him vaccinations. The test will cost more than a vaccination would, but the health benefits to your new pup will be worth it. I have had a titer run on my adopted dog, Kona, for both distemper and parvo for the past seven years. He is thirteen years old now and has not required a booster for either disease since I decided to start titering when he was six years old. When I first requested this service, the folks at my veterinary office thought I was crazy; it was not a common procedure at that time. However, over the years they have become accustomed to my taking an active role in my pets' health care choices and because they know I have my pets' best interests in mind, they welcome my input, questions, and concerns.

Vaccination Failures

Vaccinations can be extremely effective and have saved thousands, if not millions, of dogs' lives. Unfortunately, even with all their successes, vaccinations are not a magic wand and are not always effective. Vaccinations can fail for many reasons, including:

- The mother dog's antibodies. Puppies will continue to be protected by their mother's antibodies until between ten and sixteen weeks of age. Vaccinations given before the mother's antibodies have disappeared will be ineffective.
- A depressed immune system. If the dog has an immune system disorder of some kind, the vaccinations will probably not cause the immune system response necessary to protect the dog.
- The dog is sick. A dog that is sick should rarely be vaccinated, as the dog's immune system may already be too stressed. Your veterinarian will need to weigh the pros and cons before deciding to proceed.
- Handling the vaccines. Vaccines can be very fragile and must be handled correctly during manufacturing, transportation, and at your vet's clinic. If they aren't, their effectiveness can be compromised.
- Administering the vaccine. Some vaccinations should be injected via needle and syringe under the skin, while some need to be injected directly into the muscle. Other vaccinations come in mist or liquid form and are squirted up the nose. Although some dog parents give

their dogs vaccinations themselves, it is important to do so correctly. If given incorrectly, the vaccine will be less effective or potentially completely ineffective.

Vaccinations are important; they save dogs' lives by preventing many serious diseases. However, vaccinations should not be taken lightly; they are serious medicine and over-vaccination (giving too many in too short a time, giving unneeded vaccines, or giving boosters when they aren't needed) definitely has the potential to cause health problems for your dog. So talk to your veterinarian, ask for her vaccination recommendations, and then ask for her reasoning. Don't be afraid to ask questions; you are responsible for your dog's continued good health and your veterinarian should welcome your interest, concern, and questions.

Signs and Symptoms of an Injury or Illness

You may know when your adopted dog had his last vaccinations but you will not know whether his parents were healthy nor whether he's had any health crises earlier in his life. Sometimes it's easy to tell when your adopted dog needs veterinary care, but at other times you may not recognize a potential problem. Some symptoms can be very clear while others may be subtle; it can be tough to be a responsible pet parent.

Listed below are some signs and symptoms that you may see in your dog. These will be described briefly and a few possible problems will be listed. Then you will be advised as to what action to take: to treat this as an emergency and get your dog to the emergency clinic immediately; to call your veterinarian right away for guidance; to call your vet during the next business day; or to call when it's convenient. This listing is not designed to replace your veterinarian's advice, but instead, to help you make a decision as to what needs to be done.

When you call your veterinarian, always be prepared to give very detailed information. Don't try to make the vet guess why you're calling! Depending upon the reason for your call, your vet will want to know:

- What is the specific problem?
- What made you notice it? What are the symptoms?

- What is the dog's temperature?
- Has the dog eaten today? If so, how much? Is that normal for him?
- Has there been any vomiting? How much? What was in the vomit?
- Has there been any diarrhea? How much and how often? What was in the diarrhea? Was there any mucus or blood?
- Has the dog been anywhere or done anything that could have caused this problem?
- How long has the problem been going on?
- Any change in his activity level in other behavior? Is he sleeping more? Hiding?

If your dog is unusually lethargic, he could be sick.

The following list contains symptoms of illness, which are listed alphabetically for ease of reference.

Allergic reaction: Dogs, and particularly puppies, who require a lot of vaccinations, can have an allergic reaction to their vaccinations, so it's usually a good idea to remain at the vet's office for fifteen to thirty minutes after any vaccination. Dogs can also have an allergic reaction when they chase and catch a bee or a wasp. If you see swelling at the site of a sting or bite, panting, and any paleness in the dog's gums, call your vet immediately; this is a potential emergency. She may advise you to give your dog an antihistamine right away and to bring him directly to her office.

Appetite loss: Many dogs may refuse to eat when they have a stomachache, but it may also be a sign of something more serious. If your dog misses two meals in a row and acts as though he doesn't feel well, call your veterinarian as soon as you can. Watch puppies in particular, as they rarely refuse to eat; a good appetite usually means a healthy puppy. However, puppies may not eat when they're teething, so if his gums are red and swollen, offer the puppy an ice cube to chew on. An older dog may lose his appetite for several reasons. His teeth may hurt him, he may not feel well, or there could be something going on internally. Try warming his food slightly to see if the increased smell stimulates his appetite. If that doesn't work, call your veterinarian the next business day. Don't allow a senior dog to go for several days without eating.

Bad breath: Bad breath, which may occur more frequently in older dogs, is most often caused by dental disease. When plaque builds up on the teeth, the gums can become inflamed and infected, causing significant problems, not just in the mouth but in the rest of the body as well. If you notice that your dog has suddenly developed bad breath, his teeth have a plaque build up and his gums look red, call your veterinarian to schedule an examination as soon as you can.

Bleeding: Bleeding from minor cuts or scrapes can usually be stopped by applying direct pressure to the wound. However, if the blood is spurting, as from a damaged artery, this could become life-threatening very quickly. Apply pressure to the wound and get the dog to the veterinarian or to an emergency clinic immediately.

Body temperature: A dog's normal temperature is between 100.5 and 102 degrees Fahrenheit. If the temperature is slightly above or slightly below those values, if there are no other signs of illness, don't worry. Each body is an individual. However, if there is a significant change in body temperature—two degrees higher or lower— call your veterinarian for guidance. Whether it's an emergency depends upon how high or low the temperature, and any other symptoms there might be.

Breathing changes: If at any time your dog's breathing changes from normal, pay attention. If your dog is panting because he's been playing hard, or because the weather is hot, he's probably fine. But if he's panting for no apparent reason, if he's breathing heavily, or if he can't seem to catch his breath, call your veterinarian immediately; this is potentially an emergency.

Change from normal: Although many dogs, especially puppies, can be pretty good about showing when they don't feel well, not all are. Interpreting their signs is not always easy. If there is any change from normal—tenderness anywhere on the body, wincing, crying—and you can't figure out the cause, call your vet right away.

Coughing: A wet cough could signal a respiratory infection; this should be treated by your veterinarian as soon as possible, as older dogs may not be able to handle it well. A dry cough combined with restlessness and anxiety may be the onset of congestive heart failure. Call your veterinarian to schedule an examination.

Cuts, scratches, and bruises: As long as the bleeding stops, these are rarely an emergency and most can be cared for at home by cold-packing the wound (wrap an ice pack in a hand towel and hold it against the injury), cleaning it gently, and putting an antibiotic ointment on a cut or scratch. However, if a cut continues to bleed, call your veterinarian as soon as you determine the bleeding is not going to stop with direct pressure on the wound.

Deafness: Many dogs lose some or all of their hearing as they age. You may first notice this when your dog stops responding to his name or to well-known commands. Don't get angry or view this as disobedience. Instead, talk to a dog trainer for some assistance, and begin teaching your senior dog hand signals! Old dogs *can* learn new tricks, especially if they're lovingly taught. When you get a chance, confirm the diagnosis with your veterinarian.

Diarrhea: Your dog shouldn't have watery stools or stools with mucus or blood in them. If the dog has these stools once or twice a day, call your veterinarian for a checkup as soon as possible. If the diarrhea is very watery, lasts more than one day, contains blood or significant amounts of mucus, or has a bad odor, take your dog in right away. It often takes several months for a puppy's digestive tract to develop the beneficial bacteria needed for the correct digestion of foods, so soft (not firmly formed) stools are not unusual. However, like all other dogs, a puppy shouldn't have watery stools or stools containing mucus or blood and if diarrhea is very watery, lasts more than one day, contains blood or significant amounts of mucus or has a bad odor; or if your puppy refuses to eat or play, take him in to your veterinarian right away. If it's after your vet's regular hours, call the emergency clinic.

Eye problems: If your dog's eyes are runny or have discolored matter caked on the lashes or at the inside corners of the eyes, call your veterinarian. She may have you wipe the discharge away from the eyes and observe them for a day or so, or she may want to see your dog. Also call the vet if your dog has excessive tearing from one or both eyes, redness or swelling around an eye, or is squinting. Several things, including an injury to the eye, can cause these symptoms, but certain diseases can cause changes to the eyes as well.

Foggy eyes: Several different diseases can cause vision problems or loss in older dogs. If you see your dog's eyes begin to get a little gray or foggy, schedule an appointment with your veterinarian so that she can determine if there is a problem.

Head tilt: Your dog has a problem with one of his ears if he tilts his head to one side, bothers the ear on that side, has a bad odor in the ear, and/or repeatedly shakes his head. He may have something in the ear or he may have an ear infection. Either way, he needs veterinary help before he continues to bother that ear and hurts himself. If your dog tilts his head but does not have an ear problem that you or your vet can determine, he could have an inner ear problem or a more serious disease. Either way, call your veterinarian as soon as you notice the head tilt.

Limping: If your dog is limping on one leg, he has probably hurt it in some manner. You can try to feel the leg, gently, to find the injured area. Be careful—if the limb is very painful, your dog may try to bite. If you find the source of the problem, call your veterinarian for advice. However, if your dog is putting no weight at all on the leg, or if the leg is swollen, deformed, or obviously broken, immobilize the leg by wrapping it thickly with gauze or a towel, and call your veterinarian right away.

Lumps and bumps: Older dogs often develop lumps and bumps under the skin as they grow older. Although some of these can be cancerous, not all are. However, your veterinarian should check them just to be sure. If you feel a lump or bump and it's not painful or hot to the touch, keep an eye on it and call your vet when it's convenient. However, if a lump is hot, painful, bursts, grows rapidly, or the skin over it changes color, call your veterinarian to check it right away.

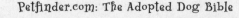

Pain: Older dogs, like older people, develop aches and pains. Their muscles aren't as strong as they once were, and if the senior dog goes out to play fetch, he may be sore the next day. Joints may ache, especially in colder weather, and many senior dogs develop arthritis. As your dog grows older and as you first begin to see signs of pain, call your veterinarian at your convenience. There are some medications and supplements available that may alleviate some of the discomfort. However, if the pain appears suddenly or seems to be more intense than an ache, call your vet right away, as it could be a sign of something serious.

Personality changes: An aging dog may get grumpy, especially if he has arthritis and it hurts to move. Dogs can also develop dementia. If you see any gradual changes in your dog's personality, maintain as normal a routine as possible, keep your senior dog comfortable, and call your veterinarian when you can. However, if your dog's personality changes abruptly, especially if he also seems to be in pain or uncomfortable, call your veterinarian right away.

Rash: A rash, redness, flakiness, or itchiness on the skin can be symptomatic of many different things. The dog may have been in contact with something that he's allergic to, or he may be reacting to a new ingredient in his food. He could have been bitten by a flea and then scratched the skin raw or he may have been stung by a bee. If there is no swelling, just redness or a rash, this is not life-threatening. However, call your veterinarian for an appointment and before you take your dog in, see if you can find out what caused the reaction.

Seizures and convulsions: Dogs can have seizures for many reasons, and just because your dog has one doesn't mean he has epilepsy. There are many different kinds of seizures, from minor trembling coupled with a blank stare to severe convulsions that cause the dog's entire body to shake and thrash. During a seizure the dog will not be aware of his surroundings, may bite out of reaction or fear, and may empty his bowels and bladder. Every seizure—no matter what its cause and how mild or severe—should be reported to your veterinarian, because it could signal a serious health problem. Most vets will want to see the dog within twenty-four hours of a seizure.

Snake bite: A snake bite is not necessarily dangerous unless the snake is poisonous. However, if you cannot recognize the snake, didn't see the snake, or you suspect that it might be poisonous, get your dog to your vet or to an emergency clinic right away.

Squinting: A dog who is squinting one eye may have something in the eye or may have scratched it. That eye needs to be examined as soon as possible, preferably before the dog rubs it and injures it even more. A dog who is squinting both eyes also needs to be seen right away as he may be sensitive to light or he may have dry eyes.

Stiffness and pain: Arthritis can cause senior dogs to move very stiffly; many may even wince or cry when they first move, especially in cooler weather. As your dog grows older and as you first begin to see signs of pain, call your vet. There are some medications and supplements available that may alleviate some of the discomfort.

Thirst: There could be several reasons why a dog drinks a lot of water and urinates often. It may be a side effect of a medication, or it may signal the start of diabetes, kidney, or liver disease. If your dog's drinking or urinating habits change, take him for an examination soon.

Urinating more frequently: If your dog has been asking to go outside more often than normal, and perhaps has even had some accidents in the house, he may have a urinary tract or bladder infection. Frequent urination can also be a symptom of other problems. Call your veterinarian and schedule an examination very quickly.

Urination is strained: If your dog is trying to urinate but cannot, or cries when he urinates, call your veterinarian and take the dog in as soon as possible. He may have a urinary tract blockage or he may have bladder stones.

Vomiting: Dogs, especially puppies, often eat things they shouldn't, so don't panic just because he throws up; it's the body's way of getting rid of something that shouldn't be there. Withhold food for about twelve hours, then offer bland foods such as rice and boiled chicken. However, if the vomiting doesn't stop after a couple of hours, call your veterinarian right away. If there is blood in the vomit, the vomiting is nonstop, or is accompanied by bloody diarrhea, this is an emergency. Go directly to the emergency clinic.

Weight gain: Dogs usually slow down as they get older and don't play or exercise as much as they used to. If the amount of food they eat remains the same, they will gain weight. This can be controlled by cutting back on calories and increasing the dog's daily exercise. However, unexplained weight gain should be evaluated by your veterinarian; call for an appointment when you can.

Weight loss: Weight loss can be caused by several different problems, including cancer. If your dog attempts to eat but drops or spits out the food, he may be having pain in his mouth. If he's eating ravenously but is still losing weight, he may have diabetes. In any case, unexpected or rapid weight loss is not an emergency but needs to be checked by your veterinarian as soon as possible.

Wounds: A cut or scrape that stops bleeding is rarely serious and can be treated at home by gently cleaning the wound, applying an antibiotic ointment, and cold-packing (wrap an ice pack in a hand towel and hold it against the injury). However, if the wound doesn't stop bleeding with direct pressure, get the dog to the vet or to an emergency clinic right away. If the wound stops bleeding but is gaping open, it needs stitches and immediate veterinary care.

Pay attention to any change in your dog's body, normal routine, energy levels, and personality. Dogs vary in their responses to injuries or illnesses; some are very stoic and won't show any symptoms until they're really uncomfortable, while other dogs will yelp or cry at the least hurt. It's important that you get to know your dog; know what's normal for him so that you can recognize when anything changes. Anything that is different from normal could signal a potential problem. And although you don't need to run your dog to the emergency room for every hiccup, don't hesitate to call your veterinarian's office for guidance if you're concerned.

First Aid 411

Even for the most diligent, responsible dog parent, accidents can still happen. Your dog might step in a hole in the ground and twist a leg, or run through bushes and scratch an eye. He might chew on a stick and swallow a splinter. Like any parent, you cannot control every environmental variable that may affect your dog. However, if you're well prepared and keep this book nearby as an easy reference, you can handle whatever occurs. Listed below are guidelines as to when to call the veterinarian should your dog hurt himself.

Call your veterinarian or the emergency vet clinic immediately and follow their directions if your dog experiences any of the following:

- Has trouble or difficulty breathing
- Has been injured and you cannot stop the bleeding within a few minutes
- Has been stung or bitten by an insect and the site is swelling
- Has been bitten by a snake
- Has been bitten by another animal (including a dog) and shows any swelling or bleeding
- Has touched, licked, swallowed, or in any way been exposed to a poison
- Has persistent diarrhea or vomiting for more than a day
- Has been burned by either heat or caustic chemicals
- Has been hit by a car
- Has any obvious broken bones or cannot put any weight on one of his limbs
- Has a seizure that doesn't stop after a few seconds
- Is panting excessively, wheezing, unable to catch his breath, breathing heavily, or sounds strange when he breathes

In these emergencies, treatment has the best chance of being effective if it is started right away, so don't delay calling your veterinarian. If it's going to take a little while for you to get your dog to the clinic, the vet may be able to tell you how to start emergency first aid on the way. Because of this, and for daily first aid needs, a well-stocked first aid kit is very important.

First Aid Kit

- Activated charcoal tablets (to help prevent the absorption of many types of poison)
- Adhesive tape, several rolls one and two inches wide (to secure bandaging or splints)
- Antibacterial ointment, safe for doggy skin and eyes
- Antidiarrheal (such as Pepto Bismol)
- Antiseptic wipes (to clean cuts, scratches, and small wounds)
- Aspirin, buffered or enteric coated, not Ibuprofen (for mild pain relief)
- Bandages: gauze, several rolls one and two inches wide, and dressing pads (for bandaging wounds)
- Benadryl (for allergic reactions, including bee stings and insect bites)
- Blanket(s)
- Bowl for water
- Cortisone spray or cream
- Cotton balls and cotton tip applicators (for cleaning wounds and for applying medications)
- Disinfectant, such as Betadine
- Disposable latex gloves
- Dosing syringe (for administering liquid medications)
- Ear cleaning solution
- Elastic wrap (for securing bandages or splints)
- Eyedropper (plastic)
- Eyewash solution
- Extra leash and collar
- First aid instruction booklet
- Hand sanitizer
- Hydrogen peroxide (3 percent) (can be used to clean wounds, and to induce vomiting in some instances of poisoning—but only use in this capacity with your veterinarian's instructions)
- Instant cold compress (to reduce pain and swelling after an injury)
- Lubricating jelly (to lubricate the rectal thermometer)

continued

- Mineral oil (can be used as a lubricant, or a laxative if given orally)
- Muzzle (to prevent your dog from biting when he's scared or in pain)
- Nail clippers
- Paper towels or rags
- Pen light (for looking into your dog's ears, eyes, or throat)
- Plastic bags (to keep wounds dry and clean, or to use as makeshift gloves)
- Rubber gloves
- Rubbing alcohol (to sterilize any tools that you might need, including the thermometer)
- Safety pins
- Saline solution (for flushing wounds or eyes)
- Scissors, both rounded tip and sharp tip
- Soap (anti-bacterial)
- Styptic powder (can be used to stop bleeding)
- Thermometer (rectal with a flexible tip)
- Tongue depressor
- Towel (to secure your dog if he is scared, or to dry him off if he's wet. A large towel can be used as a sling to carry your dog)
- Tweezers
- VetWrap (a stretchy bandage to support sprains or protect wounds)
- Water

Emergency Procedures

Emergencies happen, unfortunately, but you can deal with anything that occurs as long as you are prepared and can remain calm. A calm, gentle demeanor and the right know-how can make all the difference, and may allow you to save your dog's life. Ask your veterinarian (prior to any emergency) to show you how to check your dog's vital signs—temperature, heart rate, respiration rate—and make a note of normal ranges for each. Below are some common emergency situations, with instructions on how to deal with them, until you can get professional help.

Making a Muzzle

A dog who is hurt will be confused and
may forget his training. Even the best dogs
may snap or bite when they are in pain, so
you need to be comfortable muzzling your
dog to protect yourself while you care for
him. You can buy a canvas muzzle at most
pet supply stores, but in the event of an
emergency, you may need to improvise.
Here's how:

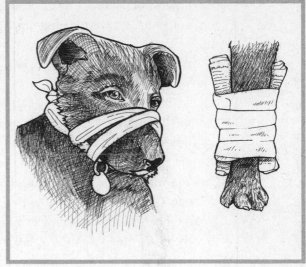

*A DIY muzzle
and an
impromptu
splint*

- ✺ Take a length of soft cloth (a leg of
  pantyhose, a length of gauze, a soft
  belt, or a bandanna). This material needs to be long enough to go
  around your dog's muzzle twice and then tie behind his head.
- ✺ Stand behind your dog and with one end of the material in each
  hand, place it under your dog's mouth and nose, near his throat.
- ✺ Gently bring it up around his mouth on each side, cross over the top
  and then below.
- ✺ Bring the ends around behind his neck, under his ears. Tie an
  easy-to-release yet secure bow.
- ✺ Check the muzzle all around, especially the knots. Make sure the
  material is snug enough so your dog can't paw it off, but loose enough
  that it doesn't hurt or choke him.
- ✺ Do *not* try to muzzle any of the snub-nosed, short-muzzled breeds,
  such as Pekingese, Pugs, or even short-nosed Boxers, as you could
  severely impair their ability to breathe.
- ✺ Never, ever muzzle your dog and leave him alone—not even for a second! It is much too easy for him to harm himself by pawing at the
  muzzle, getting a nail caught in it, scratching himself, or even impair-
  ing his ability to breathe.

Practice muzzling your dog often. Keep the training session fun; laugh
and joke with your dog and pop a treat in his mouth each time you take the
muzzle off. This has a double benefit: You will get more comfortable with the

process of making a muzzle, so you can do it easily in an emergency, and your dog will get used to being muzzled and won't associate it with anything bad.

Immobilizing and Transporting an Injured Dog

Immobilizing your dog can be hard, especially if he's scared. A small to medium-sized dog can be wrapped in a heavy towel, similar to the way you would swaddle a baby. A large to giant-sized dog can be wrapped in a blanket. Fold his legs in toward his body and wrap him snugly, but not too tightly. You want him to feel comforted, not trapped, and the wrap needs to be loose enough that he can breathe.

Then slide a board under your dog and, with the help of someone else, lift the board, using it as a stretcher and transport him to the vet's office. If you think your dog has broken a limb, see Fractures on page 284 prior to moving him.

Allergic Reactions

Many dogs chase flying insects, and sometimes they catch them. If your dog catches a bee or wasp, there's an excellent chance that he will get stung. If he begins to show signs of an allergic reaction, such as redness or swelling, give him an over-the-counter dosage of Benadryl immediately, and then phone your veterinarian. Dogs under thirty pounds should receive 10 mgs of Benadryl; dogs between thirty and fifty pounds should get 25 mg; and dogs over fifty pounds can take a 50 mg dose. After giving the appropriate medication, get your dog to the vet's office immediately.

Bleeding

Bleeding can result from a traumatic injury, such as a dog being hit by a car, or from playing too roughly with another dog. As with humans, bleeding from minor cuts or scrapes can usually be stopped by applying firm, direct pressure to the wound. Maintain the pressure for ten to fifteen minutes. Although you may be tempted, do not relieve the pressure during that time to "see if it stopped," as that can allow bleeding to resume. When bleeding has stopped, apply a topical antibiotic. Watch to see that your dog doesn't lick it off.

However, if the blood is spurting, as from a broken or damaged artery, this situation could become life-threatening very quickly. Apply pressure to the wound and get the dog to the vet or to an emergency clinic immediately. Do not apply a tourniquet except under a veterinarian's recommendation, as these can be potentially dangerous.

Breathing Resuscitation

If your dog has stopped breathing, you may need to give him breathing resuscitation to save his life. Here's how:

1. Check his mouth and nose to make sure his airways are clear.
2. Pull his tongue forward to make sure that it hasn't fallen to the back of his throat. Gently close his mouth and hold it closed.
3. Slowly blow air down his nose. A Toy dog or small breed dog will only need a gentle puff; a giant breed dog will need a stronger breath. Watch to see his side lift as you blow.
4. Release and let the air leave his lungs.
5. Repeat every five to six seconds until he begins breathing on his own or until you get him to your vet or to the emergency clinic.

Choking

If your dog is choking, he will appear to have difficulty breathing. He may be gagging or pawing at his mouth or throat, and if the airway is completely obstructed, he may pass out. Here's what to do:

1. Open his mouth and look for anything stuck in his mouth or throat. If you can see the obstruction, grab it using your fingers, forceps, or tweezers, *being very careful not to push the object farther down his throat*. If your dog is scared, you may need to prop his mouth open with something rigid as you do this, so he doesn't bite.
2. If you can't see the obstruction, or if the object is too far down his throat for you to reach, pick your dog up with his back to your stomach and chest. With a gentle but sharp motion, push upward and in on his abdomen, under the ribcage, so that the breath in his lungs will force the object out of his trachea. If you have a very large dog, you can do this while he is standing, putting your stomach

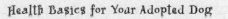

If your dog chokes...

against his behind. If you cannot visualize this, ask your veterinarian to demonstrate for you.

3. Once you remove the object, if your dog is not breathing, perform breathing resuscitation (see page 283).

Drowning

If your dog is still in the water, don't hesitate; pull him out right away.

1. Have someone call the veterinarian for advice while you work with your dog.
2. Lay your dog down with his head lower than his hips. Open his mouth so the water in his lungs can drain out.
3. Press gently on his abdomen to help the water come out of his mouth.
4. Give breathing resuscitation to help him begin breathing again.

Fractures

If one of your dog's limbs appears to be fractured, you can improvise a splint from newspaper and VetWrap or other wrapping material (torn strips of towel, a roll of gauze, or sling bandages). Roll several sheets of newspaper into two tight cylinders. Place a newspaper roll on each side of the injured leg and gently wrap them in the self-sticking VetWrap. Then get to a veterinarian as soon as possible.

Heatstroke

A dog who works or plays too hard in hot, humid weather can suffer from heatstroke. This can also happen to a dog who is confined in a hot area without adequate ventilation (such as in a car or a crate in a hot house). Symptoms include elevated body temperature (above 103 degrees Fahrenheit), rapid heart rate, extreme thirst (or no thirst at all), pale gums, weakness, collapse, and difficulty breathing.

Petfinder.com: The Adopted Dog Bible

- ❉ Call your vet right away for guidance.
- ❉ While on the phone, run cool (but not cold) water over the dog (from a hose is fine) to gradually bring down his body temperature.
- ❉ If he'll drink, offer him a very small amount of cool water, as per your veterinarian's recommendations.

Poisoning

There is no one way to treat a potential poisoning in your dog, as there are many different types of poisons. Signs of an ingested poison may be vomiting, diarrhea, lethargy, gagging, coughing, or collapse. A touched poison (such as a yard spray) may be indicated by red skin, burned skin (a contact burn), and pain. If you suspect your dog may have come into contact with any dangerous substance:

- ❉ Do everything you can to determine what kind of poison your dog has come into contact with. This is vital to his proper care.
- ❉ Call your vet immediately.
- ❉ Have the container or box or spray at hand so you can tell your vet the product name, what it does, and any other important information on the label.
- ❉ Let the vet guide you from here. Follow all her instructions, asking for clarification if you don't understand something.
- ❉ Do not make your dog vomit unless instructed to do so by your veterinarian. Some substances will do more damage if vomited back up than if they remain in the dog's digestive tract.
- ❉ If you cannot reach your vet, you can also call the ASPCA poison control center at (888) 426-4435. There may be a charge for the call, but the line is staffed twenty-four hours a day, 365 days a year, and could mean the difference between life and death for your dog.

Shock

Injured dogs, like injured people, can go into shock. If your dog is shivering, weak, and appears confused, he may be in shock. Other indications are a low body temperature, pale gums, and cold feet. If you think your dog is in shock, keep him in a quiet, warm place. Talk to and stroke him and cover him with a blanket. If he is lying down, elevate his legs on pillows to help send blood to the vital organs. Contact your veterinarian right away for further instructions.

The vast majority of emergency situations will require the assistance of your vet; very few can be fully treated at home. However, if you remain calm and know how to handle these situations until you can get your dog to the veterinarian, you can potentially save his life.

In the next chapter we will look at convalescence, and how to care for your dog when he is recovering from an injury or illness.

Dog Biscuits for the Soul: Sarah

Sarah

My husband Rich and I found Sarah on Petfinder.com. We knew we wanted a Golden Retriever because they are the sweetest dogs in the world. Sarah was somewhere between four and six years old when we adopted her, and the poor little thing had such bad skin allergies that she basically had a buzz cut. Either all of her fur had fallen out or her previous owners thought shaving her would help. It didn't. Now, with the help of doggy Benadryl and lots of love, her skin problems are in check, and she's a very happy girl. She even "smiles" when we come home and when we give her carrots, her favorite treat. I've attached a photo of her smiling. She's too cute for words and is a very healthy, happy dog. I don't know who is happier—Sarah or us. She is the best dog anyone could ask for.

Lindsay Warren, Royal Oak, Michigan
Sarah was adopted from Animal Service League in Dowagiac, Michigan

Resources

Bonham, Margaret and James M. Wingert, DVM: *The Complete Idiot's Guide to Dog Health and Nutrition*. Alpha, 2003

Eldredge, Deborah, DVM and Liisa Carlson, DVM, Delbert Carlson, DVM, and James Giffin, MD: *Dog Owner's Home Veterinary Handbook*. Wiley, 2007

Goldstein, Robert VMD and Susan Goldstein: *The Goldsteins' Wellness & Longevity Program*. TFH, 2005

Messonnier, Shawn DVM: *Natural Health Bible for Dogs & Cats*. Prima, 2001

Palika, Liz: *The KISS Guide to Raising a Puppy*. DK, 2002

Thornton, Kim and Debra Eldredge, DVM: *The Everything Dog Health Book*. Adams Media, 2005

Volhard, Wendy and Kerry Brown, DVM: *Holistic Guide for a Healthy Dog*. Howell, 2000

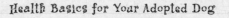

15

Helping the Healing Process

Caring for Your Sick or Injured Dog

A dog recovering from illness needs rest and love.

Let's hope your adopted dog is healthy, strong, and vigorous, and will remain that way for the rest of her life. Unfortunately, however, even the best-loved dogs do occasionally get sick, and even the most carefully supervised dogs may hurt themselves. It's very important, then, that you have a veterinarian you trust, and who you know how to work with, so that together you can provide the best care for your dog. In this chapter, you will learn how to work with your veterinarian, as well as how to nurse your dog as she heals from an injury or an illness.

Work with Your Veterinarian

There are some pet parents who begrudge the money spent at their veterinarian's office thinking that every time the vet recommends an examination, a follow-up visit, a laboratory test, or any other treatment, he is simply out to get their money. This way of thinking will not allow you to build the necessary partnership with your veterinarian and can have grave consequences for both you and your dog. If you don't trust your vet, it will be much more difficult for you to accept his help, which in turn will make it more difficult for your dog to receive the best treatment possible. If there is something about your vet that doesn't sit right with you, you need to find a new vet, someone with whom you will feel comfortable, of whom you can ask questions, and whose guidance and counsel you will trust and follow.

In addition, if you feel uncomfortable with any of the particular

Finding the Right Vet

Although you can check advertisements or contact your local veterinary association, the best referrals often come from other pet parents in the community. Ask your neighbors, friends, and family where they take their dogs. What do they like about their vet? Do they have any complaints? Another great source is the shelter or rescue group from which you adopted your dog or, if your adoption was long-distance, contact your local shelter or rescue group. They may have a relationship with a local veterinarian, and what better way to applaud a vet's decision to support homeless pets than by supporting him in turn?

Once you have two or three names, call and make an appointment to meet with each one. Go in without your dog and be willing to pay for the vet's time. Get some first impressions. Is the front office staff courteous and helpful? Is the facility clean, bright, and relatively odor-free? Is the waiting room comfortable?

Once you have a sense of the office and staff, talk to the vet himself. Some questions you may want to ask include:

continued

- **Do you have any specialties? Do you offer behavior counseling?** This can be important if your dog develops a health or behavior problem sometime in the future.
- **Have you had much of experience with this breed or mix of breeds?** Veterinarians, like everyone else, have personal preferences and are impacted by their experiences. Knowing if your veterinarian has any preconceived ideas about dogs like yours is good information. Also, many breeds are predisposed to specific health and behavior problems, and it is helpful if your veterinarian is familiar with them.
- **What are your payment policies?** Does he take the credit card you prefer to use? What happens if there is an emergency and you don't have the money? Does he offer payment plans?
- **What are your regular hours? Do you take walk-ins? What are your policies toward after-hours emergencies?** Does he take calls or does he refer to an emergency clinic? If so, which one? What can he tell you about that clinic?
- **What role do your vet techs and other staff play in caring for my pet?** What training and experience do they have?
- **How are hospitalizations handled?** Do you allow pet parents to visit hospitalized patients?
- **Do you keep animals in your office or clinic overnight and offer twenty-four-hour care if my dog is severely ill or injured?**
- **Do you offer grooming and boarding services?** This can be important if your dog needs to be tranquilized for grooming, or needs a boarding facility that provides treatment while you're away.
- **What is your policy regarding euthanasia? Will I be permitted to be in the room with my dog when and if the time comes to euthanize her?**
- **What else is important to you regarding your dog's care?** Ask those questions now.

Of the veterinarians you visited, if you are satisfied with the responses of one particular vet, you have found the right one for you and your dog.

Petfinder.com: The Adopted Dog Bible

recommendations your veterinarian makes, it is perfectly acceptable to get a second opinion from another veterinarian. Just tell your vet you would like a second opinion, and ask for copies of the pertinent parts of your pet's health record and any tests results. A good veterinarian wants what is best for your dog and should be happy to see you taking a proactive part in your dog's healthcare. He may even be able to recommend another doctor for your second opinion.

Your Partner in Your Dog's Health

Lila Miller, DVM, Vice President and Veterinary Advisor of the ASPCA in New York City, says, "Just as with humans, preventative care and early detection of medical and behavior problems are major keys to assuring our pets live a long and high-quality life. Regular veterinary visits and good home health care go hand in hand in maintaining optimal health for our canine companions." Preventative care includes:

- Vaccinations on a schedule agreed upon between you and your veterinarian and based on a thorough risk/benefit assessment.
- Good, nutritious food fed on a regular schedule in amounts appropriate to your dog's age, health and lifestyle.
- Clean water that is always available.
- Daily exercise and playtimes appropriate to your dog's breed, age, and state of health.
- Regular veterinary examinations at intervals recommended by your vet and visits at the first signs of trouble. The schedule will depend upon her assessment of your dog's health.
- Being observant to changes in your dog's normal habits and performing mini physical exams regularly to detect abnormalities when they first appear. Your veterinarian can show you how to do this.

In addition, your dog needs to spend time with you each and every day, whether during a training session, playtime, or just cuddling up on the sofa together. This is a good time to examine her, it will help you develop and maintain your relationship, and your dog needs this emotional dedication for her good mental health. I find it does wonders for my mental health, as well!

Work with Your Vet's Staff

Your veterinarian would be hard pressed to run his office and practice entirely on his own, so he probably has several people working for him. The receptionist answers the telephone, schedules appointments, and greets people and their pets as they come into the clinic. The veterinary technicians and assistant vet techs work with the pets, the people and the veterinarian. The vet techs and assistant vet techs may hold wriggling or nervous pets during examinations, assist the veterinarian in treating the pets, and help with diagnostic procedures and surgeries. Their role in your pet's health care is similar to that of a nurse in a hospital.

Many pet parents believe that only the veterinarian can answer their questions regarding their pet's care. However, some vet techs are very well educated and trained, licensed or certified through state examinations, and have worked with veterinarians for many years. Your veterinarian may have standard procedures and guidelines for his technicians regarding what advice can be offered to pet parents or what treatments the techs will or will not administer. In addition, in most veterinary clinics and hospitals, the vet techs do the actual nursing of sick or injured pets. So don't hesitate to ask the vet techs any questions you may have regarding your pet's care or treatments; if they don't have the answer, they will tell you so and will get back with you after consulting with the veterinarian. Of course, you should also feel comfortable asking to speak directly with your veterinarian at any time. Since you have chosen him to be your partner in your pet's health care, he should be happy to answer all of your questions.

When Lab Work Is Recommended

At some point during your dog's life, your veterinarian will recommend laboratory work or other tests. He may feel that X rays of your dog's hips are needed to diagnose hip dysplasia, or blood tests may be recommended to help him pinpoint a specific health problem or for routine healthcare. Ask your veterinarian:

- ✦ What is the test?
- ✦ What will the test results indicate? How will those results dictate further treatment?

- How is the test performed? What are the risks, if any? (Taking X rays or even blood may require mild sedation.)
- Is there anything you must do either before or after the test, and if so, how should you do it?
- When will the results be ready and will the vet call you?

When Medication Is Prescribed

Most prescriptions have directions written on the package, but to be certain you understand completely, there are several questions you need to ask your veterinarian.

- What is the medication? Are there alternate forms of treatment? If so, what makes this medication the best choice?
- What medical condition is it being prescribed for?
- How does the medicine work?
- How often should it be given and for how many days?
- Should it be given with food? Without food? With water? Any particular time of day?

- Are there any potential side effects to watch for?
- If your dog displays any side effects, when should you call your veterinarian? Should you continue the medication until you see the vet or should you discontinue the medication?
- What results should you see from this medication and how soon?

Make sure you understand how to properly treat your dog's injury at home.

- Is there a certain result to look for, after which you should discontinue the medication? Or should you keep administering the medicine until you've used up the dosage you've been given?
- If I miss a dose, what should I do?

✿ How much will it cost? Can I get this medication from a pharmacy with a prescription?

Give all medications according to your veterinarian's instructions and do not discontinue any medications without discussing it with your veterinarian. Antibiotics, especially, should be given in strict accordance with directions, because when antibiotics are given incorrectly, a bacterial infection may linger in the dog's body only to reappear later even stronger, and sometimes with a resistance to the antibiotic originally used. Later in this chapter you will find directions for giving your dog medication.

Follow-up Care

Make sure you understand all the directions and can repeat the care your dog needs on your own. For instance, if the vet or vet tech wants you to bandage a wound, have him show you how to do that with the materials provided to you. Ask your vet when your dog needs to come back for a checkup or for follow-up care. After a surgical procedure, most vets will want to remove any non-dissolvable stitches or simply check on your pet after seven to ten days, but this may vary according to the individual problem and your dog's state of health. If your dog needs to be seen at a specific time, make that appointment before you leave the office and mark it on your calendar as soon as you get home.

If Your Dog Is Hospitalized

If your dog is severely injured or ill enough that your veterinarian recommends hospitalization, you will need to know exactly how he handles this in his practice. Some veterinarians will keep the animals in their clinic or hospital and provide twenty-four hour care. Other veterinarians keep only office hours, and animals needing twenty four hour care will be transferred (by the vet or by the owner) to an emergency clinic for after hours care.

If your vet does not provide around-the-clock care, make sure you know where your dog will be after hours and who will transport her. Find out, too, who will be caring for your dog and where the hospital is located. Make sure to ask:

Petfinder.com: The Adopted Dog Bible

- What is the veterinarian's name?
- What is the vet's experience and references?
- Who can you contact for an update on your dog's status while in the emergency clinic?
- Will your dog be brought back to your vet's clinic in the morning?
- What happens if the next day is a weekend or a holiday?
- Will your veterinarian be called if your dog has a health crisis while at this clinic?
- If your dog requires an extended hospital stay, what are the visiting policies?
- How is the bill handled at this clinic?

Hospital Accommodations

At most clinics providing hospital care, dogs are confined to a small cage, usually just big enough for them to change position. Although some owners dislike the idea of their dog being in such a small cage, this is done for the dogs' safety. Injured or sick dogs shouldn't have the opportunity to move too much, as they might hurt themselves even more.

In addition, if the dog has an intravenous line in a vein to provide medications, a quiet, confined dog is less likely to dislodge that line. She is also going to be easier for the hospital staff to handle.

The Daily Routine

The daily routine for a hospitalized dog will vary, based on her physical condition and the reason for the hospitalization. For most dogs it will look something like this:

- First thing in the morning, the vet tech will check on the dog, make sure IV lines are working correctly, and assess the dog's condition.
- The assistant vet tech or the kennel help will clean the dog's cage, take her out to relieve herself if she is able, and clean up the dog if she has soiled herself.
- The veterinarian will examine the dog and make any adjustments to medications and treatments.

- The dog will be fed, if the vet recommends it, and the vet tech will check back to make sure the dog is eating and drinking as she should.
- This schedule will repeat throughout the day as indicated by your dog's condition.

Most veterinarians will hospitalize a dog only when the dog needs some specific care that cannot be provided at home or in the vet's office, or when the dog's health is precarious. Because many dogs (like many people) experience stress while in a hospital, most hospitals will send the dog home as soon as she is stable and when the vet is confident that you can provide continuing care at home.

Visiting a Hospitalized Dog

While in the past visitors were not recommended for hospitalized dogs, this policy has changed at many progressive veterinary hospitals where it's believed that both you and your pet benefit from being together. The decision may depend on the hospital's setup, insurance recommendations, or your dog's condition. However, it is important that, if you visit your dog, she not get excited and become too active, perhaps further injuring herself in the process. Also, hospitals may have set visiting hours and/or rules of visit length or number of visitors, so be sure to ask.

Many dogs can become depressed by being hospitalized and the resulting separation from their family. If you spend time with your dog, cuddling and petting and perhaps hand-feeding her, she may rally. If the ability to do this is as important to you as it is to me, find a hospital that will accommodate you before you are faced with an emergency. While there may be times when visiting could be too disruptive, for many pets, just as with people, a visit from a loved one is invaluable.

Nursing Your Dog

The instructions for caring for your dog as she recuperates from an illness or an injury will vary depending on the severity of the problem. You should be prepared to make adjustments as recommended by your veterinarian. She may place certain restrictions on your dog, perhaps limiting her exercise or having her eat a special diet, and it's very important that you follow these instructions. Your dog may not understand why she is being restricted, so be extra attentive and gentle with her as she heals.

Although many dogs are cooperative patients, some resist exercise and dietary restrictions or the need to keep calm. On the other hand, some dogs who have had major surgery seem to tolerate their recuperation with extremely good grace. This is just one of the wonders of dogs. Whatever your dog's temperament, you should be patient during the healing process, and always contact your veterinarian if your dog appears to be in pain or you are concerned about her recuperation.

Giving Medication

Although some dogs will take medications willingly, some will not. Nonetheless, it is your job as caretaker to get the medication into your dog with as little stress as possible. If giving your dog her medication turns into a battle of wills, it will continue to get more difficult each time. So always plan your course of action before you begin, have medications set out, measured as appropriate, and remain as calm, gentle, and firm as you can.

Pills and capsules with food. If the medication can be given with food (ask your veterinarian), hide the pill or capsule in a bit of food your dog likes. The key here is to make sure the dog eats it without suspecting that there is anything hidden in the food. Often you can hide the pill in a bit of cheese or cream cheese and your dog will gulp it down without thinking twice. A clever product known as "Pill Pockets" is a combination dog treat and pill delivery system, allowing you to insert the pill into the "pocket" and pinch it closed, leaving you with a tasty morsel to offer your dog. If she spits it out, though, or if she is clever enough to eat the treat and spit out the pill, you will need to get crafty. Ready three tidbits of food and hide the pill in one of them. Ask your dog to sit, shake hands, or do another trick that she will do willingly, and then give her a piece of food without

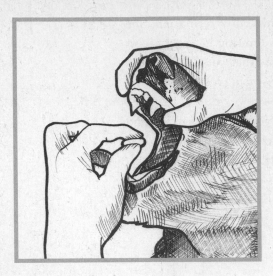

How to give a pill without food.

the pill in it. Then ask her to do another trick and pop the piece of food with the pill into her mouth, while showing her the third piece of food. She will be so eager for the third piece that she will swallow the one with the medication in it quickly.

Pills and capsules without food. If your veterinarian says that the medication must be given without food, you may need to force your dog to swallow it, especially if the medication doesn't taste good. Reach over the top of your dog's muzzle with your hand, and with your fingers on one side of her muzzle and thumb on the other side, press her upper lips against her top teeth behind the large canines. As she opens her mouth, gently tilt her head back, then quickly place the pill to the back of her throat. Close her mouth, hold it closed, and rub her throat. When she swallows, praise her.

Liquids. Liquids are best given via a large plastic syringe (without a needle) or an eye dropper. Your veterinarian will supply either of these when the medication is prescribed. (Never use anything made of glass, as your dog could bite down and shatter it, leaving glass shards in her mouth.) Put the measured amount of medication in the syringe or eye dropper and squirt it in the cheek pocket of your dog's mouth. Tilt her head back slightly as you do this, and make sure her mouth remains closed so that the medication doesn't dribble out. Rub her throat to encourage her to swallow.

Ear medication. Ear infections can be very painful, so your dog may be hesitant to let you touch her ears. Make certain your veterinarian or technician has demonstrated the best technique for treatment. You don't want to fight with your dog, as this will make any future nursing more difficult. Therefore, a good distraction is in order! Take a spoonful of peanut butter and smear it in your dog's mouth, behind her front teeth. As she licks at the peanut butter, clean and medicate one ear. Repeat for the second ear. Be very careful as you do this, because the ear canal is extremely delicate.

Petfinder.com: The Adopted Dog Bible

Eye medications. Eye medications are usually drops or ointments. These must be administered very quickly so that your dog doesn't fight you. While sitting, encourage the dog to put her head in your lap. Give her a nice massage on the head, around the ears and neck. Then, while she's relaxed, gently open one eye and administer the medication. Repeat for the other eye. Do not let the eyedropper or medicine bottle make contact with your dog's eyeball, as this could contaminate the remaining medicine.

Skin ointments. Ointments or other skin medications are usually easy to apply, unless the condition is painful or the medication stings. When either situation applies, begin the treatment with a gentle massage on a part of the dog's body that is not sore. Relax the dog (and yourself), then gently apply the medication to the affected area. Follow this with another gentle massage on the unaffected areas to relax the dog again.

If your dog snaps at you or tries to bite when you are trying to administer eye, ear, or skin medication, it's a good idea to muzzle her. Remember, she doesn't know that what you're doing will make her healthier; she just sees you coming at her with something that caused her discomfort yesterday. (For more detailed instructions, see Chapter 14). Administer her medication, take off the muzzle, and give her some love.

If you continue to have trouble giving your dog medications, talk to your vet. He may be able to show you an alternative technique, or there might be a different type of medication that will be easier for your dog to take.

Taking Your Dog's Temperature

During recuperation, your veterinarian may want you to take your dog's temperature. Although humans have many different options regarding types and insertion points for thermometers, the same is not true for dogs. Ask your veterinarian about the best kind of thermometer to use, but for the most accurate reading, many vets recommend a digital rectal thermometer. I look for a fast, accurate, digital thermometer with a flexible comfort tip for rectal use on my dogs. For safety, avoid glass or mercury thermometers.

Before inserting the thermometer, clean it with isopropyl alcohol and lubricate it slightly with petroleum jelly or K-Y lubricant. Your dog should be either standing or lying on her side. Restrain her as much as possible, getting help from a second person if you can. Insert the thermometer into your dog's rectum, and continue to hold the thermometer with one hand as the other hand restrains your dog. For a large dog, insert about half of the thermometer; for a Toy breed dog, insert no more than a quarter of the thermometer. Do not let go of the thermometer and do not allow your dog to move into a sitting position, as that could cause the thermometer to move up the dog's rectum or break inside her body. If she struggles too much, remove the thermometer. Talk soothingly to your dog throughout the process, and when you're done, pet her and praise her and give her a big treat if her condition will allow it.

Most dogs have a normal temperature between 100.5 and 102 degrees Fahrenheit. As with humans, what is normal for one dog may differ from what is normal for another. Your dog's temperature may go up substantially if it is very hot outside or she is overly excited. It's a good idea to take your dog's temperature a couple of times while she's healthy so you know her normal range.

Restricting Activity

While your dog is recovering from an illness or surgery, your veterinarian may want you to restrict her activity for a period of time so she can heal. This may be one of the hardest things you will have to do for your dog, because if she's not in pain, she will not understand why she can't run and play. It is especially important for you to be vigilant; let her know she is loved, keep her warm and comfortable, and give her extra attention, but don't let her hurt herself or delay her recovery by being more active than she should.

If your dog has been crate trained and will relax in her crate, this is one of the easiest ways to keep her calm. Make sure to ask your veterinarian exactly how much your dog can move around. If she is allowed some movement, put her in a crate that is larger than the one she would need to be in for house-training; perhaps twice her body size. You could also set up a small exercise pen. These foldable, portable fences can be found in most pet supply stores, and provide a little more room than a crate.

Petfinder.com: The Adopted Dog Bible

When you bring your dog out of the crate or exercise pen, fasten her leash on to her collar first, even if she's in the house. With the leash on, you can control her better and keep her from dashing about as she might otherwise do. Keep her on the leash as you walk her outside to relieve herself.

Special Diet

If your dog is recuperating from an injury or surgery, she may not be able to eat her normal diet so discuss feeding with your veterinarian. If your dog's activities will be restricted for a few weeks, your veterinarian may recommend that you reduce her food portions so that she doesn't gain any weight. This calls for a balancing act: while your vet may not want your dog to gain weight, adequate food is necessary for proper healing. If you have any questions as to how to handle this, discuss them with your vet.

Special diets are often recommended for dogs with certain health problems, including gastrointestinal, kidney, and heart diseases, and even obesity. Special diets are also recommended for dogs with allergies. If your veterinarian recommends a special diet, make sure you understand what this diet is, what foods your dog can or cannot have, how the food should be prepared and given, and how long your dog should remain on this diet.

Caring for a Wound or Incision

Your veterinarian or one of the vet techs will give you specific instructions as to how to care for a wound or an incision. (Instructions for emergency care are in Chapter 14.) As a general rule, if there is no discharge or bleeding, the wound will be left uncovered so it can dry and the skin can heal. In these instances, you will simply need to keep an eye on the wound, keep it clean, and make sure the dog isn't licking it or chewing on it. If the wound or the skin around the wound becomes red, hot, or swollen, or if there is blood or pus in the wound, call your veterinarian right away. It is likely that the wound has become infected.

If the wound is on an area of the leg that is always moving, your vet may decide to bandage the wound because by keeping the leg still, the wound

Elizabethan Collars

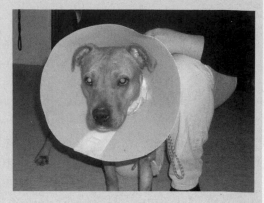

The Elizabethan Collar is one type of restraining collar used to prevent chewing of incisions or wounds.

Very few dogs tolerate bandaging well; most try to tear, pull, or chew the bandaging off. Many dogs will hurt themselves in the process—even to the point of pulling out stitches—but that doesn't seem to slow them down at all. If your dog appears to be intolerant of her bandage, your vet may recommend an Elizabethan collar. One type of the collar is a large plastic cone that attaches to your dog's regular buckle collar. Your dog can eat and drink with this cone on but cannot turn her head around enough to chew on a wound or pull off a bandage. The other type of Elizabethan collar is a padded collar that doesn't have a cone but is wide enough to limit the dog's ability to turn her head to get chewing access to her body.

Some dogs simply won't tolerate the collars, becoming obsessed with trying to remove it or becoming very depressed. If this is the case with your dog, your veterinarian can provide you with other options, like the use of a bitter-tasting cream or spray on or around the bandaging to discourage licking and biting.

can heal more quickly. If the wound will need to be immobilized for some time, you may need to change the bandage at home. Your vet or vet tech can show you how to do so, but it is extremely important to keep in mind that a tight bandage wrapped around a dog's leg or paw can easily cut off circulation. You must make sure the bandage doesn't cut off the blood flow below, and that your dog's paw remains warm and pink.

Petfinder.com: The Adopted Dog Bible

If a wound or incision is still oozing, your veterinarian may want it to remain bandaged for a few days to help keep it clean, and this will probably require you to change the bandage after a specific period of time. He may also give you instructions about cleaning the wound prior to re-bandaging it. If the injured area is small, you can bandage it by putting a gauze pad on the wound and using bandage tape to hold it in place. The tape will not stick well to your dog's coat, so trim the fur around the wound (if it hasn't already been trimmed) and apply the tape directly to her skin. If the area is not easily bandaged like this, you may need to use some rolled gauze or cling wrap (Vet Wrap) around the dog's body to hold the gauze pad or bandage in place. Your veterinarian will most likely provide the cleaning and bandaging supplies that he will want you to use; if he doesn't, ask him for a list of products that he feels are safe for you to use, and where you can find them.

Recuperation Takes Time

Healthy dogs heal very quickly, sometimes amazingly so. However, follow your veterinarian's suggestions for your dog's recuperation. You don't want to let your dog do too much too soon, because she could hurt herself or suffer a setback in her healing process.

When your vet is satisfied that your dog is healing well and can begin normal activities again, introduce those activities slowly. Don't take her out to play a spirited game of catch. Instead, gradually reintroduce more normal activities. After all, sore muscles are no more fun for your dog than they are for you!

During and after your dog's recuperation, watch her extra carefully. You know your dog better than anyone else does, so monitor the way she moves, her eating habits, her sleeping patterns, her activities, and everything else she does. If she seems too quiet, anxious, depressed, is in pain, or exhibits any other behavior that is different than normal, talk to your veterinarian. Trust your instincts and your intuition.

Pet Health Insurance

Pet health insurance works much like health insurance for people: it helps cover the cost of medical care so that care can be provided for your pet when she needs it. As with health care policies for people, the coverage and cost varies, depending upon the company providing the coverage. Unlike health insurance for people, though, it usually involves less paperwork and fewer headaches for both you and the veterinarian.

Note: When researching costs of coverage, the dog used is my three-year-old American Pit Bull Terrier named Mojo who is micro-chipped, neutered, and in good health with no known pre-existing conditions. The costs for your dog will be different; these are offered simply as a means for comparison. Keep in mind, too, that though these prices are current as of this writing, costs are constantly changing.

Veterinary Pet Insurance (VPI) offers several different health care plans. The top-level plan has two programs:

1. VPI Superior Plan offers reimbursement allowances for prescriptions, hospitalizations, office visits, surgeries, and more. There are also allowances for a variety of tests. This plan has an annual maximum benefit of $14,000 and a deductible of $50 per incident.
2. WellCare Premier and Core plans include reimbursement allowances for vaccinations, flea and heartworm preventatives, bi-annual examinations, and more.

Mojo's quote for these plans was $37.50 per month.
For more information, go to www.petinsurance.com.

AKC Pet Healthcare Plan offers five different health care plans.

Wellness Plus (the top-level plan) has reimbursement allowances for accidents and illnesses, including surgeries, prescriptions, tests, hospitalization, and more. It also has allowances for an annual physical, vaccinations and boosters, heartworm testing and prevention, flea and tick control, and dental care. The maximum coverage per policy term is $13,000 and the maximum per incident is $5,000. The deductible is $125 per year.

Petfinder.com: The Adopted Dog Bible

While the AKC Healthcare Plan does not recognize American Pit Bull Terriers as a covered breed, a pet parent could obtain coverage for an American Staffordshire Terrier for a monthly premium of $71.25 a month.

For more information, go to www.akcphp.com.

Pets Health Care Plan offers several levels of coverage.

Best Pet Insurance (the top level plan) provides coverage for illness and injury as well as wellness care. It also offers coverage for chronic and long-term conditions.

Mojo's quote was $88.31 per month.

For more information, go to www.petshealthplan.com.

Petplan offers three levels of coverage: Bronze, Silver, and Gold.

The Gold plan offers reimbursement allowances for hospitalization, surgery, tests, non-routine dental treatment, prescriptions, and alternative health care. The maximum annual benefit is $20,000 with either a $50, $100 or $200 deductible.

Mojo's quote for the Gold Plan with a $200 deductible was $37.84 a month.

For more information go to www.gopetplan.com.

Pet Health Inc. is the largest pet health care plan in Canada and the second largest in North America. Two programs are offered: Pet Care Insurance Program, which has teamed up with PETCO, and Shelter Care, which offers coverage for newly adopted dogs and cats. Both offer varying levels of coverage. The Shelter Care program was created hand-in-hand with and championed by Petfinder to raise awareness of pet health insurance and decrease euthanasia of pets due to medical costs.

Mojo's quote from Shelter Care in their Quick Care Gold Plan (which provides 90 percent coverage) was $76.90 a month.

ASPCA Pet Insurance. The ASPCA plan has several levels of coverage. The Advantage plan covers accidents, illnesses, and preventative wellness care. The maximum yearly benefits are $11,000 and the yearly deductible is $100.

The monthly premium quoted for Mojo was $35.08.

For more information, go to www.aspcapetinsurance.com.

There are many other pet health insurance companies, with more popping up each year, so take a look at all of them. Talk to your veterinarian before choosing one. Some vets only work with certain plans and some plans have restrictions as to which vet you can use. As with health care plans for people, these plans can be confusing.

Some experts suggest that making regular contributions to a dedicated savings account for pet health costs is a smarter financial choice than purchasing insurance. If you are disciplined enough to do so, or can set up an automatically recurring deposit, you should consider this option.

Finally, if you are facing unexpected or unmanageable expenses at your vet, consider CareCredit. CareCredit is a personal line of credit for healthcare treatments and procedures for your entire family, including your pets. It works like a credit card but can only be used for healthcare services and offers no-interest financing. See their website at www.carecredit.com/vetmed for more information.

Dog Biscuits for the Soul: Ralph

Ralph

I was searching to find a puppy for me and my family. One day I came across a picture of some Beagle/Lab mix puppies on Petfinder.com. I just knew one of these puppies was the dog I had been searching for. . . . The first chance I had I went to the pound to see these six-week old cuties. The moment I laid eyes on Ralph, I fell in love and adopted him. About two weeks later, he developed pneumonia, and we almost lost him. The veterinarian at the emergency vet hospital told us he didn't have a chance because he was so young. I loved this little guy, and I was determined to help him survive. With the help of a very wonderful vet and his staff, a lot of love and patience, and a makeshift oxygen tent, our puppy pulled through with flying colors. He is now a happy, healthy, spoiled, and—most of all—perfect young dog. I couldn't have wanted anything more for my family and for me. Animals will bring so much joy and meaning to your life. I couldn't imagine a single day without that little face looking at us with so much love and devotion.

Peggy Adams, Austintown, Ohio
Ralph was adopted from Mahoning County Dog Pound in Youngstown, Ohio.

Resources

Bonham, Margaret and James M. Wingert, DVM: *The Complete Idiot's Guide to Dog Health and Nutrition.* Alpha, 2003

Eldredge, Debra, DVM and Liisa Carlson, DVM, Delbert Carlson, DVM, and James Giffin, MD: *Dog Owner's Home Veterinary Handbook.* Wiley, 2007

Goldstein, Robert VMD and Susan Goldstein: *The Goldsteins' Wellness & Longevity Program.* TFH, 2005

Messonnier, Shawn DVM: *Natural Health Bible for Dogs & Cats.* Prima, 2001

Palika, Liz: *The KISS Guide to Raising a Puppy.* DK, 2002

Thornton, Kim and Debra Eldredge, DVM: *The Everything Dog Health Book.* Adams Media, 2005

Volhard, Wendy and Kerry Brown, DVM: *Holistic Guide for a Healthy Dog.* Howell, 2000

16

Managing Problems of the Outer Dog

Dogs, like people, are prone to all manner of injury and illness, from accidental cuts and bruises to disease and parasites. Most dogs, of course, experience few if any of these threats to their health and well-being, but as your adopted dog's first line of defense, you should know how to recognize potential or actual problems, and how to respond if you do. In this chapter, we will look at some of the maladies that can affect the canine eyes, ears, skin, and coat.

Eyes

Your dog's eyes, like your own, are marvelous, intricate, delicate structures. They are easy to injure, and they are often windows not only to your dog's soul, but to his health as well. Redness, swelling, excess tearing, squinting, or pawing at the face often indicate an eye problem. If your dog shows any of these symptoms, or if you see something happen to his eye, take him to the vet. Don't wait—a quick response can mean the difference between successful treatment and blindness.

Eye Lingo

Cornea	transparent front portion of the eyeball; made of several complex layers and extremely sensitive, the cornea is easily injured by trauma, infection, or disease, any of which can partially or completely cloud the cornea and interfere with vision.
Iris	colored part of the eye that prevents unlimited light from entering
Lens	transparent structure that allows the eye to focus
Pupil	aperture in the center of the iris that increases or decreases in size to control the amount of light entering the eye

Eye Injuries

Eye injuries are not everyday occurrences for most dogs, but they are fairly common. All eye injuries are serious, and canine eyes are susceptible to permanent vision loss from injury. Symptoms of eye injury or disease can include pain or tenderness, squinting, impaired vision, excessive tearing, mucus discharge, discoloration of the cornea, and conjunctivitis.

If you think your dog's eye has been injured, take him to a veterinarian as quickly as possible to prevent further injury and possible loss of vision or the eye itself. In the meantime, you must keep your dog from pawing or rubbing his injured eye. If you have a restraint collar ("Elizabethan" collar) that fits him, use it to keep his paws away from his eyes. Sterile saline solution for flushing or irrigating some types of injuries is a good addition to your first aid kit, especially if your dog has "bulgy" eyes that are more prone to injury, like Pugs and Shih Tzus. You may want to ask your vet for a referral to a veterinary ophthalmologist once the situation is stabilized.

Here are some of the most common eye injuries seen in dogs:

- Lacerations of the eyelid or the cornea.
- Blunt injury to the eyelids or to the eye itself from a direct blow.
- Punctures and other injuries from thorns, tree branches, or other foreign bodies.
- Cat claw injuries—very common, especially in puppies who don't know not to hassle the cat. A cat claw injury may at first seem to be minor, but because claws harbor vast populations of bacteria, secondary infections can devastate the eye. Introduce your dog or puppy to your cat very cautiously (see Chapter 6).
- Dog bite injuries—puppies are often on the receiving end of this type of injury when they violate an older dog's space. In some cases the injury is immediately obvious, especially if the eyeball is forced out of the socket (see the explanation of *proptosis,* below). Often, though, the extent of the damage is not apparent because the eye is squeezed and then, like a ball, returns to its round shape. Because internal injuries can be severe, any bite to the eye area should be checked by your vet as soon as possible, even if you don't see any obvious damage. Caution is always best.
- Trauma to the head or eye socket from, for instance, being hit by a vehicle or kicked by a horse, or from running into an immovable object.
- Chemical injuries to the cornea from things like shampoo, cleaners, solvents, paint, or Mace.
- *Proptosis,* is the forward displacement of the globe out of the socket. Dogs with flat faces and protruding eyes are especially prone to proptosis because their eye sockets are shallow, but any dog can experience this injury from trauma or bites. For dogs with protruding eyeballs, proptosis can occur with excessive or improper restraint. An eye that has been forced from the socket is a true emergency and must be treated by a veterinarian immediately. If possible, have someone drive you there while you keep your dog quiet and keep the eye and surrounding tissues moist with (in order of preference) sterile saline solution, eye irrigating solution, artificial tears, or water. (Do not use contact lens cleaner.) Do not let your dog rub at his eye, and do not give him any pain medicine—leave that to your vet. Don't let your dog eat or drink as he will probably have to be anesthetized for treatment.

Petfinder.com: The Adopted Dog Bible

Sometimes a proptosed eye can be saved, but even so, some or all vision may be lost. In dogs who are at risk of proptosis, such as Pekingese, Pugs, and Shih Tzus, surgical intervention can sometimes reduce the risk of occurrence.

Most dogs cope remarkably well after losing an eye.

Some accidents damage the eye so severely that it must be *enucleated* (removed). The eyelids may be sewn shut with or without insertion of a sterile prosthetic ball to fill the socket, or a prosthetic eye may be inserted and the lids left as they were. The decision to insert a prosthesis is affected by possible infection in the eye socket, as well as the depth of the socket and the owner's preference. Fortunately, dogs don't worry about how they look, and they will get along fine without the eye (see "Living with a Blind Dog" on page 321).

Conjunctivitis

The *conjunctiva* is the pink tissue lining the inside of the eyelids. It also covers and protects the front of the eyeball surrounding the cornea, and contains glands whose secretions lubricate the eyes and keep them healthy. If the conjunctiva becomes red, congested, or painful, the animal is said to have *conjunctivitis.*

Conjunctivitis can have a wide variety of causes, including bacteria, viruses, chemical or environmental irritants such as smoke, foreign matter, allergens, tumors, decreased tear production, other eye diseases, trauma, eye medication, or even birth defects. If your dog develops conjunctivitis and you think you know the cause, correct it if you can. In some cases, laboratory tests are the only way to identify the cause. In either case, your veterinarian can recommend effective treatment.

Eye Infections

Infections of the eye and surrounding tissues can be caused by injury or disease. Prompt veterinary care is essential, as an infection can progress quickly and cause irreparable, potentially blinding damage to the eye. Injuries caused by the claws or teeth of other animals are especially prone to infection because the "weapon" introduces a massive dose of bacteria. Eye infections are usually treated with antibiotics given in an eye ointment or drops that are administered several times a day or orally.

Left untreated, a corneal infection can quickly become an ulcer, or open sore. Corneal ulcers are extremely painful and can lead to scarring and permanent blindness. Symptoms of corneal abrasion or ulcer include tearing, redness, sensitivity to light, squinting, and scratching at the eye. To diagnose the problem, your vet will introduce a sterile staining solution into your dog's eye. Any break in the surface of the cornea will take up stain, making it visible.

Superficial corneal ulcers or abrasions are usually treated with antibiotic drops or ointment and if necessary, a pain medication. You may also need to put a restraint collar on your dog to keep him from pawing his eye. If the ulcer is very deep or large, or if it fails to heal quickly, your vet may draw your dog's *nictitating membrane* (see "Cherry Eye" on page 314) across the cornea and temporarily suture it into place to protect the cornea and let it heal.

Inherited Conditions of the Eyes

Inherited eye problems occur in many breeds and mixed-breeds. Some occur relatively often in certain breeds and rarely or never in other breeds, as we'll see later in this chapter. Most dogs do not experience the conditions common to their breeds, but knowing that a particular eye condition is genetic in the breed or breeds that make up your dog's ancestry can help you recognize early symptoms, which may make treatment possible or more effective.

Some of the most common eye problems in dogs are described below.

Cataracts

A *cataract* is an opaque spot on the normally transparent lens of the eye. Many cataracts are visible to the naked eye as white or bluish spots on the surface of the eye. They are not painful, but they can cause anything from mild visual impairment to total blindness. Fortunately, most cataracts develop slowly, giving the dog (and his family) time to adapt to his loss of vision. Many cataracts can be removed, which can restore a dog's vision.

Cataracts can be caused by injury, disease, environmental factors, old age, or heredity. Many different breeds have a high incidence of inherited cataracts, often referred to as *juvenile cataracts* because they develop long before the dog can be considered old. Inherited cataracts are typically *bilateral*, meaning that they affect both eyes, although they may not make their initial appearance simultaneously. In addition, inherited cataracts usually *progress*, or develop over time.

The *age of onset*, or the age at which inherited cataracts typically become apparent, varies from breed to breed. In some, they are truly "juvenile," showing up during the first or second year. In others, they don't appear until the dog is six or seven years old or even, in some cases, well into middle age. If your research into your dog's breed or breeds shows that he is at risk of inherited cataracts, consider having his eyes checked every few years by a veterinary ophthalmologist. If your dog is a purebred, schedule the first exam a year or so before the typical age of onset, or as soon after as possible. If he's a mix of breeds prone to inherited cataracts but with typically different ages of onset, use the earlier possibility as your starting point.

Some cataracts cause few problems, but others cause partial or complete blindness. There is no effective medical treatment. Cataracts can be removed surgically and the results are usually excellent. Once removed, a cataract cannot recur, but there is still some risk that the patient will lose some or all of his vision to glaucoma or retinal detachment, which can occur post-operatively.

Cataracts can cause lens induced uveitis (LIU), a serous inflammation inside the eye that can lead to glaucoma, retinal detachment, and other complications. If you choose not to have your dog's cataracts removed, your vet may prescribe anti-inflammatory eye drops and recommend regular eye exams. If you have to make a decision about surgery, keep in mind that the success rate is often higher for cataracts removed during the early stages of their development than for advanced cataracts. However, your vet may suggest monitoring the cataract to see how quickly it progresses and whether it is going to impair vision enough to necessitate surgery.

Cataracts should not be confused with *nuclear sclerosis*, a hardening of the lens in geriatric dogs. Although the eye takes on a cloudy appearance with nuclear sclerosis, vision is not usually impaired.

Cherry Eye

If you observe your dog when he's sleepy, you'll notice a gray-white membrane that slides over each eye from the inner corner. That is the *nictitating membrane*, or "third eyelid." It helps protect the surface of the eye, and it contains a tear gland, the "third eyelid gland" or TEG, which produces almost half the tears that lubricate the eye. (The remainder is produced by the *orbital lacrimal gland*.) The TEG is fastened to the eye socket by ligaments, and normally it cannot be seen.

If the ligaments that hold the TEG are weak, the gland moves out of hiding and appears as a pink or reddish tissue in the inner corner of the eye—hence the slang term "cherry eye" for the condition, which is more properly called *prolapsed third eyelid gland (PTEG)* or *prolapsed nictitans gland*. It can affect one or both eyes at any time.

PTEG is treated by surgically repositioning the gland, which is then sutured in place. Prolapsed third eyelid glands should not be removed since they contribute significantly to tear production. If the entire gland is removed, the dog can develop *dry eye* condition due to reduced tear production (see "Dry Eye" on page 319). Left untreated, the PTEG can swell, interfering with the dog's vision and causing discomfort.

Breeds Affected Collie Eye Anomaly

Collie eye anomaly (CEA) commonly affects dogs of the following breeds and mixes containing these breeds:

- Collie (Rough and Smooth)
- Border Collies
- Australian Shepherds
- Shetland Sheepdogs

Collie Eye Anomaly (CEA)

Despite its name, Collie eye anomaly, or CEA, affects many breeds and mixes. CEA is actually a complex of defects that include choroidal hypoplasia, optic disc coloboma/staphyloma, and retinal detachment. If your dog has CEA, both eyes will be affected, although the defects in each eye may differ. While some dogs with CEA are blind in one or both eyes, most have only minor visual impairment and can live happy, relatively normal lives. There is no treatment for CEA.

Petfinder.com: The Adopted Dog Bible

CEA is inherited and is present at birth, although it can be detected only by a veterinary ophthalmologist using special instruments. If you adopt your dog as a young puppy and he is at risk of CEA due to his breed or breed mix, consider having his eyes examined when he's six to eight weeks old. After eight weeks, CEA can "go normal" for a few years, meaning that the dog's eyes appear normal, but vision problems may show up as he ages.

Coloboma (Iris Coloboma)

Iris coloboma refers to a condition in which part of the iris—the colored portion of the eye—is missing. A small coloboma will not affect vision, but a large one makes it impossible for the iris to control the amount of light entering the eye. This condition is similar to having the pupil permanently dilated. A dog with a large iris coloboma will squint in bright light.

Iris colobomas are inherited and can be seen most commonly in merle, dapple, or harlequin dogs. One or both eyes may be affected. A coloboma will not necessarily affect vision, but the flood of light into the eye in bright conditions may cause discomfort and vision problems. If you take your dog to a veterinary ophthalmologist for a checkup, the doctor should look for colobomas before dilating your dog's pupils because they may not be visible once the pupil is dilated.

Merle Ocular Dysgenesis

Merle (also known as "dapple") coloring occurs in many breeds and mixed-breeds, but it is most commonly associated with the Australian Shepherd (Aussie), Border Collie, Cardigan Welsh Corgi, Catahoula Leopard Dog, Collie, Dachshund, Shetland Sheepdog (Sheltie), and a few other breeds and mixes that contain those breeds. Breeding two merle dogs increases the potential health risks for their offspring, including the risk for *merle ocular dysgenesis,* which involves some combination of the following eye conditions:

- Microphthalmia (a small eyeball)
- Eccentric pupils (irregularly shaped)
- Subluxated pupils (off center)
- Coloboma (see "Coloboma" (Iris Coloboma) above)

- ☼ Lens luxation
- ☼ Cataract
- ☼ Retinal dysplasia or detachment
- ☼ Persistent pupillary membrane
- ☼ Equatorial staphyloma
- ☼ Lack of a tapetum (the "reflector" in the back of the eye that collects light and makes dogs' eyes glow when light hits them).

Some of these problems are easy to spot, such as an off-center or oddly shaped pupil (not to be confused with a coloboma, which can occur in any color or pattern—see previous page). Others may or may not be noticeable. Under-sized eyes (microphthalmia), for instance, range from just noticeably smaller than normal to virtually nonexistent. Still other defects cannot be seen without special equipment and must be diagnosed by a veterinary ophthalmologist. The resulting loss of vision from these eye defects can vary from mild to complete blindness. Fortunately, these defects don't generally worsen with time.

There is a 25 percent chance that a breeding of a merle dog with another merle will produce a double-merle pup who, in addition to the eye problems listed, may also be deaf or partially deaf. Some breeders are willing to risk the health and lives of 25 percent of their litter for the markings of the other 75 percent. Many breeders choose to kill the pups with genetic problems who result from these breedings. However, breed rescue groups often take on the challenge of finding these special dogs equally special homes. While it would be better if these dogs were not intentionally bred, dogs with these handicaps can still make rewarding companions.

Eyelash and Eyelid Problems

Some dogs have eyelashes that grow from areas where they do not normally grow (*distichiasis, trichiasis,* or *ectopic cilia*), or eyelashes that grow from normal areas but turn in toward the eye. Sometimes the lashes do no damage, but they can scratch the eye every time the dog blinks, causing pain, inflammation, and serious corneal damage. Symptoms typically include redness, frequent blinking, squinting, rubbing, and discharge from the eye. These conditions are very common in Shih Tzus and mixes containing Shih Tzu, but they also occur in many other breeds and mixes.

Treatment usually involves surgical removal of the lashes, and antibiotics for infection if necessary. New lashes may eventually grow in, requiring another treatment, but if left untreated, the dog may suffer pain from infections and ulcers, and can eventually go blind.

Entropion is a condition in which the eyelid rolls in, which makes the hair on the outside of the lid rub against the eyeball, causing pain and potentially serious damage similar to that caused by distichiasis. Dogs with entropion typically tear profusely and squint. Entropion can be corrected in two ways: In puppies younger than six months, temporary sutures are used to roll the eyelids out. When the puppy matures, the sutures are removed, and often the puppy needs no further treatment. In older dogs, plastic surgery may be required to remove skin from the eyelid margin.

Ectropion is a condition in which the eyelid rolls out, exposing the eyeball and the inner lining of the lid. In some dogs, ectropion is mild and causes no problems. In others, the eyeball is prone to drying because tears evaporate more quickly and are not spread as efficiently when the dog blinks. Dirt and other irritants that can damage the eye also have easier access because the lid cannot block them as it should, and may even catch and hold them where they can damage the eye. In such cases, ectropion should be surgically corrected.

Eyelid tumors are common in older dogs. Although they are not usually malignant in dogs, they do grow, and as they do they can damage the structure of the eyelid and, depending on their location, can rub against the eye. Eyelid tumors can be removed surgically, preferably while they are still small. Different methods of removal are used depending on the position, size, and number of tumors. Often, eyelid tumors can be removed without general anesthesia. If general anesthesia is necessary, consider having your dog's eyelid tumors removed when he needs to be anesthetized for another procedure, such as teeth cleaning. Although tumors can recur after surgery, most do not.

Eyelid Inflammation (Blepharitis)

Blepharitis is an inflammation or infection that causes the edges of the eyelid to become red, sore, and encrusted with scales. Additional symptoms may include eyelid spasms, swelling of the eyelid, thick discharge from the eye, abscess formation, and inflammation (see also "Conjunctivitis" on page 311). Secondary injuries may result from scratching or rubbing the eye.

Blepharitis can result from allergies, insect bites, eye injuries, parasitic infection, chronic inflammatory disease, nutritional deficiencies, glandular disorders (see "The Endocrine System" on page 376 in Chapter 17), congenital eyelid problems, or bacterial infection. Treatment varies and should address the presumed cause of the inflammation to reduce the chance that it will recur. Your vet may recommend cleansing the eyelids with a special solution to remove crusts and relieve your dog's discomfort.

Glaucoma

Glaucoma is a serious, painful condition in which abnormally high pressure inside the eyeball damages the cornea, lens, and optic nerve. *Primary glaucoma* is inherited, while *secondary glaucoma* is caused by injury or disease (see also "Lens Luxation," page 319). Either way, glaucoma usually causes partial or complete blindness.

With primary glaucoma, usually only one eye is affected at first, but it almost always spreads to both eyes. In some cases the first sign of glaucoma may be blindness in the affected eye. Early signs include squinting, eyelid fluttering, and eye rubbing, either with a paw or against furniture or carpets, all undoubtedly in response to pain caused by the pressure in the eye. Other symptoms include pupil dilation, cloudiness in the cornea, or enlarged blood vessels in the white of the eye.

The pressure in the eye can build with alarming speed, sometimes within hours, so immediate treatment is essential. If you suspect that you are seeing symptoms of glaucoma in your dog, call your vet or, during off hours, an emergency vet clinic. Without treatment, the pressure in the eye will quickly destroy cells in the retina and optic nerve, and damage the iris, the cornea, and the structures that hold the lens in position, blinding the dog permanently. The eyeball will continue to swell, causing terrible pain. If caught early, glaucoma can sometimes be controlled with eye drops and medication, at least for a while. In some cases, however, the only relief for the dog comes with removal of the eye (*enucleation*).

Petfinder.com: The Adopted Dog Bible

Lens Luxation

Lens luxation is a painful condition in which the lens of the eye luxates, or moves out of its normal position behind the iris. *Secondary lens luxation* is caused by injury or disease, and is not inherited. *Primary lens luxation* is inherited and often affects terriers and terrier mixes. Without treatment, lens luxation can cause corneal edema or glaucoma and the accompanying pain and problems.

The first symptoms of primary lens luxation usually appear when the dog is between three and five years old and may include behavioral changes caused by changes in vision, such as bumping into things or having trouble catching things. Usually, only one eye will seem to be affected, but eventually (possibly within weeks or not until several years later) symptoms will appear in the other eye as well.

In some cases, special eye drops and oral medications help manage secondary problems like glaucoma, but in severe cases the lens or the entire eye may have to be removed.

Keratitis

Keratitis is an inflammation of the cornea that can cause partial or complete loss of vision. Keratitis can result from an eye injury or irritation, allergic reaction, infection, or birth defects. Symptoms include clouding, discoloration, or redness of the cornea, the normally clear covering at the front of the eye. Treatment depends on the type and severity of the individual case, but it may include surgery. Keratitis is very painful and can quickly cause permanent damage to the eye, so medical treatment should begin as soon as possible.

Dry Eye (Kertoconjunctivitis Sicca)

Dry eye occurs when tear production is absent or decreased, allowing the cornea to dry out. It is a painful condition and can cause vision loss. If your adopted dog develops dry eye, you will play a critical role in keeping him comfortable and saving at least some of his vision by lubricating his eyes regularly as recommended by your vet or (preferably) a veterinary ophthalmologist. Treatment to restore tear production may take months and is not always successful. Most vets try drug therapy first. If that is not successful, you may want to consider a surgical procedure called *parotid duct transposition* in which a salivary duct from the mouth is redirected to the eye so that saliva replaces tears.

Pannus (Chronic Superficial Keratitis)

Pannus is a degenerative disease of the cornea, conjunctiva, and sometimes the third eyelid. Although pannus most often affects German Shepherd Dogs and German Shepherd mixes, it is also seen in other breeds, including Greyhounds, Siberian Huskies, Dachshunds, Poodles, Border Collies, Labrador Retrievers, and mixes that include those breeds.

Although the precise cause of pannus is not known, it is believed to be inherited and to have an autoimmune character (see "The Immune System" on page 379 in Chapter 17). Essentially, the dog's body perceives its own corneal cells as invaders and attacks them. The symptoms of pannus seem to be more severe in dogs who live at high and low altitudes and in those who spend a lot of time exposed to ultraviolet light (direct sunlight).

Pannus is not painful, but without veterinary care, it ultimately causes blindness as the cornea loses its transparency to the intrusion of blood vessels, pigment, cholesterol deposits, and scar tissue. Some dogs with pannus also experience dry eye problems.

If your adopted dog has pannus, you will need to treat him throughout his life to preserve his vision. Eye drops or ointments, or in some cases steroid injections, are usually prescribed to decrease *vascularization* (the invasion of blood vessels), pigmentation, and scarring of the cornea. In rare cases that do not respond to medication, surgery may be recommended. In any case, pannus is typically controlled, not cured.

Progressive Retinal Atrophy (PRA)

Progressive Retinal Atrophy (PRA), also known as Progressive Retinal Degeneration (PRD), is a term used to indicate a group of inherited diseases that destroy the vision cells in the retina (the light-receptive part of the eye), causing partial or total blindness. PRA affects many breeds, but because it is a general term, the characteristics of the disease and the age of onset vary from one breed (or mix of breeds) to another.

One of the first signs of PRA is the affected dog's reluctance to go outside at night or his difficulty negotiating in reduced light because he has lost his night vision or low-light vision. As the disease progresses, he will lose all vision, and he may develop cataracts (see "Cataracts" on page 312).

It is often necessary to have an affected dog re-examined several times at intervals to detect PRA, but if you suspect that your dog is losing his vision and if his breed or breeds are prone to the disease (many are—read about your dog's breed or breeds to find out whether he is at high risk), ophthalmological examinations may be a good idea. There is no treatment for PRA, but knowing what's wrong can help prevent the development of other associated problems and also help you prepare for your dog's eventual blindness.

Resources for Owners of Dogs with Vision and Hearing Problems

For more information on canine eye conditions, visit the Canine Eye Registry Foundation (CERF) website at http://www.vet.purdue.edu/~yshen/cerf.html.

The Blind Dogs website offers information and links related to dogs with partial or complete loss of vision, an e-mail list and discussion group, and listings of blind dogs available for adoption. http://www.blinddogs.com.

For information on the BAER test for hearing loss, and to locate a BAER test, visit http://www.lsu.edu/deafness/baersite.htm.

The Deaf Dog Education Action Fund (DDEAF) offers information and links related to dogs with partial or complete loss of hearing. There is also an e-mail discussion group for owners of partially or completely deaf dogs, and listings of deaf dogs available for adoption. Visit their website: http://www.deafdogs.org.

Living with a Blind Dog

As we have seen, dogs can experience loss of useful vision for many reasons. The loss may be *bilateral*, meaning that both eyes are affected, or it may be *unilateral*, affecting only one eye. Many elderly dogs lose their vision to cataracts or other age-related causes.

The good news is that most dogs cope remarkably well with partial or complete blindness. With a few adjustments, they and their owners can live nearly normal lives. Dogs are by nature more reliant on hearing and smelling the world than on seeing it, and they can be trained to follow voice commands such as slow, right, left, step up, step down, and so forth, to keep them safe when negotiating strange terrain.

Ears

Big and floppy, small and erect, coarse-and-curly-haired, soft and silky—your dog's ears are among his most distinctive features. They are also quite vulnerable, and good ear care is an important part of grooming for good health (see "Ear Care" on page 228 in Chapter 11).

Some dogs live their entire lives with perfectly healthy ears. Others aren't so lucky, and some adopted dogs have more than their share of ear problems in the early days of their new lives because of poor care in their former lives. Fortunately, most canine ear problems can be managed with a quick response to signs of trouble and with proper care.

If your dog scratches or rubs at his ears, shakes his head a lot or holds it tilted most of the time, or if he seems to feel tenderness on or around his ears, something is wrong.

Infections

Ear infections are very common in dogs, especially those who spend a lot of time in water and those whose ear flaps hang over the opening to the ear canal, holding moisture inside. The warm, moist environment of the ear canal is a perfect breeding ground for the bacteria and yeast that cause ear infections. Allergies and hormonal problems can also cause or worsen ear infections.

If you see a discharge or notice a foul odor coming from your dog's ear or ears, take him to your veterinarian. Effective treatment depends on accurate diagnosis. Don't waste time and money on home remedies or over-the-counter "cures." Doing so just postpones effective treatment, and may actually make things worse, causing your dog unnecessary suffering and possibly damaging his hearing. Your vet will examine your dog's ears, and if indicated, take swabs and examine them under a microscope. A culture may be performed to identify the organism causing the infection. She will then be able to prescribe an effective treatment regimen.

Injuries

Ear injuries are not uncommon in dogs, especially dogs who are active outdoors, and those with hanging or floppy ears. Ticks, flies, and other bugs love to bite ears and hide under and behind them. Burrs, seeds, and other debris commonly stick into the ear's tender skin, become caught in the hair around the ears, or fall into the ear canal itself. Usually you will be able to see the object and remove it fairly easily. Occasionally, though, professional help is a better idea. If your dog has something embedded in his skin or trapped deep in his ear canal, having your vet remove it may lessen the extent of the injury and prevent complications from infection or from leaving part of the object behind.

Burrs and other types of plant matter can be very difficult to remove, especially if your dog has long, silky hair behind his ears (or elsewhere on his body) or is sensitive about having his ears handled. Some burrs are very sharp and will cut your dog's skin (and your fingers). They also pull the hair and trap moisture and dirt. If they are not removed quickly, they can injure the skin and provide a refuge for insects, fungi, and bacteria. Burrs can usually be worked out one at a time with a comb and your fingers, but if your dog picks up a lot of burrs, or if they're tangled up tight and close to his skin, you may be forced to cut them out. Be very careful not to cut your dog's skin. If you aren't sure you can do the job safely, take him to a professional groomer.

Occasionally an injury breaks a blood vessel in the ear flap and the blood pools inside the ear flap, causing a *hematoma*, or blood-filled swelling. Although unsightly and probably uncomfortable for the dog, hematomas of the ear flap are not usually serious health threats. Small ones often heal on their own. If your dog develops a large hematoma, see your vet. Treatment involves minor surgery, and it may be necessary to leave a drain in the ear for a few days to keep it from refilling with fluid. Do not attempt to treat these at home, as it will only make them worse.

Injuries to the ears can also be caused by other animals, especially other dogs. Let's hope your dog will never be in a dog fight or be attacked by another dog, but fights and attacks do happen, and the resulting injuries can be severe. For most dogs, though, bite injuries to the ears are more likely to occur during rough play. If your dog's ear leather is torn, your vet may need to suture it. All bites, even if they don't look severe, introduce vast numbers of bacteria from the biter's mouth, and risk of infection is always high. Even minor injuries to the ear may bleed excessively, especially if your dog keeps shaking his head. If bleeding has stopped and the injury is minor, clean your dog's wounds and then call your vet. (When cleaning the wound, be careful not to start the bleeding again. See Chapter 15 for more information on wound care.) She may want to prescribe a course of oral antibiotics. Be sure to discuss the pros and cons of antibiotic treatment with her. If the injury is more severe, keep your dog quiet and try to keep him from shaking his head, which can worsen the damage. Get him to your vet as soon as you can.

Deafness

It can be a shock to realize that your dog cannot hear, but the fact is that a deaf dog can live a long, happy life if you are willing to make a few adjustments. Of the parade of foster dogs who have graced my life, three have been deaf, and I didn't find their deafness to be a handicap. Deaf dogs can be trained to respond to visual signals in place of verbal commands, and hand signals and light signals are commonly used for training. Many excellent resources are available to help you if you live with a deaf dog (see "Resources for Owners of Dogs with Vision and Hearing Problems" on page 321). Remember, congenitally deaf dogs don't know that they are missing anything, and those who lose their hearing later in life don't seem to mind. Most important, deafness does not impair a dog's ability to love. If anything, I found my deaf canine friends even more cuddly than usual.

A dog with *bilateral deafness* is deaf in both ears. A dog with *unilateral deafness* is deaf in only one ear, and he may function so well with full hearing in the other ear that you won't know he's partially deaf. Even dogs with more profound hearing loss may not appear to be deaf, especially if they are living with other pets in the household, because they take visual cues from the other animals. Loud sounds also cause floors and furniture to vibrate, allowing deaf dogs to "feel" what they cannot hear.

You can perform some simple tests at home to determine whether your dog can hear, with some caveats. If he is unilaterally deaf, you probably won't learn much. The louder the test sound, the more vibration it creates, so your dog may respond to vibration rather than to sounds, and you won't

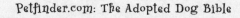

know the difference. You can increase the accuracy of the test by making sure that your dog is not looking at you or at the source of the sound, or by observing how he responds to sounds when he is asleep. When my last deaf foster pup slept through the ringing doorbell and the chaos that my other dogs create as a result, it was clear confirmation of what I already knew. Don't test your dog with other pets or small children present, as he may cue off their responses. Try the following, and see if he reacts.

- Jingle some coins or your keys.
- Squeak a toy, preferably in your pocket or behind your back so he can't see it.
- Call your dog in a normal voice when he has his back to you or is in another room.
- When he is at least several feet from you and not watching you, clap your hands or snap your fingers.
- Whistle or hum.
- Ring a bell.

If you are within reach of a testing facility and are willing to pay for the test, you can have a more accurate hearing assessment performed by a veterinarian. The Brainstem Auditory Evoked Response (BAER) test measures electrical activity in the brain in response to clicking sounds in each ear. The BAER test is designed to test hearing in human infants, so it is limited to the range of sounds that people normally hear (dogs normally hear higher frequencies than we do). Some dogs who test deaf are able to hear very high-pitched sounds that people cannot hear. However, the BAER test will tell you if your dog is deaf to most of the sounds of domestic life, including your voice. The test is non-invasive and not painful and takes about fifteen minutes. If your dog dislikes being restrained or objects to having wires attached to his head, he can be sedated for the test, although that is not usually necessary.

Inherited Deafness

Inherited (congenital) deafness, full or partial, occurs in many purebred and mixed-breed dogs and is most common in dogs who lack pigment in some or all of their fur and in their skin. In other words, it's most common in dogs who are white or have white markings and pink skin. (All three of my

deaf pooches were white.) Not all white dogs are deaf, of course, and not all deaf dogs are white, so coat color is not a foolproof indicator. However, it is a clue that the dog may be deaf.

Why, you ask, is white hair associated with deafness? The *pigment cells* that color the fur and skin in non-white dogs convert sound waves into electrical impulses that nerves then carry to the brain. When the ear lacks pigment cells, the nerve endings atrophy and die. As a result, sound waves entering the ear go no farther, and the dog cannot hear. So what about those congenitally deaf dogs who have colored ears? The pigment cells that affect hearing are deep inside the ear, and you cannot see the tiny hairs associated with them.

Not all white dogs are deaf!

Skin and Coat

Skin problems are extremely common in dogs, and some adopted dogs have more than their share because of poor care in their previous homes. In fact, some dogs end up in shelters and rescue programs because their people got tired of the constant scratching and rubbing, excessive shedding, unpleasant odor, and other results of skin problems. Ironically, many of those problems are caused or made worse by lack of care and are correctable. If your adopted dog has a history of skin and coat problems, you can do a lot to restore him to good health.

Unhealthy skin cannot support a healthy coat, so dogs with skin problems don't look their best. In fact, excessive hair loss or dull, brittle coats, and brittle, cracked, or peeling nails are often the first sign that a dog's health is not up to par. In addition, damaged skin offers an easy entry through which bacteria, viruses, and fungi can attack your dog.

The source of a canine skin problem is not always easy to identify, but if you and your vet work together and stick with it, you are likely to at least find relief for your dog, if not a complete cure. Keep in mind that whole books are

Petfinder.com: The Adopted Dog Bible

written on individual skin conditions, so the information presented here is intended just to suggest possibilities. If your dog has problems with his skin, coat, or nails, read this section and see if anything rings true for your pup. Then work with your veterinarian, or ask for a referral to a veterinary dermatologist for specialized care.

If your dog has a skin problem, don't expect your vet to diagnose it instantly or cure it overnight. She will need to evaluate the symptoms and your dog's history and may need to perform skin scrapings and other laboratory tests before she can make an accurate diagnosis and begin effective treatment. On the other hand,

Do Dogs Sweat?

We humans perspire to help keep our bodies cool through the evaporation of moisture from our skin. Dogs accomplish the same result primarily by panting, which vents heat from the body through the mouth. But dogs do have *apocrine* and *eccrine* glands that produce fluids in the skin. In people, the fluid (sweat) helps regulate body temperature. In dogs, the fluid provides a protective seal for the skin and contains *pheromones* that give the dog a distinctive odor. When the dog is stressed or nervous, glands in the pads of the feet produce a watery fluid that may improve traction and often leaves damp paw prints on the ground.

if you feel your regular vet is not progressing quickly enough, or that the treatment she prescribes is not working after a reasonable time, take your dog to a veterinary dermatologist.

Skin problems generally relate to six underlying causes: nutrition, environment, parasites, infection, allergy, and emotions.

Nutritional Dermatitis

A proper diet is essential for healthy skin. However, many problems associated with poor nutrition take some time to surface, so the connection may not be immediately obvious. Your dog may seem to do well on a particular food for a long time, then begin to show symptoms of poor nutrition or allergies.

If your dog's skin is dry, itchy, and irritated, if his coat and nails are dry and brittle, or if he seems to shed more than he should, consider his diet first (see Chapter 9). Here are the basics:

- Three of the first five ingredients in your dog's food should be meat proteins (beef, poultry, lamb, or fish)
- Many dogs are allergic to corn, wheat, and soy (see also "Allergies" on

page 334), which are used in different forms in many dog foods. Find a food that has none of these grains, which are not part of a natural diet for a canine.

☼ Supplement your dog's diet with daily doses of essential fatty acids (EFAs), which are available in capsule, liquid, and granular forms. Consult your veterinarian for product selection.

Many skin problems disappear when a dog's nutrition improves. It normally takes about four to six weeks to see a significant improvement. If problems persist after six weeks, keep your dog on a balanced diet that supports his overall health, and consult with your veterinarian to consider other possible causes for his troubled skin.

Environmental Dermatitis

Dogs, like people, can be sensitive to many things where they live and play. If such a sensitivity causes skin irritation, bumps, scratching, hair loss, open moist lesions (see "Hot Spots" on page 336), or other reactions in the skin, the dog has *environmental dermatitis.*

Many things can cause environmental dermatitis in dogs. Some of the most common triggers are lawn grasses and lawn chemicals, moisture, matted fur (see Chapter 11), tiny nicks from clipper blades ("clipper burn"), carpets and carpet cleaners or deodorizers, and plastic, especially plastic food and water bowls.

The source of an individual case of environmental dermatitis can be tough to identify, but if you're persistent you can probably find it. Your vet's experience can be a big help, especially if you provide a thorough history on where your dog spends his time.

Parasitic Dermatitis

Skin damage from parasites—including fleas, ticks, mites, lice, and others—can cause the skin to become inflamed, itchy, and sometimes smelly. (See "External Parasites" on page 337.) The dog scratches, bites, and licks himself for relief, causing more damage, inflammation, and reaction, which brings about more scratching, biting, and licking. If bacteria take hold, the dog may also develop *infectious dermatitis* (see the next section).

Petfinder.com: The Adopted Dog Bible

The first step in treating parasitic dermatitis is to eliminate the parasite that started the cycle. Again, it's essential to feed the dog an optimum diet to support his overall health, and then to treat the symptoms.

Infectious Dermatitis

Infectious dermatitis can be caused by bacterial, fungal, or viral organisms. Bacterial dermatitis can be secondary to an underlying allergy or can occur when the dog is given antibiotics to treat a different problem. Normal, healthy skin is home to a variety of bacteria that keep one another in check. When drugs (or something else) kill some types of bacteria, populations of the remaining types grow beyond normal levels, irritating the skin and making your dog itch like crazy. The affected dog licks and scratches himself raw (see also "Hot Spots" on page 336), giving the bacteria easy entry into his body. He may also transfer the infection from the original location to other parts of his body through licking and scratching. Inflammation, oozing sores, hair loss, and itching are symptoms of infectious dermatitis.

Bacterial dermatitis can be difficult to treat, but if you are persistent, it can be cleared up. Your dog's fur traps moisture near the skin, so it is important to clip the hair around the sores to help them dry. Topical and oral antibiotics may be prescribed to bring invading bacteria under control, and your dog may have to wear a restraint collar (such as an "Elizabethan" collar) to keep him from damaging his skin further. Antihistamines are often used to relieve the itching. Occasionally cortisone is used as well, but it can suppress the immune system and is usually not prescribed when infection is present. As with all treatments, it is important for you to consider the pros and cons of giving a steroid to your dog; be sure to discuss these with your veterinarian. Your veterinarian should recheck your dog during treatment to determine if any changes in medication are required. Dermatitis due to fungal or viral causes requires different therapy. Be aware, too, that if yeast is the culprit, there could be something else going on, such as allergy, hypothyroidism, nutritional deficiency, or long-term use of cortisone or antibiotics.

Allergic Dermatitis

Allergic dermatitis, or dermatitis brought on by an allergic reaction, is very common in dogs. The most common form is triggered when the immune system reacts to something the dog has inhaled, such as pollen, mold, dust, or other airborne substances. As a result, the dog licks and chews his paws and scratches and rubs his face, ears, and eyes.

Because allergies can be triggered by so many things, allergic dermatitis is often hard to diagnose and harder to control (see "Allergies" on page 334). The first step is to rule out other types of dermatitis. Once that's done, you and your vet should work together to try to identify the source of the allergy. Unfortunately, that isn't always possible, and your dog may be allergic to more than one thing, making identification even more difficult. Your vet may decide to do skin testing to identify one of the more common allergens that affect dogs. If you do identify the culprit, keeping your dog from being exposed to it will end the problem. Often, though, it's not so simple. Many common allergens, such as grass, are just too widespread to avoid.

In that case, your vet can recommend treatment to control the symptoms. Oral antihistamines, medicated baths, and topical sprays and ointments often help. Corticosteroids are sometimes prescribed, but they pose their own risks and should not be used long-term.

Neurogenic Dermatitis

Neurogenic dermatitis (neurodermatitis) involves obsessive licking and chewing of one or two easy-to-reach spots, often on a front leg. The constant licking and biting causes a *lick granuloma*, or lesion, in the skin, and then keeps it from healing. Bacterial infections are common with lick granulomas. Repeated episodes of licking, infection, partial healing, scarring, and reopening of the lesions eventually causes permanent disfigurement. Lick granulomas can be very challenging to treat.

Neurodermatitis is often linked to emotional and psychological factors such as boredom, frustration, separation anxiety, loneliness, or unreasonable confinement. Your adopted dog may have experienced one or more of these emotions in his previous situation. If he has formed a habit of self-mutilation, giving him attention, companionship, exercise, and other benefits of responsible care may help stop the behavior. Like many habits, though, obsessive licking can be a hard habit to break. Your vet can help treat the symptoms and underlying causes, but you may want to consult a qualified behaviorist to help you find a cure.

Petfinder.com: The Adopted Dog Bible

Not all cases of neurodermatitis originate with poor care, of course. Sometimes a well-cared-for dog begins by licking or nibbling a small cut or bug bite, or scratches at skin made itchy by allergies. The licking may be incited by many other causes, including infection or wounds. Unfortunately, his attention to the spot may cause his body to release histamines, which cause itching, which makes the dog lick and nibble more. A vicious cycle begins. The sooner you can break the behavior pattern and clear up the skin irritation or underlying cause of the lesion, the better the chances that you will keep your dog from becoming obsessed with licking himself. Again, a few sessions with a behaviorist may be the best thing for you and your dog.

Poor Condition from Poor Care

Well-cared-for dogs occasionally find themselves up for adoption when their owners die or for some other reason cannot continue to care for them. Many dogs in shelters and rescue programs, though, have not had very good care. If your dog was one of these unfortunates, his skin and coat are probably not in the best condition (although if he's been fostered for some time, he may be well along the road to recovery).

Don't despair! Several factors may have combined to damage your dog's appearance, and several factors will work together to restore it. Here are the keys to skin and coat repair:

- Keep your dog's skin and coat clean by regular grooming and use of appropriate dog care products (see Chapter 11).
- Keep your dog free of parasites inside and out (see "External Parasites" on page 337 in this chapter, and "Parasites" on page 353 in Chapter 17).
- Feed your dog a high-quality diet (see "Nutritional Dermatitis" on page 327 in this chapter, and all of Chapter 8).
- Give your dog proper exercise to promote his overall health.

Given time and proper care, most adopted dogs recover their healthy skin and lustrous coats. (It's rumored that frequent belly rubs are also therapeutic, by the way.)

Pemphigus Complex. This refers to four separate but related autoimmune disorders of the skin. They are usually treated with corticosteroids to suppress the immune system.

Pemphigus vulgaris (common pemphigus) causes blisters and sores in the mouth, armpits, and groin, and at places where mucous membranes meet furred skin—eyelids, lips, nostrils, anus, and prepuce or vulva.

Pemphigus vegetans causes thick, irregular lesions marked by oozing and pustules. It's thought to be a less aggressive form of pemphigus vulgaris.

Pemphigus foliaceous causes redness, crusting, scales, and loss of hair, usually beginning on the ears and face and spreading to the feet and groin. Secondary skin infections are common. In severe cases, the dog may have a fever, be depressed, and stop eating. Pemphigus foliaceous seems to be more likely to affect Akitas, Bearded Collies, Chow Chows, Dachshunds, Doberman Pinschers, Newfoundlands, and mixes that include those breeds.

Pemphigus erythematosis looks like pemphigus foliaceous and often affects the nose. It becomes worse with exposure to ultraviolet light (sunlight). It is considered to be a more benign form of pemphigus foliaceous.

Discoid lupus erythematosis (DLE). This is an autoimmune dermatitis that affects the face and nose and appears to be inherited (see the definition of *pemphigus erythematosis* above). DLE is the most common autoimmune skin problem, and German Shepherd Dogs, Collies, Shetland Sheepdogs, Siberian Huskies, and mixes that include those breeds are especially susceptible to it. DLE usually responds well to treatment with drugs that suppress the immune response.

Sebaceous Adenitis (SA). The *sebaceous* glands secrete oils that protect and lubricate your dog's skin. They occasionally become inflamed and eventually are destroyed by the inflammation. The result is a condition known as *sebaceous adenitis* (SA). Symptoms of sebaceous adenitis may include hair loss; thickened, scaly skin; an unpleasant, musty odor; and possible secondary skin infections. The cause of SA is not known, but it is not very common and is believed to have a genetic component because it occurs more frequently in some breeds and very rarely in others.

SA is diagnosed by taking a skin punch biopsy, which is then analyzed by a pathologist. The procedure requires only local anesthetic. There is no cure at present for SA, but most cases can be controlled with regular care. Weekly or biweekly baths with a hypoallergenic dog shampoo can help to control the symptoms. Many dogs respond well to twenty- to thirty-minute soaks in baby oil, which loosens dry skin scales and helps restore moisture to the skin. Oil treatments must be followed by several shampooings to remove the oil, so they are rather time- and labor-intensive.

With good care, dogs with SA can live normal lives, as the disease is essentially cosmetic (unless secondary infections become severe).

Breeds and Mixes Prone to Sebaceous Adenitis

The following breeds and mixes that include these breeds are more prone to sebaceous adenitis (SA):

- Akita
- Collie
- Dalmatian
- German Shepherd Dog
- Golden Retriever
- Miniature Pinscher
- Old English Sheepdog
- Standard Poodle
- Vizsla
- Weimaraner

Skin Cancer. *Melanoma* (skin cancer) can be either benign or malignant and is diagnosed though biopsy of the tumor to determine its type and growth rate. Benign melanomas can be unattractive, but they are not usually life-threatening. Most benign melanomas in dogs are round, firm, dark-colored masses up to approximately two inches in diameter. They are raised above the skin, and usually appear on the head, back, or toes. Benign melanomas don't usually *metastasize* (spread), but they do sometimes invade neighboring tissues. Frequent grooming, petting, and handling are good ways to check your dog for odd lumps and growths.

Malignant melanomas often appear first in X-rays of the dog's lungs or in swelling of the lymph nodes. They can metastasize to any part of the body, particularly the lungs and lymph nodes. Early detection increases the chances of successful treatment, but these cancers are often advanced before they are discovered, and are often incurable.

Melanomas are usually treated by surgically removing the tumor and surrounding tissue. If the cancer has not spread, the surgery may provide a complete cure. Sadly, malignant melanomas often spread to different parts of

Breeds at Greater Risk for Melanoma

Although any dog can develop a melanoma (skin cancer), the following breeds and mixes containing these breeds are at higher risk:

- Airedale Terrier
- Boston Terrier
- Boxer
- Chihuahua
- Chow Chow
- Cocker Spaniel
- Doberman Pinscher
- Golden Retriever
- Irish Setter
- Miniature Schnauzer
- Scottish Terrier
- Springer Spaniel

the body before the disease is discovered, making long-term survival less likely even with treatment.

Allergies

Allergic reactions, or *allergies*, occur when the immune system treats foreign proteins in contact with the body as threats, and it releases *histamines* to fight them off. Dogs and people can be allergic to many of the same things: pollen, dust mites, mold, foods, chemicals, plastic, medications, plants, animal products, and insect bites are common *allergens*. Inhalant allergies—those that are breathed in—are very common in dogs, but dogs do not get runny noses like people do. Instead, their skin becomes irritated and itchy, and sometimes, oily, raw, and infected.

What Causes Canine Allergies?

Food allergies are extremely common in dogs (see "Nutritional Dermatitis" on page 327). In addition to scratching, food allergies can cause inflammation of the ears, head shaking, licking (and if your dog has white feet, they may turn a rusty pink from proteins in his saliva), face and head rubbing, flatulence, diarrhea, vomiting, sneezing, breathing difficulty, behavioral changes, and perhaps seizures.

Finding the source of an allergic reaction can be very difficult. If you and your vet can't identify the allergen within a reasonable time span, consider taking your dog to a veterinary dermatologist for specialized testing. Testing isn't cheap, but is more cost effective (and more caring) than using an ineffective treatment for years while your dog continues to suffer.

Keep in mind, too, that allergies can develop over time. Your dog may become allergic to a stimulus that didn't bother him in the past, so keep an open mind when trying to discover what's making him react.

Treating Canine Allergies

Allergies cannot be "cured," but the substances that cause them can sometimes be avoided, and the symptoms can be treated. If your adopted dog has allergies, here are some ways to deal with them:

1. *Control your dog's environment.* If possible, remove or avoid the source. If your dog is allergic to corn, don't feed him anything that contains corn! If he scratches himself silly after you sprinkle deodorizer on your carpet, use something different or don't use a deodorizer in the future. Use a HEPA air filter to remove pollen and dust from the air in your home, and don't let your dog lie on the lawn if he's allergic to grass.

2. *Treat your dog's symptoms. Antihistamines* such as Benadryl help some dogs, but they can cause sleepiness. *Corticosteroids* such as cortisone, dexamethasone, or prednisone are sometimes prescribed to reduce itching, but they have a number of undesirable side effects, including increased thirst and appetite, which lead to increased urination and weight gain. Long-term use can suppress the immune system (see Chapter 17). As always, consult your vet before you use any products on your dog or give him any medication or "natural" product—some products could do more harm than good, especially in combination with one another.

3. *Supplement your dog's diet* with fatty acids, which are natural anti-inflammatories.

4. *Have your dog tested and treated with immunotherapy* (allergy shots). Allergy shots for dogs are safe, and are effective for some dogs. However, your dog first must be tested to determine the precise allergen, and once he begins getting the injections you may see no improvement for up to a year. Some dogs, like people, do not respond successfully to immunotherapy.

Hot Spots

Hot spots are inflamed areas of skin that often become open sores as the dog licks and chews to relieve the itching. Although any dog can develop a hot spot, they occur most often in dogs with heavy coats who have a history of allergies, flea infestations (although it only takes one or two flea bites to incite a reaction in an allergic dog), ear infections, irritated anal sacs, and tangled or matted coats. Many things have been linked to the development of hot spots, including the following common triggers:

- Lawn and garden products
- Flea or tick shampoos or medications
- Regular shampoos (especially if not rinsed thoroughly)
- Other coat products
- Cleaning products
- Flea saliva
- Food allergies
- Neurotic licking and biting

Hot spots generally appear as patches of painfully itchy, often reddened skin that has lost some or all of its hair and may be swollen and may have a smelly seepage. A hot spot can pop up in a matter of hours.

Hot spots most commonly show up initially in areas that are easy for the dog to reach—legs, paws, flanks, and rump. If not treated, though, other hot spots can appear on other parts of the body, and can become further infected, itchy, and sore. Effective treatment of hot spots can take time, and it requires a two-pronged approach.

First, the sore or sores must be treated to prevent further damage. The hair around the sore should be clipped short to help the hot spot dry and to keep the area cleaner, and the dog must be prevented from furthering the damage. Do not apply a topical ointment or cream unless your vet advises you to do so—they can seal infection in and prevent proper healing, and often encourage the dog to lick more.

Secondly, you need to eliminate the underlying cause or, if elimination isn't possible, reduce its effect. Common contributors to hot spots include poor grooming, allergies, especially to fleas, and emotional factors.

Petfinder.com: The Adopted Dog Bible

Unfortunately, adopted dogs often come from backgrounds that promoted development of hot spots. Fortunately, simply moving to a new, responsible home may make all the difference.

External Parasites

Parasites on your dog's skin, including fleas, ticks, and mange mites, are big trouble in tiny packages. They not only bite and make your dog itch, but they also open the way for infections, spread disease and other parasites to other animals and humans, and cause allergic reactions in many dogs. Dogs who come into the rescue system from neglectful homes or those dogs who have been strays may be infested with parasites. These dogs usually appear to be in less than good health. A dog with external parasites, including fleas, a heavy infestation of ticks, lice, or mites, will have a dull coat, bare patches of skin, and irritated skin. The dog may or may not be scratching or licking at his skin.

Fleas

Fleas are small black or reddish-brown insects. They are very mobile and hard to catch, and they are well-protected by hard shells. Adult fleas bite their host and ingest his blood. They lay eggs, sometimes on the host animal, but usually in the host's bedding or in carpets, and other places the host animal visits. If conditions are favorable, the eggs hatch in four to twenty-one days, but they can survive up to a year before the larvae emerge. Flea larvae look like tiny maggots, and they eat the blood-rich feces of adult fleas. The larva molt twice, then form a tough *pupa* (cocoon), where they metamorphose into adult fleas.

Fleas are more than disgusting little pests. They can also threaten both your and your dog's health. Some fleas carry disease, as well as tapeworm larvae (see Chapter 17). A large infestation of fleas can cause anemia, especially in a puppy or small dog. Some dogs are allergic to flea saliva, and even a single bite can send such a dog into a frenzy of scratching (see "Parasitic Dermatitis" on page 328). Check your dog regularly for fleas— they are easiest to spot on his belly and near his genitals—and act quickly if you find any. To learn how to keep your dog flea free, or how to deal with an infestation, see "My Dog Has Fleas—NOT!" on page 236.

Ticks

Ticks are not insects but *arthropods* (relatives of spiders and mites). Prior to eating, most ticks are round and flat. After they eat, they swell and look like beans with legs. Deer ticks are so tiny that they often go unnoticed until they eat and swell. Unfortunately, by the time any tick has filled itself with its victim's blood, it has also transmitted whatever disease organisms it carries. Ticks typically inhabit fields and woodlands, but they happily hitch rides on wild and domestic animals and on people, so you may find them in your yard or home.

Like fleas, ticks carry several serious diseases, including babesiosis, anaplasmosis, ehrlichia, Rocky Mountain spotted fever, and Lyme disease.

If you have found ticks in your yard in the past, or if you take your dog to fields or wooded areas, check him carefully when you get home and several times over the next few days. The spots ticks are likeliest to be are in or around your dog's ears, in his armpits, or around his genitals. A fine-toothed comb such as a flea comb is useful for searching through fur (see Chapter 11). If you find a tick, remove it *carefully* (see "How to Remove a Tick" on the next page).

Ringworm

Ringworm is actually not a worm but a fungus. Ringworm is highly contagious, spreading easily from one pet to another. It is one of the few diseases that can spread from your dog to you and your human family. I learned this the hard way in my early days as a volunteer with my local rescue group. It was easy for the pharmacist to identify the tell-tale ring on my *face*. Living with it until it cleared up was more difficult. Although not nearly as common in dogs as it is in cats, dogs rescued from dirty living conditions may have ringworm, which usually begins as a sore-looking bald circle. If your dog has or develops any sort of bald spot, even if it doesn't look irritated, have your vet check it.

Like all fungal infections, ringworm is hard to treat. Don't fool around with home remedies or over-the-counter treatments. Modern drugs are much more effective, and your vet can advise you on how to keep the infection

How to Remove a Tick

How to remove a tick

Tick—ick! If you find one on your dog (or yourself), remove it promptly and carefully. If it hasn't yet bitten into the skin, you can pick it up with a tissue and dispose of it. If the tick has had time to bite, though, it will be harder to remove. Here's how.

- Dab the tick with alcohol, iodine, or a strong saline solution to make it loosen its grip. Alternately, you can smear it with Vaseline, which will make it start to suffocate, also loosening its grip.

- Carefully grasp the tick's body with a tick remover, tweezers, or a tissue, and pull it straight out. Don't twist—you could leave the head embedded in your dog's skin. Don't squeeze—you may force disease-filled fluid into the victim. You need to be gentle but firm; if you pull too hard, the tick's head may separate from its body. If the head remains in your dog's skin, an infection or abscess could result, which would require veterinary treatment.

- If it's a tiny tick, show it to your vet. It may be a deer tick, in which case a discussion about Lyme disease and tick preventative measures may be a good idea. A preventative treatment won't protect your dog if he's already been bitten by a deer tick with Lyme disease, but the presence of one deer tick shows that they are a potential problem, and vaccination may be a good idea. (The vaccine works pre-exposure.)

- It's possible that pulling out a tick will be painful to your dog, although it's not likely because, like most insects, ticks inject a mild painkiller as they bite so that their host doesn't immediately scratch them off. Once you've removed the tick, check your dog's skin—you should see a small hole. If you see a black spot, you've left the head imbedded in the skin.

- Dispose of the tick carefully—remember, unless you pulled its head

continued

off, it's still alive. Drop it into alcohol to retain for your vet's inspection or flush it down the toilet.

- Clean the area with alcohol or antibacterial cleanser, dry, and apply antibacterial ointment.
- Wash your hands and any tools you used.
- Check the bite for signs of infection for a few days, particularly if the head was left behind. Call your vet if the area becomes inflamed.
- Write down the date of the bite. Tick-borne illnesses take some time to incubate and can be hard to diagnose, so knowing that your dog was bitten on a certain date could be useful if he becomes ill.

If ticks are common where you live, ask your vet to recommend a safe tick killer to use during warm weather. Additional products are available over the counter, but beware—not all are effective, and some are dangerous when combined with one another. Flea and tick collars in particular are generally ineffective and accounts of respiratory distress have been reported in some dogs after contact with them.

from spreading through your household. Treatment can last from weeks to months and may begin with clipping the hair around the affected area. (The hair must be disposed of carefully because it carries fungal spores that can infect people and other animals. Likewise, any instruments used on the infected dog must be sterilized before they are used again.) The lesions are then treated twice daily with topical ointments such as miconazole cream, Lotrimin cream, or 1 percent chlorhexidine ointment. In severe or generalized cases, antifungal shampoos and dips should also be used, and more aggressive oral antifungal medications should be prescribed.

Mange

Mange refers to several conditions caused by various species of microscopic arthropods called *mites* that live on the animal's skin and eat skin

Petfinder.com: The Adopted Dog Bible

debris, hair follicles, and tissue. Their victims typically lose hair and develop an itchy, flaky crust on their skin. Dogs with mange can scratch themselves raw, providing easy entry for bacteria, viruses, fungi, and parasites.

Three types of mange occur in dogs:

- *Demodectic mange* (demodex) is usually seen in puppies from three to twelve months old. Demodex mites live on many healthy puppies and dogs in reasonable populations that cause no problems, but an occasional puppy is less resistant, and the mites reproduce more quickly than normal, causing demodectic mange. Symptoms of demodex include thinned hair around the eyes and mouth and on the front legs. When my very first adopted puppy, Kona, started to have a "part" in the hair on his head, off we went to our vet for a skin scraping, which confirmed demodectic mange. Demodex often *resolves* (cures itself) within two to three months or when the animal reaches one year of age, but in some cases it causes oozing sores, crusty skin, and loss of hair over more of the body. Early diagnosis and treatment by your veterinarian can save your puppy a lot of discomfort. When demodex develops in an adult dog, it is usually because an underlying stressor such as cancer, hypothyroidism, adrenal gland diseases, or exposure to certain medications has compromised the immune system, allowing the previously harmless mites to reproduce rapidly. Stress from poor nutrition or other aspects of poor care can also contribute to adult-onset demodex, so it can occur in dogs in shelters or rescue programs. The underlying cause must be resolved to bring demodex under control.
- *Sarcoptic mange* (scabies) is caused by a microscopic mite that burrows under the skin to lay eggs. Within three weeks the eggs hatch and the larvae develop into adult mites who lay eggs of their own. Symptoms of scabies include intense itching, oozing sores, crusty ear tips, secondary infections, and hair loss that begins on the ears, elbows, legs, and face, and spreads over the body. Scabies is highly contagious and can affect people as well as dogs, so rapid veterinary response is critical. Unfortunately, sarcoptic mange is often misdiagnosed as allergic dermatitis because the mites that cause it burrow into the skin and are not always

evident, even in skin scrapings. Some veterinarians prefer to treat the dog for scabies, even if no mites are found, before considering allergic dermatitis. If that is the case with your dog, be aware that Ivermectin, often used to kill mites, is dangerous for some dogs (see "Dogs and Drugs" on page 387 in Chapter 17).

✻ *Cheyletiella mange* ("walking dandruff") is caused by tiny white mites that look like dandruff moving around on the dog's head, neck, and back. It causes mild itching in puppies and passes easily among dogs and to people. Fortunately, Cheyletiella is easy to cure with your veterinarian's help.

If your dog experiences any unexplained hair loss or skin irritations, take him to your veterinarian. (If any human member of your family experiences similar symptoms, see a doctor and tell her about your dog.) The sooner a diagnosis is made and treatment begun, the better for everyone.

Lice

Although it's not very common, dogs can also pick up lice. There are two kinds of lice found on dogs: *sucking lice*, which bite the dog and eat a drop of blood as they do, and *biting lice*, which eat skin dander and flakes of skin. Lice can be seen with the naked eye; if you see little white eggshells attached to your dog's hair, it's probably lice and you should contact your veterinarian right away. Lice are transmittable to other pets and people, so you need to deal with them immediately and thoroughly. Treatment generally includes a medicated bath and spray or powder. Some flea and tick preventatives have been approved for treating lice in dogs; see "My Dog Has Fleas—NOT" on page 236 in Chapter 11.

Now that we've surveyed some of the things that can go wrong with the outside of your dog, and—more importantly—some of the things you can do to keep him healthy, we'll move on to the inside of your dog. The distinction is, of course, artificial, because your dog's body is an integrated system. Injuries and infections that begin on the outside often affect internal organs, and diseases of internal organs often affect the outside of the dog as well. Learning how to keep your dog healthy inside and out is one of the most loving things you can do.

Dog Biscuits for the Soul: Sam

Sam

Sam was a twelve-year-old Yorkie whose owner died. Her son, although he promised to take care of Sam, quickly left him at a local shelter, and United Yorkie Rescue took him into foster care. Sam had a heart murmur, was blind in one eye due to a cataract, and had no tear duct in the other eye. He had hair loss due to stress, and skin tags due to old age. Sam lived a very happy two years with us and brought me so much joy. He was the best companion dog and absolutely adored car rides. He would come to the vineyards with me and loved everyone he met, including all dogs. Sam died in my arms of congenital heart failure. I would adopt ten more dogs like Sam to experience the love and joy only a rescued dog can give.

Deborah Maffettone, West Babylon, New York
Sam was adopted from United Yorkie Rescue in Indianapolis, Indiana

Resources

American Academy of Veterinary Dermatology
777 E. Park Drive, PO Box 8820
Harrisburg, PA 17105-8820
Phone: 1-877-SKINVET (754-6838)
Fax: (717) 558-7841
swilson@pamedsoc.org
aavd@pamedsoc.org
http://www.aavd.org/

WEBSITES
American College of Veterinary Dermatology
http://www.acvd.org

Skin Disorders of Dogs
http://www.vetinfo4dogs.com/dskin.html

Skin and Allergy Problems in Dogs
http://www.k9web.com/dog-faqs/medical/canine-allergies.html

Further information on breeds that carry the merle gene
http://www.lethalwhites.com/links.html

Genetics of Coat Color and Type in Dogs
http://homepage.usask.ca/~schmutz/dogcolors.html

Books

Ackerman, Lowell: *Guide to Skin & Haircoat Problems in Dogs*. Alpine Publishing, 1994
Fougere, Barbara: *The Pet Lover's Guide to Natural Healing for Cats & Dogs*. Elsevier, 2006

17

Managing Problems of the Inner Dog

Dogs and people are susceptible to most of the same health problems. Some are inherited, while others result from disease, poor nutrition, injury, exposure to harmful substances, or aging. Does that mean your adopted dog is bound to get sick? Not at all. But the wise pet parent is aware of potential problems and knows that early detection and treatment can make a significant difference in the length and quality of a dog's life. In this chapter, we look at some of the more common health problems that can affect the "inner" dog.

The Circulatory System

Heart disease is more common in dogs than was once commonly believed. It behaves differently in dogs than it does in people. Some dogs are born with *congenital heart disease*, often indicated initially by a heart murmur detected during a puppy exam. Some, but not all, congenital heart problems are inherited. *Acquired heart disease* develops as a result of disease, infection, environmental factors, inherited predisposition, or aging. Heart attacks are rare in dogs, as is coronary artery disease.

Common signs of heart disease in dogs include excessively heavy panting,

Signs of Health, Signs of Trouble

Early detection of problems is one of the best tools you and your vet have for keeping your dog healthy. A healthy dog:

- Has a temperature of 100.5–102 degrees Fahrenheit
- Takes 15–20 breaths per minute
- Has a heart rate of 70–120 beats per minute
- Has smooth pink gums, inner lips, tongue, and inner eyelids
- Smells clean and does not have bad breath
- Has a shiny coat with no sparse or bare spots (unless, of course, she's supposed to be hairless)
- Has pliant skin with no flakiness, redness, or discoloration
- Has bright, clear eyes that do not water excessively
- Has a clean, moist nose
- Has clean ears with only a faint, inoffensive, musky odor
- Is alert and reasonably active for her age

A dog who shows any of the following signs or symptoms of poor health needs to see a veterinarian to be sure that no serious problems are developing:

- Abnormally high or low temperature
- Abnormally rapid, slow, or irregular respiration or heart rate, or heavy panting (except just after strenuous exercise)
- Pale, bright red, yellow or otherwise abnormal-looking gums, inner lips, tongue, and inner eyelids
- Strong or offensive odor coming from the skin, ears, or mouth
- Dull, dry, or brittle fur or bare patches in the coat
- Inflamed, flaky, or scabbed skin; lumps anywhere on the body; change in color of skin or fur; excessive scratching, biting, or licking her own body
- Eyes that squint or appear red or swollen; eyes that have excessive or yellow or greenish discharge
- A runny or crusty nose

continued

Petfinder.com: The Adopted Dog Bible

- Ears that smell bad or have a lot of "gunk" in or near them, or ears that itch or hurt, as shown by head shaking, ear scratching or rubbing, or tenderness
- Frequent or chronic gagging, sneezing, or coughing
- Frequent or chronic retching or vomiting
- Loose or watery stools; change in frequency of bowel movements; yellow, black, or bloody stools; evidence of parasites in stools or around anus; straining to defecate
- Change in frequency of urination; signs of blood in the urine; straining to urinate; dribbling or incontinence; increase in amount of urine produced
- Sudden change in appetite or eating habits
- Increase or decrease in water intake
- Obesity, emaciation, sudden or unexplained weight loss or gain
- Broken, eroded or dirty-looking teeth; obviously irritated mouth tissues; offensive breath
- Discharge from vulva or prepuce (skin covering genitals)
- Lethargy, anxiety, aggression, stumbling, lameness, trembling, and other abnormal behavior or unexplained changes in behavior

The sooner your dog receives professional care for an injury or illness, the better her chances for recovery will be. If you want to know more about the problem and your treatment options, or if you'd like to interact with people who have been through a similar experience, search the Internet. Many veterinary schools and hospitals maintain informative websites, and there are bulletin boards and discussion lists for just about every canine health issue. Begin with the "Online Veterinary Resources" section later in this chapter.

irregular or rapid breathing, chronic coughing, enlarged abdomen, lack of stamina, or unexplained weight loss. If your dog has any of these signs, your veterinarian will probably suggest diagnostic tests, possibly including electrocardiograms (EKGs), blood tests to detect imbalances and abnormalities, chest X-rays, blood pressure measurements, or sonograms. Your vet may also refer you to a veterinary cardiologist for specialized diagnosis and treatment. If your dog's breed (or breeds) are prone to heart disease, you may want to

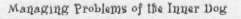

have her examined by a cardiologist, both when you adopt her and periodically as recommended, even if she shows no sign of a problem.

You can't prevent all types of canine heart disease, but you can promote heart health in your dog by keeping her at a healthy weight to reduce stress on the heart and keeping her fit through exercise appropriate to her age and overall health and condition. Her teeth and gums must be kept in good condition as gum disease can contribute to heart disease (see Chapter 11).

If your dog does develop heart disease, don't despair. Many affected dogs can be helped through diet, controlled exercise, and medication, and some congenital defects can be treated surgically.

Now let's look at some common circulatory problems that occur in dogs.

Mitral Valve Insufficiency

The *mitral valve* controls the flow of blood in the heart from the left atrium (the collecting chamber) to the left ventricle (the pumping chamber). *Mitral valve insufficiency* refers to a condition in which the mitral valve leaks.

The first indication of mitral valve insufficiency may be a *heart murmur* detected with a stethoscope. The murmur is the sound of blood flowing backward through the leaky mitral valve. At this stage, your dog may show no other signs of heart disease. Eventually, though, the leak will probably become worse, allowing blood to back up in the heart and, eventually, in the lungs. The heart slowly becomes enlarged, the lungs become congested as fluid accumulates (*edema*), and the dog is said to have *congestive heart failure* (see "Heart Failure" below). In some dogs, the situation is made worse by a leak in the *tricuspid valve*, which separates the right atrium from the right ventricle (the chamber that pumps blood into the lungs).

Valvular disease is progressive (it gets worse over time) and irreversible, but progression can be very slow and many dogs with valvular disease never develop heart failure. If the dog has no signs of heart failure, no treatment is needed. If the disease progresses to heart failure, medication and other treatments may help.

Petfinder.com: The Adopted Dog Bible

Heart Failure

Heart failure occurs when the heart becomes unable to pump blood efficiently enough to meet the body's needs. Although "failure" sounds like a situation in which the heart suddenly stops, heart failure is in fact an ongoing condition, and there may be no clinical signs for a long time. Mild to moderate heart failure typically causes enlargement of the heart, lethargy, and coughing and difficulty breathing after exercise. As heart failure progresses from moderate to severe, the dog may have more difficulty breathing even at rest and be unable to tolerate mild exercise. She may be restless and reluctant to lie down, and may stop eating. The dog's abdomen may become extended from accumulation of fluid. In some cases, the heartbeats become irregular, and the dog becomes weak. She may lose her appetite and, as a consequence, lose weight, and she may be prone to fainting.

Heart failure may be diagnosed during routine examinations even before clinical signs of disease appear. As with most health problems, the sooner heart failure is diagnosed, the more successful treatment will be.

Subvalvular Aortic Stenosis (SAS)

Subvalvular aortic stenosis (SAS) in an inherited condition that occurs in some breeds and mixes, especially the Bernese Mountain Dog, Bouvier des Flandres, Boxer, Bull Terrier, German Shepherd Dog, Golden Retriever, Newfoundland, and Rottweiler. The left ventricle of the heart pumps oxygenated blood through the *aortic valve* and into the *aorta*, the major artery carrying blood from the heart. The blood flows from there throughout the body, and then returns to the lungs for reoxygenation. *Stenosis* refers to a narrowing, in this case a narrowing near the aortic valve, which reduces blood flow. Depending on the severity of the stenosis, the affected dog may become faint at times, or may die.

SAS is often diagnosed following detection of a heart murmur, although many heart murmurs have no serious implications. If your vet detects a murmur in your dog, it may be necessary to see a veterinary cardiologist for a more definitive analysis of the problem.

Dilated Cardiomyopathy (DCM)

Dilated cardiomyopathy (DCM) is defined as enlargement of the heart. It weakens the heart muscle, making it less able to pump blood. Eventually as the heart continues to enlarge, one or more valves begin to leak, and the dog develops congestive heart failure. DCM occurs most often in middle-aged, male, large and giant breed dogs such as the Doberman Pinscher, Boxer, Irish Wolfhound, and Great Dane. DCM may have a genetic cause or in some cases may be due to a nutritional deficiency. An infection or toxin may cause the damage to the heart muscle; however, sometimes the cause of DCM is unclear.

The first indication of DCM is often reduced tolerance for exercise, although some dogs show no sign of a problem. Your veterinarian might detect a heart murmur, irregular heart rhythm or heart enlargement on a routine chest X ray. As the heart muscle becomes weaker, blood pressure will build in the veins coming into the heart. Fluid may accumulate (*edema*) behind the left ventricle, and the lungs may become congested (*pulmonary congestion*). If the right side of the heart is also affected, edema may also develop around the lungs or in the abdomen.

DCM cannot be cured, but the symptoms may be controlled with medication.

Von Willebrand's Disease

Von Willebrand's disease is an inherited bleeding disorder that occurs in a number of breeds, especially Dobermans and mixed-breeds. Signs typically include spontaneous bleeding from the nose or gums, blood in the urine or feces due to intestinal bleeding, excessive bleeding during surgery or from even small injuries, or internal hemorrhaging. Puppies born with the disease sometimes bleed to death when the umbilical cord is severed at birth.

If your dog is a breed or mix that is at high risk of Von Willebrand's Disease, you might consider having your vet perform the diagnostic blood test for the disease. Knowing that your dog is prone to excessive bleeding will be useful if she needs surgery or other risky procedures.

Heartworm Disease

Heartworm disease is caused by parasitic worms that infest the host animal's heart (right ventricle) and pulmonary artery. Heartworm disease, which is spread by mosquitoes, can affect dogs, cats, and other animals, including people. When a mosquito ingests blood from an infected animal, it also ingests heartworm larvae, which it then injects into its next victim's bloodstream. The larvae travel through the animal's arteries to the heart, where they develop into adult heartworms. As they grow, they clog the available space, ultimately causing congestive heart failure.

Fortunately, effective medications are available to prevent heartworm disease in dogs. These prescription medications are given daily or monthly in edible form. A few years ago, heartworm disease did not affect dogs in some areas of the United States, but it has now been detected in all fifty states. As a result, most dogs in the United States need to take heartworm preventative to keep them safe.

Many shelters and rescue groups have all their dogs tested for heartworm disease. Giving the preventative to a dog who has heartworms can be lethal, so if your dog is seven months old or older and has not been tested, have that done before starting her on preventative medication. Puppies should be started on heartworm prevention at eight weeks of age, and then tested at seven months. Most vets recommend retesting every year or two, even if the dog takes preventative medication regularly year-round, just to be sure. After all, no medication is one hundred percent effective. If you have a dog of a Collie breed or mix—Collie, Border Collie, Australian Shepherd, Shetland Sheepdog—beware of heartworm medications containing Ivermectin or related drugs (see "Dogs and Drugs" on page 387).

The Digestive System

Most dogs are anything but finicky eaters: Drop a sliced carrot, a cookie, one of your prescribed pills, and they're on it! When you consider the mystery items your dog may gobble outside and the zoo of parasites, bacteria, and worms that could live in your dog's digestive tract, you probably wonder how

Drugs and the MDR1 Mutation

It has long been known that certain drugs can cause seizures and death in some dogs, particularly Collie-type dogs. A few years ago, researchers identified a genetic mutation, known as the MDR1 mutation, as the source of the sensitivity. They have developed a test that can determine whether an individual dog carries the mutation.

As of this writing, the MDR1 mutation is known to affect the following breeds and mixes:

- Collies (three out of four Collies, both rough and smooth, have the MDR1 mutation)
- Australian Shepherds (Aussies)
- Shetland Sheepdogs (Shelties)
- Old English Sheepdogs
- German Shepherd Dogs
- Long-haired Whippets
- Silken Windhounds
- A variety of mixed-breed dogs, especially those whose genetic background includes any of the breeds listed here

As more dogs are tested, more breeds may be added to the list.

Drugs that are known to cause problems in dogs with the MDR1 mutation include:

- *Ivermectin*, used to prevent heartworm and to treat heartworm, mange, and other parasitic infections, can cause seizures and possible death in dogs with the MDR1 mutation.
- *Selamectin, milbemycin*, and *moxidectin*, the active ingredients in several heartworm medications, are safe for use in dogs with the MDR1 mutation if used for heartworm prevention at the manufacturer's recommended dose. Higher doses can cause neurological complications in dogs with the MDR1 mutation.
- *Loperamide*, the active ingredient in Imodium™ antidiarrheal medication, causes neurological damage and should never be given to dogs with the MDR1 mutation.

continued

Petfinder.com: The Adopted Dog Bible

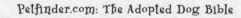

- *Acepromazine* is a tranquilizer and pre-anesthetic agent that causes extreme, prolonged sedation in dogs with the MDR1 mutation.
- *Butorphanol* is an analgesic (painkiller) and pre-anesthetic agent that causes extreme, prolonged sedation in dogs with the MDR1 mutation.
- *Vincristine, Vinblastine,* and *Doxorubicin* are chemotherapy agents that appear to be prone to causing decreased blood cell counts, anorexia, vomiting, and diarrhea in dogs with the MDR1 mutation.

Researchers also recommend exercising caution when giving the following drugs to dogs with the MDR1 mutation: Domperidone, Etoposide, Mitoxantrone, Ondansetron, Paclitaxel, Rifampicin.

The only way to know whether an individual dog has the MDR1 mutation is to have the dog tested. Testing is simple—you swab the inside of her cheek using a special brush and mail it in for analysis. Contact:

Washington State University College of Veterinary Medicine
Veterinary Clinical Pharmacology Laboratory
PO Box 609
Pullman, WA 99163-0609
Phone/FAX: 509-335-3745
Website: http://www.vetmed.wsu.edu
E-mail: VCPL@vetmed.wsu.edu

her digestive system manages to work so well. Not surprisingly, problems do occur, and here are the most common ones:

Parasites

Many species of parasites live in the digestive systems of dogs and other animals. Most worm infestations cause any or all of these signs: diarrhea, perhaps with blood in the stool; appetite and weight loss; dry hair and skin; and vomiting. However, some infestations cause few or no signs; in fact some worm eggs or larvae can be dormant in the dog's body and activated

How to Collect a Fecal Sample

Okay, it's not the most fun thing about owning a dog, but collecting the occasional fecal sample to take to your vet is a necessary part of responsible pet parenting. You should collect a fresh fecal sample about twelve hours before a microscopic fecal examination is scheduled. Here's an easy way to do it. Put your hand into a small to medium plastic bag or glove. If you use a zip-lock bag, turn it inside out first. Pick up a bit of fresh poop (it doesn't have to be a huge pile, about a teaspoonful will do!). Pull the open edge of the bag or glove over and off your hand, capturing the poop inside, and tie a knot or zip to close the open end. Voila! It is important to keep the sample cool or refrigerated until you bring it to the vet.

only in times of stress, or, in the case of roundworms, until the later stages of pregnancy, when they activate and infest the soon-to-be-born puppies.

Some intestinal parasites are visible to the naked eye, but many are microscopic. Most shelters and rescue groups either test their foster dogs for the presence of parasites or routinely administer medication to eliminate the common ones. Nevertheless, it's a good idea to take a fecal sample to your vet soon after you adopt your dog so he can do a thorough check. Some parasites are difficult to eliminate, and more than one treatment is usually necessary. Puppies should have microscopic fecal examinations performed two to four times during their first year of life. Adult dogs should have fecal examinations done once to twice yearly depending on amount of time spent outdoors where there are other animals, domestic or wild, and if they eat their stools.

If you happen to see worms in your dog's stool, take a specimen to your vet so that he can prescribe the appropriate medication. It's important to identify the parasite to combat it with the right product, so don't waste time and money or risk your dog's health by trying home remedies or over-the-counter wormers. To prevent dangerous drug interactions, consult your vet before you mix wormers or give your dog any wormer if she is taking any other medication, including heartworm preventative. Some heartworm preventatives also kill certain parasites, so be sure to discuss this with your vet. If you have other pets, ask your vet's advice on treating them and preventing spread of the parasite.

Some parasites can be transmitted to people, so be sure to wash your hands after handling your dog, at least until she gets the all clear from your vet, and teach your family (especially children) or roommates to do the same. Remove dog feces from your backyard daily, and pick up after your dog in public places to prevent the spread of parasites to other people's pets. In many cases, removal of feces from public places is required by "pooper scooper" laws.

Roundworms

Roundworms are common in puppies, even if they have had excellent care, which puppies in shelters and rescue programs may not have not had prior to their arrival. Roundworms look like white strings of spaghetti and can be up to 8 inches long. The worms do not attack the host animal directly, but eat the food being digested in the host's intestines and stomach, and are passed out in an infected dog's feces. The female roundworm can lay up to 200,000 eggs a day.

A puppy with roundworms typically develops a pot belly. She may also develop diarrhea, and if the infestation is large, she may vomit worms. As the worms take her food, she may become so ill from malnutrition that she may stop eating.

It's much less common, but roundworms can also affect older dogs (and even people, particularly children, the elderly and immunocompromised). Roundworms are transmitted via ingestion of contaminated feces or small rodents, so poop should be picked up daily, and your dog should be prevented from investigating other dogs' feces or hunting rodents.

Fortunately, roundworms are easy to eliminate. If you think your dog has roundworms, or if you see worms in her stool, take a fecal sample to your vet right away for verification and treatment.

Tapeworms

Tapeworms are segmented white worms that reach 8 inches in length and live by absorbing food passing through the host animal's intestine. Although tapeworms do not cause the host animal as much trouble as many other parasites, large worms or large numbers of worms can cause malnutrition. The tapeworm's life cycle includes an *intermediate host*, such as a flea, mouse, rabbit, or other animal. To get a tapeworm, the dog must eat the intermediate host while the tapeworms are in the larval form. Once inside the dog, the worm larvae develop into adult tapeworms.

Unlike some other intestinal worms, tapeworms rarely show up in feces, making it harder to tell when your dog has them. They do, however, shed segments, which may exit the intestine when the dog has a bowel movement. The tiny rice-like segments often stick to the fur around the dog's anus, which is usually how tapeworm infections are diagnosed.

A special wormer is needed to rid your dog of tapeworms, so if you see any segments (or, as occasionally happens, longer sections of tapeworms) in her feces or around her anus, talk to your vet. If your dog has had fleas at some time in the past—not uncommon for adopted dogs—be especially vigilant.

Hookworms

Hookworms are small, thin worms. Dogs typically pick up hookworm larvae by walking on soil that has been contaminated with hookworm eggs deposited in the feces of infected animals. Puppies, however, can also contract hookworms from their mothers before birth or through her milk. Either way, the larvae make their way to the small intestine, where they hook themselves to the walls of the intestine and suck blood. Hookworms inject an anticoagulant into their host when they bite, so when they detach and move to a new location, the old wound continues to bleed. Because of this, bloody diarrhea is usually one of the first signs of a problem.

Chronic hookworm infection can scar the lining of the intestine, and may cause blood loss and anemia as well as diarrhea, weight loss, and weakness. Hookworm infection can kill a puppy, especially if her mother didn't have the best pre- or post-natal care and the puppy has subsequently also been neglected. Hookworms are diagnosed by spotting the microscopic eggs in the dog's feces.

Whipworms

Whipworms are 1¾ to 3 inches long. Adult whipworms, which look like pieces of thread with one enlarged end, live in the large intestine, where they lay eggs. The eggs are passed with feces and develop into larvae and then adults after they are ingested by other animals. Because they can occur in small numbers and may not lay eggs continually, several fecal exams may be needed to diagnose them. Stool from a dog with whipworms often has a mucous-like coating. Whipworms often cause no symptoms, but they can contribute to intestinal problems (See "Colitis" on page 359 and "Diarrhea" on page 360).

Coccidia

Coccidia are single-celled organisms that attack the intestinal tract. Dogs acquire coccidia by ingesting fecal material from infected animals, or by eating the animal itself (commonly small rodents). In healthy adult dogs, their presence may not be noticed—in fact, some researchers believe that all adult dogs have been infected by coccidia at some time. However, for a puppy—or a dog of any age who is ill or who under stress, as a newly adopted dog may be—*coccidiosis* can cause intestinal cramps, bloody diarrhea, and weight loss.

Giardia

Giardia are single-celled parasites that inhabit the small intestine and typically spread through contaminated water and feces. An otherwise healthy dog may be infected for years without showing signs, but in puppies and in older dogs whose immune systems are impaired, Giardia can cause diarrhea, listlessness, and weight loss. Soft, mucousy, light-colored stools are a common sign of Giardia. In severe cases, the dog may also experience explosive diarrhea.

Giardia affects many species, including our own, so it's essential to keep feces cleaned up and to practice good hygiene.

Some veterinarians recommend that you bring in a stool sample for analysis three to four times per year to check for internal parasites. This may vary, depending upon your vet and the region where you live, but if at any time you suspect your dog may have parasites, call your veterinarian right away. Parasites can severely impair your dog's health, or at least make her very uncomfortable, and many are transmittable to other pets and people.

Bloat

We've probably all experienced the discomfort of *gastric distension*, or a stomach too full of food or gas. For some dogs, that feeling is more than uncomfortable—it's life-threatening. Severe distension can cause the stomach to twist, creating a condition called *gastric dilatation-volvulus* (GDV) or *gastric torsion*. In common terms, this condition is called *bloat*.

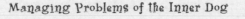
Managing Problems of the Inner Dog

When bloat occurs, the twisting of the stomach (torsion) blocks the esophagus, making it impossible for the dog to relieve the building pressure by belching or vomiting. Blood flow into and out of the heart decreases, and the heart rate may become erratic. Without blood, the stomach lining begins to die. Toxins build in the body. The liver, pancreas, spleen, and bowel are damaged, and the stomach may rupture. The dog goes into shock, suffers considerable pain, and dies.

Any dog can bloat, but dogs with deep chests are particularly at risk. Signs of bloat or impending bloat include a swollen or distended abdomen, lack of appetite, retching, drooling, restlessness, lethargy, refusal to lie down, depression, weakness, or rapid heart rate. If you think your dog may be bloating, *do not wait*. Minutes can make the difference between life and death. Call ahead to your veterinarian or emergency veterinary clinic so they know to expect a bloating dog, and get there as quickly as you can without risking an accident.

If the vet determines that your dog is about to bloat but has not yet experienced stomach torsion, he will administer intravenous fluids and steroids to treat the shock, medication to regulate the erratic heartbeat, and antibiotics to fight secondary infections. He may try to relieve the pressure by inserting a stomach tube through the esophagus or a large-bore needle directly into the stomach. If this is successful, he will probably perform a gastric lavage to clean out the stomach. He may also suggest blood tests, X-rays, and an electrocardiogram (ECG). Often, though, surgery is necessary to untwist the stomach and remove damaged tissue, followed by hospitalization for several days, a special diet at least for a while, and medications. Dogs who are at high risk of bloating, including those who have bloated once or have experienced repeated incidents of gastric distension, often undergo a *gastropexy*, a surgical procedure that anchors the stomach to the body wall so that it cannot twist.

Unfortunately, many dogs die of bloat even with surgical intervention, so prevention is by far the best medicine. To reduce the chances that your dog will bloat, feed her two or three smaller meals a day rather than one big one. If your dog gulps her food, find a way to slow her down. If you feed dry food, scatter it on the floor so she can't gulp mouthfuls, or purchase a toy that dispenses food as your dog rolls it. Postpone hard exercise and limit water intake until at least two hours after a meal.

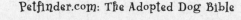

While there has been much confusion about whether or not to feed dogs from raised food bowls, a study published in the *Journal of the American Veterinary Medical Association* identified raised feeding bowls as a significant risk factor for bloat. An emergency veterinarian shared this information with me after my dog, Kona, who is not otherwise a predictable candidate for bloat, faced this emergency recently. Kona was one of the lucky ones and, as a precaution, he and my other dogs now eat from dishes on the floor.

Intestinal Obstruction

Dogs eat the darnedest things. Hand towels, golf balls, doll heads, rocks—if you can pick it up, some dog has swallowed it or part of it. And when dogs swallow strange things that cannot pass through their intestinal tract, they can suffer an *intestinal obstruction* or *blockage*.

An intestinal blockage is a true emergency situation. If you know that your dog has swallowed an indigestible object, or if she is vomiting or retching, has diarrhea, is listless, or has a tender or swollen belly, call your vet immediately. He may prefer to monitor the situation to see if the object will make its way safely through the digestive tract. Often, though, surgery or newer endoscopic procedures are necessary to remove the object and repair life-threatening damage to the intestine. Antibiotics will probably be prescribed to prevent post-surgical infection, and your dog will probably be on a restricted diet—no more rocks!—for several days.

Colitis

Colitis is a general term used to indicate a variety of problems affecting the intestinal tract, particularly the large intestine (large bowel). Colitis may be *acute* (occurring suddenly) or *chronic* (long-term and recurring).

A wide range of signs are associated with colitis in dogs. Some dogs with colitis suffer from intermittent constipation, but more commonly, the dog needs to defecate frequently and produces soft, watery stool, often with blood in it. Or she may strain, but produce little or no stool. She may become dehydrated from frequent diarrhea. A dog with chronic colitis will lose weight because of reduced appetite coupled with loss of blood and fluid and rapid movement of food through her intestines.

Colitis can have many causes, individually or in combination, including:

- ☼ Parasites
- ☼ Foreign body in the intestine (especially indigestible fiber in grass and similar things)
- ☼ Bacteria
- ☼ Chronic Inflammatory Bowel Disease (IBD) (thought to be essentially an allergic response to something in the intestine)
- ☼ Irritable Bowel Syndrome (IBS) (usually seen in dogs who are nervous or excitable and under stress, as many newly adopted and adoptable dogs are)
- ☼ *Typhilitis* (inflammation of the cecum, the canine counterpart to the human appendix)
- ☼ Cancer (especially lymphosarcoma and adenocarcinoma)

To cure colitis, it's necessary to identify and remove or cure the underlying cause, which is often easier said than done. With patience, though, you and your vet can probably find a solution. In the meantime, remember that your dog can't help it if she has an accident. Take measures to make clean up and sanitation easier, and to keep her reasonably comfortable.

Constipation

Dogs occasionally suffer from constipation. Often it is a result of eating indigestible material such as bones or plant matter, but some dogs will refuse to defecate in strange places. In either case, the longer the fecal matter remains in the large intestine, the more difficult it becomes for the dog to rid herself of that material. She may lose her appetite and show other signs of illness.

If your dog fails to have a bowel movement for more than twenty-four hours, call your vet. *Do not* give your dog a laxative unless your vet advises you to do so—if the intestine is blocked, you could cause more damage or even kill your dog.

Diarrhea

Diarrhea, the frequent passage of loose, watery stools, occurs when the small or large intestine becomes irritated. In puppies and small dogs, who can become dehydrated very quickly, diarrhea calls for immediate veterinary care. If the dog is also vomiting, you should consider this a life-threatening emergency.

Most dogs have short-term diarrhea at some point in their lives, and some dogs have repeated, infrequent, short-term bouts. As long as the duration is short and the dog seems otherwise fine, such cases are not usually serious. Withholding food for twenty-four hours to rest the intestine, followed by a bland diet of boiled rice with plain yogurt, cottage cheese, boiled hamburger, or skinless, boneless, boiled chicken for a day or two usually clears up the problem. Over-the-counter anti-diarrheal medications are sometimes given, but check with your vet first. (See also "Drugs and the MDR1 Mutation" on page 352.)

If your dog has severe diarrhea with vomiting, or if the diarrhea lasts longer than a day, get her to the vet quickly; diagnosis of the underlying cause is crucial.

Diarrhea in Dogs

Occasional rounds of diarrhea are an unpleasant but inevitable aspect of having a dog. Some bacteria can affect people, so wash carefully after handling a sick dog, and don't let your dog interact with young children until you know what's causing her diarrhea. Some of the common causes of diarrhea include:

- Stress
- Bacteria
- Viruses (particularly distemper, corona, and parvovirus)
- Parasites (particularly Giardia, Coccidia, hookworms, and whipworms)
- Change of diet
- Ingestion of garbage, grass, or other indigestible substances
- Nutritional deficiency
- Inflammatory Bowel Disease
- Toxins
- Antibiotics
- Pancreatitis

(See also "Diarrhea" on page 360, and Intestinal Obstruction" on page 359.)

Vomiting and Regurgitation

Dogs are notorious pukers, even when healthy. Everyone who has lived with a dog has had the delightful experience of hearing the dog's dinner, or that mystery item she snagged on the last outing, coming back up. This *regurgitation*, revolting as it may be, is not a cause for concern unless it happens frequently. It is often caused by eating too quickly, or drinking too much water immediately after a meal.

Vomiting, in contrast, involves *retching*, or hard contractions of the stomach that forcefully expel the contents of the stomach. Dogs often regurgitate with little warning, but imminent vomiting is usually signaled by restlessness, salivation, "smiling" as the corners of the lips are pulled back, and lip-licking.

Regurgitation and vomiting can be signs of many serious medical problems. If your dog vomits repeatedly, or if sporadic vomiting or regurgitation continues for more than a day, call your vet. If your dog retches without bringing anything up, she may be bloating, and she needs *immediate* veterinary care (see "Bloat" on page 357).

The Urinary System

The *urinary system* includes the kidneys, ureters, bladder, and urethra. Following are some of the more common problems associated with the canine urinary tract.

Urinary Incontinence

Urinary incontinence refers to *involuntary* urination. An incontinent dog cannot control the passage of urine from the bladder. (This is not the same as frequent urination in which the dog has control but has to go frequently. Incontinence should also not be confused with submissive urination—see page 143.)

Dogs can become incontinent for a variety of reasons, including:

- Deformity or disease of the bladder (holds urine), or the urethra (empties the bladder during urination)
- Injury, disease, or abnormality in certain parts of the brain or spinal cord
- Birth defect
- Partial blockage of the urethra by a tumor or a stone (see "Urolithiasis" on page 363)
- Reduction in certain hormones after altering; this occurs most commonly in female dogs and can occur weeks, months or even years after neutering (easily correctable and not a reason to avoid neutering)

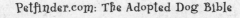

- Age-related weakening of the muscles that hold urine in the bladder
- Age-related dementia
- In females, malformation of the vagina (*vulvovaginal stenosis*), which causes urine to be trapped and to leak out when the dog stands up.

If your dog is or becomes incontinent, your vet can perform tests, which generally involves collecting a urine sample to determine the cause, depending on your dog's age, sex, and general health. Dogs with bladder infections are not truly incontinent, but they have to urinate so frequently and urgently that they have "accidents." If no infection is present, then your vet will look for other causes. You can help by providing as much of the following information as possible:

- When did your dog first show signs of incontinence?
- Is your dog typically active or resting when the incontinence occurs?
- Does your dog urinate normally at other times?
- How frequently does your dog urinate? How much?
- Does your dog seem to be comfortable when urinating?
- What color is the urine? Is any blood visible in it?
- Has your dog been neutered, or had any other surgeries or illnesses that you know of?
- What medications is your dog taking, or has she taken over the past few months?
- How much water does your dog drink?
- Does your dog have seizures?
- Does your dog show any signs of other illnesses?

If an underlying cause can be identified, it may be correctible with medical or surgical treatment. If the cause remains a mystery, the vet may recommend drugs to increase the ability of your dog's bladder to retain urine.

Urolithiasis

Urolithiasis is a disease in which stones (uroliths) form in the urinary tract. Such stones are most commonly found in the bladder. Uroliths are created following the precipitation of urinary crystals, which are formed from minerals. Stones irritate the lining of the kidneys, bladder, or urethra, causing pain, bloody urine, and changes to the lining. If the stones become large enough, they can partially or completely prevent urination. Signs of urolithiasis in a dog include some or all of the following:

- Frequent urination (often in unusual places)
- Dribbling urine
- Blood in the urine
- Straining to urinate, with or without success
- Abdominal pain

If your dog is passing little or no urine, it is likely that a stone is blocking its passage. The toxins retained in urine are lethal and your dog may exhibit weakness, depression, loss of appetite, or vomiting as symptoms of toxemia. Quick diagnosis and treatment are absolutely necessary.

Although any dog can suffer from urolithiasis, it most often affects dogs between two and ten years of age, and is more common in small dogs. Keeping your dog confined for long periods so that she urinates infrequently can contribute to formation of crystals and stones, as can lack of regular exercise and insufficient water intake. Diets containing excessive amounts of magnesium, phosphorus, and sometimes calcium can also promote urolithiasis.

To verify a suspected diagnosis of urolithiasis, your veterinarian will probably palpate your dog's abdomen to feel for stones. He may also perform a urinalysis to see if red blood cells, white blood cells, bacteria, or crystals are present. X-rays can also be used to determine whether your dog has stones and, if so, their size and location.

If your dog's urinary tract is blocked, the first step in treatment will be to remove the blockage and empty the bladder of urine. Surgery may be the best way to remove stones, but some stones can be dissolved with a special diet and/or medication. If your dog also has a urinary tract infection, your vet will prescribe antibiotics. Even after the stones are removed or dissolved, your dog may need to continue to eat a special diet to prevent new stones from forming. As always, your dog should have access to clean, fresh water at all times.

Petfinder.com: The Adopted Dog Bible

Kidney Failure

Kidney failure can either be acute or chronic. Acute kidney failure is a sudden loss of function that might be reversible; chronic kidney failure is an irreversible loss of function that occurs gradually. In both situations, the kidneys lose their ability to remove waste products from the body. A dog in kidney failure becomes *uremic* as toxic waste products build up in her blood, causing loss of appetite, vomiting, depression, and, eventually, death.

Kidney failure can be caused by many factors, including:

- Bacterial infection
- Systemic fungal infection
- Physical trauma
- Blockage of urine flow
- Metastatic cancer or leukemia
- Ingested toxins, especially ethylene glycol (found in antifreeze)
- Endotoxins (poisonous chemicals formed within the dog's own body)
- Medications, including acetaminophen
- Autoimmune disease (see "Lupus Erythematosis" on page 380)
- Inherited disorders

One of the first signs of kidney failure in dogs is increased water intake, which may also signal diabetes and other problems. When the dog drinks more water, she urinates more frequently and produces more urine. It may seem odd that a dog in kidney failure produces more urine, but urinalysis will show that the urine produced by a failing kidney is dilute, meaning that it does not contain normal levels of waste and toxins because the kidney fails to extract wastes and toxins from the blood and expel them in the urine. At the same time, failing kidneys allow some substances that should be retained to be expelled in urine, including protein and water-soluble vitamins. As a result, the dog suffers from protein and vitamin deficiencies.

Kidney failure is diagnosed through urinalysis and blood chemistry analysis, as well as by physical examination and consideration of as much of the dog's medical history as is available.

In some cases, dogs with kidney failure are treated with dialysis and even kidney transplants. Those treatments are not options for most dogs, though, in part because of the high cost and in part because by the time kidney failure is diagnosed, the dog is usually too ill to respond well to treatment. Sometimes the signs can be controlled for a while with diet and medication, but kidneys do not heal, and eventually the dog's owner must make a hard decision. Death from complete kidney shutdown is slow and painful, so euthanasia is usually the best choice.

Laryngeal Paralysis

The *larynx* (voice box) is located in the back of the throat, just above the *trachea* (windpipe). *Laryngeal paralysis* is a condition in which the nerves that control the muscles and cartilage that open the larynx do not function properly. This leads to an airway obstruction when the dog tries to breathe. The dog's bark becomes hoarse, and she makes a lot of rasping, gasping sounds as she breathes. She may gag and choke when she eats as food and water get into the trachea—they "go down the wrong pipe." In extreme cases, the dog cannot take in enough air and may suffocate.

Laryngeal paralysis occurs most commonly in older, larger dogs. In most cases, the larynx is normal at birth, but as the dog ages, the nerves and muscles that control the laryngeal cartilages fail to work properly. Occasionally, though, laryngeal paralysis occurs in puppies as young as two months (most commonly in Bouvier des Flandres, Bulldogs, Dalmatians, and Siberian Huskies, and mixes that include those breeds). Occasionally, laryngeal paralysis is caused by traumatic injury of the larynx or by hypothyroidism (see "Thyroid Disease" on page 376).

In mild cases of laryngeal paralysis, having the dog avoid excessive weight gain and stress may be the only treatment necessary. If signs become worse, certain medications may offer relief; however, surgery is recommended for many dogs. Most often, *arytenoid lateralization* ("laryngeal tie-back") surgery is performed to suture the cartilage open to allow more air to pass through the larynx. Most dogs recover well from the surgery.

The Respiratory System

Like humans, dogs' respiratory systems consist of an upper and a lower respiratory tract. The upper respiratory tract is responsible for bringing air from the outside world into your dog's lungs. Air enters a dog's respiratory system through the nostrils and travels through the nasal cavities, which consist of various bones and glands that produce mucus to trap dust, microbes, etc. Next, air travels past the larynx, which controls the flow of air and contains the vocal cords. The larynx leads to the trachea. The lower respiratory tract consists of the bronchi and lungs. Bronchi carry air from the trachea into the lungs. Ultimately, air is delivered to alveoli—where oxygen is transferred to the blood and carbon dioxide is removed to be exhaled.

All parts of the respiratory system must work together for your dog to breathe properly. While some breathing changes, such as normal panting, are caused by environmental factors like heat or strenuous exercise, other changes may indicate a chronic medical condition or emergency. Obstructions of the respiratory tract can cause choking; for information on how to help a choking dog, see page 283 in Chapter 14. Rasping, gasping sounds, along with a hoarse bark, can be signs of laryngeal paralysis, a condition that affects the nerves and muscles that open the larynx (see page 366). Excessive heavy panting, coughing, and irregular or rapid breathing, as well as other symptoms, can signal heart disease (see Signs of Health, Signs of Trouble, page 346).

Infections of both the upper and lower respiratory tracts can also pose a serious threat to your dog's health. Nasal discharge, coughing, sneezing, or labored breathing can signal respiratory infection or other health concerns. Canine infectious respiratory disease complex is commonly referred to as *kennel cough*. This disorder may be caused by viral agents including parainfluenza and adenovirus. Bordetella can be a bacterial component of *kennel cough*.

Can My Dog Get a Cold?

If you think your dog's cough, running nose, sickly eyes, or fever signals a cold, think again. The cause of the human cold, the human rhinovirus, is not considered to be a risk for transmission to canines. Your dog's symptoms may indicate a more serious and progressive illness, so call your vet for a thorough examination and recommendations regarding diagnostic testing and treatment.

The Musculoskeletal System

Problems affecting the bones, joints, and supporting soft tissues are fairly common in dogs. Some of these *orthopedic* problems can affect any dog. Some are more common in large dogs, others in small dogs. Some are relatively common in certain breeds and practically unheard of in others.

Many orthopedic problems are linked to a common affliction of humans as well as pets: obesity. Excess weight puts excess strain on all of the body's systems, including the bones, joints, muscles, and ligaments. In addition, many injuries occur during infrequent spurts of exercise because the dog is not in proper condition for that level of exertion. Good reasons to keep your dog fit and at a reasonable weight!

Osteochondritis Dissecans

Osteochondritis dissecans (OCD) is a disease in which the cartilage that helps normal joints move properly grows abnormally or is damaged. If the cartilage breaks free, it floats between bones in the joint, causing pain and potentially further injuring the joint.

Although OCD most commonly affects the shoulder joint, it can also appear in the *elbow* (the joint at the top of the long vertical bone of the front leg) or the *hock* (the joint at the top of the vertical bone above the paw on the hind legs). Lameness caused by OCD usually appears when the dog is between four and eight months old. OCD occurs primarily in large and giant dogs, although it can affect smaller animals as well.

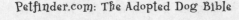

How to Ease the Pain of Bone or Joint Problems

You can't always prevent bone or joint problems, but you can do some things to reduce your dog's risk and to ease her discomfort. Here are some suggestions:

- Keep your dog at a healthy weight. Excess weight increases the stress on joints and bones.
- If you adopt a puppy, avoid injuries to developing bones and joints by postponing activities that involve jumping or twisting until the growth plates close, which occurs on average by twelve months for most dogs, but ask your vet about your individual pup.
- If your dog has an orthopedic problem, give her enough *moderate daily* exercise to maintain or increase muscle tone and strength to provide better support (after checking with your vet). Don't allow your dog to jump, play rough with other dogs, or otherwise overdo it. Swimming is excellent for building muscle without over-stressing bones and joints.
- Keep your dog warm. Cold, damp weather can exacerbate aches and pains.
- Give your dog a bed made of firm orthopedic "egg-crate" foam, which is designed to distribute weight and reduce pressure on joints. You can find egg-crate foam in many stores that sell bedding for people and cut it to fit into a dog-bed cover, or you can purchase a dog bed filled with egg-crate foam from a pet supply store.
- Elevate your dog's food and water bowls so she won't have to bend down, especially if the problem is in her neck, spine, or front legs.
- If steps or stairs are hard for your dog to negotiate, try a permanent or portable ramp.

Degenerative Joint Disease

Degenerative joint disease (DJD), commonly known as arthritis or osteoarthritis, is caused by deterioration of the smooth cartilage that covers the end of a bone in a *synovial* (movable) joint. DJD is painful and progressive; that is,

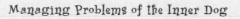

it worsens with time. Primary DJD results from normal wear and tear on an otherwise normal joint as the dog ages. Secondary DJD results from another condition affecting the joint (see "Elbow Dysplasia" on page 371 and "Canine Hip Dysplasia").

DJD cannot be cured, but weight control, moderate exercise, nutritional support, drug therapy, and sometimes surgery can slow its progress and make your dog more comfortable. (See "Treating Orthopedic Problems in Dogs" on page 372.)

Lyme Disease

Lyme disease (Lymes) is transmitted by ticks (see "Ticks" on page 338 in Chapter 16) and can cause generalized illness in animals and people. In the United States, Lyme disease occurs predominantly in Atlantic coast states, the Midwest, and less frequently on the Pacific coast. The bacteria that cause Lyme disease live in mice, deer, and other small mammals without making them sick. When a tick feeds on the infected animal, it picks up bacteria, which it transmits to the next animal it feeds on. You cannot get Lyme disease directly from your dog. You must be bitten by a tick carrying the disease.

The most common sign of Lyme disease in dogs is arthritis, which causes lameness, pain, and sometimes swelling in one or more joints. The disease may also cause fever, lack of appetite, dehydration, inactivity, and swollen lymph nodes. Lyme disease in dogs is easily cured with antibiotics. Without treatment, however, Lyme disease becomes chronic and can cause kidney damage.

The best way to prevent Lyme disease is to avoid tick-infested areas, especially in the spring when the young ticks are most active. If you do spend time in a tick-infested area, check your dog and yourself thoroughly and remove any ticks as soon as you find them, before they have a chance to spread disease. (See "How to Remove a Tick" on page 339 in Chapter 16.) Most veterinarians do not recommend vaccinating dogs in areas where risk of exposure is low, and some do not believe the vaccine is effective in any case. There are also many effective veterinary products that will kill ticks on your dog before the tick can transmit the bacteria. Check with your vet for the latest recommendations.

Rheumatoid Arthritis

Rheumatoid arthritis occurs mostly in small dogs, beginning at about five years of age. In this disorder, overreaction of the immune system causes inflammation of the joints, loss of joint cartilage, and can also affect other organs. The impact of this painful swelling ranges from stiffness to severe lameness. Initially, decreased appetite, fever, or enlarged lymph nodes might also be present. Diagnostic tests for rheumatoid arthritis include radiography, blood work, and analysis of joint fluid or tissue. While rheumatoid arthritis currently has no cure, the best you can do for a suffering dog is try to control the symptoms. This may be accomplished through anti-inflammatory or immunosuppressive drugs. Agents that help protect cartilage may prevent further damage to a dog's joints. Weight control should also be considered, as extra weight puts more stress on the animal's joints.

Elbow Dysplasia

The term "elbow dysplasia" is used to describe four conditions that can affect the elbow joint individually or in any combination. They are: *Osteochondritis dissecans (OCD)* in the elbow; *fragmented medial coronoid process (FCP)* and *ununited anconeal process (UAP)*, both deformations of the *ulna* (longer bone of the foreleg); and abnormal alignment of the bones within the elbow joint.

Elbow dysplasia is inherited, and a dysplastic puppy may be limping by four months of age. Left untreated, the dog will be crippled. Treatment of elbow dysplasia is often a combination of medical and surgical management.

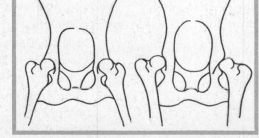

Healthy   **CHD**

Hip Dysplasia is one of the most common canine afflictions.

Canine Hip Dysplasia (CHD)

Canine hip dysplasia (CHD) is an inherited condition in which the bones of the hip joint do not fit together correctly, which can result in potentially crippling arthritis. Hip dysplasia can occur in any breed or mixture of breeds, but in tiny dogs it may not cause clinical problems because there is so little

Treating Orthopedic Problems in Dogs

Many treatments are used for dogs with orthopedic problems. Here are some that have been found effective in some cases. As always, ask your veterinarian before giving your dog any supplement or medication.

- *Biotin* and *essential fatty acid* supplements work together to strengthen supportive tissue, and have reportedly helped some dogs with DJD.
- *Non-Steroidal Anti-Inflammatory Drugs* (NSAIDs) are non-hormonal products that prevent or control pain and swelling. Common NSAIDs include buffered or enteric aspirin, Deramaxx, Metacam, EtoGesic, Piroxicam, Rimadyl, Zubrin, and Butazolidin. All NSAIDs have the potential to cause stomach and intestinal problems and to interfere with blood clotting. Some NSAIDs should not be used at all in dogs. Check with your vet before giving your dog any NSAID, or if your dog develops dark stool or stomach problems while taking an NSAID.
- *Chiropractic treatment* and *massage therapy* help some dogs with orthopedic problems. In most cases these should supplement, not replace, veterinary care, and should be performed by a properly accredited practitioner. See Chapter 18 for holistic alternatives.
- *Corticosteroids* are used as anti-inflammatory painkillers. They have a number of short- and long-term side effects, and should be used only when other painkillers don't work, and preferably for short periods only (see also "The Immune System" on page 379).
- *Glucosamine* and *Chondroitin* are widely used to treat arthritis in animals and people. Glucosamine is a component of cartilage. Chondroitin promotes formation of healthy cartilage and inhibits enzymes that break down cartilage.
- *Vitamin C* is sometimes recommended to prevent or treat orthopedic problems in dogs. There is no scientific evidence that it works, but reasonable doses don't appear to do any harm.
- *Opioids*, including morphine, codeine, tramadol and other prescrip-

continued

> tion products, may be prescribed to control severe pain in some cases.
> - *Antidepressant medications* are sometimes prescribed to control severe chronic pain.
> - *Surgery* is an effective treatment for many orthopedic problems. It is best performed by a board certified orthopedic veterinary surgeon experienced in doing such surgeries.

weight on the joint. Even some larger dogs with dysplasia never show any signs, but others suffer extreme disability, sometimes beginning when they are as young as five months. Hip dysplasia can be treated medically or surgically. Many surgical procedures can be utilized. Your veterinarian can determine which treatment will be most likely to yield the best result.

Panosteitis

Panosteitis, often called *pano,* is a bone disease that is most common in large breed dogs between six and eighteen months of age. A migrating limp or shifting leg lameness is typical of pano—the puppy limps on one leg today, a different one tomorrow. Non-steroidal anti-inflammatory drugs may be prescribed to control pain; however, pano normally resolves (heals itself) as the dog matures.

Ruptured Anterior Cruciate Ligament (ACL)

The *anterior cruciate ligament (ACL)* is a fibrous, slightly elastic tissue that helps stabilize the knee joint. If the ACL ruptures, or tears, the *femur* (the long bone running from the pelvis to the knee) rubs against the *tibia* (the thick inner bone running from the knee to the *hock,* the equivalent of your ankle), causing inflammation, pain, and, if left untreated, debilitating arthritis. When an ACL tears, there is also often damage to the *meniscus* (supporting cartilage in the knee). Ruptured ACLs are one of the most common serious orthopedic injuries in dogs.

ACL injuries are treated surgically. The specific procedure used depends on the extent of the injury, the dog's size and activity level, and other possible factors. If your dog tears an ACL, prepare yourself—a large percentage of dogs who tear one eventually tear the other.

Patellar Luxation

Patellar luxation is a painful inherited condition in which the *patella* (kneecap) *luxates* (slips out of its proper position). In a normal canine knee (or *stifle*, the joint at the front of the curved portion of the upper hind leg), the patella slides along a groove in the *femur* (thigh bone). If the groove in the femur is too shallow or is otherwise malformed, the patella may slip out of it. Sometimes, the patella can return to a normal position, but it can get stuck out of position. Over time, abnormal movement of the patella can cause wear, leading to painful arthritic changes. A luxating patella also predisposes the dog to tears in the anterior cruciate ligaments that attach the upper and lower leg bones to one another. Patellar luxation is most common in small breeds and mixes, but can occur in larger dogs.

In some dogs, luxating patellas cause little if any real disability, and can be treated with weight control and reasonable exercise. In others, surgery may be necessary to relieve chronic lameness, pain, or secondary knee injuries and to restore normal movement.

Intervertebral Disc Disease

Intervertebral disc disease is caused by biochemical changes that cause degeneration of the discs that normally lie between the vertebrae and allow for flexibility of the spine. As the discs degenerate, they become vulnerable to further injury, and even normal activity causes the disc to extrude (push out) into the spinal canal, putting pressure on the spinal cord and surrounding nerves. Blood vessels are compressed, cutting off the normal flow of oxygen and glucose to the spinal cord. In common parlance, this condition is known as a ruptured, herniated, or slipped disc. Unless you have your dog's spine X rayed, you may not see signs of disc disease until a rupture occurs. Extruded discs usually occur when the dog is between three and nine years old. The majority of problems occur in the back, with most of the rest affecting the neck.

Petfinder.com: The Adopted Dog Bible

Any dog can experience intervertebral disc disease, but certain breeds and mixes that include them are especially prone to problems. Dachshunds are at extremely high risk. Other breeds (and mixes that include them) that have more than their share of disc disease include Basset Hounds, Beagles, Bulldogs, Lhasa Apsos, Pekingese, Poodles, Shih Tzus, and Corgis.

Canine disc disease is a serious problem requiring immediate care. A ruptured disc presses against the spinal cord and surrounding nerves. In people, extruded discs cause shooting pain, but in dogs, the pain is accompanied within a few hours by paralysis. The quicker the response, the better the chances that the dog will make a partial or full recovery. Delaying treatment can leave the dog permanently paralyzed.

Treatment for intervertebral disc disease depends on its severity and other factors. If pain seems minimal and the dog has few neurological signs, your vet may ask you to simply have her rest (preferably in a crate to limit her activity) to give the injury a chance to heal. If the signs are more severe, you may want to consider the following possible treatments, individually or in combination: surgery, hydrotherapy (swimming), physical therapy, chiropractic, acupuncture, drug therapy, and massage therapy. Some dogs never regain the use of their hind legs, but if they are not in pain, they can still live happy lives. There are companies that make carts for dogs who have lost the use of their hind legs.

Legg-Perthes Disease

Legg-Perthes disease, also called Legg-Calve-Perthes (LCP), is an inherited condition of the hip joint. The hip joint is a ball-and-socket arrangement, with the head of the *femur* (thigh bone) functioning as the "ball" that fits into the "socket" of the pelvis. In Legg-Perthes, the head of the femur slowly dies and disintegrates, causing pain, arthritic changes, and lameness.

Lameness and pain, the main signs of Legg-Perthes, usually appear when the dog is six to twelve months old. The disease is usually treated by surgically removing the head of the femur, after which the muscles form a "false joint" and, once healing is complete, the dog is able to move freely.

The Endocrine System

Endocrine glands secrete *hormones*, which are chemicals transported in the blood stream to "target" organs, where the hormones help regulate the body's processes. The thyroid gland is often called the master gland because it affects the whole body, so we'll start there.

Thyroid Disease

The *thyroid gland* is in the throat, just below the larynx. It produces hormones that control growth and development, and the metabolism of proteins, carbohydrates, and lipids (fats). *Hypothyroidism*, or lack of sufficient thyroid hormone, can negatively affect the dog's physical and emotional life. Signs may include hair loss, obesity or weight gain, lethargy, inflamed ears, abnormally cool skin, or itchy, inflamed, crusty, or scaly skin. Hypothyroidism has also been linked to the development of corneal dystrophy, and to grumpiness or outright aggression. *Hyperthyroidism* (overactive thyroid gland) is rare in dogs; when it does occur, it is often associated with cancer.

Hypothyroidism can be difficult to diagnose because many of the signs suggest other problems, and because other illnesses can affect hormone levels. A simple thyroid test (T4) is often performed, but it is not very reliable. More accurate results can be obtained with a complete blood panel that measures total T4, free T4 (the usable T4 in the blood), TgAA (thyroglobulin autoantibodies), cTSH (canine thyroid stimulating hormone), and sometimes T3 and free T3. Thyroid disease can be slow to develop, so if your dog tests negative but the signs persist and seem not to indicate another condition, have her retested in six to twelve months. Blood for the test should be drawn when the dog is otherwise healthy and not taking steroids, non-steroidal anti-inflammatories, or anti-seizure drugs.

On a more positive note, once a diagnosis of hypothyroidism is made, relatively inexpensive treatment with a hormone supplement, usually L-thyroxine, is usually effective. One to two months after beginning therapy, your vet may want to retest your dog to adjust the dosage if necessary. After that, your dog should be retested once or twice a year.

Petfinder.com: The Adopted Dog Bible

Diseases of the Adrenal Glands

The *adrenal glands*, located near the kidneys, produce hormones that help control the balance of water, salt, and sugar in the body. One of the hormones produced by the adrenal glands is *cortisol*, which helps the dog deal with stress.

Addison's disease (hypoadrenocorticism) is caused by abnormally low production of adrenal hormones. Addison's disease is most common in young to middle-aged female dogs and can cause weakness, depression, loss of appetite, vomiting, diarrhea, dehydration, weak pulse, and sometimes slow, irregular heart rhythm, and occasionally increased thirst and frequent urination. Dogs suffering from Addison's disease have trouble dealing with stress.

If your dog is very ill with Addison's, she may need to be hospitalized for administration of intravenous fluids, cortisol-like drugs, and drugs to regulate the heart. Long-term treatment usually involves hormone therapy. Owners are also advised to reduce their dogs' stress as much as possible and to give high levels of hormones when stress cannot be avoided (as when traveling or moving, for instance). With proper treatment, a dog with Addison's can still live a long, happy life.

Cushing's disease (hyperadrenocorticism) is the opposite of Addison's, occurring when the adrenal glands produce too much cortisol. *Pituitary-dependent Cushing's*, the most common form, develops when the pituitary gland, located in the brain, produces too much of a hormone that determines how much cortisol the adrenal glands produce. Less common is *adrenal-dependent Cushing's*, which is caused by a tumor on one of the adrenal glands. Finally, *iatrogenic Cushing's* develops when a dog is given too much prednisone (or a similar drug) to treat a medical problem and the body reacts by decreasing the normal production of cortisol by the adrenal glands.

Common signs of Cushing's include loss of hair on the body (not the legs or head), increased appetite, increased drinking and urination, and a pot belly. Some dogs with Cushing's bruise easily. Less commonly, affected dogs may be weak and may pant excessively or have difficulty breathing.

Treatment depends on what type of Cushing's the dog has. Dogs with pituitary-dependent Cushing's disease usually take oral medication for life, under close monitoring. Adrenal-dependent Cushing's disease can be treated with surgical removal of the adrenal gland tumor or medical management. Iatrogenic Cushing's is treated by withdrawing the external cortisol, which must be done slowly so that the adrenal glands can recover. Withdrawing the drugs too quickly can have dire results, including death.

Diseases of the Pancreas

The *pancreas* is situated near the small intestine and stomach and produces several enzymes that are essential for processing proteins, fats, and carbohydrates in the diet. The pancreas also aids in the metabolism of sugar through the production of the hormone insulin.

Diabetes mellitus in most dogs results from the inadequate production of insulin by the pancreas. Signs of diabetes include heavy water consumption and, consequently, heavy urination. Obesity can lead to diabetes, but not all diabetic dogs are fat. If your dog drinks and urinates a lot and is overweight, consider having her tested for diabetes.

Dietary changes might help manage some cases of canine diabetes, but most diabetic dogs require daily insulin injections. If that is true for your dog, your veterinarian can teach you to give the injections at home and to monitor your dog's blood sugar with urine glucose strips, which are available from a pharmacy. He can also explain what to do if your dog's blood sugar drops too low. Regular veterinary visits will be necessary to be sure that your dog's insulin dosage is correct.

If you are caring for a diabetic dog, you aren't alone. You can find more information about diabetes in dogs as well as support for yourself at www. petdiabetes.org.

Pancreatitis can be a life-threatening inflammation of the pancreas that may be caused by ingestion of large amounts of fat, or by infection, medications, metabolic disorders, shock, or trauma. Signs include fever, abdominal pain, elevated heart rate, diarrhea, and vomiting.

If your dog is diagnosed with pancreatitis, she will probably need to be hospitalized. Your vet will probably administer IV fluids and electrolytes to combat dehydration and may prescribe other medications, including painkillers. He may advise you to withhold food from your dog for a short period of time to allow the pancreas to rest and heal.

The Immune System

When it works as it's supposed to, the immune system is the first defense against disease. Unfortunately, like any complex system, the immune system doesn't always function properly. We have already discussed one type of immune system dysfunction: allergies (see "Allergies" on page 334 in Chapter 16). Now we will look at another: autoimmune disease.

The immune system defends the body against invasion by threats from outside. When the threats are real, as when bacteria or viruses enter the body, the defensive response is necessary and appropriate. Sometimes, though, the immune system mistakes the body's own tissue for a threat, and it attacks and rejects the body's own tissue in an *autoimmune response*. In some cases, the target is a specific type of tissue; in others, the immune system attacks multiple tissue targets. When the immune system attacks the body in which it lives, the animal is said to have an *autoimmune disease*.

Some autoimmune diseases are believed to be inherited. Others may be the result of environmental factors, including certain food preservatives and environmental pollution. Many people believe that excessive use of vaccinations may overstimulate the immune system and trigger an autoimmune response.

Dogs with autoimmune disease suffer a wide range of health problems. We will look at common canine autoimmune problems in this section.

Autoimmune Hemolytic Anemia

Anemia is a condition in which the number of red blood cells or the amount of hemoglobin in the blood is reduced, interfering with the ability of the blood to carry oxygen. Anemia is not a disease in itself, but rather a clinical sign that disease is present.

Hemolytic anemia occurs when the immune system fails to recognize the body's red blood cells and attacks them as foreign invaders. Hemolytic anemia can be triggered by drugs, heavy metal poisoning, infectious disease, parasites, or cancer. *Primary hemolytic anemia* occurs when the immune system attacks the red blood cells without an outside stimulus. In a healthy dog, the spleen removes old, damaged, or diseased red blood cells. In a dog with

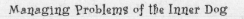

autoimmune hemolytic anemia, red blood cells are removed faster than they can be replaced, and the dog's health deteriorates.

A dog with hemolytic anemia will become weak and lethargic. She may stop eating, and her heart and respiration rates may increase. The loss of red blood cells often causes the gums and other tissues to look pale. In severe cases, the skin, gums, and eyes may take on a yellow cast (jaundice). Blood tests are used to confirm what the signs suggest.

Autoimmune hemolytic anemia is usually treated with corticosteroids or other drugs that suppress the immune system. Side effects are common with these drugs, so the dog must be closely monitored. If she does not improve with drug therapy, your vet may recommend a *splenectomy* (surgical removal of the spleen), which is the organ responsible for destroying red blood cells.

Immune-mediated Thrombocytopenia

Immune-mediated thrombocytopenia (ITP) occurs when the immune system destroys the *thrombocytes* (clotting cells) in the blood. A dog with ITP usually bruises easily and bleeds excessively if injured or after surgery. Some dogs also lose blood in urine or stool.

Diagnosis of ITP is made after other possible problems are ruled out, because clotting problems can also be caused by warfarin poisoning (a common ingredient in rat poison), hemophilia, Von Willebrand's disease (see "Von Willebrand's Disease" on page 350), bladder or prostate infection, cancer, and intestinal parasites (see "Parasites" on page 353). Your vet will recommend blood tests and possibly a bone marrow biopsy and other tests.

Treatment is the same as for autoimmune hemolytic anemia except that surgery is a last resort because of the likelihood of excessive bleeding. Transfusions to raise the number of clotting cells are often helpful.

Lupus Erythematosis

Systemic lupus erythematosis (SLE), or lupus, is a multi-systemic autoimmune disease that can be very difficult to diagnose because it mimics many other diseases. A typical sign of SLE is a fluctuating fever that does not respond to antibiotics. Dogs with SLE also often walk stiffly or have lameness that shifts from leg to leg. Muscles may become inflamed, causing pain,

Petfinder.com: The Adopted Dog Bible

muscle loss, and abnormal movement, and the kidneys may become inflamed and eventually fail. An affected dog may also be anemic, have a low white blood cell count, or have a dermatitis, especially across the bridge of the nose. SLE may be *acute* (occurring suddenly) or *chronic* (ongoing).

SLE is diagnosed with blood tests and treated with corticosteroids or other drugs that suppress the immune system. Lupus affects many of the body's systems, so additional treatments may be recommended based on the individual case. Antibiotics are often prescribed to treat secondary infections. If the dog's kidneys are affected, she will probably be given fluid therapy and a high-quality, low-protein diet. Advanced SLE may not respond to treatment, especially if the kidneys, joints, or blood are infected.

Immune-mediated Polyarthritis

Immune-mediated polyarthritis refers to several different diseases that can cause fever, joint pain and swelling, and lameness that moves from leg to leg. Sometimes the lymph nodes are enlarged, the white blood cell count may be increased, and anemia may be present. It may give rise to rheumatoid arthritis (see "Rheumatoid Arthritis" on page 371). It is treated with corticosteroids or other drugs.

Autoimmune Involvement in Other Diseases

Researchers now believe that the immune system may play a role in the development of many common diseases, including hypothyroidism, diabetes mellitus, dry eye (see Chapter 16), chronic hepatitis (liver disease), and others. This is another good reason to be a proactive and well-informed partner in your dog's health care, especially as it involves the use of vaccinations and other treatments that may compromise the immune system (see Chapter 14)

Cancer

Cancers are among the most common life-threatening diseases that affect dogs. *Cancer* is characterized by the runaway reproduction of abnormal cells and their invasion of nearby body structures. A *metastatic* cancer is one that has spread or metastasized to distant parts of the animal. Some canine cancers have a fairly high cure rate; others are more difficult to cure or control.

Cancer in dogs is treated much as it is in humans, and sometimes more than one approach is used. Your veterinarian may attempt to remove the tumor or reduce its size surgically, especially if the cancer has not spread. *Chemotherapy* drugs may be used to inhibit or kill the cancer cells and thus control tumor growth. *Radiation therapy* is also used in some cases to kill the cancer cells in a localized area. Knowing that the dog's overall health can have a profound effect on her resistance to cancer and on her chances for recovery, many people supplement conventional medical treatments with nutritional and alternative therapies. The prognosis for each dog will depend on the type of cancer, how early it is detected, the dog's age, her health prior to the disease, and other factors.

If you find any unusual lump or growth on your dog, have your vet look at it as soon as you can. As dogs age, they often develop noncancerous fatty tumors that can become unsightly, but that usually pose no health threat, so don't panic. But do be proactive on your dog's behalf. Be aware, too, that some canine cancers can be prevented. Neutered females have no risk for ovarian or uterine cancer because they no longer have those organs, and those who are spayed before their first heat have a much lower risk of mammary (breast) cancer. Neutered males have no risk for testicular cancer. Keep in mind, too, that your own lifestyle affects your dog's health. There is evidence, for instance, that dogs who live with smokers are at an increased risk for lung cancer, so if you won't quit for yourself, do it for your dog.

Now let's look at two common forms of cancer in dogs.

Bone Cancer

Any dog can get bone cancer, but it is most common in large and giant breeds and usually is seen in the long bones of the legs. There are four types of canine bone cancer:

- *Osteosarcoma* is an aggressive, fast-growing cancer that causes bony growths. It accounts for more than three out of four cases of canine bone cancer.

- *Chondrosarcomas* grow from the cartilage that covers the ends of bones at joints and are usually less aggressive than osteosarcoma.
- *Fibrosarcomas* grow from the fibrous connective tissues adjacent to bone. Although they are invasive locally and often invade nearby bone, they do not tend to spread.
- *Synovial cell carcinomas* begin in joint tissues and invade nearby bone. They are less aggressive than osteosarcomas.

A dog who loses a leg to bone cancer can function very well.

The first sign of bone cancer is often chronic lameness and perhaps swelling over a bone or near a joint. Occasionally a dog with bone cancer will suddenly become lame. X rays will likely show changes in the bone, but a final diagnosis can be made only through microscopic evaluation of a bone biopsy.

For many dogs, the first line of treatment for bone cancer is amputation of the affected leg. Unfortunately, if the cancer has metastasized, removing the leg will buy some time but will not cure the cancer. If the cancer has not spread, amputation followed by chemotherapy is often effective. Although not all dogs are candidates for amputation, those who are otherwise reasonably healthy and fit do remarkably well after losing a leg.

Lymphosarcoma

Lymphosarcoma (LSA) is one of the most common cancers seen in dogs and is caused by an abnormal proliferation of *lymphocytes* (immune system cells). LSA can affect any dog but is most commonly seen in those who are seven years old or older.

In its most common form, LSA causes an enlargement of one or more lymph nodes, which can be seen as a lump on the surface of the dog's body. Occasionally the lymph node swells so much that it prevents other body structures from working properly (by blocking airflow, for example), but usually the enlarged lymph nodes are painless.

Other forms of LSA affect the liver, spleen, bone marrow, gastrointestinal tract, skin, nervous system, or other organs. Many dogs stop eating and become lethargic. Some develop signs that relate to the affected organs, which can delay diagnosis of lymphoma while other diseases are ruled out. In the early stages, the dog may not show any obvious signs at all but may be diagnosed as a result of a vet visit for other, even routine, reasons.

LSA in dogs is not usually considered curable, but the disease can sometimes be held at bay for a while with veterinary treatment. Chemotherapy drugs generally extend the dog's life a year or more, especially if the disease is caught early. Most dogs tolerate chemotherapy well, and continue to have a high quality of life.

The Nervous System

The dog's nervous system includes the brain, spinal cord and all the sensory and motor nerves that communicate between tissues and the brain or spinal cord. While the brain and spinal cord are well protected by the skull and vertebrae of the spinal column, they can still be injured by trauma or impacted by disease or toxins. Here are some neurological disorders that commonly affect dogs and how to handle them:

Seizure Disorders

A *seizure* occurs when nerves in the brain "fire" suddenly and without normal controls, causing muscles to contract repeatedly. Seizures, although heart-wrenching to watch, are seldom fatal. However, a dog can hurt

Not All Seizures Are Epilepsy

If your dog has one or more seizures, she does not necessarily have epilepsy. Seizures can be caused by many things, including:

- Poisons
- Drugs
- Head injuries
- Fever
- Heat stroke
- Congenital defects
- Tumors
- Diabetes mellitus
- Hypoglycemia (low blood sugar)
- Kidney or liver disease
- Infectious disease

If your dog has a seizure, get her to the vet as soon as you can to determine the cause and treatment plan.

herself during a seizure, and in extreme cases, she may experience *status epilepticus* (a very long seizure or one seizure after another with no time for rest and recovery), which can cause hyperthermia (overheating), hypoglycemia (low blood sugar), exhaustion, permanent brain damage, and death.

If your dog has a seizure, stay calm. *Never put any part of your body near the mouth of a dog during a seizure*—she could bite you without even knowing it. You can gently touch your dog's body and speak to her in a calm, reassuring voice. Clear the area around her of sharp or hard objects or furniture, or pad them quickly with blankets or other cushioning materials so your dog won't hurt herself on hard edges. Turn off or remove any nearby stimuli—bright or flashing lights, for instance, or loud music or other sounds. If children are present, they need to be quiet. Be sure to time the seizures so you can report the duration and frequency to your vet.

If the seizure lasts more than fifteen minutes, or if one seizure follows another, call your vet or an emergency clinic. Wrap your dog gently in a sheet or blanket, and take her to the vet right away.

If your dog has a single mild seizure, record the date and time, and write down as accurately as possible what happened before, during, and after the seizure occurred. Call your vet as soon as possible, and let him know about anything that may have triggered the event (see "Not All Seizures Are Epilepsy" on page 384).

The first step in stopping seizure activity is to identify the cause, if possible. Be cautious about an immediate diagnosis of epilepsy or about beginning drug therapy without any attempt to find the source of the problem. Consider asking your vet for a referral to a veterinary neurologist, who has the specialized training to make a more detailed diagnosis and develop a more effective treatment plan.

If the cause cannot be identified, your dog will be diagnosed with *idiopathic epilepsy* (idiopathic means that the cause is unknown). *Idiopathic epilepsy* is believed to be inherited, and it can occur in any breed or mixed-breed. Affected dogs usually experience their first seizures when they are between one and five years old.

If your dog has seizures and the cause can be identified and removed or treated, the seizures will probably not recur. In many other cases, it may not be possible to completely stop the seizures, but they can usually be controlled so that your dog can live a reasonably normal life (unless other health problems prevent that). You will need to continue to work with your vet to ensure the dosage of medication given to your dog is enough to control the seizures, but is as low as possible to avoid potential side effects. Periodic blood chemistry and liver function analyses are usually recommended for dogs on long-term anti-seizure medications.

Other Nervous System Disorders

Ataxia is lack of normal balance and coordination of movement. Although ataxia can be caused by injury, drugs, toxins, and disease, we are concerned here about two forms of incurable, inherited ataxia that affect dogs.

Cerebellar ataxia is caused by problems in the *cerebellum*, the part of the brain that controls balance. Head trauma, toxins, and disease can cause non-inherited ataxia, but there is also a congenital, inherited form of the disease in which certain cells in the cerebellum die prematurely, causing loss of balance. Affected puppies may show signs of ataxia when they begin to walk at two to three weeks of age, or later in life. Typically such a puppy will shake, bob her head, fall repeatedly or stand with her feet far apart, and raise her feet high when she tries to walk. For some, the disease quickly worsens and for others it progresses more slowly. Some affected dogs can live for years if given special care.

Spinocerebellar ataxia has similar symptoms, but typically shows up when the puppy is about five months old. It is not as severe or debilitating as cerebellar ataxia.

Myasthenia gravis is a neuromuscular disease that interrupts the way nerves communicate with muscles. As a result, the animal cannot contract affected muscles. If only a few muscles are involved, the effects are minimal, but if many neuromuscular junctions are affected, the dog may be virtually unable to move. With proper diagnosis and treatment, however, dogs can live a long time with myasthenia gravis.

Coonhound paralysis (*acute idiopathic polyradiculoneuritis*) is caused by an allergic reaction to a protein found in raccoon saliva. The condition occurs in some dogs who are bitten by raccoons, and it appears to affect only dogs. The signs of coonhound paralysis can be similar to signs of rabies, so if your dog becomes weak or paralyzed, take her to your veterinarian *immediately*. Although coonhound paralysis cannot be cured, most dogs who receive proper treatment recover in four to six weeks. Since this is an allergic reac-

Dogs and Drugs

Dogs, like people, sometimes react badly to drugs. Drug sensitivities can simply be individual intolerance, but some breeds (and mixes including those breeds) have high rates of adverse reactions to specific drugs or families of drugs. Reactions vary from mild to fatal, so it's important to research your adopted dog's breed (or breeds and suspected breeds) so that you know if she has a higher-than-normal risk.

If you adopt from a purebred rescue program, they may be able to provide information. Otherwise contact the breed club or clubs, or search online for "breed and drug sensitivity" and similar topics. Don't rely on your veterinarian to know this by heart—he cannot possibly remember all the quirks of every breed and mix. If you find from a reputable source that your dog is potentially sensitive to a drug or family of drugs, be sure to inform your veterinarian. Have him indicate clearly in your dog's records that she should not take the drug. Then always monitor the drugs used on your dog in case someone forgets or misses the warning. If your vet trivializes or dismisses the dangers of these drugs to your dog, consider finding a new vet.

Here are some common drug sensitivities in dogs:

- Several drugs are known to cause seizures and possible death in dogs, particularly the herding breeds, some sight hounds, and mixes that include those breeds (see "Drugs and the MDR1 Mutation" on page 352).
- Certain anesthetic drugs are hazardous for sight hounds and some other breeds.
- Acepromazine is a tranquilizer that is frequently used as a pre-anesthetic agent or to sedate dogs for other reasons. Although it can be used safely in most cases, some dogs, such as Boxers or Boxer mixes, can have a negative reaction to it. Reactions may include arrhythmia of the heart, severe low blood pressure, collapse, respiratory arrest, and dangerously slow heart rate.
- Aspirin given to dogs must be buffered or enteric-coated to prevent stomach ulcers. Consult your vet for dosages.
- Don't give other prescription or over-the-counter drugs to your dog without first consulting your veterinarian.

tion, if your dog has coonhound paralysis once, a subsequent reaction will probably be more serious, so do what you need to do to prevent her from interacting with raccoons.

As we've seen in the last few chapters, there's an awful lot that can go wrong with dogs. Fortunately, there is also a lot you can do to help your adopted buddy regain good health and stay healthy the rest of her life. We've already discussed some of those things—feeding her a nutritional diet, keeping her at a proper weight, seeing that she gets enough exercise, and getting her prompt veterinary care if she shows any signs of illness or pain. In the next chapter, we'll examine some holistic and alternative approaches to canine health care that you may want to explore.

Warning: Drugs on the Internet

It can be very tempting to save a little money by purchasing medications for your dog over the Internet. If you decide to do so, though, be aware that many manufacturers do not warrant or guarantee their products if they are obtained online. This is not because they're in cahoots with the vet or trying to increase their profits. It is because medications that are improperly shipped or stored may not be fully effective, especially if they are exposed to temperature extremes.

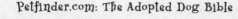

Dog Biscuits for the Soul: Oscar

Oscar

In April 2005, I was looking on Petfinder.com and saw Oscar. He had been taken to a shelter, was heartworm positive and was scheduled to be euthanized. A New Beginning Pet Care and Rescue saved him and listed him on Petfinder. Shortly after contacting A New Beginning, my father was admitted to the hospital with end-stage emphysema. The day I adopted Oscar began with a visit to the hospital. My father had always encouraged me to get another dog, and he was happy to learn I was on my way to pick up Oscar. It would be the last time I saw my father alive. Having Oscar really helped me through this difficult time. Although he was still sick from his first heartworm treatment, he was a delightful and happy boy. He goes to doggy day care while I'm at work and was selected as "Tailwagger of the Month." His day care notes that Oscar comes in with a bounce in his step and a wag in his tail. He gives kisses on his way in and out. During the day he plays very well with everyone and makes sure all new pets in the small dog area feel at home. He helps with cleanup, too, making sure that if a puppy has an accident it gets dealt with ASAP. (Yes, he actually lets the human pack leaders know that there has been an accident. I watched him do it on their web camera!) Oscar and I also do pet therapy at a local nursing home. His heartworm treatment was successful, and he is now heartworm-free. He is a wonderful example of a pet who had no future who was given a second chance by a rescue organization and a new owner, and who is now living a happy life and giving back to others. Oscar has enriched my life, and I feel lucky to have him.

Susan Tomko, Oshkosh, Wisconsin
Oscar was adopted from A New Beginning Pet Care and Rescue in Orlando, Florida

Resources

ONLINE VETERINARY RESOURCES

The Internet offers a tremendous amount of information (and misinformation) about canine health. Always check several sources before acting on what you read, and check the credentials of the site as well. Some people mean well but spread potentially dangerous misinformation. Many veterinarians and veterinary schools offer reliable online information that pet owners can find tremendously helpful. The AVMA has a list of American and Canadian veterinary schools at www.aavmc.org/students_admissions/vet_schools.htm. Here are a few to get started:

Cornell University: www.vet.cornell.edu/
UC Davis: www.vetmed.ucdavis.edu/
Tufts: www.tufts.edu/vet

Here are some other helpful online resources:

American Holistic Veterinary Medical Association
http://www.ahvma.org/

American Veterinary Medical Association (AVMA)
http://www.avma.org/

Autoimmune Diseases
http://www.canismajor.com/dog/autoimmn.html

Canine Cancer Awareness
http://www.caninecancerawareness.org/

Canine Epilepsy Network
http://www.canine-epilepsy.net/

Canine Epilepsy Resource Center
http://www.canine-epilepsy.com/

National Canine Cancer Foundation
http://www.wearethecure.org/

Orthopedic Foundation for Animals
www.offa.org

PennHIP (University of Pennsylvania Hip Improvement Program)
www.vet.upenn.edu/ResearchCenters/pennhip/

Veterinary Medical Data Basis (VMDB)/Canine Eye Registration Foundation (CERF)
www.vmdb.org/cerf.html

VetInfo.com
http://www.vetinfo4dogs.com/

BOOK
Eldredge, Deborah, DVM and Liisa Carlson, DVM, Delbert Carlson, DVM, and James Giffin, MD: *Dog Owner's Home Veterinary Handbook*. Wiley, 2007

18

Holistic Medicine

There is a paradigm shift occurring in health care today: a growing number of people are looking for alternatives to traditional allopathic medicine and seeking more natural methods for improving or maintaining their health. It's not surprising that many people want to do the same for their dogs.

What Is Holistic Veterinary Medicine?

Holistic medicine, also known as alternative therapy, has a simple yet powerful premise: treat the entire being, not just the symptoms. In fact, the word *holistic* takes its name from the Greek word *holos*, which means *total*. Holistic veterinarians, therefore, look at all aspects of a dog's life to learn about his personality, lifestyle, and diet. They will notice symptoms such as a swollen knee or itchy skin, but they mainly focus on physical, emotional, and environmental problems that may be causing illness to proliferate. Many veterinarians like Richard Pitcairn, DVM, PhD, have found holistic medicine helpful where more traditional methods have failed. In his book *Dr. Pitcairn's Complete Guide to Natural Health for Dogs and Cats*, Dr. Pitcairn states, "Since converting my practice to the use of homeopathy and nutrition, my experience of being a veterinarian has been transformed. I am really, truly seeing animals get well from conditions that are simply considered incurable or hopeless from the conventional perspective."

How Is Conventional Medicine Different from Holistic Medicine?

It can be extremely frustrating, not to mention heartbreaking, to take your adopted dog to a veterinarian where he receives a packet of pills or a series of shots to "cure" the problem, only to have another, more serious illness pop up a few weeks later. You may not associate your dog's painful limp with the allergy attack he had a month ago, but holistic practitioners realize that seemingly unrelated health problems are often connected to one another. Conventional medical practitioners, on the other hand, tend to look most closely at a patient's obvious symptoms and often prescribe a drug or medical procedure to suppress them. This doesn't mean that conventional medicine isn't important; in fact, it's indispensable for acute, life-threatening illnesses or injuries. But holistic medicine is often a gentler or more effective way to treat many common chronic ailments and mysterious conditions that don't respond well to more conventional types of treatments. For many natural remedies, there are no side effects, and an overdose is much less likely.

The combination of conventional medicine and holistic therapies is called *integrative medicine.*

Many dogs can benefit from holistic medicine used with traditional medicine.

Types of Holistic Medicine

Keep in mind that alternative therapies, while powerful, often take time to work. Be patient and persistent, and soon you'll begin to notice positive changes in your dog's overall health and well-being. *Important note: Always consult a qualified holistic veterinarian or certified herbalist who consults with a veterinarian before starting any type of natural treatment for your dog.*

Acupuncture

Acupuncture (for both people and animals) has been practiced in China for thousands of years. It wasn't until the mid-twentieth century, however, that the study and practice of acupuncture gained greater understanding and acceptance in the United States.

Ancient Chinese doctors observed that stimulation of specific areas on the body's surface could relieve pain and internal discomfort for a number of maladies and assist in general healing as well. These *acu-points* are organized into relationships called *meridians*. Acupuncture needles are placed into specific acu-points along these meridians to encourage the body to overcome pain, become balanced, and heal itself. Modern research indicates that acupuncture stimulates the release of hormones known as *endorphins* that relieve pain naturally, enhance immunity, and improve blood circulation.

Veterinary acupuncture can treat arthritis, the discomfort associated with hip dysplasia, joint pain and weakness, and immune system disorders. It can also help with recovery and rehabilitation after an injury or surgery, and it has proven a viable means of treating more serious diseases such as organ failure and cancer. Acupuncture may be used as a primary treatment or in conjunction with conventional methods.

Finding the Right Holistic Veterinarian

Choosing a holistic veterinarian is much the same as choosing a traditional veterinarian. For guidance, see Chapter 15. In addition, the References section at the end of this chapter lists many national holistic veterinary organizations that can direct you to a veterinarian in your area.

As with a traditional veterinarian, your holistic vet will be your partner in your dog's health and well-being, so be sure that he or she is someone whose advice and council you will be comfortable taking.

Aromatherapy

Plant extracts, known as essential oils, are used in aromatherapy to help strengthen the immune system, assist with healing a variety of physical ailments, and diminish emotional upsets. For instance, lavender has sedative properties that help to alleviate hyperactivity and nervousness, while peppermint eases nausea and repels insects. Knowing which type and amount of oils to use can be tricky, so you may wish to seek the advice of a qualified herbalist or holistic veterinarian. If you're the do-it-yourself type and would like to create your own remedies at home, here are a few tips to help you get started.

Since there are many brands of essential oils available, spend some time doing research online or ask a knowledgeable sales clerk at your local health food store for a recommendation. Once you have determined which essential oil to use, place two to four drops in a teaspoon of witch hazel extract or a tablespoon of a "base" oil (such as almond oil) to create a half-and-half dilution, then apply it directly to your dog's skin and fur. Essential oils are irritating to the skin and will burn your dog if used straight from the bottle, so proceed slowly until you know how your dog will react. Apply this 50/50 dilution only where your dog can't lick it off but can still inhale the scent, such as the inside of his ear. The preparation can also be added to a diffuser and allowed to evaporate slowly, or placed in a mister along with water and a few drops of biodegradable liquid soap and sprayed directly onto your dog's bedding. You can also try dabbing the essential oil on a kerchief your dog wears around his neck. Essential oils work quickly, last only a few hours, and should only be used three times a day for one or two days. If you see no improvement, talk to your veterinarian for further help. For best results, follow the directions on the label and remember to use only high-quality, pure essential oils.

Bach Flower Remedies

Dr. Edward Bach, a Welsh medical doctor and surgeon, discovered the healing properties of flower essences—or flower remedies, as they are sometimes called—more than seventy years ago. Dr. Bach became dissatisfied with traditional forms of medical treatment and believed that all physical illnesses were manifestations of emotional upsets such as worry and fear. Dr. Bach began to look to nature for answers, and over a period of several years, he found thirty-eight different flowers and plants that helped to ease negative emotions and allowed peace and happiness to return, thus allowing the body to heal itself.

Flower essences, which can be purchased at many health food stores or online, may be administered both orally and topically. The person or dog touching the essence is thought to benefit from the effect, so the drops should ideally only come in contact with the dog, not be rubbed on with human hands. Bach essences do not need to be ingested to work—drip some on your dog's nose, on the pads of his feet, or on the fur between his eyes (wherever the fur is thin). It's best to dilute these essences rather than using them straight from the bottle. Do this by adding two to three drops of the full-strength essence (your "stock bottle") to a second dropper bottle, add spring water, and shake ten times. Use this as your treatment bottle. Veterinarians recommend giving one to three drops a day until your dog feels better. You may also add a few drops to his morning drinking water.

Rescue Remedy, perhaps the most well-known of the flower remedies, can be used for any severe emotional or physical trauma. It may be used to calm hyperactive dogs, reduce excessive barking, and ease stress. See the "Bach Flower Remedies" chart on the next page for a list of common emotional upsets and the suggested remedy and outcomes for each one. Even if you choose the wrong one, it won't hurt your dog. Flower essences are safe, and typically work quite quickly if you've chosen the right remedy.

Chiropractic Care

Chiropractic care focuses on the connection between the spinal column and the nervous system and the crucial role of this relationship in the maintenance of flexibility and overall health. If the spine is improperly aligned, there is interference between normal nerve function and blood circulation. During a treatment, a chiropractor will identify *subluxations*, subtle misalignments of the spine, and manipulate or "adjust" the spine to restore alignment of the vertebrae and musculoskeletal system.

A number of conditions, including arthritis, hip dysplasia, epilepsy, lameness, rear-end weakness, and other orthopedic problems respond well to chiropractic care. Dogs who have suffered any major trauma (such as being hit by a car) or minor upset (such as slipping or falling on a slick surface or colliding with another dog during play) also respond well to treatment. If your dog is reluctant to run or jump, or if he walks with an unsteady gait or obvious discomfort, he may benefit from chiropractic care, as it improves flexibility and eases pain, often reducing the need for pain medication. Like other holistic treatments, chiropractic care works well in conjunction with acupuncture, herbal medicine, and other alternative therapies.

CHART: BACH FLOWER REMEDIES

INDICATION	BACH REMEDY	OUTCOME
Vague or unaccountable fears, especially when afraid of something unfamiliar. Appearing agitated for no apparent reason. Helpful for noise phobias and separation anxiety.	**Aspen**	Provides a sense of security and fearlessness so the patient may face challenges and difficulties more easily.
Intolerance toward animals, people, events, and situations. Helpful for introducing new pets.	**Beech**	Makes the patient more tolerant of other animals and people.
A loss of self-control; animal violently scratching himself, excitable urination, fear-related aggression.	**Cherry Plum**	Causes the animal to be more self-controlled.
Repeated unsuccessful behavior patterns; doesn't learn from past mistakes. Useful in conjunction with behavior modification and training.	**Chestnut Bud**	Helps the animal to learn from experience so he stops repeating the same mistakes.
Possessive, manipulative, or territorial nature, appears to be jealous.	**Chicory**	Makes the animal more unselfish, self-assured, and loving.
No apparent interest in the world around him, sleeps all the time, has trouble paying attention, or seems to live in a dream. Helpful when training.	**Clematis**	Enables the animal to develop a more lively interest in the world around him and enjoy and participate in life.
Obsessive cleanliness, fastidiousness, excessive grooming. Also used for dogs with rashes or body odor.	**Crab Apple**	Relaxes the animal, helping him to accepting himself and his imperfections.
Overwhelmed by a demanding situation, such as travel, competition, or trip to the groomer.	**Elm**	Restores confidence, positive outlook, and coping capabilities.

Continued on next page

CHART: BACH FLOWER REMEDIES

INDICATION	BACH REMEDY	OUTCOME
Despondency or lethargy due to a setback, e.g. loss of loved one, chronic disease.	**Gentian**	Restores optimism. (May also need Honeysuckle.)
Overly concerned with companionship. Constant barking.	**Heather**	Helps the animal not need to be the center of attention.
Jealousy of other animals or a new baby in the home. Angry growling, barking, snapping, or unprovoked attacks.	**Holly**	Makes the animal more compassionate and willing to share with other animals.
Homesickness or over-attachment to the past, exhibiting grief with illness, kennel stays. Loss of owner or home.	**Honeysuckle**	Causes the animal to become self-assured, helps him adjust to a new home or environment. (May also need Walnut.)
Lethargy or lack of enthusiasm, physical or mental exhaustion.	**Hornbeam**	Restores vitality, enthusiasm, and spontaneity. (May also need Wild Rose.)
Impatient and seeming to have boundless energy; can't wait to go for a walk or rushes ahead. Impatient, irritable, nervous.	**Impatiens**	Helps the animal to become more patient.
Lack of self-confidence or avoiding situations where he has to perform, for animals that cower in submission, good for abused animals.	**Larch**	Boosts self-esteem, confidence, and determination.
Shy, timid, and afraid of specific, identifiable things. May shake or shiver when confronted, or urinate in submission.	**Mimulus**	Increases confidence and courage; allows the animal to enjoy life without fear.

Continued on next page

CHART: BACH FLOWER REMEDIES

INDICATION	BACH REMEDY	OUTCOME
Exhaustion, fatigue due to overwork: for working animals or those involved in racing, competitive events, or shows.	**Olive**	Restores strength and vitality. (Always ensure proper nutrition as well.)
Stressful situations: visits to the vet, being left alone, adapting to new surroundings. Fear of loud noises, such as fireworks and thunder. Excessive barking. Any trauma (being hit by car, injured, etc.)	**Rescue Remedy**	Brings about an immediate calming effect.
Stubborn animals that resist breaking old bad habits.	**Rock Rose**	Helps them be more flexible and willing to learn.
An animal who can't make up his mind; any swinging behavior pattern (eats/doesn't eat, sleeps a lot/doesn't sleep), for pets with severe mood swings, helpful for motion sickness.	**Scleranthus**	Results in a more decisive and balanced animal.
Abused, mistreated in the past. Trauma or shock.	**Star of Bethlehem**	Neutralizes the effects of shock or trauma.
Enthusiastic, always wants to be involved, high strung, hyperactive, intense.	**Vervain**	Assists the animal in becoming more calm and able to relax.
Authoritative, dominant, even over his owners.	**Vine**	Helps the animal to be determined, not domineering.
Animals undergoing any period of change.	**Walnut**	Eases him into new surroundings or situations.

Continued on next page

CHART: BACH FLOWER REMEDIES

INDICATION	BACH REMEDY	OUTCOME
Unfriendly, standoffish; does not invite or welcome cuddles, petting, or obvious affection.	**Water Violet**	Produces a compassionate and sociable animal.
Loss of sense of direction or purpose; depressed, bored, especially good for working or show animals who are being retired.	**Wild Oat**	Restores ambition and sense of purpose. (May also need Walnut.)
Lack of energy or enthusiasm; submissive and disinterested.	**Wild Rose**	Creates a lively interest in life.

Source: The Original Bach Flower Essences, www.bachflower.com

The American Veterinary Chiropractic Association (AVCA) can refer you to a veterinary chiropractor in your area. See the Resources section at the end of the chapter for contact information.

Cold Laser Therapy

Cold laser therapy, or low-level light therapy, is the use of low-level laser energy to treat soft tissue injuries. The term "cold laser" is used to distinguish it from hot lasers, which are commonly used in surgery, hair removal, and tattoo removal in people. Cold laser therapy has been used successfully in both humans and animals to treat a variety of ailments such as arthritis, tendonitis, and plantar fasciitis (pain in tissues on the bottom of the foot), as well as pain in the back, knees, neck, and jaw.

Herbal Therapies

In *The Complete Holistic Dog Book*, authors Jan Allegretti and Katy Sommers, DVM, describe herbal therapies this way: "Using herbs to treat illness is the purest, simplest way to use medicine just as nature intended. It can be as easy as picking a sprig of parsley from your garden and adding the leaves to your dog's dinner."

Herbal therapies are drugs and can be used to treat anything that conventional medicines treat, from digestive problems and minor colds to nervousness and weakened immunity. A veterinarian should properly diagnose your dog's illness before you administer an herbal remedy.

Keep in mind that dogs do not metabolize drugs—or herbs—in the same ways people do. Herbal remedy dosages cannot always be based on how much less your dog weighs compared to a person. In addition, herbs can have interactions with other medications and even vitamins. That means combining an otherwise safe "natural" remedy with a conventional drug could cause an overdose of one or both treatments and be dangerous for your dog. For this reason, always discuss herbal treatments with a veterinarian before deciding on doses.

If you don't have access to fresh herbs from a garden, quality herbs can be found at most health food stores or online from a variety of companies. When choosing herbs as medicine for your pooch, it's best to buy organic to avoid any chemical contaminants from pesticides and fertilizers. Herbs are available in many forms, the most common being tinctures (also called liquid extracts), whole herbs (fresh or dried), capsules, and tablets.

Tinctures are highly concentrated liquids made by soaking an herb in a solvent—usually alcohol and water—so that the active ingredients of the plant are extracted into the solvent. Glycerin is often added to these extracts to improve taste. They have a shelf-life of five to seven years and because they are so highly concentrated, just a few drops are often all that's needed. Like Bach Flower Remedies, the tincture may be added to your dog's food or placed directly into his mouth.

Whole herbs have many healing properties, in addition to adding flavor to food. Fresh herbs can be dried and mixed into your dog's food or they can

Petfinder.com: The Adopted Dog Bible

be brewed into a tea (also called an infusion) and then added to your dog's drinking water.

Capsules contain finely powdered herbs and are available at most health food stores and some grocery stores. To give your dog the remedy, pull the capsule apart and sprinkle the contents onto your dog's food or hide an entire capsule in a yummy treat. Keep in mind that capsules have been formulated for humans, so the dosage may be too high for your dog. Only your holistic veterinarian should recommend the proper doses for your dog.

Tablets are highly compressed herbs and can be given whole (by hiding the tablet in a treat), or you can crush them and add the powder to your dog's food. Whole herbs, capsules, and tablets remain optimally effective for approximately six months.

Dosage amounts and frequency depend on the size of your dog. Keep in mind that smaller dogs may actually metabolize herbs more quickly than larger dogs, so you may need to give your dog a larger dose than you anticipated. Always follow the advice of a holistic veterinarian.

Homeopathy

Homeopathy is a holistic medical system that uses doses of certain plants or minerals that would, if used full strength, produce symptoms similar to those of an illness or disease. These diluted substances stimulate the body's own natural healing powers. To fully understand the principle of homeopathy, we need to look at the work of Dr. Samuel Hahnemann, a medical doctor who lived during the eighteenth century. Dr. Hahnemann became discouraged with the medical practices available at the time, and he began to seek a more natural method of treating illness and disease. He called his new medical system *homeopathy*, which is based on the principle that "like cures like." In other words, he found a substance that *caused* symptoms of disease to occur at normal doses could be used to *eliminate* those same symptoms at homeopathic (very diluted) doses. As an example, if pure sulfur is applied to the skin, it has an irritating and caustic effect, but when a weakened amount is applied, sulfur actually soothes dry, itchy skin and helps eliminate mange and ringworm. In homeopathy, the more *dilute* the remedy becomes, the more *potent* it is—and the better it works.

The process used for making homeopathic remedies is called *succession*. First, a pharmacist places a small amount of the original substance in a liquid—usually water or alcohol—to make a solution. Then she pounds or shakes the solution vigorously. That solution is, in turn, diluted and shaken, and the resulting solution is once again diluted and shaken, over and over again. This is repeated until perhaps only a single molecule of the original substance remains. The process is said to encode the "memory" of the original substance, which the body recognizes and reacts to, but without the danger of a harmful dose. The result is called a *potentized solution*.

You may be wondering how such a small amount of a natural remedy can be effective. Homeopathic practitioners believe that these solutions contain the *energy* of the original substance. It is this energy, they say, that stimulates a patient's *life force* to begin the healing process.

Homeopathic remedies can be used to treat a wide variety of maladies, but they appear to be particularly effective for chronic conditions and mysterious illnesses that don't respond well to the usual allopathic treatments. Dogs with allergies, arthritis, nervousness, or stress (often seen in shelter dogs), and skin problems can often be helped by homeopathic remedies. These remedies are safe and nontoxic, with no side effects, and it's impossible to overdose on them.

Light/Color Therapy

Researchers have long known that light has healing properties. Light directed into the eye, for example, can stimulate the pineal gland to produce melatonin, a hormone that controls the sleep/wake cycle. Today, many holistic veterinarians are employing the use of light and color therapy to treat a variety of ailments in dogs.

Different colors of light have different effects. For example:

- Yellow light positively influences the nervous system and eases depression
- Green light relieves tension, stabilizes blood pressure, and is a general healing stabilizer
- Red light is stimulating and also helps stabilize the immune system

☼ Blue light soothes fevers and areas of inflammation and can prompt the pituitary gland to produce calming hormones

When used properly, light therapy can rebalance a dog's natural energy and help restore him to peak physical and emotional health.

Magnetic Therapy

Magnets help the body heal by reducing inflammation and restoring circulation. Two types of magnets are used in magnetic therapy: static magnets and electromagnets. Static magnets can be applied directly to the skin, while electromagnets are used in conjunction with electricity. Both types of magnets work by increasing blood flow to an injured or diseased part of the body, thus bringing in essential nutrients that aid healing. Magnets can be helpful in easing pain associated with arthritis, hip dysplasia, sprains and strains, as well as a variety of vertebral disorders. Magnets *should not* be used on pregnant females or dogs with cardiac pacemakers. Always consult with a holistic veterinarian before trying magnetic therapy on your dog.

Massage

Massaging your dog is a terrific way for you to bond with him and help him relax, and it also has many health benefits. Massage improves circulation, boosts the immune system, eases pain and stiffness, and promotes emotional and physical relaxation. You can hire a professional massage therapist to give your dog a massage or do it yourself. If your adopted dog is a little skittish about being touched or petted, wait until he feels more comfortable around you before trying any massage techniques. You can also review the techniques in Chapter 8 on helping shy dogs get over their fear of being touched.

Most people already do some sort of massage technique when they pet their dogs (think tummy rubs). To give your dog a great massage, first settle into a quiet room together and turn off the telephone so you won't be disturbed. Have him lie on his side, and sit or kneel next to him. Take a few deep breaths and then begin to gently stroke your dog's fur. Start at the top of his head, and run your hands down the length of his body to the tip of his tail. Always move in the direction of his fur.

Using your finger pads, palms, and fingertips, massage all the muscles in your dog's body. You can also use a brush to gently caress and soothe his tired muscles. Try alternating between using your hand and a brush—one long stroke with your hand, then one long stroke with the brush. Apply more or less pressure according to your dog's responses. Have him turn over to his other side and repeat the process. You don't need to spend a lot of time massaging your dog (although he probably won't want you to stop!)—in as little as five or ten minutes, you can help him relax and foster a closer bond between the two of you.

Nosodes

Nosodes, from the Greek word *nosos*, meaning *disease*, is a homeopathic remedy made from the pathological specimen (such as blood, tissue, pus, or other body secretion) of a sick animal. For example, the saliva from a rabid dog is used to create a rabies nosode. Homeopathic veterinarians sometimes use nosodes in place of traditional vaccines to immunize a dog against a specific illness. Like vaccines, nosodes sensitize the body to a particular disease, so the immune system can quickly build a defense against the disease. While proponents claim that nosodes are as effective as vaccinations, there have been no long-term studies conducted on their efficacy or safety.

Nutrition Therapy

Feeding your dog nutritional foods is one of the most important things you can do to help him live a long and healthy life. Unfortunately, many commercial dog foods on the market today are loaded with chemicals, preservatives, and other ingredients that are considered harmful by many. Plus, they are processed at high temperatures, which may destroy many important nutrients.

If your dog suffers from allergies or other chronic conditions, the food he is eating may be the cause. See Chapter 9 for a full discussion of nutrition and how to feed your dog.

Dog Biscuits for the Soul: Arnold

Arnold

Arnold came into our lives very quickly. He was rescued from a puppy mill in Missouri and was brought to New York by way of Flaw Dogs Rescue and Green Mountain Pug Rescue. He was in foster care for six weeks, and had all but eight of his teeth removed the day of his neutering. He was covered in sores and was scratching himself constantly. Arnold is now receiving weekly acupuncture treatments to relieve his discomfort and malformed legs (from years of living in a crate). He also received a chiropractic adjustment, and now his elbows are working better. He has even started massage therapy. He is living the life of a pampered pug! Arnold had made our world complete. He fits perfectly into our family, a middle child with Pugsley and Daisy. He can be seen running in the yard with his sister, walking up and down stairs, and can even go for short walks now. He has even learned the act of pug begging. Arnold will only know the pampered life from here on out. He brings a smile to our faces each and every day.

Heather McFarland, Clifton Park, New York
Arnold was adopted from Green Mountain Pug Rescue, Lyndonville, Vermont

Resources

Academy of Veterinary Homeopathy
www.theavh.org

American Academy of Veterinary Acupuncture
www.aava.org

American Holistic Veterinary Medical Association
www.ahvma.org

American Veterinary Chiropractic Association
www.animalchiropractic.org

International Veterinary Acupuncture Society
www.ivas.org

Veterinary Botanical Medical Association
www.vbma.org

Books

Allegretti, Jan and Katy Sommers, DVM: *The Complete Holistic Dog Book: Home Health Care for Our Canine Companions*. Celestial Arts, 2003

Ballner, Maryjean: *Dog Massage: A Whiskers-to-Tail Guide to Your Dog's Ultimate Petting Experience*. St. Martin's Griffin, 2001

Pitcairn, Richard H., DVM, PhD and Susan Hubble Pitcairn: *Dr. Pitcairn's Complete Guide to Natural Health for Dogs & Cats*. Rodale, 2005

Schwartz, Cheryl, DVM: *Four Paws Five Directions: A Guide to Chinese Medicine for Cats and Dogs*. Hay House, 2002

Shojai, Amy D. and the Editors of *Prevention for Pets: New Choices in Natural Healing for Dogs & Cats*. Rodale, 2001

19

On the Road (or Plane, Train, or Boat) with Your Dog

Dogs have been an integral part of family life for ages, so it's no surprise that more and more of us are bringing them along when we travel. Dogs are always ready for a new adventure; it's a chance to spend quality time with their favorite human companions, make new friends, and explore new places. Like us, dogs can get bored with the same old routine and yearn for something new and exciting from time to time. Traveling can help you both feel relaxed and refreshed.

Canine Cruising

While "cat" and "car" don't usually fit well into the same sentence, the same doesn't hold true for dogs. At the mere mention of the words "car ride," most pups will hightail it out the door faster than you can say, well, "car ride." But if your dog is a bit of a scaredy-cat when it comes to the car, don't worry. There are things you can do before she ever sets a paw inside to make the trip more pleasurable for both of you.

Ideally, you should begin getting your dog used to cars when she is a puppy. That's not always possible with rescued dogs, as they may be adopted

Anywhere you go, he'll follow you.

as adults and you may know not know if they are accustomed to automobiles. As we discussed in Chapter 6, adopted dogs in particular may be wary of cars, because of negative memories they could associate with driving. Slowly introduce your new family member to the car by allowing her to sit inside with you while the engine is idling. Buckle her in a safety harness or place her in a traveling crate (more on this in a moment), and reassure her if she seems a little nervous. Once she appears relaxed, begin taking short jaunts around the block or perhaps to the pet store to pick out a favorite treat. This will help your dog to start associating car rides with good things.

Crates Are Great

For safety reasons, a dog should always be properly restrained whenever she rides in a car, and one of the most common ways to make sure your pup is safe is to put her in a crate. Make sure you have a crate that is large enough for your dog to sit, lie down, and turn around in comfortably. (For more on choosing the right crate for your dog, see Chapter 4.) For added safety in the car, secure the crate in place using bungee cords or rope. If a collision were to occur and the crate was not tied down, a dog will essentially become a "marble in a can," getting tossed around within the crate, which can cause serious injury not just to her, but to anyone else in the car as well. Before a car trip, allow your dog ample time to check out the crate so that she's feeling comfortable with it. Put her favorite blanket or toy inside, as this can help reduce her anxiety level.

Buckle "Pup" for Safety

Safety harnesses or "doggie seatbelts" are another viable means of protecting your dog while traveling in the car. This simple safety device, which can be purchased online or at most pet stores, easily attaches to a car's seatbelt and safely restrains your pup from roving about the car.

Important Note: As stated in Chapter 6, the safest place for a dog to travel is in the middle of the backseat of an automobile.

Just as with an infant or small child, *never* place your dog in the front passenger seat. If an accident occurs, a deployed air bag can prove deadly.

Do not ever permit your dog to travel in the bed of a pickup truck even if she's tied. Besides being illegal in many places, it is not safe for your dog, who could fall or jump out of the truck and injure, strangle, or even kill herself.

One final word of caution: It may look cute when your dog hangs her head outside the car window, but it's a dangerous practice. You may not have a full view from your side or rearview mirrors, and your dog will not only be subjected to inner ear damage and lung infections, but she could also be injured by flying objects. All hands and feet (and paws) inside the vehicle at all times.

Car Travel Dos and Don'ts

About three or four hours before you get on the road, feed your dog a light meal and give her some water to drink. Just before departing, take her for a short walk to "take care of business." Once you're on the road, stop the car every few hours so both of you can stretch your legs and get some fresh air. If your dog suffers from motion sickness, avoid feeding her just before and during a trip (even if it's a long drive), and open the car windows a little to allow fresh air into the vehicle. Many puppies outgrow their tendency to get queasy in the car.

When you reach your destination, remove your dog from her crate or safety harness and fasten her leash to her collar *before she jumps out of the car.* She's probably as excited as you are to explore the new surroundings, and she may inadvertently run into traffic or become lost.

If you plan to travel across state lines, bring along your dog's rabies

Natural Calmers: Bach's Flower Rescue Remedy

If your dog becomes anxious when she travels, you may consider giving her a homeopathic medicine, such as Bach's Flower Rescue Remedy, to calm her nerves. Flower remedies, or flower essences as they are commonly called, can be administered on an ongoing basis for a variety of behavior issues (such as separation anxiety), as well as short-term for potentially stressful situations, such as traveling. Depending on your dog's temperament, you will see results within a few minutes to a few hours of administering an essence. (More detailed information on flower essences and other holistic remedies is found in Chapter 18.)

vaccination record, as some states may require proof at certain interstate crossings.

Cool Tips for Hot Cars

When the mercury rises outside, you need to take extra precautions to ensure your dog's safety. ***Never leave a dog alone in a vehicle, even if the windows are partially open.*** In hot weather, a car can quickly become a furnace, with interior temperature rising to 160 degrees in as little as ten minutes. (Don't leave a dog alone in a car in cold weather, either, as a car will act as a refrigerator and hold in the cold, which can cause a dog to freeze to death.) Since dogs can't sweat (they pant to dissipate heat), they can quickly become overheated in a hot car. Dogs who are young, elderly, or overweight are particularly at risk of overheating, as are those with thick or dark-colored coats and breeds with short muzzles. Parking in a shady area with the windows rolled down offers little protection, as the sun shifts during the day. Even though you may plan to be gone for only a few minutes, that quick trip to pick up a carton of milk can quickly extend into fifteen minutes or more if the store is crowded or you stop to ask for help in locating the item. These extra minutes could prove deadly to your pup, so never, ever leave her alone in the car.

Here are some additional hot weather tips:

- ☼ Bring along plenty of water from home (stored in plastic jugs or a thermos). When a dog drinks water that she's not accustomed to, she could get an upset stomach.
- ☼ Keep your dog's fur cut short during the summer to prevent overheating (but don't shave the fur down to the skin, as this will put her at risk for sunburn).
- ☼ Carry sunscreen, and rub the lotion on your dog's most vulnerable spots such as her ears and nose. Pediatric or children's sunscreens work well as they are less likely to be irritating and are usually unscented. Try to purchase a product that is waterproof, such as Water Babies® or Bullfrog®, as they're also dog-saliva-proof.
- ☼ Don't force your dog to exercise in hot, humid weather (especially after she has eaten). Limit exercise time to the cooler early morning or evening hours.

Petfinder.com: The Adopted Dog Bible

Note: Snub-nosed dogs such as Bulldogs, Pekingese, Boston Terriers, Lhasa Apsos, Shih Tzus, and mixes that include those breeds are especially susceptible to hot weather problems or ailments.

- Never tie up your dog and leave her standing on the sidewalk. The hot concrete (asphalt becomes even hotter) can burn the pads of her paws if she remains in one spot too long. You also run the risk of her being stolen.

Be careful not to over-exercise your dog in the heat!

- Don't take a dog to the beach unless you bring along an umbrella for shade and plenty of fresh water to drink. After a romp in the ocean, wash the salt water off her fur as soon as you can.

Flying the "Furry" Skies

While some dogs enjoy air travel, others find it stressful, especially if they are traveling in the cargo area of an aircraft. While this section of the plane normally has proper ventilation, air pressure, and heating and cooling systems, the fact remains that this area is where the baggage is stored. Do you really want your dog flying by herself without you nearby to reassure her during the inevitable in-flight turbulence and scary take-offs and landings?

The International Air Transport Association (IATA), which oversees air travel for pets along with the United States Department of Agriculture (USDA), estimates that while 99 percent of all pets reach their destination safely, 1 percent (or approximately 5,000 animals) are lost, injured, or killed each year during air transport. Given these sobering statistics, you should proceed with caution whenever you are considering air travel with your dog.

Information About Airline Policies

Every airline has a different policy about traveling with dogs. For the most up-to-date information, visit the website of your preferred airline or call its customer service number. If your dog is small (under twelve pounds), she can usually fly with you in the cabin of the aircraft, but ask the airline about their size restrictions for dogs and the required type of carrier. Find out the cost of a puppy plane ticket and how far in advance the airline requires you to make your reservation. Some airlines only allow a certain number of dogs on any given flight, so you may need to book farther in advance to guarantee your pup's spot. Have proof of inoculations handy in case you are asked for this information. You can also visit a website such as PetFlight (www.petflight.com/airlines) for information about a variety of different airlines.

Note: Service and seeing-eye dogs are always allowed in the cabin of the plane with their human guardians.

Preparing for Air Travel

There are some additional precautions you can take to ensure your dog's safety and well-being when traveling by plane. If she is accompanying you in the cabin, you can quickly ascertain if she appears ill or agitated and take steps to make her more comfortable. On the other hand, if your dog is flying in the cargo area of the aircraft, you won't know if something has gone wrong until it's too late. That's why it's important for you to schedule direct flights whenever possible, as most problems occur when there is a layover and your dog's carrier sits on the tarmac or is transferred to another airplane. Early morning flights are best, especially during the summer months when temperatures rise dangerously during mid-day and afternoon hours.

Veterinary exam and vaccination records. Prior to your flight, make an appointment with your dog's veterinarian for a check-up and any necessary vaccinations. Obtain a health certificate no earlier than ten days before your departure date. If you haven't already done so, ask your veterinarian (or groomer) to bathe your dog and take care of any routine procedures such as ear cleaning, flea and tick treatment, and nail trimming. You'll want your dog looking and feeling her best when she meets friends in new locales!

Petfinder.com: The Adopted Dog Bible

Current identification. Make sure your dog is wearing a collar and up-to-date identification tag. The tag should include your dog's name and destination information as well as your name, address, and telephone number. This information is vital in the event your dog is lost or injured.

Proper crates. If your dog is small enough to travel in the cabin with you, consider using a soft-sided carrier that will easily fit under the seat in front of you. Check with the airline in advance to ensure that your carrier conforms to its regulations. Absorbent liners come with most soft-sided bags and are required by airlines for in-cabin use.

If your dog is medium to large in size, she will need to travel in the cargo area of the airplane. In this case, you will need to purchase a USDA-approved shipping crate (available online or from any pet supply retailer). The crate should be roomy enough to allow your dog to sit, stand, and change positions comfortably. Use a permanent marker to write LIVE ANIMAL on the outside of the crate (on both the top and sides), and draw arrows to prominently show the upright position of the crate. In addition, attach a luggage ID tag on which you type or print your dog's name, your name and address, an emergency telephone number, and your final destination.

For your dog's comfort, line the crate with shredded paper, a towel, or a favorite blanket. Once she has settled into the crate, make sure to securely close the door, but DO NOT lock it. Airline personnel may need to open the door in case of emergency.

Food and water. The crate should contain two dishes, one for food and one for water. Do not simply set the dishes inside the crate (they're likely to tip over); make sure they are attached securely to the inside of the crate. Freeze the water before a long flight so that it will not splash out during loading, but will melt by the time your dog is thirsty. For longer trips, attach a sealed plastic bag with your dog's dry food on top of the carrier with feeding instructions. Do not feed your dog for at least four hours before departure.

Tranquilizers. Sedating your dog prior to travel is not usually recommended, as the medication can have adverse effects at high altitudes. But if your dog is high-strung or becomes agitated in new situations, talk to your veterinarian about medication options.

Other vital information. As a general rule, puppies, females in heat, and elderly, ill, or pregnant dogs should not fly. In addition to the stress of air travel, changes in altitude and cabin pressure can have adverse affects on these more sensitive canines. Also, snub-nosed dogs (such as Pugs and

Bulldogs) should never fly in the cargo area of the aircraft. These breeds have short nasal passages, which restrict their intake of oxygen.

Finally, it's important that your dog be on the same flight with you. If she is flying in the cargo area of the aircraft, try to personally supervise her crate being loaded onto the plane. As soon as you board the aircraft, notify a flight attendant that your dog is on the plane. When the plane lands, make immediate arrangements to pick up your dog from the baggage claim area. Take her out of her crate (remember to clip on her leash first!) and allow her to stretch her legs and go outside for a potty break.

Trains, Boats, and Buses

As of this writing, neither Amtrak (rail carrier) nor Greyhound (bus service) allows dogs on board. In addition, most cruise lines do not accept dogs (although many local harbor cruises do permit dogs on short excursions). By law, however, all trains, boats, and buses must allow seeing-eye and service dogs.

Please note: Many train and bus services in Europe do allow dogs. If you are traveling overseas, check with your travel agent or the country of your destination for current rules and regulations.

Foreign Travel

Before embarking on a vacation to a foreign country, consult with your travel agent or contact your destination's consulate or embassy for information concerning their requirements for bringing dogs into the country. A listing of consulates can be found at www.state.gov/s/cpr/rls/fco. Every country has specific health requirements for the entry of animals, and their requirements change frequently. Check the United States Department of Agriculture website (www.aphis.usda.gov) for the most current information.

Many third-party companies can also assist you in making travel arrangements for your dog to a foreign country. Conduct an Internet search for "pet movers" or "pet shippers" to learn more about this.

Sniffing Out Pet-Friendly Hotels and Resorts

Whether your vacation includes a stay in a hotel, motel, or bed and breakfast, inquire prior to arrival about the establishment's policy on dogs. There are many good books and websites to assist you in finding pet-friendly lodging throughout the country (see the Resources section at the end of this chapter for more information), but always make sure to contact the establishment well ahead of time to obtain current information.

During your stay at a hotel or motel, always adhere to the following travel "petiquette" guidelines:

- When outdoors, keep your dog on a leash at all times.
- Always, always, always clean up after your dog.
- Never leave your dog unattended in your room (some dogs may bark or become destructive).
- If you must leave for a short time, put your dog in her crate and hang a "Do Not Disturb" sign on your doorknob. (Note: Some hotels offer short-term pet sitting; ask the concierge if this service is available.)
- Bring a blanket or towel for your dog to sleep on. This will protect the furniture from muddy paws and pet hair and will give her something familiar to cuddle up with.
- If possible, arrange to have your room cleaned while you're there or take your dog for a walk when the housekeeping staff arrives. Hotel employees may be frightened of dogs, even if yours is friendly.
- A well-trained dog makes an excellent travel companion. Consider investing in obedience training classes before embarking on your next journey with your pup, and see Chapter 7 for basic obedience training.

Time for a Break: Traveling Without Your Dog

Sometimes you will find it necessary to leave your dog at home when you go out of town. In these cases, it's important to select a suitable kennel, boarding facility, or pet-sitter for your dog. The following information will help you find the perfect person or place for your pooch.

Travel Checklist—Everything You Need for Life on the Go with Your Dog

We put a lot of thought into what items we'll put in our suitcases or duffle bags. Just as we spend time packing essential items for our trip, we should also think about what we'll pack for our pooches. Items should include:

— A first aid kit for dogs. Purchase a pre-packaged kit or make one of your own (see Chapter 14 for more information).
— A blanket or sheet to cover the backseat of your car. (Many companies offer custom-made, washable, removable seat covers specifically for dogs. Check online for manufacturers.)
— A reflective collar (with current identification tag) and leash for nighttime walks.
— A recent photo of your dog and a travel identification tag (allows you to store travel itinerary and contact information to help you recover your dog if she should get lost).
— A list of veterinary clinics and/or emergency veterinary hospitals in the area(s) where you will be traveling, including name, address, phone number, and hours of operation for each.
— Extra towels for drying off after a trip to the beach or lake.
— Non-breakable or collapsible food and water bowls. (Don't forget to bring along a container of fresh drinking water and a can opener and spoon for wet food.)
— Plastic or biodegradable bags for waste cleanup.
— Paper towels or wet wipes.
— Sunscreen (for your dog's ears and nose).
— A lint brush for clothing and furniture in hotel rooms.
— Any medications your dog is taking.
— Toys and treats.
— A digital or disposable camera to record all the happy memories of your trip!

Eileen Barish, the author of several travel books for dog lovers, offers this great suggestion: "To keep things simple from vacation to vacation, I restock my dogs' travel bags at the end of each trip. That way, I'm always prepared for the next adventure."

Finding the Best Kennel or Boarding Facility

Most towns and cities offer at least a few boarding facilities or kennels for dogs. Look online or in the yellow pages of your telephone book for the nearest one, or ask friends, family members, your veterinarian, or groomer for a recommendation. Also check with your local Humane Society; they may offer boarding services, and discounts usually apply for members.

Visit several facilities before making your selection. Here are some things to look out for when you go.

- **Staff.** Is the staff friendly and knowledgeable, and do they interact well with the dogs?
- **Cleanliness.** Are the kennels clean and free of odor? Is the building well-maintained? Are the fences, gates, and latches in good repair?
- **Climate.** Is the indoor temperature properly controlled by a heating and air-conditioning system? Are there trees or umbrellas outdoors to protect dogs from direct sunlight?
- **Exercise area.** Are the dogs free to roam around, or are they confined to a kennel?
- **Sleeping area.** Is the area clean, dry, and large enough for a dog to stand, sit, and stretch out comfortably? Are there comfy blankets and pillows for lounging?
- **Food.** Will the staff feed your dog her regular food? (You may need to bring a supply.)
- **Water.** Is there plenty of water available? Does the water (and bowls) look clean?
- **Emergency.** Does the facility have a policy in place for emergencies such as a natural disaster? If your pet becomes ill, do they have a veterinarian on call? If necessary, will they transport your dog to an emergency hospital?

Ask a staff member or manager how far in advance you should make your reservation (facilities will fill up fast during the summer months and holiday seasons). When you check your dog into the facility, remember to bring along

Every Dog Should Have Her Day ... Spa

For something a little more luxurious, you might consider checking your four-legged friend into a dog spa or resort. Many spas and resorts allow your dog to stay for a day, a week, or even longer. Amenities vary, but most establishments include overnight boarding (some places even have staff members who will sleep with your dog!), oodles of play time with two- and four-legged friends, a pool, grooming and training services, transportation to and from your home, a web cam so you can check on your dog while you're away, and massages to ease sore muscles after a "ruff" day of play.

Pricing for dog spas varies greatly, depending upon the area in which you live and the amenities you choose. As a general rule, rates begin at $25.00 for a half-day pass and go up as high as $75.00 for an overnight stay. Other services such as grooming range from $25.00-$50.00, depending on the coat length and size of the dog; a pedicure or nail trim is $15.00-$20.00; training ranges from $40.00 per hour (group session) to $150.00 per hour (private session); and massage is $50.00-$75.00 per hour.

her vaccination records, emergency contacts, any special food or medication she is taking (along with detailed instructions for administering the medication), and a blanket or favorite toy to make her feel at home.

Many dogs who were adopted from a shelter (no matter how nice the shelter was) may feel abandoned at a kennel or boarding facility. In this case, hiring a pet-sitter may be a more appropriate choice.

Finding the Best Dog Sitter

Some dogs find unfamiliar surroundings stressful and would be more content remaining at home when you're away. In a survey conducted in 2007 by FETCH! Pet Care, a whopping 82 percent of respondents selected in-home pet-sitting at the pet's residence as "the most convenient, healthful, and nurturing method of pet care." If you count yourself among that majority, then perhaps it's time to seek the services of a professional pet-sitter.

The last several years have seen a dramatic rise in the popularity of professional pet-sitting services. Organizations such as Pet Sitters International (www.petsit.com) and the National Association of Professional Pet Sitters (www.petsitters.org) list thousands of pet-sitters across the country on their websites. You can also ask a friend, family member, or veterinarian for a recommendation.

Do your homework before selecting a pet-sitter. You may wish to interview several candidates by telephone before asking a potential sitter to visit your home. Here are some questions to ask during your telephone conversation:

- Is the sitter bonded and insured?
- Does he keep regular business hours?
- What are his qualifications?
- Is he experienced with specific breeds and various medical conditions?
- How would he handle an emergency?
- Is he qualified to administer pet first aid and CPR?
- Is he a member of a reputable pet sitting association?
- Will the sitter leave a "report card," detailing the duties performed each day?

The most well-traveled dogs are well-behaved.

Once you have narrowed down your choices, arrange for in-home interviews with one or two pet-sitters to discuss services and fees (most sitters offer an initial complimentary visit). Observe how the sitter interacts with your dog to be sure they are comfortable together. The pet-sitter should have a written contract that spells out the terms of the job, including fees, dates of service, contact information, emergency information, and specific notes for caring for your dog. A good sitter will call you before the date of service and after you have returned home to confirm you arrived safely. Finally, ask for references and check them.

Depending on where you live and the level of service requested, in-home care rates typically range from $15.00 to $30.00 per visit. Unlike kennels, which usually charge a daily rate for each dog, pet-sitters normally charge a flat rate per visit, making in-home care especially affordable for a multi dog household.

Dog Biscuits for the Soul: Belle

Belle

Belle was rescued from a backyard breeder along with her sister, mother, and father. She is a Shih Tzu/Poodle mix (Shih Poo), which is a so-called designer dog—except when one needs to be rescued. Everywhere we go, people make a fuss over her and ask if she is a Yorkie. I explain what she is, adding that I adopted her at eleven weeks from a rescue group. It shocks them that such a beautiful puppy could end up needing to be rescued. Belle is a happy and very playful gal. She loves being with her big brother Buddy and riding in the car. Sometimes she even sits in her own car seat!

Samantha Wilson, Woodstock, Georgia
Belle was adopted from Pawing at Your Heart Inc., Winder, Georgia

Resources

HELPFUL WEBSITES
Bring Fido: www.bringfido.com
Dog Friendly: www.dogfriendly.com
Fido Friendly: www.fidofriendly.com
People with Pets: www.peoplewithpets.com/travel.asp
PetFlight: www.petflight.com
PetsWelcome: www.petswelcome.com
PetVacations: www.petvacations.com

FURTHER READING
Kein, Tara and Len: *DogFriendly.com's United States and Canada Dog Travel Guide.* Dogfriendly.com, 3rd Edition, 2006
Automobile Club of America (AAA): *Traveling with Your Pet.* AAA,10th Edition, 2008
Barish, Eileen: *Vacationing with Your Pet.* Pet Friendly Publications, 2006

20

Changes at Home

Dogs generally don't like change. They crave structure and routine. They count on the same things happening in the same place at the same time every day. For a dog, consistency equals security. And when it comes to security, most adopted dogs haven't had very much of it. All have lost at least one home; some have been homeless more than once. Many have spent periods of uncertainty in an animal shelter. Unfortunately, some have endured neglect or cruelty at the hands of human beings. With that kind of a past, an adopted dog isn't likely to understand why change might be necessary, and he certainly doesn't realize that by living with you, any changes in his life from now on will be for the better.

This chapter will help you help your adopted dog deal calmly with changes in the place that's most important to both of you: your home.

Back to Work, Back to School

Ah, sweet summer. If your canine companion joined your household during summer's dog days or just before, he's probably been thrilled to have members of his new pack around to play with, cuddle with, and just hang out with. But now the real world is about to intrude: You're going back to work, the kids are going back to school, and your dog will be home alone.

Such developments will not thrill your canine adoptee. He's not going to breathe a sigh of relief because he finally has the house all to himself and can get some peace and quiet. And it isn't as if he can whip out a cell phone and send a text message to all his friends when he's in the mood for company. Instead, he may feel distressed at being left alone—and he may deal with that distress in a way that leaves your house looking as though half your local high school decided that your home was Party Central. In other words, your dog may cope with his sudden solitude by exhibiting a frustrating disorder called *separation anxiety*.

Research has shown that an adopted dog has a higher risk of developing separation anxiety than a dog who hasn't had to change homes. If that adopted dog suddenly finds himself alone, his chances of developing separation anxiety are even greater. That is not to say, however, that all or even most adopted dogs will exhibit separation anxiety. In fact, pet parents who are distressed on their dog's behalf at the prospect of leaving them by themselves can actually increase the likelihood that a dog will become anxious. So the first step toward preventing separation anxiety is to relax. Your dog will likely follow suit.

There are many ways to alleviate separation anxiety.

If he doesn't, however, you may have some work to do. If your dog is excessively vocal when you leave, this is a likely indicator of separation anxiety. Another, less common signal of this condition is when a dog engages in destructive behavior when left alone. Other signs may include pacing and house-training accidents.

Treating separation anxiety can be difficult but not impossible. Here's what to do.

Downplay Arrivals and Departures

If you lavish affection on your adopted dog just before leaving the house and as soon as you arrive home, you may be contributing to his anxiety. By making a huge fuss over your dog upon your arrival home, you may be reinforcing his belief that your absence is a terrible thing and that your return is worthy of celebration. Be more matter-of-fact in your comings and goings, and you may find that your dog becomes more matter-of-fact about them, too.

Add Some Variety

Dogs are excellent observers. If you do the same things the same way each time you leave the house, your dog will figure out that you're preparing for a departure several minutes before you actually leave—and those several minutes give him plenty of time to start worrying. To break this pattern, try changing your routine a little. If you always put on your lipstick and pick up your keys before leaving, try keeping your keys in your handbag and putting on your lipstick after you leave. Varying your pre-departure routine keeps your dog guessing as to what your intentions are, and gives him much less time to become anxious.

Give Him Something to Do

Find an activity that will occupy your dog for at least some of the time that you're gone. A food puzzle toy (such as a Kong or Buster Cube) that's filled with treats can keep him so busy that he'll forget he's alone in the house. Make sure your dog only gets these special treats when he has to be alone, so he really looks forward to them.

Limit the View

Your dog may be overwhelmed by all the activity visible from the window of your home. Neighbors coming and going, mail carriers and delivery people, joggers, bicyclists, and pets taking their people for walks may all combine to overstimulate your dog, causing him to bark or act destructively. I recommend limiting your dog's view by closing blinds or sequestering your dog in a quiet area of your home. Of course, you need to be certain that wherever your dog is, you can count on him to not wreak havoc on your home and belongings, nor injure himself.

Make Some Noise

Sometimes a dog who becomes anxious when left alone relaxes when he hears familiar sounds. Your best bet is to make a recording of sounds that occur when your family is in the house, participating in your normal activities. Another good option is to turn on the television at a low volume. Make sure not to just turn on the TV when you're about to leave, however, or this could become a cue for separation anxiety. You want your dog to hear noises that commonly occur in the household, so if you usually have the TV on in the background when you're home, leave the TV on when you leave. If the radio is usually on when you're around, leave the radio on when you're not. Give your dog whatever he can associate with normal social time.

Get Him Moving

Dog trainers say that a tired dog is a good dog, and they're right. The value of exercise in helping a dog modify his behavior cannot be stressed enough. Try taking your dog for a brisk walk or run, or play fetch with him for a while each morning. Make sure you give him a good workout, though, because a *little* exercise could actually serve to arouse your dog and further his agitation. You should strive for a long, exhaustive exercise session, complete with a half hour of cool-down time, before you leave your dog alone. You want to tire him out enough that, after you leave, he'll take a nap instead of pining for you.

Take Him with You

More and more workplaces these days allow employees to bring their canine companions to work. If your adopted dog is well-behaved and properly trained, ask your employer whether the dog can join you at your office. Your co-workers may thank you! Another alternative is to work from home for at least some of the time; many employers will consider a telecommuting arrangement if it's practical for your job.

Petfinder.com: The Adopted Dog Bible

Take Him Somewhere Else

If your adopted dog is somewhere else during the day, he can't trash your house. Perhaps a neighboring dog parent who is home while you're at work would be happy to have your dog over as a playmate for hers. Another option is to take your canine companion to a doggy day-care facility. Make sure, though, that the facility you choose has no more than ten dogs to each human employee, that employees do not use physical force on any dog, and that big dogs and little dogs are kept apart from each other. In addition, dogs in day care need in-person supervision—remote cameras and/or video monitoring aren't sufficiently hands-on to keep the canine clients safe and prevent problems.

While some pet parents report that doggie day care is a lifesaver and helps entertain their dog while they're at work, others find that day care seems to only further arouse their dog. So try doggie day care for a week or so, and see if it will be what your pup needs.

Get Help

If day care or bringing your dog to work isn't feasible, and nothing else you've tried is helping, it's time to consult a veterinarian. A vet can prescribe medication that will help your four-legged friend relax a bit when you're not in the house. The meds alone won't cure separation anxiety, however, so for these acute cases, you will also need a behaviorist. But beware that nearly anyone can claim to be a dog behaviorist or a canine

Desensitization 101

A dog with an entrenched case of separation anxiety will often respond to a technique called *desensitization*. The objective here is to help the dog feel more comfortable with being alone by exposing him to solitude a few minutes at a time, eventually getting him used to being left alone.

Start by teaching your dog to sit (or lie down) and stay, as described in Chapter 7. Once your dog is proficient in this maneuver, place him in a sit/stay and leave the room. Return after only a few seconds; if he's stayed in place, reward him with a tasty treat and then release him.

Keep practicing this routine, working up to as long as a half hour. (This may seem like an unattainable goal, but with patience and consistent practice over time, your dog can do it.) Most dogs with separation anxiety do their damage within a half hour after their person's departure. Once your four-legged friend can deal comfortably with spending a half hour by himself, he's much less likely to panic when left alone for real.

psychologist. True behaviorists have had post-graduate training and are certified by either the Animal Behavior Society or the American College of Veterinary Behaviorists. Using medication in conjunction with a behavior modification program that you, your vet, and a behaviorist develop together can do a lot to restore harmony to your home and soothe your solitude-averse pup. We do not recommend a jump to medication as the solution for every pup, but recognize that some adopted dogs can really benefit from it.

Time to Move

Moving from an old home to a new one can be stressful for everyone involved—but for an adopted dog, the stress can be magnified. Consider the situation from his point of view: he's finally figured out what's what in his post-shelter home. He knows exactly where everything is and where everyone sleeps. He's determined exactly when and where the sun hits the floor in the afternoon (great for napping). He's become familiar with the smells in every corner of the house, and he knows which trees or signposts to "autograph" when you take him for a walk. A move to a new apartment or house means all that familiarity is gone, and with it, your canine adoptee's sense of comfort and security. He will need extra attention from you to help him adjust to the new home—at a time when you may feel you're too busy to give him that sort of additional consideration.

If you don't take the time to pay some extra attention to your dog now, however, he could become stressed—and chances are, that stress will take forms that you'll find highly inconvenient, at best. Signs of such stress usually include destroying parts of the new home, be it new carpeting, brand-new wallpaper, freshly painted molding, or even furniture from the old home that's gracing the new one. Other manifestations of doggy distress can include house-training accidents, loss of appetite, and refusing to let you out of his sight. He may appear to be disoriented—perfectly understandable, since he hasn't figured out what's what in his new digs. He may also try to find a place to hide from all the chaos of the move, which may seem just fine until you become frantic when you can't find him.

These scenarios don't have to happen. You can minimize the stress of a move on your adopted dog—and, in doing so, you will also minimize the stress on yourself. Here's how:

Plan Ahead

Take the time to get your dog accustomed to his new life before it actually begins. Figure out where you are going to put your dog's things in the new house, get him accustomed to car travel and spending time in his crate, and show him where his new outdoor bathroom is going to be. If his only car rides have been to the vet, take him for car rides to destinations that have more positive associations, like a park or a play date. If he's not happy being in a crate or in one room by himself, give him a refresher course in crate training or in being independent. (Chapter 7 gives you the lowdown on crate training; to encourage independence, see "Desensitization 101" on page 425 in this chapter.)

Take Him on a Walk-Through

If you've bought a new home or condominium, bring your four-legged friend on the pre-settlement walkthrough; if you're renting, ask your landlord if you can bring your dog over for a look around before you move in. While you check to see that everything is up to snuff in your new home-to-be, your dog can acquaint himself with his new digs by scoping out all the new smells. Make sure, though, that you have him on a leash, and that he's had a chance to do his business before you both go inside.

Get Him New Tags

Because your dog is more likely to get loose during the first few days in a new home than at any time in the previous home, it's crucial to change his identification tags before you move. Moving is a chaotic process, with doors opening and closing and people going in and out all the time, and not everyone is going to be careful enough about keeping track of the dog. In addition, if he does get out, it will be much more difficult for him to find his way back home, since this is a new neighborhood, and likely a place he's never been. So as soon as you know your new address, buy a new identification tag that has your dog's name, your new address, your phone number and, if possible, your cell phone number. If your dog has a microchip, be sure to contact the company and have them update your dog's identification information in their database.

Find Him a Safe Place

During the chaos that inevitably accompanies a moving day, bring your dog to a place that will feel familiar and safe to him. Some dogs find that just being in their familiar crate works well (make sure to take him for a potty break and give him some attention every couple of hours, though!). He may feel even better if you give him one or two familiar objects, such as a couple of toys that he'll recognize by smell or sight, to help him understand that this new home is still his home. Others do better being someplace else altogether: a trusted neighbor's house, day boarding at the vet's, or a doggie day care.

Be Extra Security Conscious

The first few days in a new home can spook even the most easygoing dog; for an adopted dog, such spooking is much more likely. Make sure your dog's collar fits him securely, so that he can't slip out from underneath it and run away. And unless you know that the backyard at your new home is securely fenced (check beforehand), leash him up before you take him outside to his new potty place. Be especially careful when opening the door to enter or leave the house; make sure your four-legged friend doesn't take advantage of the open door to make a quick exit.

Continue with Business As Usual

Maintain your dog's daily routine as much as possible: feed him, play with him, and exercise him at the same times you usually do. Such consistency will reassure him as he navigates this change in his life.

Spend Extra Time with Him

You may think you have no extra time to spare—but that box of dishes doesn't have to be unpacked *right now* and those clothes can wait a *little* while longer before being put into the closet. Take frequent breaks to talk to and pet your dog. This will help him stay calm, and it will help you relax, too.

Your New Relationship: Dog Versus Date

Of course you love your dog—but if you're single, you might be thinking of expanding your pack of two to a pack of three. Finding that special person to become that third pack member generally is easier said than done, but this time, you've lucked out. You've met someone who you think could become a very Significant Other—a possibility that's making you quite happy. However, you should not expect your adopted dog to share your happiness, at least not until you show your canine adoptee how he might benefit from this new relationship.

Fortunately, most dogs can be persuaded to share their special people with other humans, and even enjoy doing so. Here are some tips:

Meet on Neutral Turf

For many dogs, meeting new people is more comfortable when those initial meetings occur outside their homes. When your date meets your dog for the first time, take that meeting to neutral territory, such as a nearby park. After your date and your dog exchange greetings, the three of you should walk to your apartment or house together. If meeting outside your home isn't feasible (for example, if it's raining), place your dog in another room or in his crate before your date enters your home. After a couple of minutes, let your dog come out to greet your guest.

Distract the Dog

If you think that hosting a new visitor will cause your canine adoptee to become anxious, have your date provide a distraction that will help the dog forget his anxiety. A great diversionary tactic is for your date to drop treats around the floor. Not only will your dog shift his focus from the new visitor to the treats—he also may begin to associate your date with the goodies.

Let Your Dog Set the Pace

Forcing your dog to make friends with your date isn't a good idea. Pushing your dog to make nice before he's ready could cause him to become even more fearful or hostile than he may already be. Ask your date to not reach for the dog or even offer the dog a hand to sniff until the dog makes a clear overture. Avoiding direct eye contact and full frontal body positioning will help keep your dog from considering your date a threat.

Be Patient

Some dogs need to take their time allowing themselves to make a new human friend. If your dog is one of these individuals, respect his wishes; with time, he's more likely to learn to like your date as much as you already do. The same applies to having your dog meet your date's dog or other pets. For information on orchestrating successful dog-to-dog or dog-to-cat introductions, check out Chapter 6.

And Baby Makes . . . ?

For the humans in a household, the birth of a baby is a joyful occasion. For your adopted dog, however, the new family member may represent an unwelcome change. He may not be happy having to compete with a noisy, stinky, demanding little human interloper for the attention that had been devoted to him alone. He may relieve his distress by chewing things he shouldn't, barking excessively, or having house-training lapses. But don't despair: with careful planning and a little empathy, you can help your dog deal with a new baby's arrival more calmly than you expected. Here are some ways to do just that:

Go Back to School

Taking your dog to a group obedience class before the baby is born can be both fun and helpful. The classes will help strengthen your bond with your four-legged friend, and will also help you see which of his skills are strong and which need a little remedial work.

Do a Dry Run

Parents-to-be can purchase a realistic baby doll from most toy stores. Look for one that will cry and possibly move its arms and legs. You can use this to train your dog to do things like "down-stay" while you change the baby's diaper and not to jump up as you carry around a crying baby. This will help your dog to associate the attention you give the "baby" with showering the dog with treats. You can also identify major potential problems with your dog and the baby before the actual baby arrives.

Introduce "Scents-Ably"

You can introduce your dog to your baby before your infant is even born. Start by using some of the baby products you intend for the baby—like baby lotion, powder, and diaper cream—on yourself and on your tester doll, which will allow your dog to become familiar with these scents. Then, before bringing the new addition home, show your dog a T shirt the baby has already worn in the hospital and let him sniff it. That way, the dog will be familiar with the baby's scent before he meets the actual baby.

Get Him Moving

If your dog has been spending most of his time by himself since the baby's been born, have someone take him out for a long walk before mother and baby come home. Doing so will allow your dog to expend some of his pent-up energy and will help him behave calmly when the rest of the family arrives.

Let Him See Mom First

Before your dog meets the new baby in person, let him have some one-on-one time with Mom while someone else holds the baby in another room. This tête-à-tête will remind him that he is loved, and will help him be more relaxed when he meets the baby.

Introduce Carefully

While Dad or another person holds the baby (who should be in a blanket with just her face showing), Mom should leash the dog and bring him into the room. Allow the dog to sniff the baby, making sure that Mom continues to hold on to the leash. Stay calm, and do not yell at the dog or jerk his leash. That will turn the encounter into a stressful situation for your pup, and make him associate anxiety with the baby. After a few minutes, end the session.

Be Inclusive

Try to include your dog in baby-care tasks. While you feed the baby, pet your dog; talk to your dog during diaper changes; bring your dog along when you walk with the baby in a stroller. By including your dog at such times, you'll teach him that good things happen when the baby's around.

Be Vigilant

Even if the introductions have gone well, never leave your baby (or any child under the age of six) alone with your dog, not even for a minute. Young children often fail to realize that dogs are living beings who don't like to be teased, grabbed, pinched, or even hugged—and the dog may retaliate in a manner that could have tragic results for all concerned. One of the most common reasons that adopted dogs are returned to shelters is that "something happened" between dog and child when an adult was not in the room. So use common sense: Nana the Saint Bernard may have made a great nanny for the Darling children in *Peter Pan*, but real-life dogs are not baby-sitters, and should not be expected to be.

Babies are great, but don't forget about your pooch!

Dealing with Divorce or Death

While some changes are characterized by arrivals, others take the form of departures. A reconfiguration of a household that involves the departure of a family member—whether by death, divorce, departure for college, or moving into assisted living—can be very hard on a dog, especially a canine adoptee.

Just as people grieve such losses, so do dogs. Common symptoms of canine grief are lethargy, loss of appetite, and house-training lapses. Most of the time, however, a grieving dog responds well to a little attention and help from one or more remaining family members. Here are some ideas to help him beat the blues.

Plan Ahead

If you know that an important person in your dog's life will be leaving the household, start making sure that others in the family begin spending more time with the animal before the departure occurs. For example, if an elderly family member must give a dog to someone else in the family before entering assisted living, that family member should begin caring for the dog part-time before the older person leaves.

Re-Establish a Routine

Your dog may be more upset by the change in routine caused by a person's absence than by the absence itself. Re-establishing the old routine—or, if that's not possible, creating a new one—can go a long way toward easing canine grief. By feeding, walking, and playing with the dog at the same times every day, you'll give him the consistency he needs to help him recover from his loss.

Avoid Coddling

Although spending extra time with your dog is important, you'll put that time to better use if you get the dog moving rather than sitting on the couch and consoling him. Exercise can make a dog feel better (or at least too tired to act out), just as a person often feels better after a workout.

Monitor What Goes In and What Comes Out

Keep tabs on how much food your dog is eating, as well as any changes in his bathroom habits or output. If your dog's appetite takes a nosedive

Who Gets the Dog?

Not so long ago, the only custody cases that turned up in divorce courts involved human children. But in the last ten years or so, another kind of custody case has begun to occupy divorcing spouses and their attorneys: the question of which spouse gets to keep the dog that both parties love.

This development shouldn't be surprising. The status of dogs and other companion animals has changed considerably in recent years. Although the courts once considered pets solely as property that didn't merit consideration in divorce settlements, nowadays, many judges realize that many people view their pets as full-fledged members of many families, and so treat them differently than the rest of the parties' assets.

In many cases, the court will ask divorcing spouses to at least initially try to work out their own arrangements for custody of the family dog, or to use the services of a mediator. When those options fail, however, some judges will base their rulings on what they consider to be the best interest of the animal. The court will pay close attention to which party has been more involved in the dog's care, and which party is more able to provide financial support for the dog. And just as with children, custody need not be an either/or issue: Judges may award shared custody to divorcing dog parents.

If you and your spouse are divorcing and haven't decided where your dog will go, start by trying to come to some agreement between yourselves. A mediator can also be of some help. But even if you and your estranged partner find yourselves asking the court to decide who gets Fido, make sure that whatever you do is in Fido's best interest, not just your own.

or his bathroom habits change radically for more than a couple of days, call your veterinarian. What appears to be canine grief may actually be the onset of a serious condition that only your vet can diagnose and treat.

Dog Biscuits for the Soul: Koda

Koda

In 1995, I found a garbage bag with five puppies in it—only two were alive and only one survived. That little guy, who I named Koda, became my best buddy at a very difficult time in my life. In 1998 I married my husband and moved to Florence where we lived on a farm. Koda loved it there! He became my husband's running partner. One day in 2000, while they were out running, Koda chased something into the woods and disappeared. We searched everywhere, put up posters, and even offered a $2000 reward. We got a few calls, but he never turned up. We were devastated, but never stopped looking. Even as recently as a few months ago I saw a dog that looked like I figured he would at the age of twelve, but it wasn't him. Then, a few weeks ago, I was looking for some information on the Home Away From Home website on Petfinder.com. I came across a picture that bore an uncanny resemblance to Koda. I called Kathy at Home Away From Home. The dog had been there for four years! She had taken him from a shelter. Their records said a person who lived about two miles from our house had surrendered him to the shelter. We can only guess that his break-away collar with his tags had come off in the woods. My husband and I went to Kathy's the next day. We were pretty sure it was Koda, although after seven years he was a lot heavier and much grayer. When we got to our driveway, he got very quiet and started looking around. The reaction of our old bloodhound, Rosie, confirmed it was Koda. She knew him at once.

Kathleen Streett, Florence, South Carolina
Koda was at Home Away From Home Rescue in Florence, South Carolina

Resources

Dodman, Nicholas: *The Dog Who Loved Too Much*. Bantam, 1997

Donaldson, Jean: Shelter Behavior: Behavior Problems in Dogs. Maddie's Fund
http://www.maddiesfund.org/organizations/shelter_behavior_dogs.html

Eisenberg, Arlene, Heidi Eisenberg Murkoff and Sandy Eisenberg Hathaway: *What to Expect When You're Expecting*. Workman, 1988

Elgin Veterinary Hospital: Moving with Your Dog
http://www.elginveterinaryhospital.com/index.php?view=pageView&pageid=100001838

Gallagher, Cynthia P.: Pets on the Move
http://www.petfinder.com/journal/index.cgi?article=861

Tischler, Joyce and Bruce Wagman: Lawyers Must Plan for More Custody Cases.
Animal Legal Defense Fund, http://www.aldf.org:80/news/details.php?id=192

Wright, John C., with Judy Wright Lashnits: *The Dog Who Would Be King*. Rodale, 1999

21

When You Must Give Up Your Dog

Most people who adopt a dog hope to forge a lifelong bond with that animal. Sometimes, though, life seems to have other ideas.

Maybe you're moving overseas, and either you can't bring your dog with you or you've concluded that the move will be too stressful for her. Or perhaps you've lost your job, and with that loss you find that you can't afford to keep your pet. Or your marriage may have ended, and you need to downsize your home to a place that's not suitable for your four-legged friend. Other lifestyle changes can also make having a dog difficult or even impossible, such as starting a new job that requires frequent travel and leaves you little or no time to spend with your canine companion.

And sometimes, sadly, the problem may be with this particular dog in your particular home. Perhaps she's more hyperactive or destructive than you anticipated, and you're at a loss as to how to deal with her. Or maybe you or another member of your family has developed a serious allergy to her. Another problem might be that your canine adoptee doesn't get along with the other animals in the house. At such times, the best option may appear to be finding a new home for your adopted dog. If you're facing that decision, what should you do?

Can You Keep Her?

Deciding whether to keep a dog or find her a new home can be a difficult one, and for good reason. On the one hand, you've made a commitment to this dog; you've invested time and love and have at least begun building, if not firmly established, a strong bond with your canine adoptee. You know that she looks at you as her whole world. On the other hand, problems have developed that are forcing you to question whether she should remain in your home.

All too often, frustrated or exasperated folks decide that they cannot deal with their dog's behavior and that the only option is to "get rid of her." If that's your situation, we hope to offer you some alternatives. Also, bear in mind that your dog will take her behavioral issues with her to her next home. Dumping your dog and her problems onto someone else—unless that someone else knows about and is willing to deal with them—is unfair to both that person and your dog. As the person who knows her best, you are in the best position to help your dog. In doing so, you might even find that you can keep her after all.

Giving up your dog is a last resort: Even a rambunctious dog can be trained.

To give your dog the help she needs, you may need some help, too. Fortunately, plenty of such assistance is at hand. Here are some people who can help you determine whether you can give your dog another chance.

Your local animal shelter. Many animal shelters have trainers on staff who can help you figure out how to solve your dog's behavioral problem. No shelter wants to see an adopted dog surrendered back to the shelter by an unhappy person. Shelter staff will want to work with you to fix the problem—particularly if the shelter you contact is the shelter you adopted your dog from in the first place.

Your veterinarian. Sometimes a dog's behavioral problem can be corrected medically. For example, an intact male dog may become much less aggressive when he's neutered. A dog who is prone to sudden aggression may have a thyroid gland that's not secreting quite as much thyroid hormone as it should, and a veterinarian's prescription can supply what your dog's system cannot. If your dog is destroying your house when she's left alone, medication and re-training (see Chapter 20) can help her overcome the separation anxiety that may be prompting her destructive rampages. In any case, before you give your dog to someone else, take her for a checkup so that a new owner will have the medical information he needs to take the best possible care of her—and to see if she has a correctable medical problem that enables you to keep her.

A trainer. Even if your dog has already had some schooling, a trainer can do a lot to help you deal successfully with her behavioral issues—including hyperactivity, failure to get along with the other animals in the household, and other not-so-desirable traits. Generally, your best bet is to find a trainer who's willing to come to your home and watch how the dog acts in her natural environment. Once the trainer sees your dog and understands from you what her problem is, he can help you understand if the problem is one that can be solved or managed, what will be involved in resolving her behavioral issues, and whether you will be able to keep the dog. Often, what seem like insurmountable issues can be resolved with the right assistance. However, in extreme cases, particularly where aggression is an issue, you may not be able to resolve the issue safely. In these traumatic cases, know that the best thing you can do is to be honest with the shelter when you return the dog so that they do not unwittingly adopt her out to another family who will have to face what you have faced.

To find a trainer in your area, log onto the Association of Pet Dog Trainers website at www.apdt.com, and use the group's searchable online database. (See Chapter 8 for information on how to choose a trainer.)

The World Wide Web. Many animal shelters, rescue groups, and individual trainers have websites that offer information on how to combat common canine behavioral problems. Start with national organizations such as Petfinder, which offers a library that's chock-full of sound advice on dealing with dogs' behavioral issues, including access to many videos on dog behavior and training. Your local shelter and humane association may offer similar information on their websites as well.

Other problems may lend themselves to in-home solutions, too. If someone in your home has developed an allergy to your dog, moving the dog's sleeping area, and frequent bathing and brushing (of the dog, not the human) can usually alleviate some of the affected person's symptoms. A hyperactive dog having difficulty learning may benefit from a change of diet. Speak to your veterinarian (conventional or holistic) or a veterinary nutritionist for some suggestions.

Sometimes, though, even your best efforts aren't enough to help your dog become the kind of animal companion you'd like her to be. Other times, changes in your own circumstances may be forcing you to give up your adoptee, no matter how well behaved she is. Either way, if you've concluded that you absolutely cannot keep your dog, you still have one last responsibility toward her: to find her the best possible new home, or to place her with those who can find that home for you.

Neuter Now!

Now that you've made the decision to find your adopted dog a new home, you might be a little reluctant to spend any more money on her care. At the same time, if she hasn't already been neutered, perhaps you're thinking that someone might be interested in breeding her. *Please* think again.

You want someone to adopt your dog as a companion, not as a breeding animal. You're much more likely to find a responsible, permanent home for your adopted dog if you do the right thing and have her neutered. This will rule out anyone who might view your dog as a way to make money, and who will not be interested in providing her with the loving home she needs. Moreover, neutering reduces the risk that your dog will run away from her next home and helps ensure that she won't mark her home with urine and find herself homeless yet again.

Right now, no one wants your dog, not even you (that's why you're trying to find her a new home, right?). That being the case, it makes no sense to allow someone to breed her and bring more unwanted animals in a world where even great pets may have a hard time finding a home. Have your dog spayed or neutered now, before you start looking for a new home for her. You may even find that when your dog recovers from the procedure, she'll be a mellower companion—and that you might be able to keep her after all!

Read Your Contract!

As talk show host Ellen DeGeneres discovered, you need to read the adoption contract that you signed before making any decisions about where your adopted dog's next home will be.

In late 2007, DeGeneres found that the small dog she'd adopted from a rescue group did not get along with her cats. When DeGeneres learned that her hairdresser was looking for a dog for her two school-aged daughters, she gave the dog to the hairdresser. Meanwhile, the rescue group contacted DeGeneres to inquire how the adoption was working out. DeGeneres told the group what she had done, and the rescue group reminded DeGeneres that the adoption contract she'd signed required that, if things didn't work out, she had to return the dog to the group rather than find a new home for the dog on her own. The group then removed the dog from the hairdresser's home, leaving two young girls broken-hearted in the process. A tearful televised plea from DeGeneres to return the dog to her hairdresser's family fell on deaf ears. The rescue group insisted that the contract be honored, and placed the dog somewhere else.

Don't let this happen to your adopted dog. If you cannot keep the dog yourself, re-read your adoption contract before you take any action. Contact the shelter or rescue group from whom you adopted your dog. It may be that if you have another potential home for your dog, the shelter or rescue group would love to meet them. If you can offer to continue to care for the dog in your home and assist in finding a new home for her, many overburdened shelters or rescue groups will really appreciate your efforts.

Finding Prospects

If your adoption contract does not insist that your dog be returned to the place you adopted her from (most do)—and if you are *sure* that you cannot keep the dog—you need to start looking for a new home for your canine adoptee. If your dog is neutered and has not bitten anyone, you can probably handle the re-homing yourself. Here's what to do:

Start with your own family. If you cannot keep your dog, would your parents, grown children, or siblings be able to do so? Such a solution might work well if, for example, you are moving overseas temporarily and cannot bring your dog with you. Your family might even agree to return the dog to you when your foreign assignment or deployment ends.

Make a poster. Shelter dog expert Sue Sternberg suggests taking some color digital photographs of your canine adoptee and uploading the best one onto a poster that you create on your home computer. Include a list of your four-legged friend's best traits and most endearing qualities, and guidelines for the best possible home. Such guidelines might be "needs someone who's home a lot," "no children under six," "no other pets," or "experienced owners only." Note, too, that your dog has been neutered. Include your phone number and/or e-mail address. Then, tack up the completed posters around your neighborhood, at your vet's office, at your pet supply store, and in any other local areas that have community bulletin boards, such as a café, supermarket, or pharmacy.

Network, network, network. Tell your neighbors, your co-workers, your kids' friends' parents, your veterinarian, and anyone else you can think of that you need a new home for your dog. Think of the effort to re-home your dog as a campaign that's similar to a job hunt. When someone looks for a new job, word-of-mouth networking often brings faster results than simply scouring the want-ads on Monster.com, much less your local print newspaper.

Advertise with care. Newspaper ads can help you locate potential adopters, but such ads need to be worded carefully. For example, don't offer to give your dog "free to a good home." Such phrasing might attract people who aren't looking for a canine companion, but rather a guard dog, a fighting dog, a research tool, or even a meal. Instead, focus on your dog's best attributes as a companion, be honest about her shortcomings, and charge a reasonable adoption fee. If you are so inclined, you can choose to donate the adoption fee to your local shelter. They can always put it to good use.

Go online. In addition to local networking and advertising, consider placing a free classified ad with a nationwide adoption site. Guidelines for posting a classified ad at Petfinder can be found by logging onto www.petfinder.com/classifieds/prepost.html.

Once you've collected a list of prospective adopters from those who've responded to your networking and advertising, you can begin the next phase of your effort to find a new home for your dog.

Dealing with Applicants

You've been networking diligently, you've placed your ads, you've tacked up your posters—and now your phone is ringing and you are receiving e-mails from people interested in adopting your dog. If you are lucky enough to get multiple responses you need to sift through the candidates and figure out who can offer her the best home. Here's what to do:

Create an application. When you adopted your dog, you undoubtedly had to fill out an application or questionnaire from the shelter or rescue group, which asked questions about your family, lifestyle, housing arrangements, and previous experience with dogs. Now, as the one-person shelter for this dog, you need to do the same for those who'd like to offer her a new home. So fire up your computer, open your word processing program, and create an adoption questionnaire. Ask for the following information:

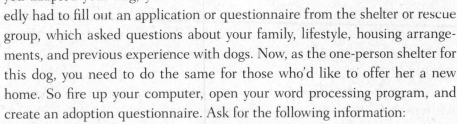

Re-Homing the Aggressive Dog

If you decide you can't live with your dog because she's aggressive, don't try to find her a new home all by yourself. Pushing your dog's problems onto another person is not only terribly unfair, but also may be in violation of state and local laws. To protect yourself, your dog, and any potential new owners, contact a trainer and ask for a behavioral evaluation. Trainers are professionally equipped to assess your dog's behavior objectively, and to advise you on how to proceed.

- ❁ Applicant's name, contact information and age (the applicant should be over 21).
- ❁ The applicant's housing arrangements—does he own his own home, rent a house or apartment, live with his parents, live with his spouse and family, or live by himself? There's no right or wrong answer here; you're just trying to learn more about his living situation.
- ❁ If he rents his dwelling, ask for his landlord's name and telephone number, so that you can confirm that the tenants are allowed to keep dogs.
- ❁ How long he's lived at his current address. Someone who doesn't stay in any one place for long may be less likely to bring a dog with him each time he moves.
- ❁ Whether every member of the family or household wants a dog.

- Whether other pets live in the home, whether they are neutered, and whether they are comfortable around other animals.
- What happened to the applicant's most recent dog, and how many dogs the applicant has owned.
- At least two references, one of which should be from a veterinarian.
- Information as to whether the dog will live indoors or outdoors, where the dog will sleep at night, how often the dog will be left alone and for how long, and how the dog will be cared for when the owner goes out of town. Here you're looking for someone who will keep his dog with him in the house, who will let the dog sleep in the house (preferably in the owner's bedroom), and who is home most evenings, if not most days.
- Whether the applicant objects to your visiting his home.

Screen calls and e-mails. Sternberg suggests telling each person who e-mails or phones you that someone has already come to meet your dog, but that you are still taking names, numbers, and references so that you can return their call or e-mail. This tactful tactic gives you an instant out if you think the caller isn't right for your dog, without hurting anyone's feelings.

Assess the applications. You may choose to send an interested party a written application or to ask him your questions over the phone. If the latter, be sure to write down the answers so you can review them later. Read all of the applications you receive, and pick several that you think represent a good home for your dog. Then invite these applicants to come and meet her, and see how they interact.

Visit the finalists. Before you agree to allow any individual to adopt your dog, visit that individual in his home—and make sure that all family members, human and non-human, are present. Bring your dog with you. You want to see not only what the applicant's living situation is like, but also how your dog gets along with everyone in the home.

The information you collect from the applicants and from your visits should help you make an informed decision about who can offer your dog the best possible home. But you're still not done. You need to perform a few more tasks before your job as your dog's guardian is complete.

Petfinder.com: The Adopted Dog Bible

Finalizing the Adoption

Before allowing a new person or family to take permanent custody of your adopted dog, make sure that you are giving your four-legged friend the best possible send-off. Here's how to ensure that your dog has a smooth transition from one home to the next.

Get her records. Make a final trip to your veterinarian to obtain your dog's medical records. This information will ensure that your dog's next veterinarian will have all the information needed to maintain a high level of health care.

Prepare instructions. Write down your dog's usual schedule, how often she goes out, feeding times, and what you feed her. Note if she is taking any medications, and how to administer them. Here, too, is a good place to note any food allergies as well as behavioral quirks and preferences—for example, that your dog is used to sleeping on your bed, or that she doesn't like to be watched while she potties. Include your dog's veterinary records and your vet's contact information.

Pack her stuff. Gather your dog's leash, food, treats, toys, crate, bedding, and any other accoutrements, and give them to her new people. Having familiar food and objects around will help her make a smooth transition to her new home.

Update her tags. Before your dog goes to her new home, prepare an identification tag with her name, new address, and phone number, and place the new tag on the dog's collar prior to her move. Re-homed pets have a higher risk of running away or getting lost than those who are staying in their accustomed homes; with an up-to-date tag, your dog has a better chance of being returned to her new home should she become lost. If your dog is microchipped or tattooed, make sure the microchip database or tattoo registry receives information about the dog's new home. Also be sure to give the new pet parents the microchip company's information, so they can update her information if they move.

Follow up. Once your dog has gone to her new home, check in with her new family to see how things are going. Doing so gives the new guardian a chance to ask any questions that he may have and also helps to reassure you that your dog has adjusted well to this change in her life. One schedule often employed by shelters for checking in with a new family is to call after

What to Give Your Dog's New Family

When your dog goes to her new home, make sure she doesn't go there by herself. Send her with the following items and information:

- Veterinary records
- Information on any behavioral quirks and/or allergies
- Leash, collar, and updated tags
- A few days' supply of food and treats
- Water and food bowls
- Feeding instructions
- Toys
- Crate and any other bedding
- Any medication she is taking, with instructions for administration

three days, three weeks, and three months. Since you only have one dog to follow up on, you might consider additional calls at the end of weeks one and two, just to offer support and see if any questions or issues have arisen.

Using a Shelter

If you're unable to find your dog a new home on your own, taking her to a shelter may be an option—but only if you choose that shelter carefully. Of paramount importance are the shelter's adoption and euthanasia policies. Sternberg notes that a "no-kill" or limited admission shelter might seem like a good bet, but only if that shelter is equally and actively committed to finding homes for all the adoptable dogs that come through their doors. All too often, shelters that don't euthanize adoptable dogs may not have the means to find homes for all of their guests. The results are often tragic, with dogs suffering great mental and emotional stress from having to spend the rest of their lives in concrete-and-chain-linked shelters, rather than in the loving homes that they deserve.

If the shelter does euthanize dogs that aren't adopted, find out how many days the shelter waits before euthanizing. Find out, too, whether any shelter personnel or volunteers implement socialization or even training programs for the dogs in their care. Such programs can help a dog handle the stress of shelter life more easily—and a dog's display of good manners and training can help make that dog more adoptable.

Find out whether the shelter has a foster care program. Many shelters send dogs and cats with special needs—or those animals they believe are adoptable but no longer have room to keep—to private homes for homestyle foster-care TLC. Such care, like in-shelter training and socialization programs, helps a homeless dog put her best paw forward to prospective adopters and helps her find that forever home more quickly.

Another possibility is to contact a rescue group. While many rescue groups dedicate themselves to re-homing purebred dogs, more than a few are also willing to help mixed-breeds. Log on to Petfinder for a list of all-breed, mixed-breed, and purebred rescue groups that will work with you to provide a permanent new home for your dog and, in many cases, a foster home while she's waiting.

Remember, though, that shelters and rescue groups are often over-full with dogs needing homes. Don't expect that they will be able to take your dog in and care for her with little or no notice. If you find yourself with no possibility of being able to keep your dog or of finding her an appropriate home, please do allow time to work with local shelters and rescue groups. Some may have waiting lists or ask that you act as your dog's foster home while they help you find her an appropriate home. You will often find extremely helpful and resourceful individuals willing to help you fulfill your responsibility to your dog—if you are willing to put in the time and energy the task requires.

Dog Biscuits for the Soul: Coby

Coby

I found Coby on Petfinder.com, applied online, and hoped to meet him soon. To my surprise and delight, I received a call from Kari Whitman, founder of Ace of Hearts, approximately ten minutes later. Kari asked if my wife Robin and I could meet Coby in a half hour, as he was at a vet's office in our area.

continued

We promptly got dressed and rushed to meet him. I fell in love with Coby upon first sight. I had learned in my courtship of my wife that she takes much longer to admit love than I do. Well, I assure you, now there is no turning back for either of us.

Our first weekend with Coby was difficult. He was disobedient, he broke free from his crate, and he damaged and urinated in our house. Coby was unruly on his leash and was aggressive toward other dogs. By Sunday night, I reluctantly agreed with my wife that we had to return Coby to his foster parents. It turned out, however, that the fosters had a work conflict and could not take him back, and they said we would have to keep Coby until a suitable replacement family could be found to adopt him.

Knowing we had failed as Coby's third adoptive family made my heart heavy. I felt that if Coby could speak, he'd say, "Please, Eric, don't give up on me!" As we awaited a new family, I noticed that Coby had started to settle into our household. At the request of Ace of Hearts, we met with a dog behavioral expert who provided us with rules, boundaries, and limitations for Coby. After the consultation, I noticed an immediate change in Coby's demeanor onleash, in the house, and with other dogs. When we reported this success to Ace of Hearts, they offered Coby a scholarship to a training program, if we would agree to keep him. After some thought, we accepted.

As a graduate, Coby has become a loved member of our family and a pleasure in the house. He is a kind dog who gravitates toward people. He's fantastic with kids and has made great strides in getting along with other dogs. I should also mention that Robin and I had struggled with pregnancy for over eighteen months. Coby's arrival brought us a new set of responsibilities which helped mitigate our pregnancy focus. My wife became pregnant just about the time we were struggling with Coby. Clearly, rescuing (and keeping) Coby was one of the best things that ever happened to our family.

Eric Garfield, Redondo Beach, California
Coby was adopted from Ace of Hearts, Beverly Hills, California

Petfinder.com: The Adopted Dog Bible

Resources

How to Find Homes for Homeless Pets
http://www.petfinder.com/journal/index.cgi?article=709

Tips For Finding a Home for a Pet
http://www.petfinder.com/journal/index.cgi?article=704

McCullough, Susan: "Physical Causes of Aggression." *Your Dog*, August 2006
    Medford, MA: Tufts Media, Cummings School of Veterinary Medicine, Tufts University

McCullough, Susan: "Giving Fluffy Away." *Animal Watch*, Summer 2003
    New York, NY: American Society for the Prevention of Cruelty to Animals (this magazine
    folded in October 2004)

Sternberg, Sue: *When You Decide to Give Up Your Pet*
http://www.petfinder.com/journal/index.cgi?printer=1&article=699

22

The Toughest Word: Euthanasia

"Dogs' lives are too short. Their only fault, really."
—Agnes Sligh Turnball

There will come a time in every pet parent's life when we must say good-bye to a beloved canine companion. That dogs live such short lives compared to our own has always seems a cruel fact to me, yet it is a fact we must face. When a dog passes away—either through an accident or illness, whether we've had time to prepare or if the loss is sudden—feelings of confusion, anger, denial, and guilt are common. In fact, our special relationship with and attachment to our dogs is so deep that experts have spent considerable time exploring what they call the *human-animal bond*. Is it any wonder that when this bond is severed, our sense of despair is overwhelming? We ride the intense waves of emotion, hoping that our pain will miraculously disappear overnight. If only it were that easy.

It's not unusual for individuals to feel that losing a much-loved dog is more painful than losing a human family member. It is said that the depth of grieving one encounters is relative to the depth of the relationship that has been severed. Why do we have such strong feelings for our canine companions? The answer in two words: *unconditional love*. Webster's dictionary defines the word *unconditional* as: "Being without conditions or limitation:

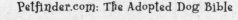

absolute." What an apt description for the non-judgmental, unqualified love and emotional support that only a dog can give. Without a doubt, we have all experienced this much-talked about phenomenon with our pets. It's the unbridled joy our dog expresses when we return home after a long day at work or school; it's the late-night "therapy sessions" where we confide our innermost thoughts and concerns to our dogs without feeling judged; and it may even be our reason for living when illness or depression causes us to withdraw from the world.

A senior dog is a treasure; treat him like one.

Losing a dog is like losing a part of yourself. If you're like most people, you probably associate many places, feelings, and events with your dog. After all, our dogs are there to share in the joy of our first home or the birth of our first child. They kiss away our tears when a close relationship or marriage ends. They help us celebrate job promotions or a move to a new city. They comfort us when we receive a scary medical diagnosis. In short, dogs are devoted companions, confidantes, and best friends.

Unfortunately, the reality is that the dogs we love have much shorter life spans than we do, and it's likely that we will outlive several special dogs in our lives. Many of you reading this chapter may have already experienced the death of a beloved dog, while some of you are preparing for that inevitable day when you must say your final good-bye. The information in this chapter will help you determine when it's the right time to put your dog to sleep, understand the actual euthanasia process, and decide what to do with your dog's body. It also will give you practical tools for dealing with your grief and ideas for ways to memorialize and celebrate your canine companion's life. Finally, there are sections on helping children and other animals deal with this loss.

"How Do I Know When It's Time?"

Deciding exactly when—or if—you should put your dog to sleep is never easy. We don't want to do it too soon and we don't want to wait until his quality of life has deteriorated to the point that he's in constant pain. If you are having trouble making this crucial decision, it may be helpful to ask yourself this question: *What would I want for myself if I were in this situation?* You will likely decide that if your dog has stopped eating, is vomiting, cannot hold his urine or feces (or cannot go at all), or appears to be in pain, then it is time to release him from his suffering. On the other hand, if your dog has a good appetite, has control of his bowels and bladder, is sleeping well, and is still finding pleasure in at least some of the same activities he has always enjoyed, you may wish to take a "wait and see" approach. Remember, each case is different. You can also ask for your veterinarian's support to make the critical decision about euthanasia.

Questions to Ask Your Veterinarian (and Yourself) About Euthanasia

When you are faced with your dog's impending death, it's helpful to have a knowledgeable, caring veterinarian with whom both you and your dog feel comfortable. Your veterinarian should be able to answer all of your questions and concerns about your dog's situation and about what the actual euthanasia process is like. Begin by asking:

- What is the prognosis of my dog's injury/illness?
- Is there a chance he will recover? If not, how long is he expected to live?
- What are the treatment options? How long can I take to make a decision about treatment?
- Do you believe my dog is in pain? Is he likely to experience significant pain? What symptoms should I look for to indicate whether he is hurting?
- If this were your dog, what would you do? (While your veterinarian may be understandably reluctant to make the final decision for you,

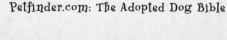

she may be willing to give you suggestions based on your dog's prognosis or level of discomfort. However, remember that it is up to you to be your dog's advocate, and in the end you will need to do for him what you believe is best.)

Euthanasia Versus a Natural Death

If there are no dogs in Heaven, then when I die I want to go where they went.

—Will Rogers

The term "euthanasia" comes from the Greek words "eu" and "thanatos," which combined means "good death." Euthanasia is the practice of quickly and painlessly ending a life. In most parts of the world, euthanizing a person for any reason is against the law, but it is a common practice for animals who are critically injured or suffering from an incurable disease.

For many people, having the ability to euthanize a companion animal who may be in pain and is not likely to recover is the final gift we can offer them. Still, making the decision to deliberately end another creature's life, much less that of one you love so deeply, will surely be one of the most difficult choices you ever face. Doubt may arise and you'll wonder if you did the right thing. You may ask yourself, "Did I put my dog to sleep too soon?" "Did I wait too long?" "If only I had done this (or hadn't done that) . . ." Feelings of guilt are a natural part of the grieving process, and we'll discuss ways to help you move through your grief a little later in this chapter. Remember, if your dog was suffering, euthanasia was likely the kindest, most loving gift you could give him.

Some pet parents choose to either postpone euthanasia or to let nature take its course and allow their dog to die a natural death at home. For these dogs, veterinary hospice care may be an option. As with humans, veterinary hospice care allows a dog to remain at home, cared for by his family—with veterinary supervision and adequate pain management. Recognizing the demand by pet parents for this option, the Nikki Hospice Foundation for Pets (NHFP) was formed. NHFP is a non-profit organization whose mission is: "Promoting the right to make personal choices concerning a terminally ill companion animal, maximizing quality of life and informing the veterinary community and the public about the value of hospice care." Information on veterinary hospice care can be found on their website at www.pethospice.org. At the urging of NHFP, the American Veterinary Medical Association created guidelines for veterinary hospice care. These are available on their website, at www.avma.org.

Whether and when to opt for euthanasia is a highly personal and difficult decision. While most of us would probably prefer that our pets die a natural and peaceful death when the time comes, the reality is that it is a rare occurrence when a dog passes peacefully in his sleep. The same sophisticated level of veterinary care that allows our pets to live longer than ever before also provides greater opportunity for them to wind up with painful and debilitating diseases at the ends of their lives. In keeping with the relationship of unconditional love you have always shared with your dog, keep his comfort and quality of life foremost in your mind when making this final, painful decision.

Preparing for the Inevitable

As with any death, you need to make arrangements for disposal of your dog's body. If possible, you should make preparations ahead of time so you don't have this added burden to deal with on top of your grief. With animals, you have a number of options: burial, cremation, or rendering. The choice you make will likely be based on your personal beliefs regarding death and spirituality, as well as practical concerns of cost and availability.

Burial

Some people would like to bury their dog in one of his favorite spots, perhaps a sunny patch of grass or beneath a tree where he liked to nap. However, keep in mind that many municipalities throughout the country do not allow property owners to bury an animal, even if the burial site is located on their own property. (If you wish to bury your dog on your property, call your town or city's zoning department to inquire about laws relating to such a practice.) Pet cemeteries do exist if you wish to have a place to go to remember your dog. You may have the option of an individual burial with a marked plot or a communal burial. This is, again, a very personal decision.

Cremation

Cremation, or the burning of a body, can occur in two ways: individually or communally. Individual cremation means that your dog will be cremated by herself. Her ashes (called *cremains*) will be returned to you either in a wooden box or an urn (again, make your selection in advance). You may also order a plaque to be placed on the box or urn with a favorite sentiment, poem, and your dog's date of birth and death.

If you do not need or want your dog's remains, you may opt for a communal cremation. This means that several pets are cremated together and crematoriums or pet cemeteries scatter the ashes at sea or in a natural setting. Some people believe that spreading the ashes allows our dog's spirit to be free, rather than confined to one spot in the ground. Others select a burial in a pet cemetery, which will give you the option to visit the grave. Whether you choose to bury or cremate your dog's body, keep in mind the words of author Cleveland Amory, "I have always believed that the best place to bury your animal is in your heart."

Rendering

If you don't specify how your dog's body should be handled, the veterinary clinic will likely give the body to a rendering company, who will take it to an industrial site where the bodies are used to make various products including commercial pet and livestock feed, fertilizer, and soap and other toiletries. Some people are repulsed by the idea of their dog being used in such a way, while others are not concerned with what happens to the dog's body once he is dead or view the practice as a good way of reusing or recycling the body.

Saying Good-bye

If you choose to have your dog euthanized, you may wish to have your veterinarian come to your home, a park, or another favorite location that you and your dog enjoyed visiting together. For some of us, the thought of witnessing our dog's death is deeply unsettling. For others, we cannot imagine not being there to cradle his furry body in our arms and gaze into his loving eyes as the veterinarian administers the euthanasia solution. Deciding to be present during the actual procedure is a choice only you can make.

Many veterinarians will assume that you don't want to know what happens during the euthanasia process, so if you do, it's important to ask questions. If you don't feel comfortable making inquiries, we offer this explanation to tell you exactly what happens when your dog is "put to sleep." The procedure is very simple. Your veterinarian or assistant will shave a small section of fur from your dog's foreleg where a catheter will be taped in place. A sedative is often given to help your dog relax. Your dog is not feeling any pain; he is already starting to drift off to sleep. Your veterinarian will then give a lethal injection of barbituates (typically sodium pentobarbital) to painlessly and quickly stop the heart. Your dog's heart will stop beating within a few seconds. The body may twitch slightly and may even let out a short gasp. These are normal responses and in no way indicate that your dog is experiencing any pain or fighting for his life. Your dog's bladder and bowels may void as all of the muscles have relaxed (place several towels or plastic bags under your dog's body to make clean-up easier). You or your veterinarian can now gently close the eyelids.

You may wish to have some private time with your beloved friend to say your final good-byes. Most veterinarians are sensitive to your feelings and will allow you as much time as you need. At this point, you are likely experiencing a flood of emotions: perhaps guilt for making the decision to end your dog's life combined with relief that he is no longer suffering. Remember, you have done something truly loving and selfless; you allowed your dog to die with dignity.

Coping with Your Loss

It is not just that animals make the world more scenic or picturesque. The lives of animals are woven into our very being—closer than our own breathing—and our soul will suffer when they are gone.

—Gary Kowalski, *The Souls of Animals*

After a pet's death, it's natural and normal to experience feelings of sadness and despair. As with any great loss, you may suffer any number of symptoms of grief. If you have learned that a pet is ill and likely to die, you may begin to experience anticipatory grief prior to the loss. Here are some of the more common symptoms and feelings resulting from grief:

Physical Reactions

* Crying
* Dry mouth, difficulty in swallowing
* Little or no appetite (or overeating)
* Lack of energy
* Sleeping too much (or not sleeping at all)
* Inability to concentrate, forgetfulness
* Aching heart, chest pains and/or an empty, hollow feeling

Emotional Reactions

* Feelings of detachment from others
* Thoughts of "no one cares"
* Worrying that other loved ones will die
* Fear of loving again, fear of loss

If you have experienced even a few of these physical or emotional feelings, you're not alone! Everyone, at some time in his or her life, has felt the same way after the death of a loved one. Every person—just like every dog—is unique and will deal with grief in a different way and on a different timeline. Some people may shed a few tears (or none at all) and move on rather quickly. Others may spend a few days, weeks, or months mourning the loss of their friend. Some of us will adopt another puppy or dog within a few days of our former dog's death, while others will wait several months or years, or may decide never to adopt another animal companion. Many older people have said they won't bring another canine companion into their lives because of their own failing health, while a few will adopt an adult or older dog, so they may enjoy their golden years together.

Keep in mind that there is no right or wrong way to grieve; there will be days when you feel like yourself, and other days when you feel weepy or numb. You may worry that you're grieving too much or not enough. Again, remember there are no set rules for grieving; we all say good-bye and mourn our loss in different ways.

Important note: If you are contemplating suicide, *please* seek the help of a qualified counselor or therapist *immediately*. A trained professional will be able to help you sort out your thoughts and feelings and may prescribe an anti-depressant medication temporarily until you feel better equipped to deal with your loss.

Expressing Your Grief

> If I have any beliefs about immortality, it is that certain dogs I
> know will go to heaven, and very, very few people.
>
> —James Thurber

There is no doubt that losing a pet is a painful, life-altering experience that can make you feel as though you're on an emotional roller-coaster ride. Healing is a process that can only begin when you acknowledge your grief and give yourself permission to express it. It hurts to lose a beloved dog; don't hesitate to say so in whatever way is helpful to you. The following are some ways you may be able to express your grief:

Talk. Share your feelings of sadness with your family, your co-workers, members of a pet loss support group or hotline (you can find a list of pet loss support hotlines at the end of this chapter), or with a counselor or therapist. You'll be surprised at how much the simple act of sharing your thoughts with a caring individual can help you heal. Keep in mind, though, that not everyone may be as understanding as you think they should be. Unfortunately, it's not uncommon for unwitting friends, coworkers, or even family members to make hurtful or callous remarks along the lines of "it was just a dog . . ." Do not allow insensitive words or attitudes to interfere with your very real need to grieve this very real loss. Anyone who has been lucky enough to have a dog as part of their family will respect this need, and as more people become educated about the importance of the human-canine bond, the more they will come to have a greater respect and appreciation for the depth of the relationships we have with our dogs.

Write. Purchase a journal at a gift shop or bookstore and spend a few minutes each day writing about your dog. Remember the way he smelled after a bath or the joyous sound of his bark when you returned home after being gone for a few hours? Put those images on paper and reread your words often. Don't focus on the death itself; instead, remember the good times you shared with your dog and include those in your journal. Journaling is an excellent way to release and reflect upon your emotions, and it can be an important part of the healing process.

Memorialize. Many of us find solace and closure when we create a funeral or memorial service for our deceased dog. Philip Gonzalez of Long Island, New York, honored his beloved Schnauzer–Siberian Husky mix, Ginny, with a beautiful service at a pet memorial park. The seventeen-year-old rescued dog, who became famous as "the dog who rescues cats," passed away in Philip's arms on a late summer day in 2005. A touching tribute to Ginny, which is posted on her website (ginnyfanclub.com), reads, "A memorial service was held for Ginny on August 27, 2005, at the Regency Forest Pet Memorial Park where she was surrounded by friends, family, and a blanket of rose petals. Ginny was laid to her final rest in the Kitty Korner section of the park, where she can be among the cats she loved for all eternity."

Your own service can be as simple or as elaborate as you wish. If your dog was cremated, you may want to spread his ashes along a favorite hiking trail or next to a new tree you planted in memory of your special companion. If you invite friends and family members to the service, encourage them to reminisce and share uplifting stories about your dog. Laugh, cry, and hug each other. This final act of love is a tribute to the love and respect you and your dog shared.

Ritualize. You may wish to create a special ritual to honor the memory of your dog. Remembering a beloved companion through memorials or rituals is a way of healing your grief. Rituals, such as lighting a candle on each anniversary of your dog's death or posting a loving note on a pet loss website, can help to calm and center you and allow healing to take place. You may choose to make a monetary donation to a favorite animal shelter or charity in your dog's name, or create a scrapbook or collage with your favorite pictures, letters from friends, poems, or song lyrics.

Pamper. Be extra kind to yourself during this difficult time. Treat yourself to a massage, take a long walk at the park or beach, or go to lunch and a movie with a good friend. Many people feel guilty for laughing or indulging in a fun activity when their dog has just died. You need to ask yourself, "Would my dog want me to suffer this much?" In your heart, you will undoubtedly answer, "No."

Adopt. There is no doubt that you can never replace a beloved companion with another dog. However, for some people, there is no better way to honor their dog's memory than to offer a loving home to another dog in need. But when and whether to do so is a very personal decision. Some families need time to grieve and heal first. Take all the time you need; you shouldn't feel rushed to get another pet. However, some people find that caring for a newly adopted dog helps fill the void left by their departed companion. Occasionally people express guilt about bringing another dog into the home so soon, but if you believe that you are ready to welcome another dog into your home and heart, without expecting him to live up to your previous dog's memory, I encourage you to act and adopt. I certainly believe that your previous adopted dog would applaud that decision.

Helping Other Animals in the Household

> Unlike some people who have experienced the loss of an animal, I did not believe, even for a moment, that I would never get another. I did know full well that there were just too many animals out there in need of homes for me to take what I have always regarded as the self-indulgent road of saying the heartbreak of the loss of an animal was too much ever to want to go through with it again. To me, such an admission brought up the far more powerful admission that all the wonderful times you had with your animal were not worth the unhappiness at the end.
> —Cleveland Amory

Like their human counterparts, many dogs don't spend their lives as only "children"; rather, they share a home with other four-legged siblings. When one dog dies, the loss can be devastating to the other pets in the home. Dogs—like people—form close emotional bonds with one another, and the death of one animal can be traumatic for the remaining pet(s). Because dogs form a social hierarchy, the death of one dog can have a profound impact on the others.

Keep in mind that, while you're dealing with your own feelings of loss and loneliness, your surviving animals are doing the same. They are also acutely sensitive to your moods and will sense when you are upset or sad. They may cuddle up closer to you than usual or jump in your lap (when they normally wouldn't do so). Some animals will exhibit a searching behavior, where they run through the house or yard looking for their missing friend. If they seem restless or uninterested in eating, you can help ease their anxiety by maintaining as normal as routine as possible. Keep feeding and exercise times the same and give them extra petting and treats. If you feel comfortable doing so, allow your pets to witness the euthanasia procedure (this can most easily be accommodated at home). Let them see and sniff the deceased pet. If that isn't possible, allow them to smell your dog's collar or blanket. Animals can smell minuscule chemical changes in the body and will know that something has happened to their pal. Animals have an amazing ability to understand things like illness and death. By including them in the process, you can help them find closure as well.

Helping Children Deal with Grief

> Many who have spent a lifetime in it can tell us less of love than
> the child that lost a dog yesterday.
>
> —Thornton Wilder

A child's first experience with death is often through the loss of a beloved dog. But sometimes parents become so involved with their own grief that they give inadequate attention to how their children are feeling. It is common to try to protect them from this "grown-up experience," but if children are old enough to reason, they will know when they are being left out of important discussions that involve them. In an attempt to shield a child from grief, parents sometimes make the mistake of using euphemisms like, "Buddy ran away," or "We put Buddy to sleep." Young children may think they did something wrong to make their dog leave, or may begin having sleep disturbances because they believe that if they go to sleep, they will never wake up. Instead of using confusing language, it's important to speak frankly and honestly with your child by saying something like, "Buddy is very sick and cannot get better. We're going to give Buddy a medicine that only dogs take; it will help him to go to heaven." You can modify your language to be congruent with your spiritual or religious beliefs.

The loss of a pet can be a significant source of grief for the whole family. Children—like adults—will need support and reassurance to cope with their feelings. Spend time talking to your child about illness and death, purchase children's books that deal with pet loss, as well as death and grief generally, and encourage your child to write a letter to their dog or help them create a scrapbook or plant flowers in a spot that was favored by their dog. The process will be therapeutic for all of you.

If Your Dog Dies Unexpectedly

So far, we have talked about dogs who have suffered a long illness and then passed away, either through euthanasia or by natural means. But what if your dog dies suddenly, while at home or elsewhere? We don't want to think about it, but there is always a possibility that our beloved companion will be hit by a car, attacked by another animal, or be poisoned. In rare instances, a young, healthy dog may fall victim to a fatal illness such as a heart attack or stroke. In all cases, we will likely experience feelings such as guilt (as if we somehow contributed to the death), anger (if another person or animal caused the death), and denial. We often find ourselves saying over and over again, "But he was just fine a few minutes ago." We feel as though we didn't have adequate time to prepare for our dog's untimely departure from our lives and we feel bad that we were unable to say good-bye in the way we would have liked.

If you discover that the "self-care" measures described in this chapter are not enough to fade the disturbing mental images of your pet's death from your mind, you may find the following tips helpful to your recovery process.

❀ Immediately make arrangements for your dog's burial or cremation. Many communities have a twenty-four-hour emergency hospital

Dog Biscuits for the Soul: Dexter

Dexter

A middle-aged Pit Bull mix named Dexter came to DAWG (Dog Adoption and Welfare Group) in Santa Barbara, California, and was soon sent to be fostered at a local veterinary clinic. There, the good-natured canine served as the official greeter for both dogs and humans. More importantly, Dexter also served as the resident blood donor for dogs in need. Nuetzie Jasiorkowski, a longtime DAWG volunteer who would soon become Dexter's foster mom, had this to say about her friend: "Dexter saved a lot of dogs . . . and helped out when they had emergency situations where they needed blood."

Late in 2005, Dexter himself needed help. He was diagnosed with bone cancer and his left hind leg had to be amputated. With the help of Eddie's Wheels for Pets, Dexter was soon able to resume his favorite activity—his daily walks with Nuetzie and the rest of her pack—in his customized wheels.

Dexter must have had lots of good doggie karma stored up from the dogs he helped, because when he was first diagnosed with cancer, veterinarians gave him a life-expectancy of three to six months. With his will to live and with the nurturing love and care of Nuetzie, this plucky pup continued to love life for the next twenty-one months!

Dexter finally lost his valiant battle against cancer on April 25, 2007. As sad as it was to say good-bye to such a courageous little man, it gives everyone great joy to know just how much Dexter loved the time he shared with Nuetzie and his adopted canine brothers and sisters.

"Dexter was such an inspiration," says Nuetzie. "He was always so grateful . . . I was blessed to have him in my life. . . ."

continued

where you can take your dog's body if your regular veterinarian is not available (such as at night or on weekends).

- Stay busy. Clean your house, wash your car, or work out at the gym. Keeping yourself occupied will help dissipate some of the physical reactions you are experiencing.
- Avoid the use of drugs or excessive alcohol to numb your pain.
- Maintain a normal schedule; continue to go to work or school. You may wish to talk with a trusted friend or co-worker about your loss.
- Eat healthy foods, even if you don't have an appetite.
- Get plenty of rest. If you can't sleep, get up and watch a funny or uplifting television show or movie until you feel tired.
- Seek the help of a trained mental health professional who can guide you through specific modes of treatment, such as cognitive behavioral therapy, biofeedback and relaxation training, and eye movement desensitization and reprocessing (EMDR).

There's no doubt that the sudden death of a beloved dog is a traumatic, life-altering event. Give yourself permission to grieve and follow the tips highlighted above. Eventually, you will be able to focus on the joy and happiness your pet brought into your life, rather than on the final moments of his life. It may seem difficult to believe, but in time, you *will* begin to feel better.

It is never easy saying good-bye to a loving, loyal canine friend, but bit by bit, day by day, you will move through the pain and heartache until you begin to feel whole again. As you look back on your arduous journey through pet loss, remember the simple and the sublime moments spent with your beloved companion—the endless games of fetch with a slobbery tennis ball, the long, meandering walks in the late afternoon sun, the rainy evenings curled up together in front of a roaring fire, warm fur pressed closely to warm skin. You will always carry the memory of your dog's soulful eyes and soul-filled spirits with you. In time, I hope that you will even welcome a new, rescued bundle of fur into your life. What a joyous day that will be!

Dog Biscuits for the Soul: Moose

Moose and his parents

My husband and I had to put down Jack, our thirteen-year-old Giant Schnauzer mix, in February of 2007. He had fought a long battle with soft tissue sarcoma (cancer). My husband was heartbroken as Jack had been his best friend. He had found Jack at a local diner, eating biscuits and gravy, and brought him home. We often said that Jack was a man in a dog suit. After we had Jack euthanized, my husband wanted to find a dog who looked exactly like our old Jack. I was browsing Petfinder on a Saturday night and spotted Max's photo. We called down to Darlington and spoke with Susan, a volunteer. She sent us more photos and we fell in love. My husband and I left on Friday night and drove the twelve hours to Darlington. We were greeted at the shelter and picked up our new addition. Since we already had a sixteen-year old Schnauzer named Max, we renamed our new friend Moose. He is everything we wanted and needed.

Suzanne Smith, New Palestine, Indiana

Moose was adopted from Darlington County Humane Society, Hartsville, South Carolina

Resources

Without a doubt, losing a beloved canine companion is one of the most heartbreaking experiences we will ever face. Friends and family may try to be supportive, but after a while, they may not understand why you don't just get over it and move on. Talking to someone who understands your anguish is an important part of the healing process. If you don't have an understanding friend, trusted veterinarian, religious figure, or therapist you can turn to, you may find it helpful to talk with a trained professional at a pet loss support center. The ASPCA has a pet loss support program that offers help with the following issues:

- Assistance with the decision to euthanize
- Comfort and support at the time of euthanasia
- Help with grieving
- Advice on dealing with children, the elderly or disabled individuals who are facing a death of a companion animal
- Helping the surviving animals in the household to cope
- Assistance in establishing a relationship with a new pet

For further information about the ASPCA Pet Loss Support program, call their Pet Loss Hotline at (877) 474-3310. You can also visit them online at www.aspca.org/site/PageServer ?pagename=pets_petloss.

In addition, several veterinary schools across the country operate hotlines that can be an indispensable lifeline to grieving pet parents. Their mission is to help callers deal with their personal responses to grief as well as to help prepare veterinary students for the emotional side of veterinary medicine. Students go through extensive training with professional counselors and veterinarians. These professionals provide insight into the grieving process so that students will be equipped to assist callers through the fog of anguish they are experiencing.

Most hotlines are available to the community as a whole; callers do not need to be a client of a particular university's veterinary hospital or live in the same city as the university to take advantage of their invaluable service. Calls, which usually last between twenty and thirty minutes, allow people to talk about a cherished pet who has passed away or to discuss their feelings about an animal who is seriously ill. It is common for volunteers to talk with people who are struggling with the decision of when, or if, it's the right time to euthanize their pet. At a time when distressed pet parents are most in need of support, the trained volunteers at pet loss support hotlines are there to comfort, to listen, and to understand.

One volunteer veterinary student expresses her feelings this way: "Being a member of a pet loss support hotline is never easy, but it has taught me the power of the human spirit and the giving nature of the human heart. It has reminded me how powerful love truly is and how those who live inside of our hearts are never truly forgotten. It has, in the process, taught me how I can be a better, more compassionate veterinarian."

BEREAVEMENT HELPLINES, STATE BY STATE:

Below you will find a list of hotlines for several veterinary schools. Hours of operation vary and calls are usually free, other than normal long-distance charges.

California

University of California at Davis School of Veterinary Medicine

1-800-565-1526

Illinois

University of Illinois Veterinary Medical Teaching Hospital

1-877-394-2273

Iowa

Iowa State University College of Veterinary Medicine

1-888-478-7574

Massachusetts

Cummings School of Veterinary Medicine at Tufts University

(508) 839-7966

Michigan

Michigan State University College of Veterinary Medicine

(517) 432-2696

New York

Cornell University College of Veterinary Medicine

(607) 253-3932

Ohio

Ohio State University College of Veterinary Medicine

(614) 292-1823

Virginia

Virginia-Maryland Regional College of Veterinary Medicine

(540) 231-8038

Washington

Washington State University College of Veterinary Medicine

(509) 335-5704

Many veterinary colleges, animal shelters, and humane societies across the country accept monetary donations in memory of a beloved pet. Check with organizations in your town or city for more information. In addition, the Petfinder.com Foundation welcomes donations in honor of a special pet or person. For more information, visit www.petfinder.com/foundation or mail a donation to: Petfinder.com Foundation, PO Box 16835, Tucson, AZ 85732-6395.

FURTHER READING

Reynolds, Rita M.: *Blessing the Bridge: What Animals Teach Us About Death, Dying, and Beyond*. NewSage Press, 2000

Kowalski, Gary: *Goodbye, Friend: Healing Wisdom for Anyone Who Has Ever Lost a Pet*. Stillpoint Publishers, 1997

Carmack, Betty J.: *Grieving the Death of a Pet*. Augsburg Fortress Publishers, 2003

Greene, Lorri A. and Jacquelyn Landis: *Saying Good-bye to the Pet You Love*. New Harbinger Publications, 2002

Sife, Wallace. PhD: *The Loss of a Pet*. Howell Book House, 3rd edition, 2005

Congalton, David: *Three Cats, Two Dogs, One Journey Through Multiple Pet Loss*. NewSage Press, 2000

PET LOSS WEBSITES

Animal Love & Loss Network
www.alln.org

Argus Institute for Families and Veterinary Medicine (Colorado State University):
www.argusinstitute.colostate.edu/grief.htm

Association for Pet Loss & Bereavement
www.aplb.org

Delta Society
www.deltasociety.org

Guardian Animal Aftercare
www.guardianaftercare.com/bereavement.htm

Shiva's Center for the Human-Animal Bond
www.shivascenter.org

SPECIAL HOLIDAY

National Pet Memorial Day (second Sunday in September)

Appendix
Saving Dogs on a Larger Scale

We at Petfinder.com get so many e-mails from adopters who say, "I wish I could help all the dogs who need homes!" It's hard not to feel that way if you've visited a shelter or a foster home, or even if you've just looked at online listings of all the dogs who have lost their homes through no fault of their own. Every one of these loving canines deserves to have a forever home, even though you have only one such home to give.

But even if you can adopt only one or maybe two dogs, you can still help lots of others—by working with us at Petfinder. Helping dogs (and cats and other companion animals) is what we do. We've matched millions of home-less dogs and other companion animals with adopters like you—people who, by offering their homes and hearts to these needy creatures, receive a life-time of love and loyalty in return.

Here are some great ways you can help us with our work, and make a lot of canine tails wag in the process!

More Time Than Money? Volunteer!

If you've got more time than money to give to a cause that's important to you, the shelters and rescue groups that Petfinder helps to support need you. These organizations depend on volunteers to do some of the heavy lifting required to care for homeless animals and to find those animals the permanent homes they need and deserve.

Volunteering at a Shelter

Shelters often need volunteers to help perform the following tasks:

Socialization and training. Shelter professionals know that a friendly, mannerly puppy or dog stands a far better chance of being adopted than a dog of any age who, simply through lack of discipline and attention, is clueless about how to behave. For that reason, many shelters hire professional dog trainers to create teams of volunteer trainers and socializers. Volunteer trainers teach individual dogs to respond to basic cues, such as coming when called, sitting, and lying down. Socializers spend time interacting with shelter dogs and puppies, giving them the one-on-one attention that will help them thrive during their shelter stays. Both types of volunteers generally complete an orientation and training period before beginning to work with a shelter's canine residents. The required time commitment varies, but shelters generally prefer volunteers who can help out on a regular basis for a reasonable duration, such as an hour a week (or month) for three to six months or so.

Housekeeping. Shelter dogs can't stay healthy if their shelters are dirty. At many facilities, volunteers improve shelter conditions by cleaning cages, washing towels and dog dishes, and making sure that dog feces and urine are dealt with promptly. Here, too, dependable volunteers are preferred, especially those who can commit to a certain number of hours per week or month for at least several months.

Logistics. Handling the logistics of animal adoption is just as important as working one-on-one with shelter dogs or keeping the facilities clean. Shelters need detail-oriented volunteers who may assist in interviewing potential adopters, contacting the references specified on adopters' applications, performing home visits, and transporting dogs to adoption events in the community. Required time commitments for these tasks may be more flexible than for tasks that involve one-on-one interaction with the dogs in the shelter.

Administrative tasks. Are you a writer? A bookkeeper? An event planner? Your local shelter may be a place where you can leverage your professional expertise to help countless dogs and other animal companions. Writers can produce newsletters, proposals, and letters that generate community interest and financial contributions to the shelter. Bookkeepers and accountants can help shelters keep track of where every dollar comes from, and where it goes. Event planners can help shelter staff organize exciting, pet-friendly fundraising events. Think about what you're best at, and talk to the shelter staff to see if you can turn that into a volunteer opportunity.

Volunteering to foster a dog is a wonderful way to save a life.

As with logistical tasks, the required time commitments for administrative tasks may be more flexible than for tasks that involve interaction with the shelter dogs.

Volunteering with a Rescue Group

Rescue groups also welcome volunteers, but their needs differ somewhat from those of shelters. Here are the most common volunteer jobs offered by rescue organizations.

Foster care. Rescue groups can't do any rescuing without their networks of foster homes. A foster care provider is responsible for offering a temporary home for an adoptable dog who has entered the foster care program. Foster homes provide a rescue dog's day-to-day care, including feeding, grooming, exercising, socializing, and training. These foster parents may also take the dogs to the veterinarian for vaccinations and other health care. While associated costs are usually covered by the rescue group, it is important to discuss this with the group with whom you are volunteering. Some foster care providers also screen potential adopters. The time commitment required of foster care providers is considerable, particularly if the dog has health or behavioral issues. There is an emotional cost as well, because a foster parent must be able to bond with the dog in her care, but be willing to relinquish that dog to a permanent home once one is found. But to the dogs, a foster parent is worth her weight in gold. Fortunately, the reward is great, as well, since a foster parent is directly responsible for helping her charge find their new "fur-ever" home. Many new adopters enjoy staying in touch with their dog's prior foster home, providing cheerful updates, photos, and heart-felt thanks.

Logistics. Rescue groups also need volunteers who can handle the many other tasks that keep the organization afloat. Such responsibilities include helping to set up adoption events at local stores, transporting dogs to their new foster homes, and visiting homes of prospective adopters to be sure that they are prepared to accept their rescue dogs. The required time commitment for a logistical volunteer is considerably less than for a foster care provider, and there's much more flexibility as well.

Administrative tasks. As with shelters, you might be able to apply your day-job skills to tasks that rescue groups value. A writer can edit a newsletter, a bookkeeper can track income and expenses, a grants specialist might map out a fundraising campaign. Best of all, these tasks probably won't require much of your time—and you'll probably be able to set your own hours. So be creative! Think of a way to apply your personal skills to helping rescued dogs, and contact some rescue organizations to discuss it.

How do you find a shelter or rescue group that needs you? One way is to contact local shelters or rescue groups directly—starting with the shelter or rescue group from which you adopted your new four-legged friend. But if you want to cast a wider net, log onto Petfinder.com. First you'll need to register at http://users.petfinder.com/visitors/userRegistration.cgi. After that, log in at http://users.petfinder.com/visitors/volunteer.cgi to register yourself in the site's volunteer database. Shelters and rescue groups in your area search for people like you who want to make a difference for homeless pets in your community.

More Money Than Time? Donate!

If you're pressed for time but have even a little money to spare, you can still be part of what we do. Here are ways to put your money to work for the animals that Petfinder, animal shelters, and rescue groups are constantly working to find homes for:

Sponsor a pet. As you browse through Petfinder's listings of available dogs, do you see one who you can't adopt but who melts your heart? You can still help. Just look for the "Sponsor Me!" icon that appears on the "Pet Notes" pages for a dog who interests you, click the bar and follow the prompts. Another way to find a dog who needs a sponsor is to log onto Petfinder.com's Sponsor-a-Pet page (www.petfinder.com/foundation/sponsorapet.html), and use the search feature at the bottom of the page to find shelters that participate in the program. Each shelter or rescue group listed has a link to take you directly to its online listings of available dogs. By clicking on a dog's name or photograph, you'll hop on over to the "Pet Notes" page, where you'll not only find more info but also the "Sponsor Me!" icon.

Become a supporter. If you'd rather have your donation applied to where the need is greatest, you can contribute directly to the Petfinder.com Foundation, which allocates donations on the basis of need. To make a donation to the Foundation, log onto www.petfinder.com/foundation and click the "Make a Donation" button at the bottom of the page. If you're uncomfortable making donations online, you can send your check to:

The Petfinder.com Foundation
P.O. Box 16385
Tucson, AZ 85732

Honor someone special. Would you like to honor someone who cares about animals for his or her birthday or a special occasion? Do you have a special companion animal you would like to honor or memorialize? Simply indicate this when you send in your contribution. Please include the names of the people or animals in whose honor or memory the gift is being made, as well as the name and address of the person or the family to whom we should acknowledge the gift.

Double your money. You can often increase your donation with matching corporate gifts. Many companies match the charitable contributions of their employees. This doubles (or sometimes more) your financial support and is relatively easy to obtain. Contact your company's human resources department to find out more about this benefit and to pick up your company's matching gift form.

Leave a legacy. You can leave a legacy that provides support and hope to thousands of homeless animals and animal shelters through your estate planning. Consider designating in your will a specific amount or percentage of your estate to be donated to the Petfinder.com Foundation or another reputable animal charity. A charity may also be designated as the beneficiary to your life insurance policies or investment funds.

Shop for the animals. By purchasing products from the companies that sponsor Petfinder, you'll also be contributing to the welfare of homeless animals. For example, Merial, the maker of HEARTGARD® and FRONT-LINE® brand products, will allocate up to $1 million to provide disaster relief to needy pets when pet parents redeem coupons and rebates for those products. And if you buy anything from The Animal Rescue Site store at http://shop.theanimalrescuesite.com/store/site.do, part of the money you pay will be used to support the Petfinder.com Foundation's shelter care and feeding program. These programs may change from time to time, but you can find updated information by visiting Petfinder.com.

No single individual, or even a single group, can help all the needy animals of the world. But by working together, we can go a long way toward making sure that every adoptable animal gets the forever home that he or she deserves.

Resources

Gillette, Kristin: "Helping Homeless Dogs and Cats"
http://www.mylifetime.com/lifestyle/relationships/portrait/helping-homeless-dogs-and-cats

Saunders, Kim: "Petfinder.com Gives Shelter Pets New Byte"
http://www.petfinder.com/press.html

Petfinder.com: "Ways You Can Help"
http://www.petfinder.com/foundation/donate.html

Index

accidents, 17, 141
acepromazine, 353, 387
activity, restricting, 300–301
acupuncture, 393
Addison's disease, 377
adolescent dogs, 33
adoption(s)
    after a pet's death, 460
    applications, 4, 9, 443–44
    costs, 17–19
    events, 91–93
    placement groups, 6–8
    pledge, 38–39
    procedure, 3–4
    re-homing and, 445–46
    rights, 94
Affenpinscher, 53
Afghan Hound, 45–46, 257
age, of dogs, 34, 84
aggression, 50–51, 439, 443
agility, 209, 211
Airedale Terrier, 48, 334
air travel, 411–14
Akita, 55, 316, 334
Alaskan Malamute, 55, 249, 251
Allegretti, Jan, 400
allergic reactions, 271, 282
allergies, of dogs, 334–37
    dermatitis and, 327–28, 329–30
    food, 172–74
    home-cooked food and, 170
allergies, of humans, 334
    sleeping arrangements and, 101–2
Alliance for Contraception in Cats and Dogs
    (ACC&D), 245–46
American Animal Hospital Association
    (AAHA), 242
American Bulldog, 49

American College of Veterinary Behaviorists,
    152, 426
American Eskimo Dog, 58
American Humane Association (AHA), 242
American Kennel Club (AKC), 55
    CGC program, 130–32
    early age neutering and, 242
    Rally O and, 210
American Pet Products Manufacturers
    Association, 180
American Pit Bull Terrier, 47–48, 252
American Society for the Prevention of
    Cruelty to Animals (ASPCA), 2, 242
    Poison Control Hotline, 79, 285
American Staffordshire Terrier, 47–49
American Temperament Test, 50
American Veterinary Chiropractic Association
    (AVCA), 399
American Veterinary Medical Association
    (AVMA), 242
American Water Spaniel, 43
anal glands, 215, 235
Anatolian Shepherd Dog, 53, 55
anemia, 162, 379–80
Animal Behavior Society, 426
Animal Hospital Association Vaccine
    Guideline, 267
animal hospitals, 72
Animal Rescue Site, 474
animal shelters, xxiii, 1–6, 138
    finding, 5
    guidelines, 86–91
    kill v. no-kill, 3
    open-admission, 3
    questions, 84–86
    re-homing and, 446–47
    volunteering at, 470–71
animal welfare agencies, 13

antibiotics, 282
antidepressants, 373
antifreeze, 74, 76
antihistamines, 330, 335. *See also* Benadryl
anxiety, 103, 195. *See also* separation anxiety
    bathing, 225–26
    medications and, 297–98
apartments, 21–22. *See also* homes
appetite, 160, 271–72
applications for adoption, 4, 9, 443–44
aromatherapy, 393–94
arthritis, 157, 371
aspirin, 387
Association for Pet Dog Trainers (APDT), 91,
    150–51
Association of American Feed Control
    Officials (AAFCO), 164–65
Australian Cattle Dog, 55–56
Australian Shepherd, 55–56, 220, 221, 251,
    257, 314, 315, 351, 352
Australian Terrier, 48
autoimmune disease, 379

babies, 430–32
baby gates, 66, 106
Bach, Edward, 394
Bach flower remedies, 394–99, 409
background of shelter dogs, 84–85
bags, plastic, 68–69
balls, 70, 208
Barish, Eileen, 416
barking, 27, 104, 135
barrier frustration, 199
Basenji, 46
Basset Hound, 45–46, 251, 258, 375
bathing, 31, 66–67, 225–28
Beagle, 44–46, 251, 258, 375
Bearded Collie, 56, 316
Beauceron, 57
Bedlington Terrier, 47–48
begging, 147–48
behavior
    capturing, 203–4
    changes, 271
    consequences and, 125
    evaluation, 85
    genetics and, 26–27
    problem, 113, 143–50
behaviorists, 152, 425–26
Belgian Malinois, 57
Belgian Sheepdog, 57
Belgian Shepherd, 249, 251, 255
Belgian Tervuren, 57
Benadryl, 282, 335

Bernese Mountain Dog, 55, 258, 349
Bichon Frisé, 57–58, 220
Big Black Dog Syndrome, 4
Billinghurst, Ian, 175
biofeedback, 464
Biologically Appropriate Raw Food (BARF)
    diet, 175
birdfeeders, 78
bittering spray, 75, 144
Black and Tan Coonhound, 46
Black Russian Terrier, 55
bladder stones, 362–63
bleeding, 272, 282–83
blindness, 36, 321–22
blinking, 86–87
bloat, 54, 205, 357–58, 359
blood, 271
Bloodhound, 45–46
boarding facilities, 417–18
boats, 414
body language, 197–98
body temperature, 272, 280, 299–300, 346
bonding, 33, 71
bones, 173, 175
booties, 206
bordatella, 264, 266
Border Collie, 56–57, 251, 257, 314, 315,
    351
Border Terrier, 48, 257
Borzoi, 46
Boston Terrier, 57–58, 334, 411
Bouvier des Flandres, 57, 349, 366
bowls, 63, 105, 157, 359
Boxer, 55, 219–20, 259, 281, 334, 349, 350
Boyle, Stephen, 245
Brainstem Auditory Evoked Response (BAER)
    testing, 321, 325
breathing, 250
    changes in, 272
    emergency procedures and, 280
    resuscitation, 283
breeding, 244–45, 248, 316
breeds. *See also* cross-breeds; *specific breed*
    groups
    brachycephalic, 249
    exercise and, 204
    grooming and, 216
    groups, 41–42
    intelligent, 35
    knowing, 109
    obesity and, 177
    questions about, 84
    SA and, 333
brewer's yeast, 168, 237

Briard, 57
Brittany, 43
Brittany Spaniel, 246
brushes, 67, 216, 220
brushing, 219, 222. *See also* grooming
Brussels Griffon, 53
budgeting, 17–19
Bulldog, 49, 189, 249, 255, 366, 375, 411
Bullie sticks, 144
Bullmastiff, 55
Bull Terrier, 47–49, 349
burials, 454–55
burrs, 323
buses, 414
Buster Cube, 71
Busy Buddies, 144

CA. *See* infectious canine hepatitis
Cairn Terrier, 48
California Veterinary Medical Association
    (CVMA), 242
calming, 117–18
Camp Gone to the Dogs, 204
Canaan Dog, 57
cancer
    skin, 333–34
    spaying and neutering and, 241
    types, 381–84
canine adenovirus, 263–64, 266, 267
Canine Distemper (CDV), 262, 266, 267
Canine Eye Registry Foundation (CERF),
    321
Canine Good Citizen (CGC) program,
    130–32
canine hip dysplasia (CHD), 26, 42–43, 54,
    371, 371–73
canine influenza, 262
canine parainfluenza, 264, 266
canine parvovirus, 263, 266, 267
"capturing a behavior," 203–4
carbohydrates, 163
cars, 12, 98–99, 407–11
castrating. *See* spaying and neutering
Catahoula Leopard Dog, 315
cataracts, 312–13
cats, 105–6
Cavalier King Charles Spaniel, 53, 194
Certification Council for Professional Dog
    Trainers (CCPDT), 151
chasing, 127, 201
check-ups, 109
chemotherapy, 382
cherry eye, 314
Chesapeake Bay Retriever, 44, 220

chewing, 143–44
    bittering spray and, 75
    dog-proofing and, 74
    stress and, 104
    toys and, 70
chews, 179
Chihuahua, 29, 52–53, 95, 194, 251, 253, 334
childproof latches, 75
children, 20, 82–83, 85, 88–89, 193, 196–97.
        See also babies
    dog-proofing and, 75
    pet death and, 461–62
Chinese Crested, 53
Chinese Shar Pei, 58, 256–57
chiropractic care, 372, 395–99
chocolate, 173
choking, 283–84, 284
chondroitin, 372
Chow Chow, 57–58, 316, 334
circulatory system, 253, 345–51
classified ads, 4, 8–13
cleaning
    in dog parks, 200
    ears, 228–29
    house-training and, 141
    supplies, 67–68
clickers, 64–65, 117, 119–20
clipping, 217, 223–24
    dermatitis from, 328
    ear hairs, 229
    nails, 231–32
Clumber Spaniel, 44
coats, 217–24
    bathing and, 225
    brush type and, 220
    color of, 258–59
    conditions of, 326–34
    patterns of, 258–59
    stripping, 223
    types of, 256–58
Cockapoo, 60
Cocker Spaniel, 43, 194, 334
cold laser therapy, 399
colds, 368
cold weather
    exercise and, 206–7
    house-training in, 142
    walking in, 194
colitis, 359–60
collars, 11–12, 17–18, 64, 65, 115–16
Collie, 56–57, 221, 251, 314, 315, 316, 334,
    351, 352
Collie Eye Anomaly (CEA), 314–15
combs, 67

come command, 124–26, 127, 130
Comfort Zone, 136
commercial dog food, 164–66
The Complete Holistic Dog Book (Allegretti &
    Sommers), 400
conditioner, 227
conjunctivitis, 311
consequences, 125
consistency, 117, 138
constipation, 360
contracts, 93, 441
Coonhound, 251
Coonhound paralysis, 386–88
coprophagia, 149
corneas, 309
Coronavirus, 264–65
corticosteroids, 329–30, 332, 335, 372
costs, 17–19
    of hospitalization, 295
    of medications, 294
    of veterinarians, 290
coughing, 273
crates, 66, 72, 115
    air travel and, 413
    cars and, 408
    house-training and, 140
    recuperation and, 300–1
    training, 128–29
cremation, 455
cropping, of ears, 252
cross-breeds, 26, 52–53, 60
crowds, 130
crying, 272–73
cupboards, 75
Curly-Coated Retriever, 44
Cushing's disease, 377–78
custody, 434

Dachshund, 44–46, 219–20, 315, 316
Dalmatian, 58, 258, 334, 366
dancing, 209–10
Dandie Dinmont Terrier, 48
D.A.P., 136
dating, 429–30
day care, 425
Deaf Dog Education Action Fund (DDEAF),
    321
deafness, 36, 273, 324–26
death, 432–34
    coping with, 456–61
    natural, 453–54
    preparing for, 454–55
    unexpected, 462–65
Degenerative Joint Disease (DJD), 369–70

DeGeneres, Ellen, 441
dehydration, 206
dental care, 216, 230–31, 348
dermatitis, 327–31
desensitization, 425
dewclaws, 234, 256
diabetes mellitus, 378
diarrhea, 271, 273, 360–61
    causes of, 361
    internal parasites and, 353–57
diet. *See* food
dieting, 177–78
digestive system, 254, 351–62
digging, 104, 148–49
dishes. *See* bowls
Dis-Taste, 149
distractions, 123, 130
divorce, 432–34
Doane Pet Care Center, 167
Doberman Pinscher, 55, 252, 257, 258, 316,
    334, 349, 350
Dock Dogs, 153
dog parks, 190, 200–2
dog-proofing, 74–79
dogs. *See also* adolescent dogs; older dogs;
    special needs dogs
    after death, 460–61
    age of, 34, 84
    approaching, 11–12
    evaluation of, 3–4
    growth, 34
    ignoring, 113
    lifespan of, 34
    meeting with, 11
    other, 131, 197–99
    picking up, 98–99
    qualities of, 24–37
    size, 29–31
    talking to, 86–87
    testing, 87
    types, 3
dog sitters, 418–19
dog sports, 22, 209–10
dog-to-dog introductions, 104–5
dog walkers, 190
dog washing centers, 67
dominance hierarchy, 113–14
Donaldson, Jean, 150
donations to shelters and rescue groups,
    472–74
doorbells, 134–35
doors, 76
down command, 122–23, 130
drowning, 284

Dr. Pitcairn's Complete Guide to Natural Health for Dogs and Cats (Pitcairn), 158, 391–92
drugs. *See* medications
dry eye, 314, 319–20
drying, 227
Dutch Shepherd, 251

ears, 251–52, 322–26
  care for, 228–29
  cropped, 252
  medications for, 298
  water in, 226
E. coli, 174, 175
edema, 348, 350
elbow dysplasia, 371
electrical cords, 74–76
electronic fencing, 78
elimination diet trial, 172–74
Elizabethan collars, 302
emergencies, 17–19, 72, 127, 278, 280–86
endocrine system, 254, 376–78
English Bulldog, 58
English Setter, 44
English Shepherd, 251
English Springer Spaniel, 43
English Toy Spaniel, 53
enzymatic odor neutralizers, 67–68
epilepsy, 384–85
euthanasia, 290, 452–54
examinations, 291
exercise, 27–28, 108, 204–7, 291, 424
  obesity and, 177
  pens, 66, 115
  time and, 19–20
  walking and, 188
expressing, 235
eye contact, 86–87
eyelids, 316–18
eye movement desensitization and
    reprocessing (EMDR), 464
eyes, 252–53
  care of, 229–30
  conditions of, 308–22
  foggy, 274
  medications for, 299
  problems with, 273–74
EZ Walk, 191

fats, 162–63, 168
fatty acids, 164, 335, 372
fear
  of sounds, 134–36
  of strangers, 195
fecal samples, 354

feces. *See also* house-training
  bird, 78
  cleaning, 67–68
  eating, 149
  removing, 68–69
  tapeworms and, 355–56
feeding, 156–60
  during hospitalizations, 296
  time and, 19
fees. *See also* costs
  adoption, 5–6
  rescue group, 7–8
  special needs dogs and, 37
feet, 255–56. *See also* paws
fencing, 77
fertilizers, 76
fetching, 70, 208
FETCH! Pet Care, 418
fever, 271, 272
Field Spaniel, 43–44
Finnish Spitz, 58
fireworks, 135–36
first aid, 72, 278–80
fixing. *See* spaying and neutering
Flat-Coated Retriever, 44
flea combs, 217, 237
fleas, 214, 236, 337–38, 355
flowers, 79. *See also* Bach flower remedies
follow-up care, 294
food
  air travel and, 413
  allergies, 172–74
  amount of, 108
  begging and, 147
  bowls, 63
  buying, 63
  changing, 158
  dangerous, 173
  home-cooked, 170–72
  house-training and, 139
  human, 116
  hypoallergenic, 172–74
  ingredients, 168–70
  kosher, 180
  labels, 168–70
  low-calorie, 178
  "people," 171–72
  portions, 158–60
  quality of, 291
  recalls, 167
  during recuperation, 301
  toys and, 71
  types of, 161–76
  vegetarian, 181

Food and Drug Administration (FDA),
    164
For-Bid, 149
foster care, 7, 91–93, 471–72
Foxhound, 46, 251, 258
Fox Terrier, 48
fractures, 284
freestyle, 209–10
French Bulldog, 58, 251, 257
Frisbees, 208
fruit, 79, 175
fur. *See* coats
furnishings, 221
furniture, 146

garages, 76
gardens, 35–36, 78–79, 148–49
genetics, 26–27
    bathing and, 225
    deafness and, 325–26
    eye conditions and, 312
Gentle Leader, 191
German Pinscher, 54
German Shepherd Dog, 56–57, 59, 220, 249,
    251, 255, 257, 258, 316, 334, 349, 352
German Shorthaired Pointer, 44
German Wirehaired Pointer, 44
Giant Schnauzer, 55, 252
Giardia, 265, 267, 357
glaucoma, 318
Glen of Imaal Terrier, 48
glucosamine hydrochloride, 169, 372
Goldendoodle, 60
Golden Retriever, 27, 43, 44, 58–59, 220, 255,
    286, 334, 349
Gonzalez, Philip, 459
Gordon Setter, 43, 44, 255
Great Dane, 29, 55, 252, 350
Greater Swiss Mountain Dog, 55
Great Pyrenees, 55
Greyhound, 44, 46, 107, 194, 219
grief, expressing, 458–60
grooming, 31, 130
    breeds and, 216
    health and, 214
    hot spots and, 337
    mitts, 219
    professional, 215
    supplies, 66–67, 214–17
    time and, 19
gunfire, 135

Hahnemann, Samuel, 401
hairlessness, 228

hand shyness, 137
hand signals, 114
harnesses, 115–16
Harrier, 46
Havanese, 53
health, 23
    certificates, 151, 412
    grooming and, 214
    issues, 85–86
    monitoring, 346–47
heart disease, 345–51
heart failure, 348–49
heart rate, 280
heartworm, 36, 108, 351
heat, 410–11
heatstroke, 284–85
heeling, 120, 191–92
hematomas, 323
hemophilia, 380
hepatitis. *See* Infectious Canine Hepatitis
herbal therapies, 400–1
herding group, 55–57
hip dysplasia. *See* canine hip dysplasia
holistic medicine, 391–404
homeopathy, 401–2
homes
    dog-proofing, 74–75
    dog size and, 30
    first 24 hours and, 99–101
    leaving, 423
    moving, 426–28
    new, 426–28
    size of, 21–22
hookworms, 356
hospice care, 453–54
hospitalizations, 290, 294–96
hotels, 415
hot spots, 336–37
hound group, 44–46
house-training, 69, 138–42, 189
howling, 45
hugging, 137
human-animal bond, 450
Humane Society of the United States (HSUS),
    2, 242
Hurricane Katrina, xxiv
hydrogen peroxide, 175
hyperactivity, 27
hyperthyroidism, 376
hypothyroidism, 43, 376

Ibizan Hound, 46
identification tags, 11–12, 65
    air travel and, 413

fireworks and, 136
moving and, 427
illness. *See also* vaccinations; *specific illnesses*
chronic, 36
cost of, 17
hereditary, 26
infectious, 261–65
recuperation from, 296–303
symptoms of, 270–77
immobilizing, 282
immune system, 162, 254, 269, 378–81
immunotherapy, 335
Imodium, 352
infections, 261–65
anal glands and, 235
ear, 228, 322
eye, 229, 311–12
fungal, 338–40
oral, 231
Infectious Canine Hepatitis (CA), 262–63, 266
injuries
ear, 323–24
eye, 309–11
hospitalization from, 294–96
immobilizing and, 282
recuperation from, 296–303
signs of, 270–77
transporting and, 282
insurance. *See* pet health insurance
integrative medicine, 392
intelligence, 34–35
International Air Transport Association
(IATA), 411
International Association of Animal Behavior
Consultants (IAABC), 151
Internet, xxii–xxiii
adoption events and, 92
classified ads, 8–11
medications on, 388
re-homing and, 442
intestinal obstruction, 359
invertebral disc disease, 45, 374–75
invisible fencing, 78
Irish Setter, 44, 255, 334
Irish Terrier, 48
Irish Water Spaniel, 44
Irish Wolfhound, 46, 350
Irritable Bowel Syndrome (IBS), 360
Italian Greyhound, 53

Japanese Chin, 53, 249
jogging, 204–5
*Journal of the American Veterinary Medical
Association*, 359

jumping
dog-proofing and, 75
on furniture, 146
on strangers, 196

Keeshond, 58
kennel cough, 263–64, 367
kennels, 417–18
Kerry Blue Terrier, 48
kidney failure, 365–66
Klee Kai, 133
knees, 256
knocking, 134–35
Komondor, 55, 257, 258
Kongs, 144
Kuvasz, 55, 258

Labradoodle, 60
Labrador Retriever, 44, 219–20, 255
lab work, 292–93
Lakeland Terrier, 48
laryngeal paralysis, 366
last resorts, 438–40
lawns, 35–36
laxatives, 360
leashes, 64, 65, 115–16
cars and, 98–99
cost of, 17–18
house-training and, 141
loose, 191–92
recuperation and, 301
retractable, 64
legacies, 473–74
Legg-Perthes disease, 375
legs, 255–56
leptospirosis, 263, 266
Lhasa Apso, 57–58, 375, 411
lice, 342
licensing, 17, 108, 200
lick granuloma, 330
lifespan, 24, 34
life vests, 194
light/color therapy, 402–3
limping, 274
linoleic acid, 164, 169
liquid medications, 298
Listeria, 175
litter boxes, 69, 74
Löwchen, 58
lumps, 214, 274
lupus, 380–81
lures. *See* rewards
Lyme disease, 264, 266, 338, 370
lymphatic system, 254

magnetic therapy, 403
Maltese, 53, 220, 221, 260
Malti-Poo, 52, 60
management tools, 115–18
Manchester Terrier, 48, 53
mange, 341–42
marijuana, 79
massage therapy, 372, 403–4
Mastiff, 30, 55
MDR1 mutation, 352–53
medical records, 98, 108
medications, 293–94
  administering, 109
  giving, 297–99
  sensitivity, 387
  separation anxiety and, 425
melamine, 167
memorials, 459
Menu Foods, 166, 167
Merial, 474
microchips, 13, 17, 65, 136
Mine! (Donaldson), 150
minerals, 163–64
Miniature Bull Terrier, 48
Miniature Pinscher, 257, 334
Miniature Schnauzer, 48, 252, 334
mites, 341–42
mitral valve insufficiency, 348
Mixed Breed Dog Club of America
  (MBDCA), 210
mixed breeds, 58–59. *See also* cross-breeds
  purebreds *v.,* 25–27
  terriers and, 47
mosquitos, 351
mouthing, 144–45
moving, 426–28
musculoskeletal system, 253, 368–75
mutts. *See* mixed breeds
muzzling, *281,* 281–82

nail care, 231–35
nail clippers, 67, 216
names, changing, 110
National Association of Professional Pet
  Sitters, 418
National Organization of Dog Obedience
  Instructors (NADOI), 151
Nature's Miracle, 67
Nature's Recipe, 181
Nature's Variety, 175
nausea, 99
Neapolitan Mastiff, 55
negative reinforcement, 152

nervous system, 254, 384–88
Nestlé Purina Pet care, 176
neutering. *See* spaying and neutering
neuticles, 244
Newfoundland, 55, 316, 349
nictitating membrane, 312, 314
Nikki Hospice Foundation for Pets (NFHP),
  453
non-sporting group, 57–58
non-steroidal anti-inflammatory drugs
  (NSAIDs), 372
Norfolk Terrier, 48, 255
Norwegian Elkhound, 46
Norwich Terrier, 48, 255
Nova Scotia Duck Tolling Retriever, 44
nutrition. *See* feeding
nutrition therapy, 404
Nylabones, 144, 179–80

obesity, 176–78, 378
odors. *See* smells
ointments, 299, 336
Old English Sheepdog, 57, 334, 352
older dogs, 34
  feeding, 158, 160–61
  puppies *v.,* 32–33
opioids, 372–73
Orbees, 144
orthopedic treatments, 372–73
Osteochondritis disease, 368
Otterhound, 46
overexertion, 204
overheating, 223

pain, 275, 276, 369
pancreatitis, 378
panting, 250, 327
Papillion, 53, 258
parasites, 174
  external, 337–43
  internal, 353–57
parks, 192–93. *See also* dog parks
Parson Russell Terrier, 48, 59
parvo. *See* canine parvovirus
paws, 231–35. *See also* feet
  poisons on, 234
  trimming fur in, 207, 234–35
Peke-a-poo, 60
Pekingese, 53, 189, 249, 281, 311, 375,
  411
personality changes, 275
pesticides, 76, 78
pet cemeteries, 454–55

Index

Petfinder.com
  adoption events and, 92
  donating to, 472–74
  history of, xxii–xxv
PetFlight, 412
Pet Guard, 181
pet health insurance, 304–6
Petit Basset Griffon Vendeen, 46
Pet Sitters International, 418
pets, other, 23–24, 104–6
  death and, 460–61
  dog size and, 30
pet store adoptions, 10
petting, 88, 130, 137–38
Pharaoh Hound, 46
pheromones, 136, 327
physical contact, 87–88
pig ears, 180
pigment cells, 326
Pill Pockets, 297
Pit Bull, 7, 47, 49–51, 61, 219–20
Pitcairn, Richard H., 158, 391–92
place training, 126–27
plaque, 230–31
playing, 27–28, 207–10
  in dog parks, 201
  mouthing and, 144–45
  with other dogs, 198
  testing, 89–90
  toys and, 71
pledge, for new adopters, 38–39
Plott Hound, 46
Pointer, 44
Poison Control Hotline, 79, 285
poisons
  chewing and, 144
  cleaning supplies and, 68
  control, 72
  digging and, 148–49
  dog-proofing, 74
  in gardens, 78–79
  on paws, 234
  pet food recalls and, 167
  treatment for, 285
Polish Lowland Sheepdog, 57
Pomeranian, 53
Poodle, 27, 57–58, 220, 256–57, 375
Poodle, Standard, 334
Poodle, Toy, 53
pooper scoopers, 68–69
Portuguese Water Dog, 53, 55
potty time
  command, 142

feeding frequency and, 157
first 24 hours and, 100
time and, 19
walking and, 188–89
preventative care, 291
proteins, 162, 365
Pug, 53, 249, 253, 255, 281, 309, 311, 405
Puggle, 52, 60, 249
Puli, 57, 257
pulling, 64, 191–92
punishment, 152
pupils, 309
puppies
  appetite loss in, 271–72
  feeding frequency, 156
  food portions for, 159
  older dogs v., 32–33
  roundworms and, 355
puppy pads, 102
purebreds, 2–3
  mixed breeds v., 25–27
  rescue groups and, 7
Purina Incredible Dog Challenge, 209

quarantining, 12
questions
  for adoption, 25
  about age, 84
  animal shelters, 84–86
  about breeds, 84
  classified ads and, 10
  for dog sitters, 419
  for hospitalizations, 295
  for veterinarians, 290

rabies, 12, 263, 266, 267
radiation therapy, 382
Rally O, 210
rashes, 275
rawhide bones, 180
recalls, pet food, 167
recipes, 183–87
recuperation, 296–303
references, 4
regurgitation, 361–62
re-homing, 438–47
rendering, 455
rescue groups, xxii, 6–8, 13, 471–72
resorts, 415
resource guarding, 88–89, 150
respiratory system, 254, 367
resuscitation, 283
retrieving. See fetching

rewards, 116–17, 119
  begging and, 147
  training without, 129
Rhodesian Ridgeback, 44–46
Rheumatoid Arthritis, 371
rights, 94
ringworm, 338–40
Rocky Mountain spotted fever, 338
rodents, 106
Rottweiler, 55, 258, 349
roundworms, 355
routine, 114
  hospitalizations and, 295–96
  house-training and, 138
rubber curries, 219
rules, 83

safety harnesses, 98–99
Saint Bernard, 30, 54, 55
salmonella, 174, 175
Saluki, 45–46
Samoyed, 55, 255, 258
Saul, Betsy, xxii–xxiii
Saul, Jared, xxii–xxiii
scabies, 341–42
scent hounds, 44–45
Schipperke, 58
school, for dogs, 421–26
Scottish Deerhound, 44, 46
Scottish Terrier, 48, 334
scratches, 273
Sealyham Terrier, 48
seatbelts, 408–9
sedatives
  air travel and, 413
  fireworks and, 136
  professional grooming and, 215
seizures, 275, 384–86
self-exercise, 27–28
self-mutilation, 330
separation, 132
separation anxiety, 422, 425
sex, of dogs, 35–36
shampoo, 67, 217, 225–26
shaving, 223
shedding, 31, 217, 221, 257–58
Sheltie. See Shetland Sheepdog
Shetland Sheepdog, 55–57, 221, 251, 314, 315,
  316, 351, 352
Shiba Inu, 58, 257
Shih Tzu, 53, 253, 309, 311, 316, 375
shock, 285–86
Siberian Husky, 55, 249, 251, 257, 316, 366

sight hounds, 44
Silken Windhound, 352
Silky Terrier, 53
sirens, 135
sit command, 121–22, 130
skin, 256
  bathing and, 225
  care, 217–24
  conditions, 326–34
  flaky, 214
  of hairless dogs, 228
  ointments, 299
skunks, 224
Skye Terrier, 48
sleep arrangements, 101–2
smells, 224
smell, sense of, 250
snake bites, 276
sniffing, 198
snow, 194
socialization
  of adolescent dogs, 33
  classes, 199
  with other dogs, 104–5, 197–99
  in parks, 192–93
  with strangers, 193–97
Society for the Prevention of Cruelty to
  Animals (SPCA), 2
Soft Coated Wheaten Terrier, 48
Sommers, Katy, 400
sounds, 134–36, 424
spas, for dogs, 418
spaying and neutering, 240–42
  early age, 242–43
  fees, 6
  future of, 245–46
  myths, 243–45
  nonsurgical, 245–46
  re-homing and, 440
  scheduling, 108
  vouchers, 107
special needs dogs, 36–37
Spinone Italiano, 44
splints, 281, 284
splitting, 168–70
sponsorships, 473
sporting group, 42–44
Springer Spaniel, 334
squinting, 276
Staffordshire Bull Terrier, 47–49
Standard Schnauzer, 54, 252
stay command, 123–24, 130
sterilizing. See spaying and neutering

Sternberg, Sue, 86, 442
stiffness, 276
stitches, removing, 294
strangers, 90, 130, 193–97
strays, 11–13
stress
    check-ups and, 109
    managing, 104
    moving and, 426
stretches, 203–4
stubbornness, 51
stud tail, 241
submissive urination, 143
suicide, 458
sunscreen, 228, 410
supplies, 62–72
    checklist, 73
    grooming, 214–17
    training, 115–18
surgery, 373
Sussex Spaniel, 44
sweat, 327
sweaters, 142, 194
swimming, 369

tails
    docking of, 255
    grooming, 221
    types of, 254–55
    wagging, 105
tangles, 217–18
tapeworms, 355–56
target sticks, 117
target training, 120–21
tattoos, 13, 17
tearstains, 230
teeth, 250
teeth cleaning. See dental care
teething, 271–72
temperament, 50
    choosing, 28–29
    genetics and, 26–27
    of hound dogs, 45
    of other pets, 23
tenderness, 272–73
terrier group, 47–48
testing, 87–88
    BAER, 321
    diagnostic, 347
    lab, 292–93
    urinary incontinence, 362–63
    veterinarian, 108
tethering, 101

theobromine, 173
therapy, dog-assisted, 22
thermometers, 299–300
thunderstorms, 135
thyroid disease, 376
Tibetan Mastiff, 55
Tibetan Spaniel, 58
Tibetan Terrier, 58
ticks, 338
    in ears, 323
    Lyme disease and, 370
    removing, 339–40
time, 19
    adoption process and, 90–91
    dog's needs and, 19–20
    moving and, 428
    recuperation and, 303
titer testing, 108, 268–69
touching sensitivity, 137–38
tourniquets, 283
Toy Fox Terrier, 53
toy group, 52–53, 69
Toy Manchester Terrier, 53
toys, 69–71
    chewing, 144
    puzzle, 423
    as rewards, 116–17
trainers, 150–52
    agility, 209
    knowledge of, 117–18
    as last resort, 439
    socialization classes and, 199
training, 113–14
    baby gates and, 66
    basic behaviors, 121–29
    CGC program and, 131
    choosing, 91
    classes, 6
    ease of, 34–35
    muzzling and, 281–82
    problem behaviors, 143–50
    puppies v. older dogs, 32
    supplies, 64–65
    techniques, 119–21
    time and, 19–20
    treats and, 71–72
    voice and, 117–18
    without rewards, 129
    working dogs, 56
travel, 22
    air, 411–14
    in cars, 407–11
    checklist, 416

travel (*continued*)
  crates and, 66
  with dogs, 30–31
  foreign, 414–15
  with injuries, 282
  without dogs, 415–19
treats, 71–72, 179–81
  offering, 89
  reducing, 177–78
trimming, 207, 223–24, 234–35
trucks, 98
trust, 102–3
Tuffies, 70

Ultimate Raw Food Plan, 176
umbilical cording, 101, 139
unconditional love, 450–51
United Kennel Club, 210
United States Department of Agriculture
    (USDA), 164, 411, 414
urinary incontinence, 362–63
urinary system, 254, 362–66
urine, 35–36, 143, 276. *See also* house-training
  cleaning, 67–68
  testing, 108

vaccinations, 107–8, 265–66
  boosters, 268–69
  core, 266–67
  failures, 269–70
  noncore, 266–67
  proof of, 151, 412
  reactions to, 268
  schedules, 267
vacuum cleaners, 68
vascular disease, 348
vegetables, 78–79, 116, 175
vegetarianism, 181
veterinarians
  aggression and, 439
  calling, 270
  cost of, 290
  dental care and, 230–31
  euthanasia and, 452–53
  finding, 289–90
  first visits to, 107–9
  holistic, 164, 393
  during hospitalizations, 295
  pet health insurance and, 306
  strays and, 12–13
  working with, 289–91

veterinary staff, 292–94
VetWrap, 284, 303
views and overstimulation, 423–24
vinegar, 67, 237
vital signs, 280, 346–47
vitamins, 163–64, 365, 372
Vizsla, 44, 334
Volhard Diet, 176
Volhard, Wendy, 176
volunteering, 2, 469–72
vomiting, 271, 276–77, 361–62
Von Willebrand's disease, 350, 380

walking, 90, 130, 188–93
warfarin, 380
warm-ups, 203–4
water, 161–62
  air travel and, 413
  availability of, 291
  bowls, 63
  in ears, 226
  exercise and, 206
  Giardia and, 357
  heatstroke and, 285
  location, 156
weight control, 177–79
Weimaraner, 44, 258, 334
Welsh Corgi, 57, 59, 315
Welsh Springer Spaniel, 44
Welsh Terrier, 48, 255
West Highland White Terrier, 48
Whippet, 46, 352
whipworms, 356
Whole Dog Journal, 165
Whole Prey Diet, 176
wincing, 272–73
windows, 76
Wire Fox Terrier, 257
Wirehaired Pointing Griffon, 44, 257
Wolfhound, 44
work, 421–26
working group, 53–55
World Canine Freestyle Organization,
    209–10
wounds, 277, 301–3

yards, 21–22, 77–79
yes command, 124
Yorkie-Poo, 52
Yorkshire Terrier, 53, 220, 221, 343
Yuck!, 144